THE FORMATION OF MODERN LEBANON

The Formation of Modern Lebanon

MEIR ZAMIR

CROOM HELM

London · Sydney · Dover, New Hampshire

© 1985 Meir Zamir
Croom Helm Ltd, Provident House, Burrell Row,
Beckenham, Kent BR3 1AT
Croom Helm Australia Pty Ltd, First Floor,
139 King Street, Sydney, NSW 2001, Australia

British Library Cataloguing in Publication Data

Zamir, Meir
    The formation of modern Lebanon.
    1. Lebanon – History – French occupation,
    1918-1946
    I. Title
    956.92'035   DS86

    ISBN 0-7099-3002-X

Croom Helm, 51 Washington Street,
Dover, New Hampshire 03820, USA

Library of Congress Cataloging in Publication Data

Zamir, Meir
    The formation of modern Lebanon.
    Bibliography: p. 299.
    Includes index.
    1. Lebanon – History – French occupation, 1918-1946.
I. Title
DS86.Z36   1985   956.92'035   85-358
ISBN 0-7099-3002-X

Printed and bound in Great Britain

CONTENTS

To Angela, Sharon, Tal and Yaniv

PREFACE

This study examines a vital period in the political development of modern Lebanon, a period during which its existence as a separate independent state was secured, its borders defined and its political structure shaped. If there was one single act which, more than any other, determined the character and development of the Lebanese state, it was undoubtedly the establishment of Greater Lebanon on 1 September 1920. On that date, the coastal area and the Beqa'a Valley, with their large Muslim populations, were annexed to Mount Lebanon, with its predominantly Maronite Christian population and its tradition of autonomy and close links to the West. This act, which totally violated Muslim aspirations, had far-reaching consequences for the development of Lebanon, whose subsequent history has been dominated by political, social, cultural and economic conflicts between Christians and Muslims and by repeated unsuccessful attempts to find a solution that would integrate the latter community into Lebanese life.

In spite of these efforts Lebanon has never really succeeded in overcoming the repercussions of the events of 1920. This failure has been manifested ever since in the continuous tension between the Christians and Muslims in Lebanon and between Lebanon and the Arab Muslim world, particularly Syria. The civil war of 1958 and that of 1975/6, which in fact has not yet ended, were rooted in the expansion of Lebanon's borders. It can thus be claimed that in the very creation of Greater Lebanon were sown the seeds of destruction for the independent Christian entity it was designed to guarantee.

This book falls into four parts. The first chapter surveys the emergence of a special Lebanese Christian entity and its transformation, by the eve of the First World War, into a national movement. It analyses its three goals: an independent state, extended borders and French protection, and the Muslim reaction. The second chapter studies the factors behind the French decision to establish Greater Lebanon in 1920. This decision is examined in the context of general French policy and interests in the Levant during and after the War, Franco-British rivalry over the Middle East, the post-war conflict between France and the Arab national movement led by Faisal, and the role of the Lebanese Christians, in particular of the Maronite

Church, in the formation of an independent Greater Lebanon. The third chapter is concerned with the repercussions of the extension of Lebanon's borders on the demographic and political structure of the new state, examines the stand of the major communities, especially of the Maronites and Sunnis towards it, and traces its political development during the early years of the mandate. The fourth chapter describes Lebanon's political development between 1923 and 1926, the effect of the Druze and Syrian uprising of 1925/6 on Syro-Lebanese relations, particularly on the territorial dispute between the two states, and the attempts to detach some of the annexed areas and to attach them to Syria. This section ends with the elaboration of the Lebanese Constitution of May 1926 and the establishment of the Lebanese Republic.

I am indebted to many friends and colleagues who helped me throughout the preparation of this book, especially to Professor Elie Kedourie of the London School of Economics and Political Science, and to Professor Moshe Ma'oz of the Hebrew University of Jerusalem. In my research I was greatly assisted by various institutions, libraries and archives in France, England and Israel. I acknowledge with gratitude the aid I received from the Centre International des Etudiants et Stagiaires under the auspices of the French Foreign Ministry, which enabled me to stay at the Centre de Hautes Etudes sur l'Afrique et l'Asie Modernes. I am grateful to Mr G. Malécot, its director, and to the staff, who were always ready to help. I would like to thank the directors and staffs of the Archives du Ministère des Affaires Etrangères in Paris, the librarians of the Bibliothèque Nationale, the Service Historique de l'Armée in Vincennes and the Archives Départementales de la Corrèze in Tulle. My thanks also to the Central Research Fund of the University of London for its support, to the staffs of the Public Record Office in London and of the Middle East Centre, St Antony's College, Oxford. I owe particular gratitude to the Ben-Gurion University of the Negev in Beersheba, and to the Harry S. Truman Institute for the Advancement of Peace of the Hebrew University of Jerusalem for their assistance and support in the preparation of this study for publication. Above all I am indebted to my wife Angela without whose constant help and encouragement this book would not have been possible.

Meir Zamir
Ben-Gurion University of the Negev
Beersheba

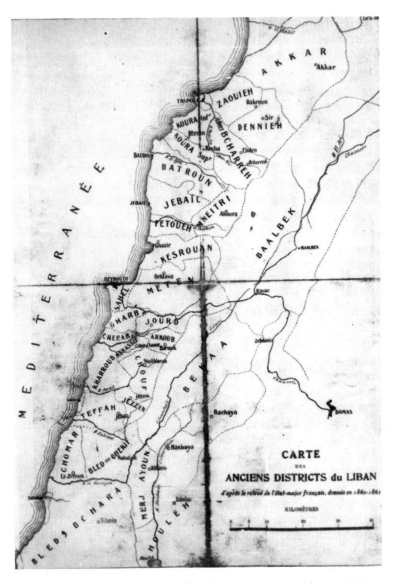

A copy of the map presented by the first Lebanese delegation to the Paris Peace Conference.

1 THE EMERGENCE OF A LEBANESE ENTITY

The modern state of Lebanon was established on 1 September 1920 at the end of a two-year period which shaped the political character of the present-day Middle East. These two years had begun in October 1918 with the capture of Damascus and Beirut by the Allied Forces, thus terminating 400 years of Ottoman rule. They ended with the defeat of Faisal's Arab government in July 1920, opening the way to the partition of the Middle East between England and France and to its subsequent division into nation-states.

The creation of 'Grand Liban' by General Gouraud, high commissioner for Syria and Lebanon, was the first step taken by France, the mandatory power, to fulfil its pledges to its traditional Lebanese Christian protégés. For the Christians, especially the Maronites, the establishment of an independent Christian state with extended borders and under French protection was the realisation of a centuries-old dream. For the Muslims in Syria and the areas newly attached to Lebanon, however, it was the final blow in a series of demoralising events which had begun six weeks earlier with the defeat of the Arab army at Maisalun, the subsequent occupation of Damascus by the French and the expulsion of Faisal from Syria. Fervent Muslim hopes for an independent united Arab state, which had begun to seem realistic after Faisal's triumphant entry into Damascus two years before, were suddenly shattered. The establishment of a Christian state in Lebanon by the foreign Christian power which had just overthrown the Muslim state in Syria symbolised not only their own defeat, but a victory of Christianity over Islam. It was in such circumstances that modern Lebanon came into being as the only independent Christian state in the Arab Muslim world.

The conflict between Lebanese Christians and Syrian Muslims was only one of many which characterised those crucial years. In the area known as 'geographical Syria'[1] foreign powers and local forces were scrambling for advantage in the vacuum created by the Ottoman collapse. The nineteenth-century rivalry between Britain and France for control of the Asiatic Ottoman territories now came to a climax. On another level British and French ambitions both clashed with the aspirations for independence and unity of the Arab Muslims, the majority of the population. This clash was expressed in the struggle of the Arab government in Syria against France between 1918 and 1920, and the Iraqi revolt against Britain in 1920.[2] On still another level the Arab Muslim majority had to contend with powerful minority groups trying to realise their own national aspirations, such as the Maronites in Lebanon and the Jews in Palestine, as well as with 'compact' groups like the Druze and Alawites and 'scattered' groups like the Greek Orthodox and Greek Catholics, who were not really seeking self-determination but were anxious to secure their position and interests in any future Sunni-dominated Arab state.

Conflicting communal interests led to a rapid deterioration in relations, particularly between Muslims and Christians in Lebanon and Muslims and Jews in Palestine. Violence soon followed; in April 1920 clashes broke out between Muslims and Jews in Jerusalem, while in late 1919 and early 1920 Muslims attacked Christian villages in Lebanon. In the most serious incident, more than 50 Christians were massacred in the village of 'Ain Ibel in south Lebanon in May 1920. Muslim-Christian relations in Lebanon had not been so bad since 1860.

The age-old religious and communal gap between Muslims and Christians had grown wider in the second half of the nineteenth century as Lebanon, together with the rest of the Ottoman Empire, underwent profound changes. Nevertheless the Ottoman social and administrative system still provided some basis for co-existence, as centuries of common life had produced a viable balance of rights and obligations between the various communities. This relatively stable situation ended abruptly with the defeat of the Ottoman army and the Allied occupation of Syria and Lebanon. The Christians had little difficulty adjusting to the new situation but the Muslims were most apprehensive for their future under foreign Christian rule. Tensions and suspicions were exacerbated by post-war confusion.

The rapid spread of nationalism also poisoned relations between the Muslims and the Christian and Jewish minorities. The new secular rhetoric could not conceal the essentially religious-communal nature of Arab Muslim, Lebanese Christian and Zionist Jewish nationalism. The fact that the three movements emerged and expressed their national aims almost simultaneously further aggravated relations between them.

Muslims regarded the Lebanese and Zionist movements as obstacles in the path of their legitimate aspirations; the unity and independence of the Arab Muslim world was endangered by the call for separate Christian and Jewish states in areas the Muslims saw as integral parts of their own territory. They regarded these movements as tools of the foreign powers. Indeed, the Lebanese Christians and the Zionist Jews finally realised their national aspirations not by agreement or compromise with the Muslims but with the aid respectively, of France and Britain.

Between 1918 and 1920 the Christian demand for an independent state in Lebanon appeared to the Muslims in Syria as a more immediate and serious threat than the corresponding Zionist demand in Palestine. The Lebanese Christians, particularly the Maronites, were a large, well-established community, while the Zionist movement was still in its infancy and the number of Jews in Palestine was relatively small. The Lebanese Christians, moreover, were supported by France, whose colonial ambitions seriously threatened Arab national aims. The Zionists, on the other hand, were supported by Britain, the Muslims' ally, who had initiated and encouraged the Arab Revolt and backed Arab claims against France.

Rivalry between Britain and France added yet another element to the religious, sectarian and now national conflicts between the Lebanese Christians and the Syrian Muslims. In its struggle for influence and control each power used propaganda and subversion to undermine the position of the other. The British used both Zionists and Arab Muslims under Hashemite family leadership in an attempt to circumvent the terms of their War agreements with the French on the partition of the Middle East; the French supported the Lebanese Christians in order to strengthen their own claims in Syria and Lebanon.

It is therefore not surprising that from the moment it was established as an independent Christian state, Lebanon's existence has been challenged from within by its own Muslim population and from without by the Muslims of Syria. Even before the creation of the Lebanese state Faisal, the leader of the Arab national movement, declared his opposition to the Lebanese Christian national movement in an interview with the American Commission of Inquiry on 3 July 1919: 'This, the movement of separation recently arisen in an unnatural idea inspired by the occupying authority and supported by a section of the clergy and their followers, is rejected by the broad-minded and intellectual.'[3]

The Damascus Programme, approved by the General Syrian Congress the previous day, also opposed the separation of Palestine and Lebanon from Syria, as did the March 1920 Declaration of Independence, which was to serve 'as a programme for Arab nationalists for the next twenty-five years'.[4] Arab nationalists have continued to describe the Lebanese state as an artificial creation, the product of a French plot against the Arabs.[5] They have never ceased to challenge its political legitimacy; Syria, in fact, has never officially recognised Lebanon as an independent state.[6]

To what extent were these accusations valid? Was Lebanese nationalism really an artificial cause inspired by France and attracting only a small minority of Christians, mainly Maronites, or was it a genuine national movement? Did a Lebanese entity already exist at the end of the First World War? What role did France play in the establishment of Lebanon? Did that role reflect direct colonial interests, or was it the culmination of historical processes in which the Lebanese themselves played an important part? Answers to these questions are essential if one is to understand the political development of modern Lebanon.

The political aspirations of the Lebanese national movement during the first two decades of the twentieth century were summed up in the oft-cited 'formula': 'an independent Lebanon within its historical and natural boundaries under French protection'.[7] This formula consisted of three separate demands: an independent state, a Greater Lebanon with its more extensive borders, and French protection. One must ask whether the demands for an independent state and a Greater Lebanon were of equal importance for the Lebanese and whether the request for French protection was only a means to achieve the first two demands. Were the Lebanese Christians aware that a Greater Lebanon would contain a large Muslim population which could endanger the character and independence of a Christian Lebanese state? Was there not a contradiction between 'independence' and 'French protection'?

The history of Lebanon as a separate entity began neither in 1920 with the creation of the modern state, nor in 1861 with the establishment of the autonomous Sanjak of Mount Lebanon (the Mutasarrifiya). In fact it is doubtful whether any other country in the Middle East apart from Egypt can claim such a long, continuous history as a political entity. Certain unique features had already appeared as far back as the Mameluke period; but a truly Lebanese entity, the Imarah, emerged only in the late sixteenth and early seventeenth centuries during the reign of Fakhr al-Din II. It has been claimed: 'Within the limits of this territory an evolving form of political authority has continued without interruption from the early seventeenth century to our own time, giving Lebanon a separate and distinct identity.'[8]

The Imarah took shape when one feudal family, the Ma'nids, managed to establish its hegemony over the other local families and bring the Maronites and Druze together in a close political association. This association served as the basis for the Imarah for two-and-a-half centuries, first under the Ma'nids and later under the Shihabists. During this period (1590–1842) Lebanon acquired its special character as a separate political entity with a tradition of autonomy. It was these two factors which gave rise to the Lebanese claims for a state of their own.

The drive for autonomy stemmed from the particular nature of the Druze and Maronite communities. One Muslim heterodox, the other Christian Uniate, these sects had resisted any central government authority for centuries. This was what had first led them to seek refuge in the isolated and inaccessible Lebanese mountains. The Imarah provided a unifying, acceptable political authority. Its autonomy had its limits, however. The Ottoman sultan was still recognised as the sovereign; each new emir had to be invested by the sultan and was required to pay annual taxes to the Ottoman treasury.

Up to the eighteenth century the Imarah was under Druze hegemony. It was not until the reign of Bashir II (1788–1840) that its Christian character was finally determined and Mount Lebanon began to be regarded as a homeland for Christians, in particular for Maronites. The shift in the balance of power from the Druze to the Maronites was the culmination of political, social, economic, cultural and demographic changes. A large population increase led many Maronites to migrate from the north of Mount Lebanon to the predominantly Druze areas in the central and southern regions. At the very time the Maronites were becoming the largest and most widespread community in Mount Lebanon, many Christians were migrating into the area from the Syrian interior, often settling in Beirut and the other coastal towns. Lebanon could soon boast the largest concentration of Christians in the Middle East.[9]

Maronite political, economic, social and numerical dominance was of vital importance to Lebanon's development as a Christian entity. The Maronites were the driving force behind the Lebanese national movement; it was thanks to their efforts that the Lebanese state was established in 1920. What kind of people were they? They have been described as

. . . a national group. They reflect distinctive ethnic character-istics, a single religion, and a long history; for centuries they lived in one compact area and once had a distinct language and memories up to the recent past. In addition to this, they once enjoyed a political history and life of their own, the memory of which they translated into a national myth.[10]

The Maronites possessed a strong sense of particularism, ethnic unity and pride. Their geographical situation enabled them to develop their own special characteristics that distinguished them from the other Christian sects in Syria. Unlike these other sects, who lived mainly in towns, the Maronites were warlike mountain peas-ants with strong ties to the land; they were consequently less vulner-able to outside attack. Their attachment to Mount Lebanon, which they regarded as their homeland, their strong spirit of independence and their particularism were to blossom into a full territorial and ethnic nationalism.

Like the other Christians, the Maronites feared Muslim domina-tion, but their geographical situation helped them withstand Muslim pressure. They developed the notion of resistance to Islam into a myth, expressed in the Mardaite idea.[11] They did not regard them-selves as Arabs, nor their community as an integral part of the Arab world. They felt superior to Muslims in religion, culture and education and opposed assimilation into Muslim society. Their close ties with the West and their identification with the European powers, in particular France, further strengthened their feelings of particularism and their resistance to Islamisation.

The Maronites were also unique in their strong attachment to their Church:

More even than other Syrian sects they were dominated by their clergy. The priests were national leaders, the centre around which turned the struggle of the community to survive and retain its identity; and the Maronite Patriarch, the only Patriarch residing in Lebanon itself, was a temporal as well as a spiritual power. . .[12]

The Maronite Church and its patriarch played prominent roles in shaping Lebanon's political history during the nineteenth and early twentieth centuries; the establishment of a Christian state in Lebanon in 1920 was largely the successful culmination of their efforts.

It was the Church that preserved the community's faith, unity and identity, and first gave voice to a Maronite ideology, through the medium of the clergy's historiographic writings:

> The traditional historiography of the Maronites seems to have come into being as an expression of Maronite national pride. As a small, closely-knit community surrounded by enemies . . . the Maronites tended to be deeply interested in their own history, taking pride in having retained their identity through centuries of vicissitude.[13]

The aim of these authors was not so much to record history as to establish the claims of their community. Their writings stressed a strong sense of ethnic unity and a feeling that their community was 'a rose among thorns': they were not Arabs; they had managed to preserve a separate national and religious identity in a Muslim milieu. The claims of Mardaite or Phoenician ancestry originated in these writings. The clergy were also the first to develop the idea of a Maronite state, claiming that Mount Lebanon had for centuries been an independent or autonomous Maronite homeland. The reign of Fakhr al-Din II was portrayed as the high point in Lebanese history, when an independent polity covered the entire country. These arguments were intended to give historical depth to the demand for a separate Maronite entity; they would later be used by Lebanese Christians to counter the demands of Arab nationalists. Enshrined in the historiographic writings, all these ideas profoundly influenced the whole Maronite community. The Church dominated the educational system; generation after generation of young Maronites were inculcated with these values and beliefs, which shaped their conception of themselves, their community and their surroundings.

By the first half of the nineteenth century a Lebanese identity had begun to emerge; the main foundations of Maronite nationalism were all in place: a people — the Maronites; a territory — Mount Lebanon; and an ideology aspiring to political autonomy. The Church had been the driving force behind the demand to establish a Maronite princedom under a Shihabi Christian emir who was expected to co-operate closely with the clergy.[14] Extensive social and economic changes, including the emergence of an independent peasantry and middle class, contributed to the further spread of Maronite nationalism.[15]

It took two decades of bitter civil war, however, for the Maronites to secure their dominance over Mount Lebanon, the core of their future state. Ten years of Egyptian rule in Syria and Lebanon (1831–40) had exacerbated the already strained relations between Maronites and Druze. By the end of the occupation relations had deteriorated into violent conflict. In the 20 years which followed three outbreaks of civil war (in 1841, 1845 and 1860) led to a complete transformation of Lebanon; the Imarah collapsed, the feudal system was abolished and the Druze lost their superior political and economic position in the Mountain.

The conflict began as a struggle for political, social and economic dominance, but it soon developed into a religious and confessional war; this would not be the last complex Lebanese struggle to manifest itself in such terms. Apart from the increase in the Christian population and its spread southwards into Druze districts, some of the factors behind the fighting included the increasing involvement of the Church in political and economic affairs, in particular its close ties with the peasantry; the emergence of a Christian middle class which did not fit into traditional feudal society; the decline and collapse of the authority of the Shihabi emirs after the expulsion of Bashir II; the Ottoman government's attempts to restrict the autonomy of the Mountain; and the growing rivalry between Britain and France in the area.[16]

The civil war reached its climax in 1860, when within a few weeks over 10,000 Christians in Lebanon were massacred and another 100,000 made homeless. The massacre was a traumatic event for the Lebanese Christians; it strengthened their communal consciousness and became the '*terminus a quo* from which all political thinking starts'.[17] The tragedy proved the need for an autonomous Maronite entity, which the Church had been seeking since 1840.

Out of the ruins of civil war the autonomous Sanjak of Mount Lebanon emerged in place of the defunct Imarah and the short-lived unsuccessful 'Double Caimacamia' regime.[18] The main objective of the new administrative system was to restore stability and peace to the Mountain and to prevent further confessional conflicts. And indeed, a new equilibrium was achieved that lasted for more than half a century (1861–1915). In this peaceful climate a Christian entity separate from the rest of Syria gradually matured; it became the foundation for the modern Lebanese state. Many of the political, social and economic characteristics that set modern Lebanon apart first appeared in this era, such as the role of the confessionalist principle in political life and the dominant position of trade, finance and services in the economy.

The Règlement Organique of 1861 and its modification three years later provided the legal basis for the Mutasarrifiya.[19] The Règlement was drawn up by an international commission set up in Beirut in 1860 with representatives of the Ottoman government and of five European powers: France, England, Russia, Austria and Prussia. It made Mount Lebanon an autonomous Ottoman province, ruled by a non-Lebanese Ottoman Christian governor; the area's special status was to be guaranteed by the European powers.[20] The new arrangement involved in fact a series of compromises: between Druze and Maronite interests; between the Lebanese, in particular the Maronites, who demanded complete autonomy, and the Ottomans, who sought to restrict it; between the Ottomans, who wished to retain full sovereignty over the area, and the European powers, who sought to intervene; and between the great powers themselves, each with its own interests and its own protégés: for France, the Maronites, for Britain, the Druze, and for Russia, the Greek Orthodox community.[21]

In spite of its shortcomings this arrangement had clear advantages for the inhabitants of the Mountain. Although autonomy was not complete, the Ottomans were far from having a free hand in its internal affairs, and their sovereignty in the Mountain was greatly reduced. The appointment of the Ottoman governor was subject to the confirmation of the signatory powers, and his authority was hampered by the constant interference of their representatives. Only a small Ottoman garrison could be stationed in the Mountain. The autonomous Sanjak had its own council, administration and French-trained militia; it drew up its own budget, and its inhabitants enjoyed tax privileges and exemption from military service.

The Règlement Organique represented an official recognition by the Ottomans of Mount Lebanon's unique autonomous status, at the very time they were advocating a centralisation policy for the Empire as a whole. It can be argued that one of the main achievements of the Mutasarrifiya was to maintain Lebanon's autonomy until circumstances permitted the Lebanese to renew their demands for full autonomy and even independence.

For the first time, Lebanese identity now had a legal definition. To be Lebanese was to be a citizen of the Mutasarrifiya and to enjoy the privileges that entailed. The Lebanese benefited from a modern system of administration while the inhabitants of the rest of Syria were still subject to the backward and corrupt Ottoman governmental system. The privileges they enjoyed, together with economic prosperity, reinforced their feelings of distinction and superiority. Their desire to safeguard the special status of the Mountain and their fear of Ottoman attempts to restrict or even abolish it became the main political issue of the time. The formal guarantees of the European powers bolstered their tendency to rely on the West, with whom they now developed stronger political, religious and linguistic ties. The spread of education and Western ideas changed their outlook and further strengthened their feelings of distinction from the rest of Syria. Most Lebanese Christians did not even regard themselves as Ottoman citizens.[22]

The Mutasarrifiya put the final seal on the Christian character of Mount Lebanon. Its territory was limited to the predominantly Christian areas and the Maronites now became numerically, politically and economically dominant.[23] Now more than ever they regarded Mount Lebanon as their homeland, and the Mutasarrifiya as a stepping stone towards the establishment of a state of their own. The element of territorial nationalism was strengthened, as was opposition to any attempt to jeopardise the territorial integrity of the Mountain.[24] Moreover, the existence of a strong and prosperous Christian entity gave confidence to the Christians in the surrounding areas which had not been included in the Mutasarrifiya. Envious of the privileges enjoyed by the inhabitants of the Mountain, many of them, especially the Maronites and Greek Catholics, wanted their own areas annexed to the autonomous Sanjak.

Yet in spite of the advantages offered by the new system, the Maronites' reaction to the Règlement was far from favourable. The arrangement did not satisfy their demands for complete autonomy under a Shihabi Maronite governor, nor did it formally recognise their supremacy. They resented the appointment of an Ottoman governor, whom they chose to regard merely as Istanbul's representative in the Mountain. Active opposition to the compromises in the Règlement Organique came mainly from the Maronite patriarch and from a movement led by Yusuf Karam. Both elements were motivated in part by private interests and ambitions; the former was anxious to safeguard the influence and power of the Church, which the new statute restricted, while Karam aimed at becoming governor. Nevertheless, nationalist considerations also played an important part in their opposition. With the backing of the Church and the support of the majority of the Maronites, Karam openly rebelled against the Ottomans. He and his supporters were attempting to realise the goal of a Maronite state as inspired by such Lebanese historiographers as Niqula Murad.[25] Although they failed to achieve their objective, their movement inspired the Maronites with enduring patriotic feelings. Karam himself became a popular national hero;[26] the strong support he continued to receive even after his expulsion proved how deeply nationalist ideas were already rooted in the Maronite community.[27]

Unlike Karam, the Church could not openly rebel against the Ottoman authorities, and it eventually resigned itself to the Règlement Organique. As it had feared, its influence in political affairs was curbed by the Ottoman governors, especially Da'ud Pasha, but it did succeed in retaining much influence in the Maronite community. The Church remained the major centre of opposition to the Ottomans; it was better able than other sectors of the population to resist the temptation of bribes and offers by the governor of high positions in the administration. It continued to see itself as the only agency responsible for the community's interests, and as the embodiment of the Maronite demand for full autonomy and eventual independence.

The vacuum left by the collapse of the Imarah and the abolition of the feudal system was filled by the Ottoman governor and by the Administrative Council of Mount Lebanon, an advisory body consisting of twelve representatives elected by the sheikhs of the villages, with proportional representation for all the sects of the Mountain: 4 Maronites, 3 Druze, 2 Greek Orthodox, 1 Greek Catholic, 1 Mutawalli and 1 Sunni. The Council provided a col- *(ie Shi'i)* lective secular political leadership. Although its powers were limited, it acquired a large degree of influence in the Mutasarrifiya. Its members were drawn primarily from those feudal families which had succeeded in retaining their positions by joining the new administration, and from families of traders, financiers and entrepreneurs. The latter class was to benefit the most from the new system, and its members acquired a personal interest in safeguarding the privileges of the Mountain. Toward that end, they adopted principles of political compromise and balance between the representatives of the various sects; both practices would long remain central features in Lebanese politics.[28] Along with the Maronite Church, the Administrative Council became a firm defender of the special status of the Mountain's inhabitants, as when it opposed their participation in the Ottoman general elections of 1876 and

1908. But while the Church represented only the Maronite community, the Council represented all elements of the ' Lebanese entity'.

The Mutasarrifiya could have been viewed as one stage in the
realisation of Maronite national aspirations; alternatively, it could
have been seen as a new political arrangement for securing harmony
and balance in a multi-confessional society. The outcome in the first
case would have been a Christian Maronite state; in the second it
would have been a pluralistic state not necessarily dominated by the
Maronites. In fact the Mutasarrifiya provided the basis for both
possibilities. Its creation, after 20 years of civil war, was an
acknowledgement of the difficulties involved when a variety of sects
lived under one political system. The attempts to secure a Christian
majority, the appointment of a Christian governor, and the guarantee by the powers were all originally aimed at protecting the Christians from any resurgence of religious and sectarian conflict. Nevertheless the Mutasarrifiya's success in fostering political and social
equilibrium among the various sects through 50 years of peaceful
co-existence encouraged the development of a pluralistic society,
which was further facilitated by the spread of secularist ideas
towards the end of the century. Whether the Christian or the inter-
denominational aspect would prevail ultimately depended on how
the borders of the state were drawn.

Therein lies a paradox. Although the Règlement Organique
provided a more or less acceptable solution to the problem of
autonomy, it created a new problem: that of borders. This was to
become one of the main concerns of the Lebanese Christians; by the
turn of the century, extension of the borders of the Sanjak and
reform in its administration took priority over the question of independence. The arrangement of 1861 restricted the autonomous
Sanjak to the mountainous area of Mount Lebanon, as the International Commission wanted to include in the Mutasarrifiya only
those regions with a clear Christian majority. This policy was
promoted by the British representative in hopes of forestalling
any further confessional conflict. It was also supported by the
Ottoman government, which sought to limit the area within which
its sovereignty would be restricted, and to reduce the revenue
loss ensuing from the economic privileges granted to the area's
residents.[29]

The autonomous Sanjak was consequently smaller than the
Imarah had been, and now covered only about 4,000 sq. km. Its
boundaries, which were never clearly defined, stretched from the

districts of Tripoli and 'Akkar in the north to the district of Sidon in the south, which remained attached to the vilayet of Beirut. In the east, the Sanjak bordered the districts of Ba'albek, Beqa'a and Marjayoun, which were part of the vilayet of Damascus; while in the west it extended at two points to the Mediterranean. Beirut became an enclave separated by the Mutasarrifiya from its dependent districts in the north and south.

The Maronites opposed this reduction in territory from the start; it was one of the main reasons the Church rejected the Règlement Organique. Maronites repeatedly called for the return of four regions which they regarded as integral parts of Lebanon: Tripoli and the district of 'Akkar in the north; the Beqa'a Valley in the east; the districts of Hasbaya, Rashaya and Jabal 'Amel in the south; and in the west, the coastal towns of Tyre, Sidon and, most important of all, Beirut.

Lebanese Christians resorted to historical, geographical and economic arguments to justify their claims over these areas. The historical argument was the first to be heard. The Christians noted that the Mutasarrifiya covered only a part of the area formerly included in the Imarah; they demanded a return to historical boundaries, in particular those prevailing under Fakhr al-Din II. The historical boundaries of the Imarah have been defined as '. . . the whole territory from the crest of the Anti-Lebanon to the sea, which normally felt the impact of Ma'n and Shihab government — a territory which, in extent, did not differ much from present-day Lebanon'.[30] In fact, the Imarah had never possessed such defined or permanent borders, although at various periods its emirs did extend their control beyond Mount Lebanon, sometimes with the agreement of the neighbouring Ottoman valis and at other times without.

Another argument, that of 'natural-geographical boundaries', was marshalled to reinforce the historical claim. The geographical limits of the country were said to be Nahr-al-Kabir in the north, the crest of the Anti-Lebanon in the east, the Litani river in the south and the Mediterranean in the west.[31] It was further claimed that most of the Christians living in the four regions, especially in Beirut and the Beqa'a Valley, favoured annexation to Mount Lebanon.

Finally, and most insistently, it was said that the reduction in area was detrimental to the economy; in order for Lebanon to become economically viable, it would have to return to its 'historical and natural boundaries'.[32] Economic problems, which gradually intensified towards the turn of the century, proved that the Mountain alone could never be completely autonomous or independent. These problems affected the daily lives of its residents, especially traders, financiers and other entrepreneurs, whose opportunities within the narrow confines of the Mutasarrifiya were limited. These businessmen became the driving force behind the demand for a Greater Lebanon, and in particular for the inclusion of Beirut within the Sanjak.

The main problem was the shortage of arable land. There were no open plains for the cultivation of cereals or for pasture, such as could be found in the neighbouring 'Akkar region or in the Beqa'a Valley. The Mountain had to purchase grain from the Beqa'a and the Houran and had to import much of its meat supply. The shortage of cultivated land became more acute towards the end of the century owing to the rapid population growth, which made the Mountain the most densely populated area in Syria.[33] The shift to commercial crops such as silk and tobacco further increased the dependence on imported food and made the Sanjak more vulnerable to crop failure in both the Mountain and the neighbouring areas. At the turn of the century the economy was further affected by a reduced demand for raw silk products, previously the main source of income.[34]

The Mountain also suffered from a lack of sea-ports. Its natural outlets in Beirut, Sidon and Tripoli lay outside its borders, and residents had to pay high customs duties to the Ottoman authorities. To facilitate a growing trade with Europe, several governors pushed for the right to open a new port within the territory of the Mutasarrifiya; they all ran into stiff opposition from the Ottoman government. In 1902, for example, Muzaffar Pasha proposed the opening of a port in Junieh, a small town north of Beirut; he too was unsuccessful. The lack of a port was to become a major grievance of the residents of the Mountain against the Ottomans.[35]

The most pressing economic problem was the separation from Beirut, the Sanjak's natural capital and port. In rejecting the Maronites' 1861 demand for its annexation, the Ottomans pointed out that the city had a large Muslim population and provided services for the whole of Syria and even Mesopotamia. Beirut had already become a prosperous economic centre and an important source of revenue for the Ottoman government.[36] By 1900 it had become the major political, cultural and economic centre for the Levant. Most of Syria's trade with Europe passed through the town, thanks to its modern harbour and its rail link to Damascus and the interior. Foreign banks and trading companies set up branches in Beirut and a large foreign community established itself there. Without an urban centre of its own, the Mountain depended completely on Beirut, with which its economy was closely linked. Thousands left the Mountain to take advantage of the opportunities provided by its prosperous economy. The lack of a commercial tribunal in the Mountain increased its dependence on the town even further.

The shortage of land, the lack of economic opportunities and the steady population growth led to a rapid increase in emigration after 1860. Towards the turn of the century thousands of Christians left Lebanon and Syria for Egypt, the United States, South America and West Africa. Between 1900 and 1914 an estimated 100,000 Lebanese, about a quarter of the population, emigrated. The phenomenon was increasingly cited as a major argument for extended boundaries. Christians claimed that more territory would not only greatly reduce emigration, but also enable those Lebanese who had already emigrated to return to their homeland.[37]

The heavy weight of economic considerations in Maronite arguments for expansion should not be allowed to obscure the underlying political motivations. For the Maronites and their Church, the establishment of an economically viable 'Grand Liban' was merely a precondition for the achievement of their goal of full political autonomy and subsequent independence.

The close connection between political and economic independence for Lebanon was probably best expressed in a book published in 1908 by Bulus Nujaim, under the pseudonym M. Jouplain. The author was a Lebanese Maronite with close ties to the government of the Mutasarrifiya.[38] His book analysed in detail the history of Lebanon from 1831, examined the various aspects of the Lebanese question and proposed a plan for political, economic and territorial reform. The case for extended boundaries was carefully presented. Nujaim's formulation was to become the basis for Lebanese Christian arguments in favour of a Greater Lebanon. It stressed the national rather than economic aspects of that goal. Only extended boundaries would enable Lebanon to exist as an independent state. In Nujaim's words: 'Il faut l'arracher à la misère, et lui donner les moyens de vivre et de prospérer. Le droit à la vie, à l'existence, n'appartient pas seulement à l'individu, il appartient aussi aux nations.'

Nujaim told the European public that the Lebanese question

required a definite solution: the establishment of an independent Christian state. As for its borders: 'Il faut reconstituer le Liban avec les frontières qu'il avait sous le grand émir Fakhr al-Din et sous les émirs Chéhab. Ce sont ses frontières naturelles.'[39] The way to achieve this was clear. In 1861 the European powers, particularly France, had failed to ensure either full autonomy for Lebanon or the protection of its natural boundaries. As the traditional protector of the Maronites, France now had to shoulder the task of helping the Lebanese Christians realise their aspirations for a state of their own.[40]

The appeal for French intervention seemed quite natural to Nujaim and his fellow Maronites. Their centuries-old attachment to France was based on religious, cultural and economic ties as well as a history of French moral and legal protection. The French may have used this relationship to justify their claims for domination in the Levant, but the Maronites and the other Christians in Lebanon saw it differently.

French and Lebanese historians trace the tradition of French protection back to the Crusades or even to Charlemagne, but it is generally accepted that France's claim to a Catholic protectorate in the Levant was based on the Capitulations of 1535 and other later capitulations. French protection became more explicit in 1649 when Louis XIV, in response to an appeal by the Maronite patriarch, granted his patronage to the Maronite Church and community. This royal protection was renewed by succeeding kings so that by the eighteenth century the tradition was well-established.[41] In the 1840s, after Lebanon became entangled in the 'Eastern question', France became generally recognised as the protector of the Maronites. This period also saw the beginnings of Maronite activity within France aimed at mobilising governmental, parliamentary and public support; this was later to become an accepted way of trying to influence French policy.[42] French protection became more overt in August 1860 when an expeditionary force of 6,000 men landed in Beirut to defend the Maronites and other Christian inhabitants against the Druze and Muslims. French support was again demonstrated during the deliberations of the International Commission in Beirut, when French representatives endorsed the Maronite demands; it was mainly due to France's efforts that the Mutasarrifiya was established.

The Règlement Organique of 1861 granted international recognition to the principle of European protection over the Lebanese

Christians. Although France was only one of the signatory powers, the Maronites continued to rely on it as the sole protector of their autonomy and privileges. For the Maronites, who completely identified with France and who often described themselves as the 'French of the Levant',[43] French occupation or even annexation was a national goal. Such a step would rescue them from Ottoman Muslim rule which they had always resented, and place them under a Christian power with whom they already had close cultural, religious and economic ties. The decline of the Ottoman Empire towards the end of the century and the rapid growth of France's economic and cultural interests in Lebanon made occupation seem possible. As the empire's weakness became more apparent, the Maronites increased their appeals to France for direct intervention. This became an immediate goal in the second decade of the twentieth century, as they believed that France would help them to achieve their aspirations for an independent Christian Greater Lebanon.

At the beginning of the twentieth century, the general Maronite demands for full autonomy leading ultimately to independence, extended boundaries and French protection had not yet been consolidated into a defined political programme. The Ottoman Empire, although weakening, still maintained its sovereignty and administrative control over the area. This situation changed dramatically in July 1908, as the Young Turk revolution opened a new chapter in the history of Syria and Lebanon; the years that followed were to be decisive in determining future political developments. The revolution ended three decades of 'Abd al-Hamid II's conservative rule and eventually led to the final collapse of a system of government which had lasted for centuries. Waves of enthusiasm and hopes for radical political and administrative change spread rapidly throughout the empire, followed by an upsurge in nationalist ideas. The Arab national movement took shape in those years as most of its political aims were defined. Lebanon became engulfed in the general turmoil; its Christians consolidated a separate national movement aiming for an independent Christian state.

The Young Turk revolution raised new hopes and opened new opportunities for the Christians, but it also presented new problems. The restoration of the Constitution and the promise of change encouraged some Lebanese to seek the administrative reforms they had been demanding since the turn of the century. In September 1908 a group calling itself the Liberal Party laid siege to the governor's residence in Beit a-Din; they demanded the dissolution of the Administrative Council, new elections, an increase in the Council's power, the dismissal of corrupt officials and the abolition of new taxes. Under the threat of violent demonstrations the governor, Yusuf Franco, dismissed the vice-president of the Administrative Council and other high officials.[44]

On the other hand, a Young Turk demand that the Mountain participate in general elections and send representatives to the Ottoman parliament, sparked off the first major conflict between the Lebanese and the new regime. Some Lebanese supported participation, which had indeed been one of the original Liberal Party demands, but as in 1876 the majority were against it. The split assumed a sectarian dimension. Opponents came mainly from among the Maronites, in particular from the clergy, who feared that participation in the Ottoman parliament might undermine the Mountain's autonomy and privileges; Turkish insistence on this issue only increased their fears of ulterior motives. The Greek Orthodox, who resented Maronite domination of the Mountain, were willing to take part in the elections, but only if the Mountain's autonomy and privileges were fully guaranteed. The Druze, Mutawallis and Sunnis unconditionally supported participation, as they were prepared to support any step that might weaken the Christian majority and undermine Maronite domination.[45]

Thousands of Maronites led by the Church and members of the Administrative Council joined together in a popular movement to oppose participation. Petitions were sent to representatives of the European powers, in particular to the French and British consuls. By the middle of November 1908 Cumberbatch had received 195 such petitions with 30,000 signatures,[46] A new organisation, the Alliance Libanaise was formed to counter Ottoman efforts to persuade the Lebanese to participate, and to demand continued autonomy and privileges for the Mountain and reform in its administration. In October 1908 the Administrative Council passed a resolution stating that '. . . the inhabitants persist in their refusal. . .to elect representatives for the Ottoman parliament in order to safeguard their privileges'.[47] The Ottoman authorities continued their compliance efforts, and in December 1908 the minister of the interior informed the governor that the cabinet had instructed him to '. . . take the necessary measures for the election of Deputies; the Lebanon being an integral part of the Empire's domination and provinces'.[48] The Maronites, however, remained steadfast; in the end, their dominant position was confirmed: the Mountain failed to take part in the elections and remained unrepresented in the Ottoman parliament.

This controversy helped shape Lebanese attitudes towards the Young Turk regime. It seemed more urgent than ever to secure reforms to safeguard autonomy. There was, in fact, some basis for these fears, as the Young Turks advocated centralisation and opposed foreign intervention. The Turks may even have offered, as some Lebanese claimed, to expand the borders of the Mountain in exchange for a surrender of privileges. Some residents, including Christians, would probably have been prepared to support such a step. Lebanese fears increased when Turkish land forces and warships entered the Mountain and its territorial waters to prevent the opening of the port of Junieh. These fears were exaggerated, however, as the Ottoman government could do little without the approval of the signatory powers.[49]

Relations between the inhabitants of the Mountain and Yusuf Franco became strained. The part he played in the elections controversy proved to the Lebanese that he was no more than a representative of the Ottoman government. The governor, now backed by the central government, refused to comply with the demand for comprehensive administrative reforms; on the contrary, he heavy-handedly attempted to impose the principles and policies of the new Turkish regime upon the Mountain. The tension, however, was due less to Yusuf Franco's policies than to the attitude of the Lebanese, who were becoming increasingly impatient with and hostile towards the Ottoman authorities. The political freedom they enjoyed after the revolution had raised their hopes for reform, while they saw the unrest and political turmoil throughout the empire as an opportunity to press their demands for greater autonomy.[50]

Relations between the Administrative Council and the governor openly deteriorated. Council members regarded themselves as the true representatives of the Mountain's inhabitants and demanded reforms and greater autonomy. They sought to restrict the governor's power and upgrade the Council from an advisory body to a legislature. The fight against the governor led to open hostility and even contempt towards the Ottoman authorities. Yusuf Franco reacted by dismissing some Council members and threatening to dissolve the body altogether. The strained relations were aggravated by the internal rivalries and conflicting personal interests which characterised Lebanese politics. Cumberbatch, who followed closely the worsening relations between the Council and Yusuf Franco, sympathised with the latter and expressed his doubts as to the real motives of the Council members.[51]

The issue of a new Lebanese port once again emerged as a major complaint against the Ottoman authorities. In mid-1909 a group of Lebanese entrepreneurs attempted to open the port of Junieh to large ships without the consent of the authorities. The Ottoman government replied through a cabinet resolution of September 1909, which reiterated its opposition to the opening of a port to general navigation. Actually, the Ottomans were under counter-pressure from groups in Beirut who feared that a new port might jeopardise their own interests. The government's decision evoked vehement protest, especially from a self-constituted group called the National Committee for the Development of the Trade and Commerce of the Lebanon, one of whose members was Bulus Nujaim. The group mainly comprised inhabitants of Junieh, but it also drew support from the Administrative Council and from entrepreneurs in the Mountain. It sent petitions to the representatives of the European powers, asking them to support the opening of a new port. In April 1910 an Ottoman warship tried to prevent a Belgian ship from entering Junieh. This aroused further protests from the Lebanese, who saw the action as a violation of their autonomy.[52]

Other issues which aggravated relations between the Lebanese and the Ottoman authorities included the levying of additional taxes by the governor despite strong opposition from the Administrative Council, and the refusal of the Ottoman government to contribute towards the deficit in the budget of the Mountain, as laid down in the Règlement Organique. The introduction of identity cards became another source for complaint, as many Lebanese denied they were Ottoman citizens. Others feared that the cards might be used in the future for conscription and taxation. Their introduction coincided with a new law which required non- Muslims throughout the empire to serve in the Ottoman army: they had hitherto been exempt from service upon payment of the Bedel, the Military Exemption Tax. Lebanese residing in the Mountain continued to be exempt, but the Ottoman authorities insisted that the thousands of Lebanese who had settled outside the Mountain, many of them in Beirut, serve in the army and pay full taxes like all other citizens.[53]

When Yusuf Franco's five-year term of office ended in July 1912 the Lebanese seized the opportunity to press their demands for administrative change. They found in France a faithful ally, who with the support of the other signatory powers proposed a comprehensive programme for reforms in the Mountain. France refused to ratify the appointment of a new governor without prior approval of the reform programme. The Ottoman government on the other hand, said it would be prepared to discuss the requested reforms only after the appointment had been approved.[54] During the negotiations, which lasted until the end of the year, the Mountain remained without an Ottoman governor. For part of this time, the functions of governor were performed by the vice-president of the Administrative Council, Sa'adalah Hawayik, the Maronite patriarch's brother, a fact which further encouraged the inhabitants to demand full autonomy. At this time widespread rumours throughout Lebanon that France was pressing for the appointment of a French governor moved the vali of Beirut to inform the Ottoman government of the urgent need for a new governor.[55]

Under pressure from France and the other signatory powers, the Ottoman government yielded and on 22 December 1912 approved a new Protocol, which included the appointment of a new governor and a programme for reforms. The fact that the Union Libérale of Kamil Pasha, which favoured decentralisation, was then in power in Constantinople facilitated the reaching of an accord. The Protocol provided for the first major modification of the Règlement Organique since 1864, and fulfilled several basic Lebanese demands: the power of the Administrative Council was increased, its electoral system was modified, and an additional Maronite representative was included; a commercial tribunal was set up in the Mountain; and the opening of two Lebanese ports was approved, one for the Maronites in Junieh and the other for the Druze in Nabi-Yunis. The demand for extended boundaries, however, was not accepted.[56]

The return to power the following month of the Young Turks, who advocated centralisation, underlined the special position that Lebanon had managed to secure. France's prestige was greatly enhanced in the eyes of the Lebanese Christians, who regarded the achievement of the reforms as further proof that France was their defender and protector. Nevertheless, the reforms proved to be too modest and too late. The Lebanese were no longer content with administrative adjustments; they now aspired to radical political and territorial change. Autonomy under Ottoman rule was no longer sufficient; they now wanted an independent Christian state with extended boundaries under French protection.

The escalation of Lebanese Christian political ambitions resulted from the rapid decline of the Ottoman Empire, particularly after its crushing defeat in the Balkan wars, which put its very existence in jeopardy. The Lebanese felt that the time had come to realise their aspirations. They were greatly encouraged by French policy in the Levant. Faced with the impending collapse of the empire and growing rivalry from other European powers, France hastened to demonstrate its presence in an area it regarded as its own sphere of influence. French representatives intensified their activities among the inhabitants; French warships visited Lebanese ports more frequently, their commanders often paying ceremonial visits to the Maronite patriarch. In France itself there was increasing interest in the affairs of Syria and Lebanon as the press embarked upon an intensive campaign in support of French domination in the Levant. Statements by French politicians, in particular the speech of Premier Poincaré in the Senate on 21 December 1912, convinced the Lebanese Christians that France was preparing the ground for the occupation of Syria and Lebanon.[57]

The last two years before the World War saw the consolidation of political processes which would later bear fruit in the establishment of Lebanon. The Administrative Council, which during the previous five years had been constantly struggling against Yusuf Franco to retain its power and influence, now became the main political force, its authority unchallenged by the new governor Ohanes Pasha. Separatist tendencies became more pronounced; the Lebanese Christians, particularly the Maronites, now regarded independence not as a distant goal but as an immediate political objective. They appealed both openly and secretly to France to occupy Lebanon and establish an independent Christian state under its protection. They worked to persuade all the Lebanese Christians to support such a move, including those, in particular in the Greek Orthodox community, who were hesitant. They now phrased their aspirations in modern secular and national terms rather than in religious and confessional language. Many educated Lebanese ceased to regard themselves as members of a minority group seeking autonomy and foreign protection, but as part of a nation demanding its own independent state.

In the absence of modern political parties various societies and committees were formed as centres for political activity and tools to help achieve the desired goals. Despite their small membership, they had a significant influence on the crystallisation of Lebanese

Christian aspirations in national and secular terms, as many of their members were Western-educated lawyers and journalists. Their importance would become apparent during and after the War, when they became directly involved in the creation of modern Lebanon. One of the first societies was al-Nahda al-Lubnaniyah (The Lebanese Revival), established at the beginning of the century by the Khazin brothers, one of whom, Philippe al-Khazin, owned and edited the Christian newspaper *al-'Arz*. The society's objective was an independent Lebanon within extended boundaries under French protection; some of its members held secret contacts with French representatives before the War.[58]

Similar societies were established by Lebanese emigrants in Egypt, France, the United States and South America. These emigrants maintained close ties with their homeland and were an important source of financial aid. The concept of an independent Greater Lebanon was particularly strong among the emigrants, who were more exposed to western ideas and culture. Some historians have even suggested that Lebanese nationalism arose not in Lebanon itself, but among these societies abroad.[59] The groups were in close contact with one another; they co-ordinated their efforts to solicit the support of foreign governments and to influence local public opinion on behalf of Lebanese aspirations. One society active both in Lebanon and abroad was the Alliance Libanaise. It had originally been formed in Lebanon in 1908 in opposition to the demand for Lebanese participation in the Ottoman elections. In February 1909 branches were established in Cairo and Alexandria by Lebanese emigrants influenced by the Egyptian nationalist ideas of Mustafa Kamil. The society had a strongly nationalist character and was dedicated to the independence of Lebanon within extended boundaries.[60] But the most influential group was the Comité Libanais of Paris, whose president was Shukri Ghanem and whose members included Khairallah Khairallah and George Samné. It succeeded in establishing close ties with French politicians and groups with colonial interests; together, they founded the Comité Central Syrien, which played a prominent role in enlisting the support of the French government and public for the Lebanese cause during and after the War.

The efforts of the Lebanese Christians to establish a state of their own became increasingly nationalist in character as political and nationalist activity increased among their Muslim neighbours in the coastal area; the latter began to press their own demands for autonomy and even separatism, especially after the Balkan wars. The attempts of the Muslims of the coast to make the vilayet of Beirut an autonomous province with its own rights and privileges could hardly have been viewed favourably by the Christians in the Mountain, who wanted to annex the area to Mount Lebanon. The development added a sense of urgency to Christian demands.

The change in Muslim attitudes was even more threatening for the Christians of the coast and the Beqa'a Valley. They had already been badly affected by the new Ottoman laws, particularly by the introduction of compulsory conscription of non-Muslims into the Ottoman army. Thousands of young Christians began to emigrate for fear of conscription, and the trend increased after the Balkan wars. The massacres of the Armenians, the growth of anti-Christian feeling and the rise of nationalist and separatist tendencies among the Muslims, fed their growing fear and insecurity.[61] Although some Christians, in particular the Greek Orthodox community, were willing to co-operate with the Muslims on a national and secular basis if equality were respected, the majority regarded Muslim aspirations with suspicion and anxiety. The Christians on the coast were prepared to join their Muslim neighbours in the struggle to obtain autonomy and decentralisation from the Turks, but they regarded this co-operation as a short-term tactical move. Most of them continued to aspire for incorporation with Mount Lebanon in a Christian state under French protection. Even while co-operating with the Muslims of Beirut in the reform movement, some of their leaders secretly continued to pursue policies aimed at the annexation of the area to Mount Lebanon, with the active support of many inhabitants of the Mountain and Christians in the Beqa'a. The Christians in the Mountain had been sorely disappointed when the Protocol of December 1912 failed to provide for extended borders, but their success in safeguarding and even increasing their autonomy and privileges strengthened the desire of the Christians on the coast and in the Beqa'a for annexation so that they too could enjoy these privileges. They stepped up their pleas with French representatives for French occupation and for annexation to the Mountain as the basis of an independent state under French suzerainty.[62]

So far, our discussion has centred on the Christians in Lebanon and the emergence of a Christian national movement on the eve of the First World War. Mount Lebanon, however, was not an isolated area, but an integral part of Ottoman Syria in which the majority of the population was Muslim. The Muslims were divided into several sects of whom the Sunnis were dominant, like the Maronites among the Christians. The Sunni reaction to the emergence of a strong Christian Maronite entity in their midst, demanding not only independence and foreign protection but also the annexation of areas in which many Muslims lived, was to become a vital factor in the political development of modern Lebanon. After 1920 the Sunnis came to replace the Druze as the Maronites' main partners; since then the Lebanese political scene has been dominated by the relationship between these two communities.

The Sunnis lived mainly in the coastal towns of Beirut, Tripoli and Sidon. They regarded their community as an integral part of the Muslim population of Syria, and they had strong family, social and economic ties with the Syrian interior. Many were prosperous merchants who conducted commerce between the coastal area and the hinterland. As in the rest of Syria, they were the mainstay of the Ottoman government and the politically dominant community.

The extensive social, cultural and political changes of the second half of the nineteenth century led to increased hostility between the Muslim majority throughout Syria, including the Sunnis of the coast, and the Christian minority. The Muslims considered the religious equality granted to Christians by the Tanzimat reforms as an affront to their religion and to the Muslim character of the state as a whole. Religious and political opposition to the Christians was bolstered by economic, social and cultural factors. Muslims envied the commercial success of the Christians who had begun to dominate the economy of the area, in particular the trade with Europe. Muslim notables feared that the now rich and Western-oriented Christians might try to gain control with the aid of the European Christian powers. The Christians' rapid cultural Westernisation increased Muslim hostility and further widened the gap between the two communities.

The strong ties of the Christians, especially the Maronites, with Europe led the Muslims to identify them with the European powers, in particular with France, and to regard them as potential traitors. Their fears increased as the Ottoman Empire continued to decline in the second half of the nineteenth and in the early twentieth centuries, and as the political, economic and cultural activities of the European powers in the area intensified. The Christians, with their newly-acquired equality, education and prosperity, often behaved in a superior and provocative manner, further increasing Muslim hostility, which was manifested in such outbreaks of anti-Christian violence as the massacres in Aleppo in 1850 and in Damascus and Mount Lebanon in 1860, which in turn widened the gap between the two communities. These outbreaks amplified Christian fears of their Muslim neighbours, which were to re-emerge repeatedly in the following years.[63] An American eye-witness observed at the time that

> These panics among the Syrian Christians are terrible and uncontrollable. Usually in other lands, when a riot occurs, the people turn to the government and the military to restore order. But here in Syria, where the military are all Muslims, the Christian people are as much afraid of the soldiers as of a mob of Muslim roughs, and they can never forget that regular troops joined in the awful massacres in Damascus, Hasbeiya and Deir el Kamer in 1860.[64]

The geographical situation of the Muslims along the coast made them feel particularly vulnerable to domination by the Christians and their European allies. Unlike their co-religionists of the interior, they did not constitute the overwhelming majority. In fact in Beirut they formed less than half the population. Beirut became a Christian town; the many Christians who moved there from all parts of Syria and Lebanon settled in separate quarters in the east. By the beginning of the twentieth century the contrast between the prosperous Christian quarters in the east and the poorer Muslim area in the west had aroused the Muslims' hostility against their more affluent neighbours.[65] Moreover, their proximity to Mount Lebanon, an autonomous militant Christian entity whose inhabitants, together with many of Beirut's Christians, openly expressed their desire to be united into one Christian state under foreign protection, reinforced their fears of becoming a minority under Christian domination. The Christians' close contacts with the politically and economically powerful West made the Muslims more aware of their own weaknesses. Their exposure to the Western culture and ideas which were far more evident in Beirut than in the other towns of Syria, drove them to seek changes and reforms in their own society. It was in Beirut that the idea of Arab nationalism arose. Muslim notables from Beirut were the first to establish, in 1874, a society to improve education for Muslims.[66] The same milieu provided the leaders of the reform movement before the War.

The growing Muslim sense of vulnerability fostered two contradictory approaches. On the one hand, fear and insecurity drove the masses to fanaticism, sometimes to the point of anti-Christian violence. On the other hand, the same vulnerability, combined with the growth of secular Western ideas of equality and brotherhood without regard for religious or confessional differences, increased their desire for peaceful coexistence with Christian neighbours. Both of these contradictory attitudes would become especially conspicuous in the period from the Young Turk revolution to the outbreak of the War.

The restoration of constitutional government was enthusiastically received by the Muslims, who were now predisposed to a particularly friendly attitude towards the Christians. In Beirut Muslim leaders such as Shekib Arslan acclaimed the new era of 'liberty, equality and fraternity' and praised the 'breaking down of all the barriers distinguishing between Muslims and Christians'.[67] Shortly afterwards, however, a local incident between a Muslim and a Christian in Beirut led to an anti-Christian demonstration by 500 Muslims. Communal tension increased in the months following the massacre of Armenians in the provinces of Adana and Aleppo in April 1909. This and several other local incidents added to Christian fears of a Muslim uprising and led many Christians to seek refuge in Mount Lebanon.[68] The difficulties in bridging the traditional hostility and suspicion again became apparent in 1911 and 1912 during the wars against Italy and the Balkan states. Fear of foreign occupation, together with Turkish pan-Islamic and anti-foreign propaganda, increased the already strong anti-Christian feeling among the Muslims of the coastal towns. Foreigners and Lebanese Christians living there grew anxious, and both France and Britain found it necessary to send warships to the Lebanese coast to deter possible attacks against them.[69]

The 1911–12 wars were a turning point in Arab Muslim attitudes towards the Ottoman Empire. The defeat and humiliation suffered by the Turks demonstrated that the empire was no longer able to fulfil its role of defending the 'ummah (Muslim community) against the ambitions of the Christian powers.[70] The majority of Muslims were now reluctant to comply with Turkish appeals for their participation in the war effort. Describing the general mood of the Muslims in Beirut, Cumberbatch wrote that they were '. . . not so keen upon sacrificing their lives and fortunes in a war which they knew must end disastrously for them and their country'.[71] Moreover the wars, which demanded great efforts on the part of the entire empire, proved that the Turks had neither the time nor the intention to deal seriously with local demands for comprehensive reform. The strengthening of Turkish nationalism, the Young Turk policy of centralisation, the inadequate representation of Arabs in the administration and the attempt to impose the Turkish lauguage on them all increased Arab resentment of the Young Turk regime. After 1912 Arab Muslim disillusionment led many to adopt an openly anti-Turkish attitude.

By 1913 the Muslims of the coast, particularly in Beirut, were deeply discontented and in a state of political, social and economic agitation. The general atmosphere of uncertainty and unrest was accompanied by intense political activity and the spread of the new idea of Arab nationalism. Political discussions took place in the press and in the societies established to defend Arab rights; the Arabs were being called upon to take their future into their own hands.

Once again, the main source of Muslim unrest was the fear of occupation by a European power and the creation of a Christian state under its protection. Open appeals by the Christians to France to occupy Lebanon, together with intensified French activity in the area led the Muslims to assume that French occupation was inevitable.[72] Although the Muslims of Syria and Lebanon were apprehensive of any European Christian occupation, it was France they feared most of all. The French, for their part, were loath to acknowledge the extent of their unpopularity and of Muslim resentment and hostility. Even when they did acknowledge its existence, they minimised its strength and claimed it was inspired by foreign propaganda and intrigue, first Turkish and later British. However, the anti-French feeling of the Muslims was genuine and was already evident before the War. It later became a major political factor affecting relations between France and Britain in the region and colouring the relationship between France and the Muslims in the Levant throughout the Mandate period.

Hostility towards France had religious, cultural, political and economic grounds. The Muslims saw that country as an anti-Muslim Catholic power which could endanger their religion and way of life. French missionaries had for centuries been the spearhead of Western cultural, educational and religious activity in the area. French conduct in colonies such as Algeria and Tunisia was seen as proof of its anti-Muslim policy. Intensive pan-Islamic propaganda with an emphasis on xenophobia and on the danger to the faith from the Christian powers, especially France and Italy, s. the fears of the Muslim masses. This propaganda was, in fa.t, inspired by the Young Turks as a means of weakening anti-Turkish feelings among the Arab Muslims by emphasising the common religion in the face of the Christian threat. But France's own intensive economic activity, particularly in Beirut, gave rise to claims that French companies were exploiting the area and its inhabitants. The privileges enjoyed by these companies and the fact that they conducted their business mainly with local Christians added to Muslim envy and resentment.

The main cause for resentment and hostility remained the fear that French occupation would enable the Christians to realise their age-old dream of an independent French-protected Lebanon. It was France, the Muslims knew, who had sent forces to protect the Christians in 1860; it was French representatives who had defended Christian interests and rights in the area and maintained close ties with Christian religious leaders, in particular with the Maronite patriarch. The Muslims were convinced that French occupation would enable the Christians to establish their own state within extended boundaries, in which Muslims would be a minority.[73]

By 1913 the Arab Muslims knew that the Ottoman Empire was in a precarious state and that foreign intervention in Syria and Lebanon was inevitable. The question was no longer whether such intervention would take place, but when and by whom. Fear of French occupation led some Muslims in Lebanon, encouraged by Franco-British rivalry, to express pro-British sentiment openly. If foreign intervention was inevitable, they preferred Britain, whose administration in Egypt was regarded as a successful example of liberal British colonial policy. They reasoned that Britain, unlike France, was not identified with the local Christians; they turned to Britain mainly to prevent the possibility of French-aided Christian domination. They regarded British protection as a means of '. . . ensuring the continuation of Muslim rule fortified by British administrative authority which they all respect and appreciate'.[74]

These views were held only by a small number of Muslims, while the majority remained loyal to the Ottoman Empire. Nevertheless, growing disappointment with the Young Turk regime, which had failed to implement their requests for reform, combined with fear of foreign occupation as increasingly called for by the Christians and even by some Muslims, led to the formation by Beirut Muslims of a reform movement. At the centre of this movement was the Beirut Reform Society; within this group, co-operation between Muslims and Christians reached its pre-war peak. Although the demand for reform was a major factor in its establishment, and was indeed the main reason for the strong support it received from both Muslims and Christians, it was not the only goal of the Muslim notables of Beirut who initiated and promoted the movement. No less important was the desire to forestall foreign intervention and to weaken the separatist tendencies among Christians and some Muslims. Only a comprehensive programme of reform could contain the growing discontent and particularist sentiment. These considerations show up clearly in the memoirs of Salim 'Ali Salam, a Sunni notable from Beirut who was one of the initiators and leaders of the movement for reform. He described the atmosphere which led him and other notables to initiate such a movement:

> Hardly had the Balkan war started when the Ottoman army was defeated and routed; it was then rumoured that the French were going to send their fleet to this country. This made the various vilayets concerned about their future, and the vilayet of Beirut was more concerned than others, considering its geographic position and the Imperialist ambitions focused on it from the earliest times. Some friends approached me with the suggestion that an annexation to Egypt, under English protection, be requested; others expressed a desire for a French occupation.[75]

Another factor which militated in favour of immediate action was the increasingly insistent Christian demand that the borders of the Mountain be extended to include the coast and the Beqa'a Valley. Towards the end of 1912, when negotiations were being held in Constantinople for a new Protocol for the Mountain, the Christians both in the Mountain and the two adjacent regions tried to pressure the Ottoman government and gain the support of the signatory powers for annexation. The Muslim leaders believed large-scale reform was essential in order to strengthen the autonomous position of the vilayet of Beirut and help it resist such demands. Moreover, the success of the Mountain's inhabitants in extracting additional privileges from the Ottoman authorities encouraged both Muslims and Christians on the coast to redouble their efforts to obtain similar concessions. The reform movement was officially established and its programme drawn up less than a month after the new Protocol was approved.

The Muslim notables of Beirut were prepared to offer significant concessions to the Christians in order to secure their participation in the movement. Christians were offered equal representation in its General Assembly (comprised of 42 Muslims, 42 Christians and 2 Jews), and Executive Committee (12 Muslims, 12 Christians and 1 Jew),[76] even though they were only a minority in the vilayet. The Muslims were prepared to go even further. In compliance with the request of some of the Christian representatives the programme for reform presented to the Ottoman authorities on 31 January 1913 included a call for the appointment of foreign advisers and inspectors in the administration of the vilayet. Indeed, some Christians had joined the movement precisely to achieve that concession.[77]

Muslim and Christian hopes for comprehensive reform in the vilayet of Beirut suffered a serious setback when the liberal government of Kamil Pasha was overthrown by the Committee for Union and Progress (CUP) on 23 January 1913. The replacement of the vali Adham Bey, who had sympathised with the Reform Movement, by the former vali Kazim Bey, a strong supporter of the CUP who had previously been dismissed by Kamil Pasha, added to their disappointment. After the *coup d'état* Cumberbatch informed the Foreign Office that

> . . . with the return of the Union Party, a recrudescence of separatist ideas may be expected. In the town of Beirut the general feeling is that all hopes of a betterment of their position must now be abandoned, and that the occupation of this region by a foreign Power is only a matter of time. . .[78]

But the reform movement was already well-established, and despite their disappointment, its leaders continued to assert their demands for comprehensive reform. The CUP and the new vali tried to weaken the movement through pressure and bribes; when these efforts failed, the alarmed Ottoman authorities on 8 April took the drastic step of dissolving the Reform Society and banning its meetings. Several days later they arrested five of its leaders and turned them over to the military court for trial. In protest, a general strike was called in Beirut. Only the mediation of the British consul-general, who succeeded in obtaining the release of those detained in return for their promise to call off the strike, prevented further deterioration in relations between the inhabitants of the town and the Ottoman authorities.[79]

In the months that followed, co-operation between Muslims and Christians against the Turks reached its peak. Leaders of both communities sent petitions to the Ottoman government and refused to co-operate with the Ottoman vali. Attempts by the government to sow discord between them failed:

> The phase of the whole proceedings which strikes one most forcibly is the unity of purpose and the solidarity of action that seem to gain strength between the Arab Muslims and the Christians, as time goes by, notwithstanding the many subtle efforts made to divide them.[80]

The only major success of the Ottoman authorities was in persuading the Mutawallis of Sidon and Jabal 'Amel to disassociate themselves from the Beirut Reform Society; in return, the government promised to accept some of their demands, in particular that they be recognised as a community separate from the Sunnis.[81]

Co-operation between Muslims and Christians continued during the preparations for the Arab Congress in Paris in June 1913. Three Muslims and three Christians from the Beirut Reform Society were chosen to represent the vilayet. Before their departure, all six delegates received a letter from the religious leaders of the various Christian communities confirming that they were authorised to represent them in Europe.[82]

Once in Paris, however, the Muslim delegates, in particular Salim 'Ali Salam, began to question their role in a general movement for reform and decentralisation throughout the empire. Although they participated in the Congress, they continued to regard their reform movement as a local group representing local interests, particularly those of Beirut. Indeed, at the end of March they had turned down a merger proposal offered by the Decentralisation Party in Egypt.[83] The harsh Turkish measures of April had driven them to co-operate more closely with other organisations pressing for reform throughout the empire, but they really had little in common with such Christian delegates as Shukri Ghanem, Nadra Mutran or Iskandar 'Ammun, whose close relations with French officials aroused their suspicions. As for the Christian delegates from Beirut, their close ties with French officials and the rumours that they were appealing to France to annex Lebanon did not inspire confidence. In their contacts with French officials the Muslim delegates left no doubt of their opposition to any such step, and they stressed that they still regarded the Ottoman Empire as their country. In his memoirs, Salam suggests that one of the main reasons he decided to take part in the Congress had been to counteract any such activities by the Christian delegates. Speaking of their behaviour in Paris, Salam remarked: 'We did not then know that when we were in Beirut, working together in the Reform Society, they had presented a memorandum to the French consul in Beirut . . . requesting the opposite to what Mukhtar had requested.'[84] Salam's bitterness is understandable as he and his associates in Beirut had initiated the reform movement precisely to counter the threat of French occupation of the coast and annexation of Beirut to Mount Lebanon.

Towards the end of 1913 the CUP stepped up its efforts to improve relations with Arab Muslims. It adopted a more sympathetic tone, replaced the vali of Beirut and acceded to some of the Muslim demands for reform. These efforts met with some success; in consequence, Muslim-Christian co-operation, which had flourished since the end of 1912, began to weaken. The Reform Society was dissolved and distrust once more deepened between the two communities. Nevertheless, although most Arab Muslims still remained loyal to the empire, many were disappointed with the Ottoman regime and nationalist and separatist tendencies became stronger. As for the Christians, they had ceased to believe in the possibility of obtaining significant reforms. They now regarded foreign intervention and annexation to Mount Lebanon as the only solution.

The outbreak of the First World War in August 1914 and the Ottoman decision in late October to join forces with Germany and Austria was just the crisis the Christians had been waiting for and the Muslims had feared. Both groups believed that the final obstacle in the way of direct foreign intervention had now been removed; within a short time, the empire would crumble and Lebanon would be occupied by the Allied forces. The moment they heard of the outbreak of the War many Muslims, fearing an impending French invasion, fled Beirut and the coast for Damascus and the interior; the Christians remained behind to wait hopefully for their liberators' arrival. But the War dragged on for four years, bringing great suffering to the Lebanese. In the end Lebanon was occupied not by the French, but by the British, who had advanced northwards from Palestine.

The War was the turning point in the historical and political development of Lebanon, as for the whole Middle East. It marked the defeat and disintegration of the Ottoman Empire and the division of its Arab territories between Britain and France. In Syria and Lebanon, the ties between Arab Muslims and Turks were severed; but for Christians the War was an even more traumatic experience which profoundly influenced their attitude in subsequent years. For both Muslims and Christians the events of those years provided the opportunity to realise national aspirations; they also led to a final split between the two communities.

The War broke out at a time when relations between Arab Muslims and Turks were still strained followed the events of 1913. Most Arab still retained strong religious ties with the empire and remained loyal supporters of the Caliphate, but many were reluctant to participate in the War. The proclamation of a jihad (holy war) by the sultan in November roused little enthusiasm among them. They feared that the War would lead to foreign occupation of their country. Furthermore, they were soon alienated by the oppressive policies of Jamal Pasha, commander of the IVth Army and military governor of Syria and Lebanon, which grew particularly harsh after the failure of the Turkish offensive on the Suez Canal. Muslim leaders, especially members of the reform movement, suffered deportation, confiscation of property and some were even executed. Such acts antagonised the most influential group of Arabs, the very people on whom the Ottoman authorities had traditionally relied.[85] The effect was to strengthen Arab nationalism and encourage the Arabs to feel the need to establish an independent state of their own. After the Sharif of Mecca began his Arab Revolt against the Turks in June 1916, an increasing number of Muslims in Syria and Lebanon came to regard him and his movement as offering new hope for Arab self-rule and for a revived Arab Caliphate. As Arab and British forces advanced towards Syria, many Muslims on the coast began to believe that they might not be occupied by French forces after all, but liberated by fellow Arabs. These hopes were manifested in the enthusiastic welcome accorded to Faisal and his army by the Muslims of Syria and Lebanon in October 1918.

Upon the outbreak of the War the Lebanese Christians, in particular the Maronites, expected France to occupy Lebanon immediately and help them realise their aspirations. During the two months between the outbreak of war in Europe and the Ottoman decision to enter the fray, Maronites openly expressed their support for France.

Their patriarch proclaimed the attachment of the Maronites to that country, and donations were collected for the French Red Cross. A deputation told French consul-general Picot in Beirut that the Maronites were willing to volunteer for the French army. Optimistic about the future, these Christians nevertheless had to face more immediate problems. The abolition of the Capitulations by the Ottoman authorities in September raised the prospect that the government might exploit the War in Europe to terminate the special status of the Mountain. After being assured by Picot that France would occupy Lebanon within three months, some known Christian Francophiles left for Egypt, fearing reprisals by the Turkish authorities.[86]

Turkish treatment of the Lebanese Christians during the War was strongly influenced by long-standing Young Turk resentment of foreign interference in the internal affairs of the empire, which was particularly evident in Lebanon. The War gave them the opportunity to bring an end to such interference and to make Lebanon an ordinary Ottoman province. In any case, fears of a Christian uprising in the Mountain and an Allied invasion of the coast, which would cut Jamal Pasha's forces off from the north, led him to adopt harsh measures. French newspaper claims that the Maronite patriarch had promised 5,000 men to help the French occupy Lebanon seemed to confirm these suspicions.[87] Jamal Pasha wrote in his memoirs:

> About this time there was a general idea throughout Syria and Beirut that the Christians of the Lebanon would rise in the near future. I was advised on all sides to suspend the special rights of the Lebanon and issue a proclamation calling upon the civil population to deliver up their arms to the government. It was said that there were fifty thousand modern rifles in the Lebanon.[88]

Elsewhere he claimed that before the War, members of the Lebanese Revival and the Society for Decentralisation had already contacted the French representative in Egypt asking for his assistance in sustaining a revolt in Lebanon, and that they had been promised 20,000 rifles, financial aid and the backing of the French fleet.[89]

To prevent an uprising in the Mountain and to defend it against a possible Allied invasion 16,000 Turkish troops entered the autonomous Sanjak and took up positions throughout the Mountain, in violation of the Règlement Organique. To forestall any armed resistance Jamal Pasha pursued an oppressive policy aimed at rendering effective leadership impossible. His main targets were the Administrative Council and the Maronite Church, the two most influential bodies in the Mountain and the chief sources of opposition to the Turkish authorities. In early 1915 he began to restrict the authority of the Administrative Council; he later arrested and deported some of its members, including Habib Pasha al-Sa'd. In March he dissolved the Council altogether. A new Council was formed with members appointed by the Turkish authorities, but even this body was later dissolved. In June 1915 Ohanes Pasha resigned in protest; he was eventually replaced by a Muslim governor; the Mountain's autonomy was abolished as Mount Lebanon became an ordinary province under direct Ottoman rule.[90]

Parallel to these pressures against the Administrative Council the authorities went into action against the Maronite Church and Patriarch Hawayik. Monasteries and other institutions under foreign control were taken over. Members of the clergy, including the bishop of Beirut, were arrested and deported, and one priest was executed. In March 1915 Patriarch Hawayik was forced to apply for a special firman from the sultan to ratify his office. This was the first time in the history of the Maronite Church that such a document had been required; the application was intended as a symbolic act of Church submission to the Turkish authorities. In the next two years the Turks made several attempts to remove Hawayik from office and bring him to trial, but they bowed to the intervention of the representatives of Austria and the Holy See. In spite of all these pressures, the Maronite Church continued throughout the War to provide support for the community; even in these highly difficult circumstances it proved to be the only stable organisation in the Mountain.[91]

During the War Lebanon suffered from severe widespread famine. It is believed that over one-fifth of the population of Mount Lebanon, most of them Christians, died of starvation or disease. The Lebanese accused the Turks, particularly Jamal Pasha, of intentionally starving the inhabitants of the Mountain and trying to exterminate them as they had the Armenians. In any case, there were objective factors that contributed to the high number of fatalities: the cessation of remittances from abroad, which had been a main source of income for many; the collapse of the economy, especially of commerce and silk production; the inefficiency of the Turkish administration; high inflation; corruption and profiteering; and a severe plague of locusts.[92]

Wartime developments made the Lebanese Christians even more determined to realise their national aims. Without taking into consideration the impact of their experiences during the War, it would be difficult to understand their almost desperate efforts in the first two years of peace to establish a state of their own. They were determined never again to be part of any Muslim state, whether Turkish or Arab, and they vehemently opposed the steps taken by Faisal's Arab government in Damascus to establish an Arab Syrian state which would include Lebanon. Their demand for extended boundaries also took on new significance. For them, the tragic events of the War had proved their claim that Mount Lebanon had insufficient land to support its population. Now, more than ever before, they were convinced of the need for extended boundaries if Lebanon was to become self-sufficient and economically viable. Their conviction was so powerful that they totally ignored the implications of such a demand; namely the inclusion of a large Muslim population within the larger entity. Finally, the events of the War bolstered their conviction that only a European power could protect them against a recurrence of such traumatic experiences.

At the end of the War the Administrative Council, under its president Habib al-Sa'd, back from exile in Anatolia, resumed its role as the chief political organisation in Mount Lebanon; but it was no longer the main representative of the inhabitants. The Maronite Church under Patriarch Hawayik had become a major political force embodying the aspirations of the Lebanese Christians; Hawayik's personal trials during the War had strengthened his resolve to strive to turn these aspirations into facts.

2 THE ESTABLISHMENT OF GREATER LEBANON

Throughout the First World War the Lebanese Christians remained convinced that under French occupation their national aspirations would soon be realised; but even when the War was over it was to take another two years of political upheaval in the Levant before they finally achieved their centuries-old dream of a state of their own. In the interim the Lebanese question became entangled in a larger complex of international and regional issues including Anglo-French rivalry in the Middle East, the secret War agreements, Britain's pledges to the Arabs, the emergence of a strong Arab national movement in Syria led by Faisal, and the relationship of that movement with France. Only when most of these problems had found their solution was the establishment of the Lebanese state possible. True, in the end the French government and its representatives in the Levant did fulfil the hopes of the Lebanese Christians in creating the Lebanese state and giving it generous borders. But this was not merely the automatic outcome of French pledges and traditional ties to the Lebanese Christians; it also reflected France's current interests in the area, including its developing relationship with Faisal's Arab government in Damascus. The establishment of Greater Lebanon must therefore be examined in the wider aspect of French policy in the Levant during and immediately after the War.

The granting of the mandate over Syria to France at the San Remo Conference in April 1920 was an official recognition of France's long-standing ties with the Levant. The origin of its claims to a protectorate over the Catholics, in particular the Maronites, has already been discussed. But France also pointed to its cultural, philanthropic and economic interests as justification for special 'rights' in the Levant. French religious orders such as the Jesuits and Lazarists had for centuries been conducting extensive educational activities in the Levant, particularly in Lebanon, through a network of educational institutions that included the University of St Joseph in Beirut. They also founded hospitals, orphanages and other charitable establishments. Other French institutions such as the Alliance Française were also active in the region. It has been estimated that before the War, 40,000 pupils were studying in more than 80 French schools in Lebanon and that the French government was spending about one million French francs annually in their support. French had become the cultural and literary language of the educated classes and had replaced Arabic as the first spoken language among many Lebanese Christians.[1]

Apart from humanitarian considerations the French 'civilising mission' had the clear political goal of strengthening France's position in an area in which it had for centuries had an interest. In the Levant, as in Black Africa and Southeast Asia, the missionaries had been the first to lay the foundations for French colonial ambitions. Indeed, these religious orders regularly received funds from the French government. The separation of Church and State during the Third Republic did not seriously hamper such activities outside the mother country. On the contrary, it led to an intensified involvement in the Levant, as many clerics sought alternative fields of action after their activities within France had been restricted.

France also had extensive economic interests in the Levant. French banks and businesses had invested heavily in the Ottoman Empire; before the War 63 per cent of the Ottoman Public Debt was in French hands. In Syria, Lebanon and Palestine French companies held an almost complete monopoly of the railway system and had extensive interests in ports, gas and electricity companies, chemical plants, silk cultivation and various other sectors.[2] France's concern about protecting these investments had been a major factor in its opposition, before the War, to the partition of the Ottoman realm. It feared that such a partition would enable other European powers to take over large areas of the empire. Germany's increasing influence, England's growing activity in Syria and the weakness of the empire, as underlined by its defeats at the hands of Italy and the Balkan states further increased France's anxiety about its interests in the Levant. It was this concern that prompted Premier Poincaré to make his well-known declaration in the Senate on 21 December 1912 stressing France's special interests in Syria and Lebanon and its intention to safeguard them.[3]

The outbreak of the War and the decision of the Ottoman Empire to join Germany and Austria gave France, Britain, Russia and later Italy and Greece the opportunity to try to fulfil their own ambitions in the territories of the empire. However, France's options in the Levant were seriously hampered. Unlike England and Russia, it was unable to allocate substantial forces to the eastern front, as most of its troops were tied down along the German border. At the same time the French government was determined not to allow its position and interests in the Levant to be jeopardised.

France's concern, particularly in the face of Britain's large military presence and extensive activities, prompted several attempts to demonstrate at least some French military presence in the area. Immediately after the outbreak of the War France demanded British acknowledgement of the supremacy of the French navy in the eastern Mediterranean, which Britain conceded. From their base in Port Sa'id French warships participated in the blockade of the Syrian coast, and the small island of Arwad opposite Tripoli became a naval base for French intelligence activities under the command of Captain Trabaud, who was later to become the first French governor of Lebanon. The rivalry with Britain also explains France's rejection of the plan proposed by British War Secretary Kitchener to invade Alexandretta, as well as its willingness to participate in the Dardanelles campaign. Again, the despatch of a small French detachment led by Colonel Piépape to fight with British forces under the command of General Allenby in Palestine, Syria and Lebanon was intended to ensure a French military presence in the area; the formation of the Légion d'Orient in Egypt and Cyprus in 1916 from Armenian, Syrian and Lebanese Christian volunteers was no more than an attempt to overcome France's inability to allocate its own forces to the campaign in Syria. The official appointment by the French government in April 1917 of Georges-Picot as 'high commissioner in Syria, Palestine and Armenia' was a further demonstration that France intended to secure these areas under its own control.[4]

The launching of the Dardanelles campaign fostered Allied hopes for the immediate collapse of the Ottoman Empire, and prompted Russia, France and Britain to enter into negotiations over the future of the region; the talks ended in a series of secret accords. The Sykes-Picot agreement of May 1916, which carved up the empire's Arab territories between France and Britain, was particularly important. It played an essential role in French policy in the Levant for the remainder of the War and at the peace conference, and largely determined the present-day division of the Middle East into nation-states. From the moment the accord was reached France regarded it as a binding agreement and a basis for its claims over Syria and Lebanon; it firmly opposed all later British attempts to revise it.[5]

The Sykes-Picot agreement had a considerable impact on the future of Lebanon. The agreement stipulated direct French control over a 'Blue Zone', stretching along the coast from the district of Sefad in the south to Alexandretta in the north, and including Cilicia. The southern part of the Blue Zone corresponded roughly to present-day Lebanon. France was given direct control over this region mainly due to its special interests and position in Lebanon; the inclusion of Cilicia was based largely on considerations of economic potential. The separation of the Blue Zone from 'Zone A', which was to be placed under Arab administration and only indirectly controlled by France, was an acknowledgement of the special status of Lebanon. This was also expressed in the McMahon-Hussein correspondence, when Britain turned down Hussein's claim for control over Lebanon, stressing that the area could not be considered purely Arab and that France had traditional interests there.[6]

The fact that the French representative in the negotiations was Picot who had served as consul-general in Beirut before the War, further strengthened the general assumption that Lebanese Christian aspirations were being taken into account. Picot was fully aware of the precise boundaries the Christians demanded for their future state; in fact during the negotiations it was he who insisted on the inclusion of the Beqa'a Valley in the area under direct French control.[7] Sykes, at least, assumed that Lebanese Christian aspirations had some influence on the stand taken by the French; he suggested that Britain exploit French Catholic fears about a possible massacre of Lebanese Christians in order to pressure the French to adopt a more flexible stand and conclude an agreement as quickly as possible.[8]

At the time the Sykes-Picot agreement was concluded, French decision-makers had not yet necessarily envisaged the creation of an independent Christian Greater Lebanon. The French government considered Lebanon to be part of Syria, all of which, it felt, should be included in France's sphere of influence. The division of both French-controlled Syria and British-controlled Mesopotamia into two zones each had been proposed to enable Britain to reconcile its pledges to the Arabs and to pave the way for an Arab revolt against the Turks. At the time, Picot himself had in mind retaining the *status quo* in Lebanon under French instead of Turkish suzerainty. At a meeting at the British Foreign Office on 21 December 1915 attended by Picot, it was suggested 'that the Lebanon should so far as is practicable, retain its present constitution, but that it should comprise Beirut and that the Governor should be nominated by the

French government'.[9]

Nevertheless, the Sykes-Picot agreement laid the potential basis for the future Lebanese state by separating Lebanon from the rest of Syria. This would become apparent immediately after the War when Lebanon and the coastal area came under direct French control while the rest of Syria was placed under Faisal's Arab administration in Damascus. In the two-year period following the War, the precedent of Lebanon as a separate entity was established; it would contribute to France's decision to create a Lebanese state. The Lebanese Christians themselves soon realised the importance of the agreement for their own aspirations; they later used it to back their claims for an independent state, and their demands for the Beqa'a Valley.

The intensive efforts of the various French governments to secure French control over Syria were not merely the result of strategic, political and economic considerations, as was the case with British activity in the area. During the War, and in particular in the two years following the Armistice, the Syrian question became a matter of national prestige, fraught with emotion and directly involved in domestic politics. Although only a small number of groups and organisations in France had direct interests in the Levant, they succeeded, through intensive campaigns of propaganda, pressure and lobbying, in turning the question of French control over Syria into a national issue, second in importance only to Alsace-Lorraine. These groups argued that France, in addition to its vital interests in Syria which had to be safeguarded, also had 'rights' there acquired during centuries of activities. They described Syria as a 'second Alsace-Lorraine' and put pressure on successive governments to entrench France's position there, as it wished to do along the Rhine.[10] This sensitivity and emotion, coupled with France's traditional suspicion about British 'Fashodism', explains the bitterness of the Anglo-French confrontation over Syria after the War. The French public genuinely believed that Britain was trying to undermine France's control over a region which rightfully belonged to it. Faisal and his father were often portrayed as 'Beduins' subtly used by Britain to take over the region.[11] No politician in France could ignore public opinion and disregard the pressure which these groups had successfully generated. Even Clemenceau, a powerful prime minister who did not personally consider French domination over Syria to be a matter of vital importance, had to bow to this pressure and take a firmer stand on Syria at the Peace Conference. The majority of French politicians at the time, including ministers and most members of the National Assembly but excluding the Left, strongly supported France's efforts to take control over Syria, whether for political and economic gain or for moral considerations, and were convinced that France had to continue its special cultural and humanitarian mission in the Levant.[12]

Sykes referred to these groups as 'The Syrian Party' and divided them into two main categories: those with colonial, commercial and financial interests in the Levant and those with religious, cultural and educational interests there.[13] Among the former were banks and businesses involved in ports, railways, import and export, textiles and silk production, as well as various industrialists, financiers and entrepreneurs. They were backed by the Chambers of Commerce of Paris, Lyons and Marseilles and organisations such as the French Colonial League. They acted directly as pressure groups, and indirectly by supporting and financing other organisations and by waging a campaign in the French press. They saw the outbreak of the War as an opportunity to secure French control over the area they called 'La Syrie Intégrale', which included Cilicia in addition to Syria, Lebanon and Palestine. They regarded such control as necessary to guarantee the large investments already made in the area; at the same time they were attracted by the seemingly great economic potential of Syria which they considered ripe for extensive French economic activity. They saw the Levant as both a rich agricultural region abounding in raw materials such as cotton from Cilicia, wheat from Syria, silk cocoons from Lebanon and oil from Mosul, and an important market for French manufactured goods. The railway system, and the ports of Alexandretta, Beirut and Tripoli were considered to be of strategic importance to France as well as a means of spreading French influence and economic activity throughout the area. Furthermore, French control over Syria, particularly over the important Muslim centre of Damascus, was considered by the colonialists as essential in securing France's position in its Muslim colonies in North Africa. At the end of the War, Syria was compared with Algeria, and it was hoped that its great economic wealth would enable the French economy to overcome the devastating effects of the War. Only later was it realised that Syria was to bring France more burdens than benefits.[14]

In their efforts to enlist the support of the French government and public, the economic sectors capitalised on works by well-known French writers, historians and Orientalists such as Etienne Lamy, Victor Bérard and Maurice Barrès. These writers emphasised

Syria's wealth, its economic and strategic importance for France, the friendliness of its inhabitants towards the French and the historical ties between France and the area. The many journalists and writers fascinated by the East succeeded in presenting a powerful and appealing image of Syria to the French public. The economists, financiers and politicians exploited this image for their own interests. Indeed, they were influenced by it themselves; they consciously worked to realise the dreams of the writers and historians.[15]

The commercial and financial sectors were strongly supported by the French Catholic Church and its religious orders, particularly the Jesuits, Lazarists and Franciscans, whose long-standing religious, educational and cultural activity in Lebanon had been brought to a halt.[16] At the start of the War the Ottoman authorities had expelled the orders from Syria, Lebanon and Palestine, taken over their institutions and confiscated their property. Reports about the massacre of Armenians and the sufferings of Lebanese Christians spurred the Church to step up its efforts to help at least the latter. For the Catholic orders, French control over the Levant was deemed necessary both to defend Christians against Muslim domination, and to guarantee the pre-eminence of their own religious and educational activities in the area.[17]

All these interested sectors played an active role in forming French policy in the Levant. They managed to establish close ties with many members of the government, the Senate and the Chamber of Deputies, as well as with officials in the Quai d'Orsay and army officers. It would be impossible to understand France's Syrian policy during these years without taking their activities and influence into account.

One of the more active of these societies before the war was the Comité de Défense des Intérêts Français en Orient. It was established in December 1911 with the aim of promoting France's moral, political and economic interests in the Middle East. To achieve this, the Committee proposed

> . . . de faire appel à l'opinion et de seconder la politique française, en employant ses ressources et sa propagande à soutenir toutes les oeuvres qui font honneur à la France dans les pays d'Orient et contribuent à y répondre son action.[18]

One of its initial acts was to send Maurice Pernot, editor of the *Journal des Débats* on a mission in 1912 to prepare a report on the state of France's interests in Syria. The society was supported by many prominent politicians. Its president was Alexandre Ribot, who served several times as prime minister. Its secretary-general was Denys Cochin,[19] a deputy with close ties in Catholic circles, and its secretary for a short period was Robert de Caix. Among its members were Poincaré, Briand, Flandin, Franklin-Bouillon, Deschanel, Herriot and Henri Simon. The group received funds from various banks and commercial enterprises which had economic interests in the Middle East, including the Chambers of Commerce of Marseilles, Lyons and Paris.

Another society active during and after the war to secure French dominance in *la Syrie intégrale* was the Comité de l'Orient, founded in 1912. Its first president was Pichon and later, Barthou. Lebanese and Syrian emigrants such as George Samné played an important part in this group, which adopted a more liberal attitude towards the future of French Syria.[20] The Comité de l'Orient was also supported by prominent French colonialists such as Flandin, who was a key figure in the campaign to secure French control over the Levant.[21] He headed a group of senators dedicated to the defence of French interests in Syria and in 1916 organised the various societies into one coherent pressure group — the Comité d'Action Française en Syrie.

The most influential society in the 'Syrian Party' was the Comité de l'Asie Française which had been established in 1901 on the initiative of Eugène Etienne on the model of l'Afrique Française. Its aim was to further knowledge of Asia in France and to promote French interests in Asia. However, during the war, it increasingly dedicated its efforts to promoting France's position in the Middle East. Its president was Emile Sénart, and many leading politicians such as Leygues, Millerand, Poincaré, Doumer and Marin were among its supporters. The society had close ties with prominent officials in the Quai d'Orsay including de Margerie, Berthelot, Goût and Georges-Picot. With its widely circulated bulletin and close ties with prominent writers such as Lamy and Bérard and with many journalists, l'Asie Française proved very influential in shaping French public opinion. After France had established control over Syria, the bulletin proudly claimed:

> Par l'intermédiaire des journalistes quotidiens qui s'en inspirent, l'Asie française exerce une influence indirecte qui ajoute beaucoup à l'influence directe du Comité. Ses études n'ont pas

été étrangères à tel vote du parlement ou à telle décision prise par la politique française dans les affaires asiatiques.[22]

The success of the Comité de l'Asie Française can largely be credited to the efforts of Robert de Caix, its chief ideologist. He was a well-known journalist who expounded his views in its bulletin, which he founded and went on to edit for 19 years (1901–19), and in the *Journal des Débats*, where he served as foreign editor. His ideas played a crucial role in shaping France's policy in the Levant during the vital years between 1919 and 1923. As adviser to the Quai d'Orsay, he participated in the negotiations with Faisal in April 1919. Later that year he was appointed secretary-general to Gouraud, high commissioner in Syria and Lebanon, a position he held until the summer of 1923. In subsequent years he continued to advise the Quai d'Orsay on Syrian policy and represented France in the Permanent Mandates Commission of the League of Nations. De Caix admired Lyautey's policy in Morocco, and was himself active in securing the French protectorate there. In his articles before the War he often called on France to intensify its activities in the Levant to counter the growing influence of Germany and Britain. At that time he opposed the partition of the Ottoman Empire, or at any rate paid lip-service to that position, but from 1915 he advocated a policy aimed at securing direct French control over the whole of Syria. He was one of the most outspoken critics of Britain's policy in the Levant and a strong opponent of Faisal and the Arab national movement.[23]

Upon the outbreak of the War, and especially after the Dardanelles campaign had begun, these groups intensified their propaganda and lobbying campaign. At a meeting held on 21 April 1915, the Comité de l'Asie Française passed a resolution at de Caix's initiative calling for the defence of French interests in the Levant. The resolution was presented to the government. Shortly afterwards Flandin appeared before the Senatorial Group for the Defence of French Interests Abroad to make the same demand, which was rapidly echoed by the Chambers of Commerce of Lyons and Marseilles in letters presented to the foreign minister.[24]

As the War advanced and British intentions in the Middle East became clearer, these groups stepped up their activities. They vehemently protested to the French government following the publication of the Sykes-Picot agreement by the new Russian revolutionary government at the end of 1917. Shortly before the opening of the Peace Conference in Paris, which was to decide the future of the Ottoman territories, the Chamber of Commerce of Marseilles organised a congress of various societies and individuals, including representatives of religious orders with interests in the Levant, to bring France's long-standing connection with and interests in the Levant to the attention of the government and public and the participants in the Peace Conference. It was the most important congress held on the subject. It decided to organise a mission, headed by Professor Huvelin of the University of Lyons and including members of the Comité de l'Orient, to visit the area, examine its resources and clarify the state of French interests. The mission received financial support from the Quai d'Orsay. Its comprehensive report later became a basic source of information on all questions affecting French economic policy in Syria.[25]

The activities of these pressure groups created an atmosphere of sympathy and support for the Lebanese cause among the French public and in the government and National Assembly, helping to lay the groundwork for the decision in summer 1920 to create an independent and enlarged Lebanese state. These sentiments were cultivated and exploited by the Maronites and their patriarch Hawayik in 1919 and 1920, in their attempts to persuade the French government to comply with their requests. The 'Syrian Party' policy of direct French control over Syria and Lebanon was in complete accord with the aspirations of the Lebanese Christians themselves. The strong pressure against any compromise with Faisal which these groups brought to bear upon the French government was of crucial importance to the Lebanese Christians, as any such compromise would have undermined their own ambitions.

The various groups, however, did not hold similar views concerning an independent Greater Lebanon. For the commercial-financial sectors seeking French domination of Syria and Cilicia the question of Lebanon was of secondary importance. They regarded a Syrian federation under direct French control, in which Lebanon would enjoy local autonomy, as the most desirable solution to the ethnic and religious divisions of the area. In contrast, the French Catholic Church and its various religious orders strongly backed the Maronites.

During the War the Lebanese emigrant groups took over the struggle for the Lebanese cause, as the inhabitants of Lebanon themselves were cut off from Europe. Syrian and Lebanese Christian emigrants in France comprised an important pressure group with some influence on French public opinion. The pre-War activities of the Comité Libanais de Paris have already been cited. Its members now stressed the wealth of Syria and Lebanon, the loyalty of its inhabitants to France and the threat to French interests from the increasing activity of Britain and Germany. They co-operated closely with the various French societies seeking French occupation of the Levant.[26]

In June 1917 these emigrants established the Comité Central Syrien (CCS), which called for a French mandate over Syria and Lebanon and set out to gain the support of Lebanese and Syrian emigrant groups in other countries. The new group was backed by the Comité de l'Orient; George Samné held the position of secretary-general in both societies. Funds were supplied by French companies and financiers, as well as by the Quai d'Orsay. Shukri Ghanem, president of the CCS, was said to have received payment for his activities from companies in Lyons and Marseilles.[27] The French colonialists probably considered it useful that the propaganda for control over Syria emanated from the Lebanese and Syrians, as this seemed to verify the claim of the attachment to France felt by the local inhabitants. Indeed, during the Peace Conference the Quai d'Orsay itself used the CCS to demonstrate the strong support of the people of Syria and Lebanon for a French mandate.[28]

The CCS, however, was not merely a mouthpiece of the French colonialist movement or of the French government. Towards the end of the War and during the Peace Conference it established itself as an influential pressure group in its own right. Its bulletin, *Correspondance d'Orient*, and numerous articles published by its members in the French press called for a French mandate over the Levant. Its members were the first to oppose the claims of the Hashemite family over Syria, and they helped develop a hostile atmosphere in France towards Faisal and the Arab national movement. Their exaggeration of the degree of support for France in Syria and Lebanon was largely responsible for the distorted image of Syria presented to the French public. French politicians and officials such as Goût, a staunch supporter of the CCS, regarded its members as experts on Syrian and Lebanese affairs with an intimate knowledge of conditions there. The pre-War French tendency to regard the situation in Syria and Lebanon through the eyes of the Christian minorities was thus further reinforced.[29]

Towards the end of 1918 one could discern several different

trends among Christians both in Lebanon and abroad on the question of an independent Lebanese state and the means by which it might be attained. There were some who regarded the securing of a French mandate over all of Syria as their main objective; for them the demand for an independent Greater Lebanon had become, at this stage, less important. This was the stand adopted by the CCS, whose official programme advocated a Syrian federation under a French mandate in which Lebanon would enjoy local autonomy. This position was partly determined by the needs of the French business interests who backed the Committee and who aspired primarily to French domination over all of Syria; any emphasis on a separate Lebanese state would have been incompatible with their aims. CCS members raised various arguments to justify their stand and stressed that Lebanon was closely linked with the rest of Syria by economic ties.[30]

There were other Lebanese Christians who agreed that an autonomous Greater Lebanon should be included in a Syrian federation, but rejected the idea of a French mandate in favour of rule by Faisal. They argued that Lebanon should co-operate with the Arab national movement and with the Muslims and not rely on foreign protection. This stand was supported by many non-Catholic Christians, in particular by the Greek Orthodox community. Among those who promulgated such views was Iskandar 'Ammun, a member of a prominent Lebanese Maronite family, who had been active before the War in the Decentralisation Party in Egypt and had represented it at the Arab Congress in Paris. He had also been a member of the Party for Syrian Unity in Egypt, which had pan-Arabist tendencies and which supported a Syrian federation under Faisal's rule; its president was Michel Lutf'allah and among its members were Rashid Rida and 'Abd al-Rahman Shahbandar.[31] After establishing close ties with Faisal he resigned as president of the Alliance Libanaise in Egypt in June 1917 and went on to serve as minister of justice in the Arab government in Damascus. He played an important role in Faisal's efforts to persuade the Lebanese Christians to unite with Syria.[32]

In contrast, there were those who continued to regard the establishment of an independent Greater Lebanon as their main goal. For them, the call for a French mandate was of secondary importance; some even opposed it altogether. The most important group in this camp was the Alliance Libanaise of Egypt, whose activities and nationalist tendencies before the War have already been cited. Many of its members were influenced during and after the War by the anti-French propaganda of British officers. Inspired by the liberal principles of President Wilson they demanded independence and the right to self-determination. They constituted the main opposition to the CCS and strongly opposed French control over Lebanon. After the resignation of Iskandar 'Ammun the Alliance was headed by Auguste Adib Pasha, a Lebanese Maronite who held a high position in the Egyptian administration.[33] The society had branches in Buenos Aires and Sao Paulo and maintained close ties with other Lebanese emigrant groups including the Comité Libanais de Paris, an organisation headed by 'Abbas Bejani and Khairallah Khairallah.[34]

But it was the Maronites within Lebanon, under the leadership of the patriarch and the Administrative Council, who ultimately determined the aims of the Lebanese national movement. After Lebanon came under the control of the Allied Forces, they committed themselves to a major effort toward the realisation of their ambitions. They too wanted an independent Greater Lebanon, but unlike the Alliance Libanaise they continued to demand French protection. If France needed a Christian Lebanon as a base from which to secure its own influence and interests in the whole of Syria the Maronites were more than willing to co-operate, as they themselves were in need of French protection against pan-Arab and Muslim claims for a united Syria. They sought to influence the French government and public to support their cause. Between 1918 and 1920 both the Church and the Administrative Council steadfastly pursued this objective; they despatched three Lebanese delegations to Paris, whose activities became the focus of the Lebanese Christian drive to secure a state of their own.

The Beirut incident, occurring just one week after Lebanon's occupation by the Allied Forces, shocked the Maronites and made them see that even though Turkish rule had ended, the realisation of their goals was by no means assured. Symbolically, it was in the future capital of the Lebanese state that the first major clash arose between the Christians and their French ally on the one hand, and the pro-Faisal Muslims and their British ally on the other. The conflict between these camps would become the main theme underlying the events of the following two years.

Even before the occupation of Damascus by British and Arab forces on 1 October 1918, the emir Sa'id al Jaza'iri had established an Arab government there. He sent telegrams on behalf of Faisal to the mayors of the coastal towns, the leaders of the Druze and the

Maronite patriarch, calling on them to declare their allegiance to Faisal and the future Arab government. But while the Muslim inhabitants of the coastal towns, led by Beirut mayor 'Umar Da'uq, reacted enthusiastically, the Maronites and their patriarch were not in the least inclined to comply. They had not struggled against the Turks for so long only to have Turkish rule replaced by Faisal's new Arab regime. Hawayik immediately sent a messenger to the French base in Arwad requesting the advice of the French government. This was the first indication the French received that Faisal intended to take over Lebanon, in breach of their agreement with the British. Their reply to Hawayik consisted of two words only: 'Nous venons'.[35]

In spite of this assurance, the events of the following two weeks were far from encouraging for the Christians. Faisal's representative, Shukri al-Ayubi, declared an Arab government in Beirut and the coast, an area regarded by the Christians as an integral part of their future state; he even proceeded to Ba'abda in Mount Lebanon where he appointed Habib al-Sa'd as governor. His expulsion a few days later by the British and the appointment of Piépape as chief administrator for the whole of Lebanon partly renewed Christian confidence in France. Piépape's declaration restoring the Mountain's special status, which the Turks had abolished at the beginning of the War, and the reappointment of Habib al-Sa'd as president of the Administrative Council of Mount Lebanon were enthusiastically acclaimed by the Maronites.[36] Yet they still had reason for apprehension, particularly as France's position remained unclear, and Faisal and his British allies were seen as the new overlords.

Once their fears for the future of Beirut and the coast had been allayed, there arose the question of the Beqa'a Valley, which they also regarded as part of Lebanon. Faisal's representatives had established an Arab administration there. In contrast to their stand on the coast, the British agreed to leave the area under Arab control, in breach of the Sykes-Picot agreement, after Faisal threatened to resign if his representative was expelled. At the end of October Faisal visited Zahle and Ba'albek, where the Muslims gave him an enthusiastic welcome; he thereby showed that he regarded the Beqa'a as part of the area under Arab control. He now declared that the whole of Lebanon was an integral part of the future Arab state.[37]

Maronite fears further increased after the publication on 8 November 1918 of the Anglo-French Declaration, which defined the rights of the local inhabitants to self-determination, much to the satisfaction of the Muslims. The Maronites interpreted the document as a sign that France intended to give up its traditional ambitions in Syria. France's weakness seemed to be confirmed by Faisal's visit to Beirut on 17 November, which turned into a Muslim political demonstration against both the French and the Lebanese Christians. His departure from Junieh aboard a British warship a few days later in order to present Arab demands at the Peace Conference demonstrated to the Christians the precarious state of their own demands.[38]

At that point the Christians decided to send their own delegation to the Peace Conference to oppose the demands of Faisal and the Arabs. They could no longer rely solely on France, but had to act themselves without delay in both Lebanon and Europe to enlist international support for their cause. The initiative came from a number of Christian notables, particularly Maronites; early in December 1918 they proposed to Picot that they present their claims directly to the Peace Conference and ask for a French mandate. Picot saw the value of such a deputation in furthering French interests against Britain and Faisal. Foreign Minister Pichon approved the idea and instructed Picot to supply sufficient funds 'without us appearing to do so'. Pichon was clearly anxious not to give the impression that the French had organised the delegation; he recommended that they should contact the CCS rather than the government itself.[39]

On 9 December the Administrative Council authorised seven of its members to go to Paris, in a resolution that called for French protection and an autonomous, not independent Greater Lebanon. The French no doubt feared that any demand for independence could undermine France's claim for a mandate over all of Syria. Picot was able to influence the content of the resolution with the help of Habib al-Sa'd, who was anxious to demonstrate his loyalty to the French after his recent episode of co-operation with the Arab government. Indeed, the French version of the resolution was sent to the Quai d'Orsay on 5 December, although the Council only passed it, in a slightly different Arabic version, four days later.[40]

Further evidence that the Lebanese question had become entangled in Anglo-French rivalry for control over Syria was provided when members of the Lebanese delegation were held by the British in Port Sa'id on their way to Paris. The official British explanation was that the delegates held illegal *laissez-passers* signed by Picot, who had no authority to do so; they were instructed to return to Beirut. In fact both Allenby and General Clayton, his influential political adviser, were anxious to prevent the appearance of a pro-French delegation at the Peace Conference. The incident increased French suspicion about British intentions and strained personal relations between Picot and Allenby, as the latter had previously informed Picot of his objection to the departure of the delegation from Beirut. Only after France strongly protested to the Foreign Office in London did the British allow the delegation to continue on its way; but they decided to prevent the departure of any further deputations from the area.[41]

The Lebanese delegation arrived in Paris at the end of January 1919. It established contact with Shukri Ghanem, who was co-ordinating the various Syrian and Lebanese groups on behalf of the Quai d'Orsay to support a French mandate over Syria at the Peace Conference. It soon became clear to the Lebanese that they had no choice but to adopt the CCS programme, and that their main role would be to support the French stand and counter the impression made at the conference by Faisal and the British and American representatives. Da'ud 'Ammun, head of the Lebanese delegation, told the Council of Ten that Lebanon was willing to be part of a Syrian federation, on condition that Syria, like Lebanon, be placed under a French mandate.[42]

Although the delegates could do little to advance the cause of independence, the French had no objection to the demand for expanded borders, as this was compatible with their own policy of implementing the Sykes-Picot agreement to the letter, namely by annexing the Beqa'a Valley to the Western Zone. In his speech to the Council of Ten and in his interviews with French newspapers 'Ammun repeatedly called for the restoration of Lebanon's historical and geographical borders. The delegation presented the Peace Conference with a detailed memorandum on this matter dated 8 March 1919; it included a map prepared by the French expedition to Syria in 1861 that showed the borders of Lebanon before its territorial reduction. These borders were similar to those the Lebanese were now demanding. The memorandum ended by declaring:

> On voit par ce qui procède que ce n'est pas par esprit de conquête ou de mégalomanie que le Liban revendique ses

anciennes frontières, mais bien pour une raison qui domine toutes les autres considérations le droit à la vie. Sans ces frontières l'oeuvre de 1861 reste inachevée, et l'indépendance du Liban ne serait qu'une cruelle ironie.[43]

Although the delegation became a mere mouthpiece for French interests and failed to represent the genuine aspirations of the Lebanese Christians, its contribution to the Lebanese cause was by no means unimportant. It was the only delegation from Syria, apart from Faisal's, to appear at the Peace Conference, and it testified to the existence of a desire for a separate Lebanese entity. The arrest of its members by the British in Port Sa'id, widely publicised in the French press, heightened support in France for the Lebanese cause. For the general public and for many politicians the delegation represented a nation with a long-standing attachment to France, situated in an area where France had always had vital interests, which wanted to express its loyalty in the face of Britain's and Faisal's ambitions. The delegation was received by many French leaders including President Poincaré, Premier Clemenceau, the heads of the Senate and Chamber of Deputies and various ministers and politicians. These encounters, together with the wide publicity and support the Lebanese received, were the first step in the Lebanese Christian campaign of 1919 and 1920 to influence the French government.

The publication of the Administrative Council's resolution and the departure of the Lebanese delegation to the Peace Conference roused strong protests in Syria and Lebanon from those who opposed the separation of Lebanon from Syria and the creation of an enlarged Lebanese state under a French mandate. Protests were made to the British authorities by Muslims in Beirut; Druze in Mount Lebanon; Mutawallis in the Tyre area and by municipal councils in various localities in the Beqa'a Valley. Most of the protesters, including the Party for Syrian Unity in Egypt, demanded the right to send their own delegations to the Peace Conference and were bitterly disappointed when their requests were turned down by the British authorities.[44] Protests were also voiced by some Lebanese Christians, who claimed that the Administrative Council resolution and the stand taken by the delegation in Paris did not express the genuine aspirations of the Lebanese people for complete independence. These included the Alliance Libanaise and the Comité Libanais de Paris, which claimed that according to the Règlement Organique the Administrative Council had no authority to deal with political affairs, and that in any case the mandate of the present Council had already expired. Such criticism was also raised in Lebanon itself, where many Christians were beginning to realise that Lebanese and French interests were not always compatible and that in any compromise, Lebanese Christian interests would always be the first to suffer.[45]

In fact, as soon as it learned that the Allied Forces had occupied Lebanon the French government, which had been subjected to continuous pressure and lobbying by French groups and Lebanese emigrants during the War, expressed its willingness to help the Lebanese Christians realise their aspirations. Pichon informed French representatives that France intended to safeguard Lebanon's autonomy, and that it was prepared to recognise the authority of the Administrative Council over Beirut, the Beqa'a and Tripoli if their inhabitants wished to be part of Lebanon. Picot took a similar stand; he emphasised the need to demonstrate French support for the Maronites and expressed his belief that the Peace Conference would entirely change the existing borders of Lebanon. In Lebanon itself the French representatives openly declared that France intended to help the Maronites and other Christians to realise their aspirations and safeguard their interests. The French were soon to realise, however, that they were not yet the rulers of Syria and Lebanon and that the actual situation was far more complex than they had been led to believe.[46]

During the first year of their administration in Lebanon many French officials felt frustrated and disillusioned. Contrary to their expectations they were not welcomed as liberators by the entire population, and their rule over Syria, supposedly based on War agreements with the British, was not immediately recognised. In fact British officers did their utmost to undermine France's position and prestige in the area. The French were also taken aback by Faisal's success in establishing his regime in Damascus and by the enthusiam with which he was received by the inhabitants of Syria. They were convinced that Britain was plotting to use Faisal to seize territory that rightfully belonged to France; events in Damascus, Beirut and the Beqa'a only served to strengthen this conviction. No doubt there was more than a grain of truth in these claims; yet the objective conditions would have made French rule in Lebanon difficult in those days whatever Britain's policies. Unlike the British, the French had not arrived as conquerors, nor did they enjoy the advantage over the local inhabitants that naturally accrues to those in authority. During the year following the occupation General Allenby continued to hold the position of commander-in-chief and supreme authority. Forty-five thousand British officers and soldiers were stationed in Syria and Lebanon, compared with a French garrison of only 8,000, mostly colonial troops, the majority of whom were stationed in Cilicia.[47]

In November 1918 Picot became chief political adviser to Allenby in the Western Zone. He soon perceived the weakness of France's position and emphatically told his government that the only solution would be to dispatch 20,000 French soldiers to take the area over from the British. However, any plans to increase the number of French soldiers were vetoed by Allenby, who claimed that such a move would antagonise the Arabs and undermine stability.[48] In any case France had lost over a million soldiers in the War and would have found it difficult to allocate the necessary forces and funds to take over Syria and Lebanon. France also suffered from a lack of organisation, experienced staff and plans for controlling the area. By comparison the British were far more efficient in establishing their authority in Palestine. They had prepared detailed plans for relief and for the restoration of the administration and economy, and they possessed the necessary staff to implement these plans. In Lebanon, which had suffered much more during the War and whose economy and administration had nearly collapsed, French inability to mobilise sufficient resources was to have grave political consequences.[49]

By early 1919 it became clear to the French representatives in Beirut that a reassessment of their policy towards the Lebanese Christians was necessary. Picot, who daily confronted the real conditions in Lebanon, was one of the first to realise the full extent of the opposition of Faisal and the Muslims in Syria and on the coast to the establishment of a Christian Greater Lebanon. He saw that it might be possible to exploit Faisal's insistence on the annexation of Lebanon and the coast in order to further French interests. In a despatch to Pichon, he put forward three possible courses of action: to annex Lebanon to Syria and secure a French mandate over the entire region; obtain Faisal's recognition of French control over Greater Lebanon in return for France's acceptance of his rule over Syria; or to instigate opposition to Faisal in Syria in order to undermine his authority there. Picot pointed out that the first alternative would meet with strong opposition from the Lebanese Christians, while the third would antagonise the British. In fact the French were to use both these means during the following two years; in 1919 they tried to come to a compromise with Faisal, while in 1920 they worked to depose him. The middle course of action was never seriously considered, as France continued to aim for control over all of Syria.[50]

Picot's first goal was to strengthen France's position and prestige in Syria and Lebanon among both Christians and Muslims. French representatives began an intensive campaign to gain the support of the local inhabitants and to counter the anti-French propaganda spread by Faisal's agents and supporters and by British officers. In his meetings with delegates of the various communities, Picot stressed that France had no intention of abandoning Syria and that it would soon be the only suzerain there. Notables and influential religious leaders were encouraged to express their sympathy for France openly and to send petitions to the French government and to the Peace Conference.[51] Money and positions were offered to various friendly groups and individuals, while pressure was brought to bear on their opponents; for example strict censorship was imposed on Muslim newspapers in the Western Zone. Special efforts were made to gain the support of minority groups such as the Druze, Mutawallis and 'Alawites. In January 1919 a French column was sent to south Lebanon to visit Christian, Druze and Mutawalli villages, in order to demonstrate France's presence in the area. Close contacts were established with the Druze in the Houran and Jabal Druze; Picot offered them a large measure of autonomy in return for their support for a French mandate. The French also made contacts with the Mutawallis, whose influential leader Kamal al-As'ad, came to Beirut and met with Picot.[52]

The French worked intensively to weaken Muslim opposition. Picot himself was convinced of the need to gain Muslim confidence, as his close associate Sykes had been constantly urging him to do since 1917. In December and January Picot, accompanied by Sykes, visited several towns in Syria. His conciliatory speeches on France's future policy were received favourably by the Muslims, but aroused protests from the Lebanese Christians.[53] At the same time, Picot took harsh measures against anti-French elements when he considered this necessary. He arrested Salim 'Ali Salam, a prominent Sunni leader from Beirut, and resisted pressure from Allenby and Faisal to release him. Although Salam was accused of war profiteering, his arrest was clearly politically motivated. Immediately following the occupation of Beirut he had begun an intensive campaign against the

French; after Piépape's appointment, he had initiated a petition, signed by many Muslim notables and presented to Allenby, demanding a British mandate over the area.[54]

This twofold policy of reconciliation and pressure was to some extent successful. By March 1919 Picot was able to inform the Quai d'Orsay that France's position had improved and that many Muslim leaders had established contacts with the French authorities, although they were still not prepared to declare publicly their support for French rule.[55]

But the Sunnis of Lebanon were still not reconciled. Their fears of being dominated by their Christian neighbours with France's aid have already been cited. Now, with Arab flags hauled down in their towns, Faisal's representatives expelled and their region arbitrarily separated from Syria, they saw their fears being materialised. Most of the Sunnis and heterodox Muslims had been subjected for many years to continuous anti-French propaganda emphasising the French threat to their religion, culture and language. Their leaders and notables feared for the influential positions they had held under the Turks; and in fact many of those who had retained their previous posts during the first year of French rule were later ousted or had their authority curtailed by the new administration. Their bitterness would continue to be an important factor in their opposition to France throughout the mandate period. One of the main objectives behind the dismissals was to concentrate full authority in French hands, a policy that was later to arouse resentment even among the Christians. But Muslim officials suffered more, as the French tended to consider them unreliable because of the anti-French attitude many of them had adopted. The authorities preferred to work with the Christians, whom they considered more loyal and with whom they found it easier to communicate.[56] Many Lebanese Christians who had been in Egypt during the War and had established close ties with the French there returned to Lebanon and began to fill key positions in the new administration. Two of them, Emile Eddé and Bishara al-Khuri, were to play important roles in the political development of Lebanon.[57]

Whatever the Muslims of the coast may have felt about an independent Great Lebanon or a French mandate in the period between the Armistice and the expulsion of Faisal from Damascus, they were under a French administration which greatly restricted their political activities. With the establishment of Faisal's Arab government the centre of the Arab national movement had shifted from

Beirut, where it had emerged before the War, to Damascus. The Muslims of the coast began to rely solely on Faisal and his government for support in their struggle against becoming a minority in a Christian state. Throughout the period of the mandate and even afterwards, Damascus remained the main centre of Muslim opposition to a Christian Lebanon.

Faisal and the Arab national movement had emerged after the War as a powerful force among the Muslims in Syria and Lebanon; their stand concerning Lebanese Christian demands was a crucial factor in the process which finally led to the establishment of Greater Lebanon. The Lebanese question was now directly involved in the wider issue of relations between France and the Arab nationalists; the final decision to create Greater Lebanon was the direct outcome of Gouraud's victory over Faisal.

From the moment of his arrival in Damascus at the head of the Arab forces, Faisal adopted an extremely negative attitude towards the Maronite claim to an independent state under French protection. His opposition derived from complex political, cultural, religious and economic factors, at the centre of which was the conviction that the Maronites were being used by France to realise its own ambitions in Syria.[58] Faisal and the Arab nationalists regarded the Maronite claim not as a legitimate national aspiration, but as a plot to deny the Arabs their independence. It was at this stage that the rift between the Arab and Lebanese national movements developed, a rift which would be only partly bridged in 1943 by the National Pact, when Christian leaders, headed by Bishara al-Khuri, finally renounced French protection and identified Lebanon as part of the Arab world.

Faisal was somewhat more open to the Maronite demand for extended borders. He and many Muslims on the coast were prepared to accept the annexation of that area and the Beqa'a Valley to a Lebanese entity, but only if the Maronites relinquished their demand for a French mandate and became part of a Syrian federation under Faisal's rule. Their efforts to persuade the Christians to turn their backs on France and to link their future with the Arab government continued throughout Faisal's rule, and met with some success in the summer of 1920 when the Administrative Council adopted a resolution opposing a French mandate.

By the spring of 1919 French officials, who had been following the events in Syria since the previous October, began to realise how essential it was for France to try to reach an agreement with Faisal.

Despite the charge that he was being used by Britain, he remained the only leader capable of persuading the Muslims to accept a French mandate over Syria. With this in mind Clemenceau made his first attempt to reach a compromise agreement with Faisal in April 1919, while the latter was in Paris for the Peace Conference.

For Clemenceau, the entire Syrian question was of secondary importance. His main goal was to protect France's vital interests in Europe against Germany, both by territorial adjustments on the Rhine and by containing any German military resurgence. To that end it was vitally important to maintain France's unity with its two allies, Britain and the United States; the French leader was prepared to make concessions to Lloyd George in the Middle East in exchange for support on matters more essential to France. Indeed, a month before the opening of the Peace Conference he conceded the region of Mosul to Lloyd George and agreed that Palestine would be placed under a British mandate.[59]

During 1919, however, Clemenceau came under increasing pressure from the French public and press, inspire by the 'Syrian Party', to stand up for France's 'rights' in the Levant. His opponents, particularly in the National Assembly, were angered by his conduct at the Peace Conference and frequently criticised him for his insufficiently enthusiastic Syrian policy. He himself was not prepared to allow Britain to treat France as a subordinate partner in the Middle East. He became indignant at Lloyd George's blunt attempt to dominate the whole area in violation of Britain's obligations in the War agreements, and his last year in office saw repeated clashes with the British prime minster over these issues. At the same time he still hoped to reach an agreement with Faisal that would secure France's interests in Syria, weaken domestic pressures and leave him free to deal at the Peace Conference with issues far more vital to France.[60]

The difficulties in reaching such an agreement became apparent in the course of the negotiations with Faisal in April. Clemenceau left the actual talks to Tardieu, who was closely associated with the 'Syrian Party' and who had personal financial interests in Syria before the War, and to Goût and de Caix.[61] The former advocated direct French domination over the whole of Syria, while the latter, although recognising the need to reach an agreement with Faisal, did not believe that this would be possible without first achieving an Anglo-French understanding in Syria. On the Arab side, Faisal himself was not yet convinced of the necessity of concluding an agreement with France. Lawrence, who was serving at that time as an adviser to the Arab delegation, had always held anti-French views and strongly opposed the relinquishment of Syria to France.[62] Nevertheless, at a meeting on 13 April, during a particularly crucial time in the discussions over the western border of Germany, Clemenceau reached an understanding with Faisal in which he agreed to recognise Syria's independence 'in the form of a federation of local communities', in return for Faisal's approval of a French mandate over Syria. Faisal undertook to seek the support of his people for an arrangement with France. Thus an autonomous Lebanon was to become a part of Syria under Faisal's rule. The agreement embodied the first of Picot's three proposals as suggested a few months before. Picot himself was in Paris during the talks, putting his weight behind an immediate accord with Faisal.[63]

In these negotiations Lebanon was used as bait to tempt Faisal into an agreement. In short, when it came to upholding their own interests in Syria, the French had little regard for the interests of the Lebanese Christians. This was made quite explicit by de Caix, who later wrote:

> Personne en France n'était hostile au début à une entente avec Faysal. Les idées étaient encore beaucoup trop flottantes en ce qui concerne la politique à suivre en Syrie pour que l'on écartat à priori ce système qui avait ses séductions. On sentait seulement que nous ne pourrions honorablement livrer au Chérif nos vieilles clientèles, mais il semblait qu'en guarantissant contre l'excès des tendances unitaires, le Liban, qui envoya dès la fin de 1918 des députations à Paris, en ferait ce qui importait. Pour le reste, on se serait fort bien contente d'autonomies légères pour ces minorités qui étaient un des soucis de la politique wilsonienne.[64]

Rumours that Faisal had reached an agreement with Clemenceau aroused much anxiety among the Maronites. They were alarmed by the official reception accorded to Faisal by French officials when he arrived in Beirut on 30 April aboard a French warship. His declaration that the future of the area would be determined by the International Commission of Inquiry according to the will of the people, and that the independence and unity of Syria was secure, further intensified their fears. Moreover, they saw the French relax their restrictions on Arab nationalist activity in the Western Zone. Some French officers went so far as to declare that France would be ready to sacrifice the Christians in Lebanon to gain the support of the Muslims. The suspicions of a sellout were confirmed when a Maronite deputation met Picot immediately after his return to Beirut on 10 May. Picot explained that since France would have the mandate over all Syria Lebanese Christian interests would be safeguarded; thus there would be no need to separate Lebanon from the rest of Syria.[65]

The Maronites reacted strongly against the new French policy of *rapprochement* with Faisal. In May and June the Mountain became a centre of growing opposition and protest. Large demonstrations were held against the annexation of Lebanon to Syria and anti-French speeches were made. Leading this activity were the Administrative Council, in particular its president Habib al-Sa'd, and the Maronite Church under Patriarch Hawayik. On 20 May the Council reversed the earlier resolution of December 1918 and called for the complete political and administrative independence of Lebanon within its geographical and historical boundaries, without so much as mentioning a French mandate. At a ceremony in Ba'abda that same day a Lebanese flag was hoisted and the independence of Lebanon was declared, before the participants were dispersed by the French military governor. Both the ceremony and the resolution, which Sa'd asked Picot to transfer to the French government and to the Peace Conference, were manifestations of Maronite determination not to acquiesce in the new French policy.[66]

The seat of the Maronite patriarch in Bkerki became the focal point of the opposition; delegations from all over Lebanon urged the patriarch to go immediately to Paris to defend the Lebanese Christian cause at the Peace Conference. There were even some who accused him of being too passive and unwilling to act against the French. In fact, however, it was he and his bishops, in particular Mubarak, bishop of Beirut, who had mobilised the clergy and the whole community to voice their protests and demand complete independence. Hawayik encouraged deputations of notables to visit Picot and express their support for the Council's resolution. When his own meeting with Picot failed to produce any results he sent telegrams to Clemenceau and the Peace Conference, bluntly repeating the demand for Lebanese independence.[67]

Hawayik's fears of Muslim domination over Mount Lebanon and his disappointment with France were so intense that he secretly proposed to General Allenby that he go immediately to the Peace Conference and request a British mandate, in exchange for a guarantee of Lebanese independence. The British authorities, however, showed no interest in Hawayik's proposition; they advised him to put his claims directly to the International Commission of Inquiry which was due to arrive in the area shortly.[68]

In mid-June Hawayik and his bishops gathered in Bkerki to deliberate on what measures to adopt in order to pressure the French government into changing its stand. During three days of talks Hawayik repeatedly emphasised that the Maronites had no choice but to continue to rely on France; only with French assistance could they attain their national goals. He informed Picot that if the complete independence of Greater Lebanon was guaranteed, the Maronites would leave it to France to determine the specific nature of future relations between Lebanon and Syria.[69]

The new French policy towards Faisal caused many non-Catholic Christians and heterodox Muslims to reconsider their own attitudes. Sunni notables in Beirut, pleased by the new French position, stepped up their efforts to persuade the other communities to offer their allegiance to Faisal. In order to gain the Christians' support they proposed an autonomous Lebanon within the extended boundaries considered necessary for its economic prosperity, but only on condition that the country recognise the suzerainty of the future Arab government in Damascus. These efforts met with some success, especially in the Greek Orthodox community. Only one day after the Maronites attempted to declare their independence a group of Lebanese Christians met Faisal in Damascus. Their initiative evoked a strong protest from the Administrative Council to Faisal and to the French and British authorities, stating that the individuals involved did not truly represent the Lebanese people.[70]

Picot and the other French representatives in the Levant were placed in a difficult position. France's new policy towards Faisal, which had not yet produced any tangible results, had managed to antagonise the Maronites, thus endangering France's position among its most loyal supporters. But Picot was still convinced of the need to reach an agreement with Faisal; he considered the Maronite request for complete independence from Syria as incompatible with France's ambition to obtain a mandate over all Syria. In his despatches to the Quai d'Orsay, he complained that the Maronite demand was 'calculated to considerably disturb the policy of union and equilibrium which [he] was pursuing'. He accused Hawayik and Sa'd of encouraging agitation 'inspired only by the concern to protect the privileged status which circumstances had granted them in former Lebanon'. Reports from other French officials in the Western Zone also expressed open criticism of Hawayik's and the Maronite Church's intervention in political affairs.[71]

At the same time, Picot saw an advantage in the Maronite agitation against the annexation of Lebanon to Syria; it could strengthen France's position in the negotiations with Faisal by demonstrating that only France could help him to realise his ambition of annexing Lebanon and the rest of the coastal area to Syria. Similar views were expressed by de Caix, who wrote in *L'Asie française*:

> Sans abandonner le moins du monde les droits du Liban, nous pouvons les réconcilier avec l'idée d'une association avec le reste de la Syrie. C'est d'ailleurs sans doute la seule raison pour laquelle les chérifiens ont esquissé par moments un pas de notre côté.[72]

At the beginning of June Picot informed the Quai d'Orsay of his plans to restore Lebanese Christian confidence in France and thus enable the French to use Lebanon to strengthen their position in the area. Under Picot's instructions, Lebanese notables drew up a secret programme for a Lebanese state within its natural and historical boundaries. This 'state' would enjoy extensive political, executive, legislative and judicial rights but would be obliged to work closely with France, who would have the power to appoint its governor from among the Lebanese Christians. Lebanon would be part of a Syrian confederation and would send representatives to a federal council presided over by the Syrian head of state. However, if the Syrian confederation ceased to co-operate with France, Lebanon's links with the former would be severed and it would become an independent state under French protection. Picot's plan would guarantee France's position in all of Syria by using Lebanon as a perpetual inducement to Faisal to continue to co-operate. Picot was confident that the majority of Lebanese Christians would support such a solution; he suggested that it be kept secret for use as a compromise proposal at the appropriate time.[73]

Picot's plan came to nought, as it became clear that Faisal had no intention of reaching an agreement or recognising France's mandate over Syria. He decided instead to rely on the International Commission of Inquiry, which he was confident would grant Syria independence. He no longer saw the need for French mediation to gain control over Lebanon, as he was convinced that the majority of the inhabitants of the coastal area would support union with Syria under his rule. Nevertheless, not wanting to leave any room for chance, he encouraged his supporters in the Western Zone to step up their activities to gain the support of the inhabitants there for the Damascus Programme. Among those most active in this campaign were various Sunni notables in Beirut; Faisal's delegate there Jamil 'Elchi; Iskandar 'Ammun; and Yusuf al-Hakim, a Greek Orthodox and former caimacam in Mount Lebanon who was serving as attorney-general in Faisal's government.[74]

The preparations in June for elections for the Syrian Congress in Damascus gave Faisal's supporters another opportunity to increase their pressure for close ties between Lebanon and Syria and to demonstrate that the coastal area was an integral part of the Syrian state. Although the French authorities forbade elections in the Western Zone, local notables and leaders named their own delegates to the Congress. The Muslims tried to lure the Christians of Beirut into participating by offering them an equal number of seats, but most of them declined and Beirut was finally represented by nine Sunnis and two Maronites. The importance Faisal attached to Beirut and its Sunnis was evident in the fact that the vilayet was apportioned 16 seats (13 Sunnis, 2 Maronites and 1 Mutawalli), 11 of them representing the city itself.[75]

From the start the French did not favour the appointment of an International Commission of Inquiry, as they feared it would reveal that the overwhelming majority of Muslims resented any form of French mandate. In May Clemenceau demanded the replacement of the British forces in the Blue Zone by French forces as a condition for France's agreement to participate in the Commission. When his demand was rejected by Lloyd George, he withdrew the two French representatives-designate, de Caix and Goût; the British, for their own reasons, soon followed suit. The Commission which finally arrived in Damascus at the beginning of July thus consisted of only two members, both Americans.

The forthcoming Commission visit led France to change its attitude towards the Lebanese Christians. It was now crucial to be able to point to local support for a French mandate, and also vital to strengthen actual control over Lebanon in order to secure France's future position in the area, particularly in any negotiations with Faisal. The Maronite request for an independent Greater Lebanon was no longer regarded as an obstacle to French policy, but as a demand which France ought to support as it was now in line with its own interests. French officials clamped down on the activities of Faisal's supporters in the Western Zone and at the same time began an intensive campaign to persuade the various communities there to support an independent Greater Lebanon under a French mandate.[76] The French did not want to be fully identified with the Maronite cause, preferring to emphasise their impartiality towards both Muslims and Christians. But as Muslim opposition to a French mandate mounted they had no choice but to rely on the Christians, especially the Maronites, in order to demonstrate to the Peace Conference that France enjoyed support in the area. For the Maronites, on the other hand, the identification of their aspirations with French interests was a great advantage; they continually emphasised that by supporting their requests France would better serve its own interests. Picot still hoped that an agreement could be reached with Faisal, and he continued to regard his own plan as the only suitable solution, but he stressed that he would not attempt to bring both sides together until 'Faisal adopted in Syria an attitude consistent with the promises he had made to the prime minister in Paris'.[77]

The Maronites themselves were not at all inclined to leave the decision on their future in the hands of the American Commission of Inquiry. They had already expressed their reservations about a plebiscite as the method of determining the future of the area; now, after intensive propaganda by Faisal's supporters on the coast, they were even more apprehensive about the outcome of the Inquiry. They feared that the majority of the population, particularly the Muslims, in the regions they wanted to annex to Lebanon would react unfavourably. Therefore, despite their reservations concerning France's policy, the Maronite leaders once again rallied support for a French mandate. On 10 July the Administrative Council, encouraged by Picot, adopted a new resolution reiterating its request for a French mandate but stressing that this would not prejudice the independence of Lebanon; the character of the mandate would be jointly determined by the 'Independent Greater Lebanese Republic' and the mandatory power. After the experience of the previous two months the Lebanese Christians were anxious to leave no doubt about their desire for separation from Syria.[78]

The findings of the King-Crane Commission, despite all their inaccuracies, offer a unique opportunity to examine the stand taken by the six main communities in Lebanon towards the concept of an independent Greater Lebanon. True, Faisal's Arab government, the French and the British used intensive propaganda to influence the inhabitants of their respective zones, and the petitions presented to the Commission were a rather unreliable source of information, as they were easy to forge; the Commission itself pointed to the irregularities in the material it had been presented.[79] Nevertheless, these petitions, and even more the views expressed to the Commission by deputations from the various communities, can still be regarded as valid indications of the attitude of these groups. The deputations were comprised of prominent notables and religious leaders, who were best qualified to represent the views and aspirations of their communities. Along with most of the population of Syria and Lebanon, these representatives were convinced that the outcome of the Inquiry would determine the future of the whole region; they therefore attached great importance to their presentations.[80]

From the views expressed to the Commission, it is clear that nearly all the Maronites and Greek Catholics supported the concept of an independent Greater Lebanon separate from Syria and under a French mandate, while the overwhelming majority of the Sunnis on the coast strongly opposed the concept and supported a united Syria ruled by Faisal under an American or British mandate in line with the Damascus Programme. Between these two opposing stands were the differing positions of the other three sects: the Greek Orthodox, the Druze and the Mutawallis.[81]

The Greek Orthodox faced an old dilemma: they feared Muslim rule on the one hand and Maronite Catholic supremacy on the other. Those who lived in the Kura district, which had been part of the autonomous Sanjak, sympathised with the Maronites and were unmoved by the attempts of Faisal's agents, particularly Yusuf al-Hakim, to influence them. But the rich and important Greek Orthodox community in Beirut was divided. One camp, headed by Bishop Messara, followed the lead of Patriarch Haddad in Damascus, who had been co-operating closely with Faisal ever since the establishment of the Arab government and who supported union with Syria. Others, including many notables, favoured an independent Lebanon under a French mandate; they protested to the Commission that they alone were the true representatives of the 26,000 members of their community in Beirut.[82]

The Druze also feared Maronite domination and were even more resentful than the Greek Orthodox over the prospect of French rule. Most of them supported Faisal's government under a British rather than an American mandate. Some of their leaders declared that if the mandate over Lebanon was granted to France, they would choose to remain outside such a state. Druze opposition to a French mandate, and thus to an independent Lebanon, was led by the two most influential families in the area: the Junblats, traditionally close to the British, and the Arslans, some of whom held positions in the Arab administration in Damascus and were active in enlisting the support of their community for Faisal. The Lebanese Druze were also influenced by the agreement their co-religionists in Jabal Druze and the Houran had reached with Faisal before the Commission arrived, in which they were promised a large measure of autonomy. In the Druze sector the French relied mainly on Tawfik Arslan, caimacam of the Shuf district, who with the help of French officers used pressure as well as favours to obtain Druze support for France.[83]

Both France and Faisal's government attached great importance to the support of the Mutawallis. Propaganda and intimidation from both sides were particularly evident in the Beqa'a and the Tyre-Jabal 'Amel areas, where most of this community lived. As heterodox Muslims the Mutawallis were traditionally suspicious of the Sunni majority, and they continually aspired to an official status as a separate independent community. But as members of a militant Muslim sect they also resented the idea of French and Christian rule. They feared that the large measure of *de-facto* autonomy they had always enjoyed in Jabal 'Amel would be restricted by a strong French or British rule; under an Arab government, they believed, it would be safeguarded. The majority of Mutawallis thus opposed inclusion in a Christian Lebanon under a French mandate, and supported Faisal. Kamal al-As'ad, who was courted by both the French and Faisal, came out in support of the latter after a visit to Damascus, during which he was decorated and promised the position of governor of Jabal 'Amel. The French succeeded in enlisting the support of several Mutawalli notables including Muhammad al-Tammer, Kamal al-As'ad's brother-in-law, by offering them positions in the administration and other favours. They also took the extreme measure of dismissing many officials in the area before the arrival of the Commission, to suppress any possible expression of anti-French views.[84]

Thus one year before its actual establishment the Maronites and Greek Catholics fully supported a separate Greater Lebanon; the Greek Orthodox were divided; the Sunnis and most of the Mutawallis strongly opposed it, as did many of the Druze, who for the last half-century had been closely associated with the Maronites in the

Mutasarrifiya. In describing the attitude of non-Christians towards the concept of a Greater Lebanon the King-Crane Commission emphasised that

> It is apparently contrary to the wish of the majority of the people in the area itself. The Syrians outside the area are so opposed to the plan as to be inclined to make war rather than accept it . . . The separation off of the Greater Lebanon . . . would intensify the religious differences in Syria, which it is most desirable to diminish in favor of the growth of national feeling.[85]

The Commission also cited the strong anti-French feeling among Sunnis, Druze, Mutawallis and some Greek Orthodox and Protestants in the Western Zone. These feelings were a no less important factor in the opposition to an independent Greater Lebanon under a French mandate than was the fear and resentment of Maronite domination. The Commission concluded by recommending that Lebanon be part of Syria, while retaining a large degree of local autonomy.[86]

Captain Yale, an adviser to the Commission who had been in the area during the War and had close ties with Lebanese and Syrian emigrants in Egypt, took a different view. He knew that Muslims and non-Catholic Christians opposed an independent Lebanese state, but he could not believe in the existence of a genuine Syrian national sentiment or the viability of a politically united Syria. He regarded Syria as a 'crazy quilt' of religions and sects, all jealous and intolerant of one another, each more fanatical than the rest. He emphasised that the Lebanese Christians were opposed to any Muslim domination. In his words:

> Mount Lebanon is profoundly Christian and Syria profoundly Moslem: until these two civilizations can be brought closer together it would be folly to try to bind them together by artificial bonds. Such an experiment would possibly prove disastrous for the minority.[87]

He recommended that Lebanon be separated politically from Syria, and that it be extended to include Beirut and the Beqa'a Valley; Tripoli, a Muslim town, should be left as a Syrian port.

During July, feelings were running high among the Maronites. They were disillusioned by the French policy shifts of the past few

months; the visit of the American Commission, the extremely negative stand taken by Faisal and the Muslims and the lack of support
from the other sects convinced them that their goals were in danger
of slipping out of reach. Given these circumstances, Patriarch
Hawayik decided to go to Paris to try to win the support of the
French government and public and to present the Lebanese cause
before the Peace Conference. His mission proved to be the turning-
point in the course of events that ultimately led to the establishment
of Greater Lebanon. Twelve years later Shekib Arslan, an Arab
nationalist and strong adversary of Hawayik, described the patriarch as a leader '. . . who took in his hands the political destiny of
[his] people'.[88]

It was appropriate that the head of the Maronite Church, the
spearhead of Maronite nationalism since the beginning of the nineteenth century, was the figure who finally enabled the Maronites to
realise their aspirations. The community naturally turned to him as
the only leader with sufficient moral and political authority to represent them, especially after their first delegation, comprised of
secular leaders, had failed to get across their genuine aspirations.
Hawayik had made the decision to go to Paris during the discussions
with his bishops in Bkerki in June, yet he was anxious to appear as a
representative of all the inhabitants of Mount Lebanon. With this
aim, the Administrative Council passed a resolution on 16 June
granting him a mandate to represent all the Lebanese people at the
Peace Conference and instructing him to request an independent
Greater Lebanon. But his only genuine mandate was from his own
community. This was evident in the composition of his delegation,
exclusively comprised of Maronite bishops with the sole exception
of Mughabghab, the Greek Catholic bishop of Zahle.[89]

The French had no objection to Hawayik's mission, as they hoped
to use it to demonstrate to the Peace Conference the support they
enjoyed in the area. But Hawayik had no intention of being used
merely as an instrument of French propaganda. His main objective
was to secure the complete independence of Lebanon and its separation from Syria. On his way to Paris he stopped in Rome for a month
to obtain the Pope's support for the Lebanese cause. In his discussions in Rome with Barrère, the French ambassador, Hawayik
strongly criticised France's policy in the Levant, which he described
as full of contradictions; he particularly rejected France's plan to
incorporate Lebanon into Syria. He stressed the danger to French
interests posed by Britain, which was backing Faisal, and charged

that the American Commission was not qualified to examine the will of the people; most of the petitions it had received had been forged. Hawayik proposed that the Lebanese state be fashioned by France; although the majority of his people wanted a Lebanese governor, he himself preferred a French governor, as 'a Frenchman would always be less disputed and more respected than a native one and being French would give him greater prestige in the eyes of the people'.[90] The patriarch was well aware that such a proposal complied with French interests, but he was probably sincere in doubting the ability of any Lebanese politician to fill the governor's post successfully.

After arriving in Paris on 22 August Hawayik was received by President Poincaré, General Foch, Pichon and leaders of the Senate and Chamber of Deputies. His personality, and his emphasis in discussions and interviews on how the Lebanese Christians had suffered during the War because of their loyalty to France, roused much sympathy among politicians and the general public.[91] Nevertheless his efforts to secure French government support for his demands met with little success during the first two months of his mission. His contacts were confined mainly to officials at the Quai d'Orsay, in particular de Caix and Goût. It was only after repeated requests that Clemenceau received him at the beginning of October. The meeting failed to produce any concrete results, as the premier had not yet given up hope of reaching an agreement with Faisal; moreover, during August and September France was engaged in intensive negotiations with England on the future of Syria, and Clemenceau was unwilling to commit himself before the final status of Syria had been decided.[92]

On 27 October, Hawayik presented a memorandum to the Peace Conference which detailed the national aspirations of the Lebanese Christians. The memorandum asked for the complete independence of Lebanon within its historical and natural boundaries as proclaimed 'by the government and the people of Lebanon on 20 May'. Its main aim was to ward off any possibility that Lebanon might be included in a Syrian federation. Although Hawayik requested a French mandate over Lebanon, the memorandum clearly aimed at curbing the ability of the mandatory power to interfere with the independence and sovereignty of the future state. The fact that Hawayik, who had always been pro-French, could express such reservations shows how far his confidence in France had been undermined since he had declared his desire for a French governor less than three months before. Hawayik's successor, Patriarch

Arida, later even claimed that his predecessor had agreed to ask for a French mandate only after the French government had pledged to establish an independent Lebanon separate from Syria.[93]

At the end of October Clemenceau's government finally began to solidify its policy on Lebanon, adopting a positive attitude towards Christian aspirations. This was clearly expressed in Clemenceau's celebrated letter to Hawayik of 10 November 1919, the French government's first official commitment to an independent Lebanese state. Hawayik had thus achieved the main objective of his mission to Paris: French recognition of Lebanon as an independent state separate from Syria. His request for extended borders was not yet granted, however, as Clemenceau was reluctant to commit himself to specific boundaries at that stage.[94]

The change in French policy reflected both a concern for the country's own interests in the Levant and a response to domestic political pressures. Following his agreement in September with Lloyd George, Clemenceau was more predisposed to take a definite stand on the future of Syria and Lebanon. It was only then that he began to deal personally with the issue. In September he held intensive discussions with Picot, who was then in Paris. Picot, like de Caix and most of the French officials who were directly involved in Syrian affairs, was convinced of the need for a separate Christian Lebanese state, not so much to appease the Christians as to safeguard France's position and interests in the region by creating a stronghold in Lebanon. Clemenceau's desire to reach an agreement with Faisal, who arrived in Paris in October, was not compatible with such a policy. But after Faisal was abandoned by Britain, he could no longer deter France from taking a step it considered essential for its own interests.

The general elections due to take place on 16 November were another factor in the government's decision. Since the summer Clemenceau's Syrian policy had been under constant attack in the press. His agreement with Lloyd George in September aroused even stronger criticism, as it limited French occupation to the Blue Zone. A gesture towards the Lebanese Christians was deemed necessary to defuse this opposition and to demonstrate the government's determination to protect France's interests and its traditional position in the Levant. The gesture was aimed chiefly at Roman Catholic circles who had always shown concern for the fate of the Christians in Lebanon and who were anxious to safeguard their own religious and cultural interests there. Clemenceau was probably also influenced by Hawayik's presence in Paris and by the strong support he rallied among the public and among many politicians.[95]

The new French policy became evident during Clemenceau's negotiations with Faisal in November and December. The French prime minister insisted that Lebanon be separated from Syria. The only question to be discussed, he said, was that of its future borders; he suggested that Faisal recognise the independence of Lebanon under a French mandate within borders to be defined at the Peace Conference. In his counter-proposal Faisal agreed to recognise Lebanon's independence and its right to determine its own future, but only within its existing borders.

In a draft provisional accord dated 28 December, the two sides reached an agreement on this issue too. In addition to Mount Lebanon, the future Lebanese state was to include the cazas of Sidon, Tyre, Marjayoun, Hasbaya and Rashaya. The border would then follow

> the course of the Litani until five kilometres south of the railway line, Rayak station, the road and railway towards Ba'albek, then the course of the river 'Aasi, including the entrance of the Hirmil with the districts of Batrun, Zghorta, with the condition that some necessary adjustments will be carried out in the local boundary.[96]

Tripoli, the district of 'Akkar and a large part of the districts of the Beqa'a and Ba'albek would thus become part of Syria. The final draft of the agreement reached on 6 January 1920, however, left the decision on boundaries to the Peace Conference, 'taking into consideration the rights, interests and will of the population'. A letter of interpretation which Philippe Berthelot, secretary-general for foreign affairs, sent to Faisal along with the agreement declared that the boundaries of Lebanon would reflect its 'historical rights, economic interests and the free will of the people'. Although the French had assured Faisal that their stand would be impartial, their use of such Christian bywords as 'historical rights' and 'economic interests' left little doubt where their sympathy lay.[97]

The provisional agreement of 6 January was Clemenceau's last attempt as prime minister to solve the Syrian question by a compromise. The effort proved fruitless; the new French government was determined to safeguard French interests in the Levant, while Faisal for his part was unable to convince the extremist elements in his camp that compromise was preferable to military confrontation. The following months saw a rapid deterioration in relations between the French authorities in Beirut and the Arab government in Damascus.

Another act of Clemenceau's turned out to be of far greater consequence to the future of Syria and Lebanon: his appointment of Gouraud in October as high commissioner of Syria, Lebanon and Cilicia, and of Robert de Caix as Gouraud's secretary-general. Both men played an important role in defining the Syrian policy of the Millerand government. The present-day borders of Lebanon can largely be attributed to Gouraud's decisions, while the division of Syria into a federation of 'states' based on ethnic, religious and regional factors was mainly the result of de Caix's policy.

Gouraud was an obvious choice. His success during the War had won him great prestige in the army and with the French public. He could boast some colonial experience in Muslim countries, and was known as an admirer of Lyautey's colonial policy. He was also an ardent Catholic. Commenting on his appointment, the British ambassador in Paris wrote: 'In French Roman Catholic circles, where so keen an interest is displayed about Syrian matters, the appointment will be extremely well received, for General Gouraud is known for his devotion to the Church.'[98] Like many other Frenchmen Gouraud was concerned for the traditional position of France in the Levant and the safeguarding of its interests there; but judging from his declarations and actions immediately after his arrival in Beirut he supported Clemenceau's moderate Syrian policy and attached great importance to the *entente* with Britain.[99]

As a military man Gouraud gave top priority to implementing the government's decision to replace British forces throughout the Blue Zone. But his arrangements with Allenby and Faisal's aide Nuri al-Sa'id for a peaceful deployment of French forces in the Beqa'a Valley were suspended at the last minute by Clemenceau, who had reached his own agreement with Faisal in Paris. In any case, the frequent raids against French forces and positions in the Western Zone, encouraged by the nationalist elements in Damascus, rapidly quenched any spirit of co-operation he had felt towards the Arab government. Like many other Frenchmen, he had scorned the military ability of the Arabs and expected little opposition to his forces. He was therefore frustrated and humiliated by their inability to withstand Arab raids in the Western Zone and by the heavy defeats they suffered in Cilicia at the hands of the Turkish nationalists between January and April 1920. In the meantime he was continually pressed by de Caix to take harsh measures against Faisal and the Arab nationalists. Gouraud later recounted de Caix's words:

> Mon Général, dites-nous donc la vérité. Il n'est pas possible de nous faire comprendre qu'une grande nation comme la France que le général Gouraud, qui a une bonne réputation à la guerre, ne puisse pas nous défendre contre les Bédouins. Avouez donc que votre pays est épuisé et que vous ne voulez pas nous défendre.[100]

De Caix was now playing an important role in shaping French Syrian policy in both Beirut and Paris. His influence was so great, that Victor Bérard later charged that he was able to implement some of his own policies alongside those of Gouraud. In spite of his later claims to the contrary, de Caix had not really believed that any agreement with Faisal and the Arab nationalists could fully safeguard French interests in Syria, and he vigorously opposed the provisional agreement between Clemenceau and Faisal. In its place he called for military intervention. After Millerand's government came to power he concluded an agreement with the Turkish nationalists to enable France to concentrate its forces against the Arabs, and he suggested presenting Faisal with an ultimatum. De Caix had no illusions as to Syria's economic potential; his activities were motivated by a belief that to abandon Syria would undermine France's prestige as a colonial power in North Africa and as a power in post-War Europe on a par with Britain.[101]

Although Gouraud and de Caix shared a common stand on the Arab nationalists, they differed in their attitudes towards the Lebanese Christians. Gouraud's staunch support for their aspirations was to be the most important single factor in determining the borders of Lebanon. De Caix, on the other hand, was one of the first to realise the dangers of extended boundaries to the integrity of the future Lebanese state; throughout his involvement in affairs of the Levant he advocated a smaller Lebanon. Gouraud, as a devout Catholic was particularly susceptible to the pleas of the Lebanese Christians and their French supporters. For their part the Christians, particularly the Maronite Church and its patriarch, were quick to capitalise on his sympathy, and on his dismay at the Arab extremists in Damascus. Gouraud was personally impressed by

Hawayik; their mutual respect is transparent in their correspondence.[102] He was also under strong pressure from French circles in Beirut, including clerics, especially Jesuits, who had returned to Beirut after the War to renew their religious, educational and cultural activities and take part in relief operations.[103] Both the French groups and the Lebanese Christians constantly pressed Gouraud to take military action against the Arab government; the pressure mounted as security in the Western Zone deteriorated.[104]

Describing the influence of the Lebanese Christians and their French supporters on Gouraud, de Caix wrote six years later:

> L'ancien élément français de Beyrouth et les chrétiens ralliés à Rome qui assiégeaient le Haut Commisariat étaient trop imbus de la politique de clientèle, trop incapables de comprendre que le représentant de la France responsable désormais de l'ensemble de la population, avait à la dépasser, pour signaler l'obstacle au Haut Commissaire et sans doute même pour le voir. On ne lui parlait que de 'frontières historiques' dont on n'établissait d'ailleurs pas l'histoire. Le Patriarcat Maronite, avec, ce manque de véritable esprit politique qui caractérise si souvent les groupes d'hommes rusés et aptes à l'intrigue, poussait de toutes ses forces le Général Gouraud à tout donner au Liban. C'est alors, mais alors seulement que Gouraud fit la 'politique chrétienne' qu'on l'a si injustement accusé d'avoir faite; mais qu'il ne la fit même alors que croyant faire de la politique française et non pas confessionelle.[105]

De Caix himself was unmoved by this kind of pressure. Even before his arrival in Lebanon he had realised that the situation was far more complex than had been portrayed by the Christians. In the Paris discussions immediately after the arrival of the first Lebanese delegation, and again during Hawayik's visit, he had been one of the few to oppose the demand for expanded borders. He stuck to this position while serving in Beirut; when he failed at first to prevent the creation of a Greater Lebanon within the borders demanded by the Christians, he tried to detach some of the areas annexed to it by Gouraud. He condemned what he termed the 'mégalomanie libanaise' and warned that the incorporation of areas with a large Muslim population might endanger the stability and future of a Christian Lebanese state. He pointed out the difficulties involved in attaching a large urban centre such as Beirut to Mount Lebanon, with its traditional social and economic structure. De Caix's main motivation was to safeguard French interests in the area. A separate Christian entity would fit in with his policy of dividing Syria up into regions in order to weaken the influence of Arab nationalism and reduce anti-French feeling among the Muslim majority. A Christian Lebanese state under direct French rule inside realistic boundaries, would serve as a necessary base for French control and influence in the interior. Although de Caix's views on boundaries were not accepted, his policy advocating direct French control of Lebanon was eventually adopted despite strong opposition in both Lebanon and France.[106]

The replacement of Clemenceau by Millerand was to have a major influence on developments in the Levant. The new prime minister had close ties with the lobbies which advocated French control. He himself was convinced of the need for France to safeguard its traditional position and interests in the area, and he was less concerned than his predecessor about the *entente* with Britain. Thus one of the major deterrents to an extreme French policy was removed. The deterioration of relations with Faisal reinforced the new policy trends.[107]

The change in French policy became apparent as soon as Millerand's government took office in January 1920. The new prime minister backed Gouraud's firm stand in the Beqa'a Valley and hastened to allocate the additional forces and funds needed to strengthen France's position. Even more significant was his decision to give Gouraud and de Caix a free hand in dealing with affairs in Syria and Lebanon. As late as February he still regarded Clemenceau's agreement with Faisal as a possible solution, on condition that the Arab leader would be willing and able to guarantee French interests in Syria. Faisal's unilateral declaration of independence on 8 March and his coronation that day as King of Syria, Lebanon and Palestine was the last straw. It was seen as final proof that he had no intention of reaching an agreement with France. By the middle of March Millerand realised that the Syrian question demanded a military solution. However, he instructed Gouraud to take a moderate stand towards Faisal for the time being in order not to interfere with France's chances of obtaining a mandate over Syria at the Peace Conference, and in order to gain time to allow sufficient forces to be deployed in the Western Zone. At the beginning of May, immediately after France had been granted the mandate over Syria at San Remo, the policy of a military solution was finally adopted, and two months later was put into effect by Gouraud.[108]

During the crucial months from the end of 1919 through the summer of 1920, the Maronites and other Lebanese Christians proved neither willing nor able to understand the difficulties faced by the French in defining their Syrian policy. As they saw it, France, a year after the liberation of their country, was still indecisive and unable to assert either its authority or help them realise their own ambitions. They demanded the immediate fulfilment of their objectives; every delay increased their fears of a French arrangement with Faisal. The news from Paris in the middle of January that Clemenceau and Faisal had indeed reached an agreement renewed their suspicions that France had reverted to its policy of spring 1919. Further confirmation came with Faisal's declaration, on his arrival in Beirut, that he was co-operating with France and would soon return to Paris to conclude the agreement. The Christians were also anxious over the question of borders, which had been left open by Clemenceau in his letter to Hawayik, particularly as it concerned the Beqa'a Valley, which was still under Arab administration. They had hoped for French control of the Beqa'a and were bitterly disappointed when at the end of November French forces on their way to occupy the region were kept back at the last minute.[109]

It was in such circumstances, early in February 1920, that Hawayik and his bishops hastened to despatch a third delegation to Paris to ensure that the boundaries of the Lebanese state were drawn according to their demands, and especially that they include the Beqa'a. During seven months of steady lobbying in Paris the delegation succeeded in winning the support of many French politicians both in the Senate and the Chamber of Deputies. Their task was made easier by widespread feelings of anger and dismay at the anti-French attitude displayed by Faisal's Arab government. They also enjoyed the support of certain French groups who had their own interests in Syria. For these groups, the Lebanese cause was a convenient tool in convincing the government and public of the need for French control over the area, and in countering the growing body of opinion in France that opposed intervention in Syria. The strong support which the delegation mobilised, and the very presence of its members in Paris during July and August when the borders of Lebanon were finally determined, were crucial in preventing the few voices of opposition raised against a Greater Lebanon, including that of de Caix, from influencing the French government.[110]

In its memoranda to the government, the delegation brought up the same insistent demand for the recognition of Lebanon's historical and natural boundaries. It also advanced a new argument to support the inclusion of the Beqa'a in Lebanon: as the Sykes-Picot agreement assigned the Beqa'a to the Blue Zone, France had the right to direct control over the region. This was in fact a call for French occupation of the Beqa'a, in line with the policy that Gouraud and de Caix had been advocating since November 1919.[111] The demand won immediate support in a resolution adopted on 20 February by the External Affairs Committee of the Senate which demanded that

> . . . le Liban obtienne à brève échéance les limites que la France lui a reconnues et notamment les districts de Baalbeck, de la Bekaa, de Hasbaya et de Rachaya incorporées dans la zone française par les accords de 1916.[112]

A few days later Lenail,[113] a deputy from Lyons who was then playing an important part in rallying support for the Lebanese cause, questioned the prime minister in the Chamber on his Lebanon policy and called for the inclusion of the Beqa'a Valley in Lebanon. In his reply Millerand quoted Clemenceau's pledges to Hawayik, but this did not suffice for the Lebanese Christians and their French supporters, especially as the Arabs had just declared their independence. In an emotional speech in the Chamber of Deputies at the end of March, Lenail vehemently attacked Faisal and the 'Beduins' whom he accused of attempting to take Syria from France, and strongly defended the Lebanese Christians, stressing that 200,000 Lebanese had perished for their loyalty to France. Shortly afterwards Lenail presented the Lebanese delegation to Millerand, and proposed that France convene a congress of Lebanese Christians for the purpose of proclaiming a Lebanese Republic as a counter-measure to Faisal's recent moves. Millerand turned down this proposal after discussions with Gouraud, explaining that such a step would undermine France's claim to a mandate over the whole of Syria and could provoke the Muslims to step up their attacks in the Western Zone, where the French still had insufficient forces. At the same time Lenail was told to inform the delegation that France intended to honour its pledges to the Lebanese Christians.[114]

While successive governments in Paris were busy working out a

Syrian policy and trying to solve the problem of Anglo-French relations in the Levant, relations between Muslims and Christians within Syria and Lebanon were rapidly deteriorating, especially from late 1919. Tension had been mounting ever since the occupation of the area by the Allied Forces. It had already manifested itself in Aleppo, when 50 Armenians were killed by Muslims in February 1919. The visit of the King-Crane Commission, accompanied by intensive propaganda, pressure and intimidation by all sides, further exacerbated relations between the various sects.[115] Muslims increasingly tended to identify the Lebanese Christians with the French, whom they bitterly resented, and to hold them responsible for French attempts at domination. Describing the impact of Franco-British rivalry on relations between the various communities, Yale commented:

> The French were sure of the support of the Catholic elements in Syria, so when the British and the Young Arabs made it impossible for the French to obtain any support among the Moslems they have done their uttermost to rally the Christians to the French cause. In so doing they have deepened the hatred of the Moslems, created in the minds of the Christians fear and distrust of the Moslems. The result of the British and French policy in Syria has been to deepen the hatred between Moslems and Christians, increase the fanaticism of both parties, and to divide Syria along religious lines. The policy of both nations is a curse to the country and if persisted in will eventually result in massacres.[116]

Indeed, the Clemenceau-Lloyd George agreement in September on the evacuation of British forces from Syria and Lebanon and their replacement by French forces in the Blue Zone sparked an outbreak of violence throughout Syria. The withdrawal of the strong British force whose presence had prevented the eruption of hostilities left the opposing sides face to face: the Arab government in Damascus supported by the majority of the Muslims, and the French authorities in Beirut with their Christian supporters.

The Muslims strongly opposed the agreement and regarded the appointment of General Gouraud a few weeks later as proof that France had resolved to take control. Their anger and frustration found an outlet in expressions of anti-European and pan-Islamic sentiment, stoked by intensive Arab and Turkish nationalist propaganda. Extremist elements among the Arab nationalists, many of them of Iraqi origin, were anxious to prevent their movement from losing ground. They gradually began to turn the nationalist movement into an Islamic crusade. Describing the feelings among the Muslims, Major Clayton wrote:

> The Nationalist and anti-French movement, in fact, appears to be rather losing its force and should the French come in with troops, they would be unlikely, I think, to meet with any organised resistance. There is only one factor which might revive the former widespread feeling against them, and that is religion. With the vast majority of the Moslems, Arab Nationalism and Islamism are synonymous terms. This is now recognised by the Christian supporters of the Nationalist movement, and they are becoming slightly uneasy as to the possible results of their efforts to inculcate national ideas into the people of the country.[117]

Towards the end of 1919, when Faisal's brother Zayd was heading the government in his absence, these extremist elements, including members of the government and the Syrian Congress, almost succeeded in taking control of the political situation. This development proved to be of major political importance; it not only prevented Faisal from reaching an agreement with the French, but it also helped to determine the character of the Arab national movement in Syria throughout the mandate period. These nationalists were no longer prepared to wait for the outcome of the Peace Conference, nor were they willing to rely solely on political means to achieve Arab national aspirations, as advocated by Faisal and Nuri al-Sa'id. They decided instead to take immediate action to force the French out of Syria and Lebanon, and to resist any attempt by French troops to occupy the Beqa'a Valley as had been provided for in the Clemenceau-Lloyd George agreement. At the end of September Yassin Pasha al-Hashimi, chief-of-staff of the Arab army and a leading nationalist, sent reinforcements to the Beqa'a in preparation for the fight against the French; conscription was stepped up and local defence committees were formed.[118]

Although the Arab nationalists bitterly resented France, they were not yet prepared for an open military confrontation with the French army in the Western Zone. Instead they tried to cause as much disruption as possible by instigating attacks and raids, making sure to give them the appearance of spontaneous acts by the local inhabitants. From late 1919 to the summer of 1920, French positions throughout the Western Zone came under constant attack by bands from the Eastern Zone and by local inhabitants. These acts of violence had a clear political motive: to demonstrate to the French public that the occupation of Syria would result in heavy expenditure and loss of life, and thereby to pressure the French government into giving up its ambitions in the area.[119]

Faisal himself encouraged or at least indirectly tolerated the first wave of hostilities, which he thought would improve his position in the negotiations, first in London and then in Paris. But by early 1920, particularly after the fatal Marjayoun incident, he began to fear that the violence could sabotage his attempts to reach an agreement with Clemenceau. Before leaving Paris, he told a French official that he was worried that Gouraud, under the influence of some of his officers and Lebanese Christians, might use these incidents to justify a French military occupation of the whole of Syria. Back in Damascus Faisal succeeded for a while in preventing further attacks against the French in the Western Zone. But after the declaration of independence the situation got out of hand, and he was no longer able to control the extremist elements inside his own camp. That being the case, he tried once more to exploit the disorders to back his own claims over Lebanon.[120]

The deterioration in relations between the Arab nationalists in Damascus and the French authorities in Beirut had serious consequence for the various communities in Lebanon. Anti-French hostility was soon deflected towards the Lebanese Christians. Christian villages from Latakia in the north through the Beqa'a Valley to Jabal 'Amel in the south became targets for Muslim attacks and raids. Many were killed and thousands driven to seek refuge in the coastal towns. Wratislaw, the British consul-general in Beirut, wrote:

> It would appear that the word has been passed round all the non-Christian tribes — Arabs, Ansarriyeh, Mutawallis, Dandashi, etc. to cause all possible trouble to the French, and this they do most effectively, by harrying Christian villages, by holding up the roads and by acts of brigandage of all sorts.[121]

Within Lebanon itself it was the heterodox Muslim sects such as the Druze, the Mutawallis and the 'Alawites, together with Beduins from the surrounding areas, who carried out most of the attacks against both the French and the Lebanese Christians. The Druze and

Mutawallis had their own reasons for resisting a French mandate and for fearing Maronite domination in a Greater Lebanon, apart from the fact that many of their leaders were closely associated with the Arab nationalists. Their tight-knit feudal society, warlike tradition and mountainous habitat made them better able to rebel against the French than the urban Sunnis on the coast. The traditional animosity between Druze and Maronites in Mount Lebanon had always been easy to ignite, while certain elements among the Mutawallis and Beduins were prepared to raid Christian villages whenever the opportunity arose. Yet it was the Arab nationalists and their supporters within these communities who instigated the attacks. It can even be argued that the Sunnis on the coast and in the interior used the sects in their own fight against the French and the Lebanese Christians. The latter were apparently to be taught a lesson: the ineffectiveness of French protection and the need to link their future with Syria.[122]

At the beginning of 1920 the French had to send a large part of their forces to Cilicia at the expense of their military presence in Lebanon. This, together with the heavy defeats they suffered at the hands of the Turkish nationalists, encouraged the Arab nationalists and their supporters to step up their hostilities. But the French and the Lebanese Christians themselves also contributed to the violence. The behaviour of some French officers towards the Druze and Mutawallis aroused resentment against both French and Christians. Moreover, as the French authorities feared that Christian-Muslim *rapprochement* might harm their own interests, they did little to encourage it. Their arming of the Lebanese Christians for self-defence brought loud protests from the other communities. Finally, the provocative behaviour of some elements within the Christian communities, particularly after the announcement of the evacuation of the British forces, roused strong protests from the Muslims and exacerbated the already strained relations.[123]

It was the Druze in the Shuf district of Mount Lebanon who fired the first shot in the cycle of violence. The visit of the American Commission had left them divided, with one faction in particular bitterly resentful of the French and the Maronites. The first incident was instigated by certain influential Druze figures who held positions in the Arab administration in Damascus. On 24 July 1919 Admiral Mornet, commander of the French navy in the eastern Mediterranean was shot and seriously wounded as he and Picot were on their way to pay an official visit to the Druze religious leader in

Ba'alkin. The French tried to portray the episode as an accident, but in fact it was a clear attempt on Picot's life. Within a short time murder, revenge and brigandage became rife throughout the Mountain. Druze-Christian relations deteriorated further, and at the beginning of October Habib al-Sa'd's house was attacked by Druze. Many of the bands which carried out these attacks found refuge in the Beqa'a Valley. Attempts by the French and the Lebanese gendarmerie to contain the situation met with little success. A French report stressed the need 'to put an end to this agitation which is gradually spreading and causing a revolution in all Lebanon'.[124] On 14 October the French military governor of Mount Lebanon assembled the leaders and notables of both the Maronites and the Druze and warned them that unless the attacks ceased the authorities would have to take a firmer stand. The warning went unheeded, and after a series of further incidents the French did indeed respond with harsh measures against Druze villages. This in turn provoked threats of an invasion from the inhabitants of Jabal Druze.[125]

But Druze-French relations saw a rapid improvement towards the end of 1919. The British had pressed the Druze to moderate their stand. The Druze themselves had their own reasons for a *rapprochement* with the French, whom they now regarded as the new effective rulers. On their part Gouraud and de Caix attached great importance to gaining the support of the Druze by cultivating a friendlier approach. They worked to reach an agreement with the Druze in Jabal Druze, hoping that this would calm the Druze in Lebanon as well. An ally in Jabal Druze could also help the French to cut Faisal and his forces in Damascus off from the Hijaz and strengthen France's claims over Jabal Druze in its dispute with Britain. And indeed, following the understanding reached between Gouraud and the Druze leaders in Jabal Druze, relations gradually improved between the French and the Druze in Mount Lebanon as well. Nasib Junblat, their influential leader, even attempted to persuade the Druze of Hasbaya to accept a French mandate. It soon became clear that the Arab government's efforts to gain the support of the Druze had failed. In March, the Druze refrained from recognising Faisal as King.[126]

Southern Lebanon was another focus for raids and attacks which continued from the end of 1919 until the summer of 1920. In this region the perpetrators were bands of Mutawallis and Beduins. The latter came mainly from the Quneitra region in the Eastern Zone and the Hula area; they were led by Muhammad al-Fa'ur, who had close ties with extremists in Damascus, including war minister Yussuf al-'Azmah. Maronite and Greek Catholic villages were the main targets. Between 6 December and 6 January 30 villages were attacked and thousands of Christians fled to the coast. After repeated protests and appeals from the local Christians, whose leaders met Gouraud on 18 December, the French sent a punitive column to act against the Mutawalli villages which had taken part in the attacks. But when the French were forced to transfer most of their forces to Cilicia the raids and attacks were renewed in full force. French reaction was limited to the bombardment of Mutawalli villages and the distribution of arms and ammunition to the Christians.[127]

But it was not just the lack of troops which kept the French from taking a firmer stand. De Caix considered the Mutawallis in southern Lebanon, the 'Alawites in the north and the Druze in Jabal Druze as distinct groups capable of forming autonomous communities that could be separated from Syria and placed under direct French control. In a memorandum to the new government in January, in which he criticised Clemenceau's agreement with Faisal, de Caix raised the possibility of creating such an autonomous Mutawalli region in south Lebanon, or of attaching the area to Lebanon. The agreement with Faisal had stipulated that the future of the Beqa'a Valley was to be decided in accordance with the will of the inhabitants; as the Mutawallis comprised a large section of that population, their support became important for both the French and the Arab governments. French efforts met with some success as several Mutawalli notables, including Kamal al-As'ad, improved their ties with the authorities. Aware of de Caix's intentions, Faisal's government stepped up its pressure on the inhabitants of the region and encouraged attacks by Beduins to prevent any reconciliation.[128] One of the most serious incidents took place early in May, when the large Christian village of 'Ain Ibel and two neighbouring villages were attacked by Mutawallis and Beduin bands. More than 50 inhabitants were massacred; the rest fled either to the coast or to northern Palestine in the British zone.[129]

This incident, which greatly alarmed the Christians in Lebanon, was widely publicised in the French and British press. The French authorities finally decided to take firm action against the Mutawallis. Forces led by Colonel Nieger destroyed several villages whose inhabitants had participated in the attack on 'Ain Ibel, including Bint Jbayil, a main Mutawalli stronghold in Jabal 'Amel, and Taibeh, Kamal al-As'ad's village. Several leaders were sentenced to death in absentia while others were deported; their property was confiscated and their houses demolished. Most of the condemned leaders, including As'ad, along with about 20,000 followers, fled to the Eastern Zone. A fine of 100,000 Egyptian pounds was levied on the Mutawalli villages to compensate for the damage suffered by the Christians. Colonel Nieger ordered the Mutawalli notables to undertake to live peacefully with their Christian neighbours, but as the British consul-general remarked: 'It is hardly to be expected that any particular goodwill towards the Christians will result from the punishment which the Mutawallis have received.'[130]

The French had another reason for hastening to restore law and order. The attacks on Christian villages in southern Lebanon took place at the very time negotiations were being held with the British to define the border between the French zone in Lebanon and the British zone in Palestine. The lack of security in the region could strengthen British claims to the area south of the Litani; if a plebiscite were held, the majority of inhabitants, even including the Christians, might support incorporation in Palestine under a British mandate.[131]

France's military weakness in the face of a deteriorating security situation sapped the country's prestige not only in the eyes of its opponents, but even among its supporters, the Lebanese Christians. With Gouraud's arrival the Christians had been confident that the French army would soon impose its authority over the whole of Syria; thus its subsequent defeats and its inability to protect them were all the more alarming. Many Christians in Beirut feared an attack on the town by the Arab army in collaboration with Muslim inhabitants. Others believed that France, confronted with increasing difficulties in the area, would abandon Syria and Lebanon and leave the Christians to defend themselves. Reports from Paris told of growing opposition to French intervention in the Levant with its mounting toll in money and lives. The massacre in February 1920 of thousands of Armenians in Marash, after the French had evacuated the town, further amplified Christian fears. Moreover, the fact that the Christians had now become the main target for Muslim hatred and hostility undoubtedly led some of them to reconsider their relations with France.[132]

The inclusion of Lebanon in the independent Syrian kingdom proclaimed by the Syrian Congress, in which Muslim delegates from the Western Zone took part, sparked angry protests to the French government by Hawayik, the Administrative Council and various

Lebanese groups. Primed by their long-standing suspicions about a France-Faisal deal, many Christians assumed that Faisal would not have taken such a step without French compliance. This assumption was encouraged by Faisal's supporters, including the Muslim press.[133]

Gouraud was greatly alarmed by the decline of French prestige among the Lebanese Christians. From the end of 1919 his dispatches repeatedly stressed the weakening of Christian confidence in France, which he blamed largely on Clemenceau's decision not to occupy the Beqa'a. Immediately after Faisal's unilateral declaration of independence he asked Millerand to renew Clemenceau's pledges to the Lebanese Christians; Millerand complied in a letter to the Lebanese delegation in Paris. In a mid-March tour of Lebanon Gouraud made conciliatory speeches emphasising the strong ties between France and Lebanon, repeating France's intentions to remain in the area and declaring that Faisal's proclamation was null and void. With French encouragement, members of the Administrative Council and representatives from Beirut and from towns and villages in the Mountain gathered in Ba'abda on 22 March to declare the independence of Lebanon. They adopted a resolution reiterating their demand for an independent Greater Lebanon under a French mandate.[134]

The deterioration in the Lebanese economy, particularly in Beirut, was another factor that strained relations between some Christians and the French authorities. The economy, which had not yet recovered from the ravages of the War, rapidly deteriorated even further towards the end of 1919. A steep rise in prices and a severe shortage of basic commodities was accompanied by an almost complete halt in commerce between the coast and the interior, due to both the lack of security in the area and the policies adopted by the Arab government. From the end of 1919 and even more following the declaration of independence, Faisal's government began to apply economic pressure on the Western Zone. It aimed to demonstrate Lebanon's economic dependence and the impossibility of establishing a separate state without close association with Syria. The transport of commodities such as grain and cattle from the interior to the Western Zone ceased; imports and exports through Beirut rapidly dried up as the Arab government and merchants in the interior began to use the port of Haifa instead. Beirut merchants, Christian as well as Muslim, were stranded with accumulated stocks of imported goods they were unable to sell. The difficulties created by the introduction of French currency in the Western Zone in April, when the Eastern Zone was still using Egyptian currency, raised further protests from numerous sectors.[135] But the greatest harm to French-Christian relations came from the increasing French intervention in the Lebanese administration and the attempts to impose direct French control. The Christians, who had always jealously guarded their administrative autonomy, found themselves displaced from positions and influence by French bureaucrats. They resented the patronising and sometimes contemptuous attitude of French military and civilian officials, most of whom had been trained in the colonial administration in Morocco.[136]

Among the first to express concern was the Administrative Council, which on 29 November 1919, after the Western Zone had been placed under military administration, adopted a resolution calling for France to respect Lebanon's independence. Relations between the High Commission and most of the members of the Administrative Council, including its president Habib al-Sa'd, soon became strained.[137] The French scorned the favouritism and regard for personal interest which were rife in the Lebanese administration, although they themselves did not hesitate to use the same methods to further their own interests.[138] But their main objection was to the attempts made by Sa'd and other members to preserve the Council's authority as an autonomous body representing the inhabitants of Lebanon. Though personal interests were also involved, including Sa'd's ambition to become the first Lebanese governor, the Council's stand was a genuine expression of Lebanese aspirations for full independence.

A few days after the Arab declaration of independence the members of the Administrative Council met Gouraud to discuss the writing of a Lebanese constitution. Being elected representatives they considered themselves eligible to form a constituent assembly. Gouraud and de Caix had no reason to object, and saw approval as a way to defuse Christian discontent. At the same time they were anxious to see that France's own interests were protected in any such constitution. On 2 June Gouraud officially informed Sa'd that he had appointed a commission of 14 members which, together with the Administrative Council, would draw up the constitution. He explained that the commission would enable other sectors of the population to be represented, but the emphasis he laid on close co-operation between the constituent assembly and the French authorities left little doubt that their main aim was to secure French interests, in particular to ensure that the constitution would stipulate the appointment of a French governor. French officials tried to persuade the Lebanese to sign petitions in support of a French governor; they were assisted by some of the Lebanese themselves, including Administrative Council member Da'ud 'Ammun. But many Christians still held out for a Lebanese governor and strongly opposed the appointment of the commission on the grounds that only the Lebanese had the right to elect their own constituent assembly.[139]

Alarmed by France's inability to protect them or help them realise their ambitions for an independent Greater Lebanon; disappointed with the precarious political and economic situation and annoyed at French intervention in the Lebanese administration, many Christians, in particular members of the Greek Orthodox community in Beirut, began to react more positively to the attempts of Faisal and his representatives and supporters in the Western Zone to reach an agreement. These attempts were intensified after the March declaration of independence, when the Arab government tried to obtain recognition of Faisal as King by various communities and notables in the Western Zone. At the end of May Hawayik felt obliged to write to Gouraud:

Quant aux bruits que font courir certaines personnes, il ne faut pas y attacher une grande importance. Le Liban tient fortement à son indépendance et aux traditions séculaires d'attachement inébranlables à la France. Nous avons toujours soutenu cette thèse et nous ne manquerons pas de la défendre.[140]

The deterioration in relations between the Administrative Council and the French left some members particularly susceptible to Faisal's representatives. Secret contacts with the Arab government were arranged in June. Gouraud later claimed that Suleiman Kena'an, a Maronite member of the Council, was the first to be won over by Amin Arslan and Ri'ad al-Sulh, and that he then persuaded six other Council members to join him in an attempt to reach an agreement with Faisal. In June and early July rumours circulated by Faisal's government about an imminent agreement between the King and the French caused much anxiety among the Lebanese Christians. It was undoubtedly these rumours which finally prompted the seven councillors to reach their own accord with Faisal.[141]

This was the direct background of the Council resolution of 10 July, a signed advance copy of which had been taken by Ri'ad al-Sulh to Damascus.[142] In the resolution, which the Council was prepared to take to Damascus and then to the Peace Conference in Europe, the seven Council members agreed to give up the Lebanese request for a French mandate; in return, Faisal and his government recognised the complete independence of Lebanon. In a verbal agreement, Faisal apparently also agreed to the annexation to Lebanon of the whole coastal area including Tripoli, Beirut and Sidon. The episode represented an attempt by some Lebanese Christians to forego foreign protection and to link the future of Lebanon with the Arab world, 23 years before Bishara al-Khuri pursued this path to its conclusion. It is therefore understandable that in his memoirs half a century later, al-Khuri fully endorsed the earlier initiative.[143]

For Faisal, the advantages of such an agreement were obvious. A visit by the Council members of Damascus would have embarrassed the French government and seriously undermined one of its main arguments for a mandate: protection of the Lebanese Christians. Their appearance at the Peace Conference could have persuaded both the other powers and the French public that the Lebanese Christians, France's traditional supporters, had joined the Arab Muslims in Syria in rejecting a French mandate and demanding complete independence. Moreover, the annexation to Lebanon of areas with a large Muslim population would have greatly reduced its Christian majority, an advantage Faisal had already pointed out 18 months before, while in Paris for the Peace Conference.[144]

The French authorities, who were following these contacts closely, were indeed embarrassed and angered. They arrested the seven councillors on their way to Damascus on charges of high treason and conspiracy, and brought them before a military court one week later along with other Lebanese who had participated in the negotiations. The councillors were sentenced to deportation and heavy fines. The whole affair was officially presented as a plot by Faisal and a small group of notables willing to sell their country for money. In truth, Faisal's offer of 40,000 Egyptian pounds was undoubtedly a great inducement, especially in winning the councillors' consent to go to Europe. But these men were no mere insignificant figures, as the French were claiming; they were the elected representatives of Mount Lebanon, whom the French had previously recognised as such. One of them was the Maronite patriarch's own brother, Sa'adalah Hawayik.[145]

Nevertheless, the French exploited the incident to achieve two objectives. They had already, in early May, decided on a military solution and were seeking an opportunity to present an ultimatum to the Arab government. Faisal's intrigue gave them such an opportunity. Four days after the arrest of the councillors Gouraud sent his ultimatum to Faisal; it was to lead in the end to the defeat of the Arab army at Maisalun on 24 July and the occupation of Damascus by French forces the following day. The second objective served by branding the councillors as traitors was to weaken opposition within Lebanon to the appointment of a French governor. Many Christians now regarded a French governor as a necessary safeguard for the future independence of Lebanon. On 12 July Gouraud dissolved the Administrative Council altogether, thereby removing the main opposition to direct French control. A long time would pass before Lebanese Christian leaders once more attempted to seek complete independence from France with the co-operation of Syria.[146]

The defeat of Faisal and his Arab government and the occupation of all of Syria by French forces was regarded by most Maronites and other Lebanese Christians as a victory for their cause. The strong opposition of Faisal and the Arab nationalists during the previous two years had been the main obstacle to the establishment of an independent Greater Lebanon. Soon after France imposed complete control they asked for the immediate annexation of the coast and the Beqa'a Valley, and began intensive lobbying both in Beirut and in Paris in favour of the full realisation of their aspirations.[147]

In the meantime, French officials in France and Lebanon were engaged in intensive discussions on future policy in Syria, in particular on political and administrative organisation.[148] The borders of Lebanon and its future relations with the rest of Syria became one of the main issues in these discussions. Gouraud strongly supported the boundaries demanded by the Lebanese Christians, while de Caix and several other officials argued for narrower boundaries. The latter were supported by Millerand, who as premier had to take the final decision.

De Caix argued that the ethnic, religious and cultural composition of the areas proposed for annexation was so different from that of the Mountain that the two regions could not be successfully incorporated into one state. He knew how much the Sunnis on the coast would resent annexation to a Christian state; moreover, after

Faisal's defeat, he was anxious not to arouse further Muslim hostility by complying immediately with all the Lebanese Christian demands. Only six weeks before the official establishment of Greater Lebanon de Caix detailed all these reservations in a memorandum to Millerand.[149] He proposed that only the Beqa'a Valley and Jabal 'Akkar be annexed; the question of Beirut and the sanjak of Sidon should be deferred until it became clear how the first two regions had fared. Tripoli should remain permanently outside Lebanon.

From a later perspective de Caix's arguments are of special interest as they demonstrate an early awareness of the demographic problems which could arise in an oversized Lebanese state. De Caix saw no reason to refuse Lebanese Christian claims to the Beqa'a Valley, as he believed that the majority of the area's inhabitants were non-Muslims and were willing to be annexed. He went on to argue that such an annexation would also be beneficial to France, as it would facilitate the division of the former Arab state and place this strategically important region, with its network of roads and railways, under direct French control. He took a similar stand concerning the Jabal 'Akkar region in the north, believing that most of its inhabitants were Christians, mainly Greek Orthodox. By annexing this region, Lebanon would border directly on the proposed 'Alawite 'state', thereby separating the Sunni centre of Tripoli from the Muslims of the interior. On the other hand he strongly opposed the annexation of Tripoli, arguing that it was 'a Sunni Muslim centre, somewhat fanatical, with no wish to be incorporated into a country with a Christian majority'. He disputed the claim that Tripoli was necessary for Lebanon as a port, stressing that it could still be used freely as there would be no customs barriers. He also dismissed the claims made by some Lebanese Christians that they would soon be able to dominate the town. He proposed that Tripoli and the area to its north, with its 40,000–50,000 Sunni inhabitants, be granted municipal autonomy.

As for Beirut, which the Lebanese Christians were particularly anxious to incorporate, de Caix had certain reservations about whether such a large city would make a suitable capital for the Mountain. He argued that before long, Beirut would probably have half as many inhabitants as the whole of Lebanon; this would greatly alter the character of the Lebanese state. De Caix also disputed the claim that nearly all the Christians in the town, except for the Greek Orthodox, were of Lebanese origin; he doubted whether the majority of the city's inhabitants, or even those of Lebanon itself, actually supported annexation. Here too, he stressed that the Lebanese would have free access to the port of Beirut; he proposed to make the city an autonomous municipality separate from Lebanon.

On the future of the sanjak of Sidon in the south, with its 80,000–90,000 Mutawalli inhabitants, de Caix raised the possibility of creating a small autonomous Mutawalli 'state' there, with guarantees for the Christian minority. However, because of the dispute with Britain and the Zionists on the future of the area south of the Litani, he proposed to link this region as closely as possible to Lebanon.

De Caix intended to overcome the problems created by the heterogeneous character of Lebanon by establishing a 'Lebanese federation' comprising Mount Lebanon, with its clear Christian majority, the sanjak of Sidon with its Mutawalli inhabitants and Beirut with its large Sunni and Greek Orthodox communities. His memorandum was, in fact, used by the Quai d'Orsay as the basis for a plan for the administrative organisation of Syria and Lebanon, which closely followed his recommendations on the borders of Lebanon. On 6 August Millerand sent the plan to Gouraud as a guide to French policy in Syria.[150]

During this period, Gouraud's strong support for the Lebanese Christian cause became plain. He fought against de Caix's proposals and constantly pressed Millerand to allow him to set up a Greater Lebanon at once, to include all the regions demanded by the Lebanese Christians. He regarded the fulfilment of Lebanese Christian aspirations as repayment of France's moral debt to them for their loyalty and historical attachment. In a ceremony in Zahle on 3 August, he officially announced the annexation of the Beqa'a Valley to Lebanon; in a speech to the inhabitants of the town, these sentiments were clearly expressed:

> Lorsque j'ai débarqué, il y a huit mois, je connaissais depuis longtemps l'attachement traditionnel du Liban à la France . . . Pendant les huit mois écoulés, le Liban, dans son immense majorité, resta fidèle; et cette fidélité lui vaut en ce jour sa récompense . . . De notre côté nous pouvons dire, nous Français, que nous avons payé la dette que nous avait fait contracter votre antique attachement.[151]

In fact during that month Gouraud came under strong pressure from both the Lebanese Christians, headed by the Maronite Church, and French missionaries in Beirut to create a *fait accompli*. He himself was convinced of the need for immediate compliance with Lebanese Christian demands, particularly after the Administrative Council action. He believed that France had to 'grant the Lebanese state, whose interests are indissolubly linked to ours, maximum extension and power for its political, economic and social needs'. Unlike de Caix, he grossly underestimated the opposition of the Muslims on the coast to their annexation to Lebanon, and made the mistake of taking at face value the appeals and petitions presented to him after Faisal's defeat by some notables and groups there. At the same time, he erred in accepting Lebanese Christian claims about the extent of support in these areas for annexation, and about the Christians' ability to dominate the area politically and economically. This was particularly evident in his arguments for the inclusion of Tripoli. He claimed that de Caix's views were based on the situation before Faisal's defeat; now, he argued, 'the Muslims of Tripoli are willing to be incorporated in Greater Lebanon on the condition that they retain their administrative autonomy . . .' As for the problem of annexing so many Muslims to Lebanon, Gouraud stressed that there were large Greek Orthodox and Maronite communities in Tripoli, and that although Tripoli and the regions of Husn and 'Akkar would add 57,000 Sunnis to Lebanon, some 69,000 Christians would be included as well. Finally, he insisted that Beirut become the capital of the new Lebanese state and the seat of the French high commissioner.[152]

Faced with continuous lobbying by the Lebanese Christians and their French supporters, as well as pressure from Gouraud, Millerand finally authorised the latter on 21 August to extend Lebanon's borders, but he again warned him that the annexation of Tripoli and Beirut was not necessarily an advantage either for Lebanon or for the towns themselves. He recommended a trial period during which both towns would enjoy a large measure of autonomy.[153] On 31 August Gouraud signed decrees granting Beirut and Tripoli autonomous status, while incorporating them in Greater Lebanon. But it was understood by both Gouraud and the Lebanese Christians that this autonomy was merely nominal, and that the towns, together with the coastal area, were an integral part of the Lebanese state. On the following day, at a ceremony in Beirut, Gouraud formally proclaimed the establishment of Greater

Lebanon, from the Nahr al-Kabir in the north to Ras Nakura in the south; and from the Mediterranean in the west to the anti-Lebanon in the east. The centuries-old Maronite dream of an independent state was now fulfilled.[154]

The main factors behind the establishment of Greater Lebanon have now moved into clearer perspective. The traditional ties between France and the Lebanese Christians, particularly the Maronites, formed a solid basis for deep sympathy and strong support. Many Frenchmen were genuinely concerned for the future of the Lebanese Christians and even felt a moral obligation to assist them, especially as they believed that the latter had suffered during the War because of their loyalty to France. The success of French societies after the War in mobilising public and political support for French control over Syria was vital for the Lebanese Christians, as it was only through French intervention that they were able to realise all their aspirations. Moreover, these groups effectively blocked Clemenceau's attempt to reach an agreement with Faisal; such an accord would undoubtedly have prevented the Lebanese Christians from achieving their aims.

In 1919 Clemenceau's view of the French role in Syria and Lebanon, and French attempts to use Lebanon to manoeuvre Faisal into an agreement, constituted major obstacles in the path of the Lebanese Christians. But these attempts failed, mainly because of internal pressure on Clemenceau to safeguard France's rights in Syria, Faisal's short-sighted policy, the Anglo-French rivalry over Syria and the strong opposition of the Lebanese Christians and their supporters in France. At this stage many French decision-makers still tended to see Greater Lebanon as an autonomous administrative unit in a Syrian federation under a French mandate. It was primarily due to Hawayik's efforts and to France's own realisation that a stronghold in Lebanon was needed to secure its interests in the entire region, that the French government finally recognised the need for an independent Lebanese Christian state.

By the beginning of 1920 the establishment of Greater Lebanon had been secured. Clemenceau's defeat in the presidential elections in January removed the main supporter of compromise with Faisal and a more modest French involvement in Syria.[155] The new government was far more sympathetic towards the Lebanese Christians and was determined to safeguard France's interests in Syria to the full, even if force was required. After the unilateral declaration of independence by the Syrian Congress, a military confrontation between France and Faisal's government became inevitable. Indeed, it was the challenge and subsequent defeat of the Arab government in Damascus that finally enabled the Lebanese Christians to win a state of their own. The fact that they achieved this not in agreement with the Arab Muslims but by force and with the aid of a foreign power, was to colour their relations with the Muslims in both Greater Lebanon and Syria throughout the mandate period.

3 THE FIRST YEARS OF DISILLUSION

The establishment of Greater Lebanon on 1 September 1920 had far-reaching consequences for the political, social and economic development of the country. It is difficult to find any aspect of modern Lebanese life which was not influenced by the new circumstances arising from territorial enlargement. Several factors conspired to bring about this crucial decision. By creating Greater Lebanon, France hoped to establish a permanent and loyal base in the Levant, a bastion against the Muslims of the interior who were so hostile towards its political and cultural aims. But at the same time it sought to satisfy the aspirations of the Maronites, its traditional protégés, for an independent Christian state. In fact, the events which led up to the September proclamation leave little doubt that the final decision on borders was prompted more by Maronite demands than by French interests.

The Maronites saw the founding of Greater Lebanon as the culmination of their century-long struggle for independence and 'historical-natural' borders. For them the new state was the immediate successor to the Imarah and the Mutasarrifiya, and its borders recalled the historic lines of the Ma'nid and Shihabist periods. It was the culmination of a continuous historical process during which Lebanon became identified as the national home of the Christians in the Levant. The French mandate was part of this continuity; it was seen as an international guarantee for the independence, territorial integrity and Christian character of Greater Lebanon, recalling the guarantees of the six European powers, headed by France, for the existence of the autonomous Sanjak of Mount Lebanon more than half a century before. But though Greater Lebanon was indeed the immediate successor of the Imarah and the Mutasarrifiya, its establishment was nevertheless a turning-point in the political development of modern Lebanon. It marked the end of 'smaller' Lebanon, based on a close association between a clear Maronite majority and a Druze minority, and centred in Mount Lebanon, and the beginning of the pluralistic society of present-day Lebanon, centred in the city of Beirut.

Although the annexation of the coastal area and the Beqa'a Valley made Lebanon more viable economically, the old cohesion and collective sense of Lebanese identity, developed during centuries of co-existence between the various sects in the Mountain, was lost. Nearly half of the population were now Muslims who deeply resented their arbitrary annexation to a Christian Lebanese state. Paradoxically, while the expansion of Lebanon marked the culmination of Maronite aspirations, it also concealed a funda-mental threat to the country's future stability and even to its very existence as a Christian state.

In order to comprehend the problems Lebanon has had to face since 1920 it is essential to examine the demographic structure that emerged with territorial enlargement. Precise population figures are of crucial importance in Lebanon, as the political system is based on sectarian representation in proportion to the size of each community.

Table 3.1: A comparison of the Population Distribution between the Autonomous Sanjak and Greater Lebanon.[1]

Sect	The Autonomous Sanjak 1911		Greater Lebanon 1921		Greater Lebanon 1932	
	Number	Per cent	Number	Per cent	Number	Per cent
Maronites	242,308	58.40	199,181	32.70	227,800	29.11
Greek Orthodox	52,356	12.62	81,409	13.37	77,312	9.88
Greek Catholic	31,939	7.70	42,462	6.97	46,709	5.97
Other Christians	3,026	0.73	12,651	2.08	45,125	5.77
Total Christians	329,626	79.45	335,703	55.12	396,946	50.73
Sunnis	14,529	3.50	124,786	20.48	177,100	22.63
Mutawallis	23,413	5.64	104,947	17.23	155,035	19.81
Druze	47,290	11.40	43,633	7.16	53,334	6.82
Total Muslims	85,232	20.54	273,366	44.87	385,469	49.26
Total	414,858	99.99	609,069	99.99	782,415	99.99

The expansion of the autonomous Sanjak into Greater Lebanon brought a dramatic demographic change. The Christians had com-prised 80 per cent of the population of the Sanjak, but were now only 51 per cent in Greater Lebanon according to the 1932 census. Even this small statistical majority was attained only by including registered emigrants, who were mainly Christian, and Armenians who settled in Lebanon after the War. Without these two groups the

Muslims would have held the majority. In any case Christian emigration and a higher Muslim birth-rate soon shifted the balance. In Greater Lebanon the Maronites were still the largest single sect, comprising 30 per cent of the population, but they had lost the absolute majority of 58 per cent which they had held in the Sanjak. The Greek Orthodox community and the Greek Catholics maintained their former percentages of the total population, but the Druze dropped from 11 per cent to 7 per cent, becoming the fifth largest community. In contrast, the Sunnis, who had constituted only 3.5 per cent of the population of the autonomous Sanjak, became the second largest community in Greater Lebanon, comprising 22 per cent of the population, while the Mutawallis increased from 5.5 per cent to 20 per cent, thus becoming the third largest community.

When examining the demographic structure of the annexed areas according to the census of 1921, it becomes clear that the Christian claim to be a majority in these areas was unfounded. Of the 320,000 people living in the newly-annexed areas, only 35 per cent were Christians. The division between the six main sects in these areas was: Maronites, 14 per cent; Greek Orthodox, 13 per cent; Greek Catholics, 8 per cent; Sunnis, 33 per cent; Mutawallis, 27 per cent; Druze, 3 per cent. The population of the districts which had comprised the autonomous Sanjak totalled 288,000 (30,000 of whom were registered emigrants, mainly Maronites); of these, four-fifths were Christians. The division between the six main sects was as follows: Maronites, 54 per cent; Greek Orthodox, 14 per cent; Greek Catholics, 6 per cent; Druze, 12 per cent; Mutawallis, 7 per cent; Sunnis, 6 per cent. A comparison between these figures and those of 1911 shows that the Mountain's population had fallen by one-third; most of the decline was among the Maronites. The total population had dropped from 414,800 to 288,000 and the number of Maronites from 242,308 to 156,090 (present in Lebanon). The sharp decline in the number of Maronites reflected both emigration and the direct effects of the War.[2]

An analysis of the census of 1932 demonstrates even more clearly that the Muslims formed the majority in all the districts annexed to Mount Lebanon. In seven of the districts annexed in 1920, the Muslims (Sunnis and Mutawallis) comprised an absolute majority: 'Akkar, 55 per cent (Sunnis); Tripoli, 72 per cent (Sunnis); Sidon, 80 per cent (Sunnis, 18 per cent, Mutawallis, 62 per cent); Tyre, 87 per cent (Sunnis, 4 per cent, Mutawallis, 83 per cent); Marjayoun, 61 per cent (Sunnis, 15 per cent, Mutawallis, 46 per cent); Ba'albek, 79 per cent (Sunnis, 12 per cent, Mutawallis, 67 per cent); and Hermil, 69 per cent (Sunnis, 5 per cent, Mutawallis, 64 per cent). Even in the remaining two annexed districts, Zahle and Beirut, there was no clear Christian majority. In the former the Muslims were in the minority (38 per cent) only because the mainly Christian town of Zahle, which had previously been part of the autonomous Sanjak, was now included in the district of Zahle. The Christian claim that they were the majority in Beirut was also questionable. According to the census of 1921, the total population of Beirut was 94,432 (including 12,206 foreigners and 2,934 registered emigrants), of whom 41,378 were Muslims, mainly Sunnis, and 39,962 Christians. Furthermore, the number of Muslims in Beirut at that time was undoubtedly greater than these figures show, as is borne out by the figures for 1943. Although the Christians comprised 55 per cent of the total 1943 population of 169,967, compared with the Muslims' 41 per cent, the figures for the former included over 40,000 Armenians who had settled in Beirut after 1920. If this number had been deducted, the Muslims would have comprised a clear majority.[3]

The small size of the Christian majority led the French authorities and the Lebanese Christians themselves to seek ways of reversing the demographic trend. One of their first moves was to try to reduce the rate of Christian emigration. Before 1920 the Christians had often raised the issue of emigration to justify their demand for extended borders. They claimed that a larger state would enable many Christians who would otherwise emigrate for lack of economic opportunity to stay on; it would even lead to the return of thousands who had already left. In fact, territorial enlargement did little to alleviate the problem. The French tried to restrict the issue of exit permits but even this did not stem the flow of emigrants, which reached a peak of 16,000 in 1923. The numbers did fall over the following years, but this was due mainly to restrictions imposed by the countries of destination, especially the United States, and to the world-wide economic crisis of 1929. A few thousand emigrants did return to Lebanon, but between the two World Wars, net emigration averaged about 4,000 a year.[4]

Another French move to augment the small Christian majority was to encourage other Christians to settle in Lebanon, in particular the Armenian refugees who had begun to arrive in increasing numbers towards the end of the War. Following the Franklin-Bouillon agreement of October 1921 and the defeat of the Greeks by the Kemalists, thousands of Armenians fled from the areas under Turkish control and settled in northern Syria and Lebanon, mainly in Beirut. Over 30,000 Armenians were counted in Lebanon in the census of 1932. The Armenians, who added one more component to the multi-confessional society of Lebanon, were disliked by the Muslims of Beirut both because they added to the number of Christians and because they competed for employment and trade.[5]

The establishment of Greater Lebanon created a deeply divided society, not only in demographic terms. There were other basic differences between Mount Lebanon and the annexed areas. During the Imarah and particularly during the Mutasarrifiya, Mount Lebanon had developed political, administrative, social and economic characteristics distinguishing it from the surrounding areas, which remained under direct Ottoman rule. For over half a century before the War it had enjoyed a privileged status as an autonomous province. Its inhabitants had their own political and administrative system, a separate budget and a lower level of taxation. The feudal system had almost ceased to exist; the inhabitants were mainly small independent farmers whose standard of living was far higher than that of the poorer Muslim peasantry in the annexed areas. In contrast the annexed areas had remained integral parts of the Ottoman political and administrative system, as part of the vilayets of Beirut and Damascus. The social structure of peasant-tenants tied to feudal lords still existed among the Sunnis in the 'Akkar region and the Mutawallis in the Beqa'a Valley and southern Lebanon. Within the urban Sunni and Greek Orthodox communities of the coastal area there was a wide gap between the wealthy merchants and financiers and the poorer working classes, a gap which did not exist in the Mountain. The economy of most of the areas, particularly the Beqa'a, Tripoli and 'Akkar, was more closely linked to the economy of the interior than to that of Mount Lebanon. Their contrasting characters made it difficult to unite these two regions into one state.[6]

Regionalism was still another factor which hindered the integration of the various inhabitants into a cohesive political community. Religious communities in Lebanon tend to be concentrated in distinct geographical regions where they often constitute a majority: the Maronites in the north and centre of Mount Lebanon; the Druze in the Shuf district of the Mountain and the southern part of the Beqa'a Valley around Hasbaya and Rashaya; the Mutawallis in the area of Tyre-Jabal 'Amel and in the central and northern Beqa'a;

the Sunnis in the towns of Tripoli, Beirut and Sidon and in the 'Akkar district surrounding Tripoli; and the Greek Orthodox in Beirut, Tripoli and the district of Kura in Mount Lebanon. The Greek Catholics are scattered in southern Lebanon, with a large concentration in Zahle. Substantial numbers of every sect are present in Beirut, the administrative, political and economic centre of the country.[7]

The policies followed by the first three high commissioners for Syria and Lebanon in the six years following the French occupation of Syria helped determine the political, administrative and legislative characteristics of Lebanon for the next two decades. All of the three, Gouraud (November 1919-November 1922), Weygand (May 1923-December 1924) and Sarrail (January 1925-November 1925), were military men accustomed to a military hierarchy. The government in Paris usually limited itself to issuing general and sometimes vague instructions, while the high commissioners used their extensive executive and legislative powers to formulate their own programmes, each according to his previous experience, personal beliefs and political tendencies. Their frequent replacement led to acute policy changes. The appointment of Gouraud and Weygand, both ardent Catholics, was a demonstration of France's intention to pursue its traditional policy of close links with the Catholics in the Levant. A similar step had been taken by the British in appointing Herbert Samuel, a Jew, as the first high commissioner in Palestine. Sarrail, on the other hand, was known for his anti-clerical tendencies. Gouraud, Weygand and Sarrail introduced many political and administrative reforms into the Lebanese state, but it was Jouvenel (December 1925-May 1926), the first civilian high commissioner and the first to serve after the Druze revolt, who established the Lebanese Republic and gave it its constitution.[8]

For all three major forces, Maronites, Sunnis and French, whose interrelations determined the character of the Lebanese state, these years marked a period of disillusion and adjustment to harsh reality. After the first few months of enthusiasm, the Maronites were to discover that in spite of Gouraud's proclamation, neither Lebanon's independent existence nor its new borders were secured. They became aware of the enormous task involved in transforming their newly-established state into a viable political entity, and they grew increasingly disillusioned with the French mandate. The Sunnis saw their hopes in Faisal's Arab regime shattered. As they could no longer rely on Damascus they had to readjust their attitude towards the new Lebanese state and the French mandate. For the French, the disappointment was particularly acute. They had hoped that with the removal of Faisal and their occupation of all Syria their troubles would be over, but the following years found them faced with an exhausting war against Turkish nationalists in the north and continual unrest in Syria which culminated in the Druze revolt. The majority of the Muslims resented the French mandate, and Arab nationalist leaders in exile in the neighbouring countries and in Europe waged a bitter anti-French campaign in which they demanded the complete independence and unification of Syria. Furthermore, the French were soon disabused of their hopes for economic advantages stemming from their control over Syria. Having poured millions of francs into Syria and Lebanon, they had expected to reap the benefits of their investment, but it soon became apparent that Syria's economic potential and importance for France had been greatly exaggerated. Without the oil of Mosul and the rich agricultural region of Cilicia, and with the port of Alexandretta under continual threat from the Turkish nationalists, Syria could fulfil very few of their expectations. The French government and public then realised that Syria was not a second Algeria, but an economic burden that would have to be continually financed from Paris.[9]

France was then undergoing a serious post-war economic crisis and lacked the resources necessary to establish control over Syria and Lebanon. The French public began to resent the large government expenditures in areas where they felt France had no vital interests. As the difficulties confronting France in Syria became more apparent, nearly every aspect of the government's Syrian policy came under attack in the National Assembly and in the press. Moreover, after the enormous loss of life during the War the French were reluctant to send soldiers abroad to fight Turkish nationalists or Arabs for objectives that remained obscure. During the first few years of the mandate the formerly strong emotional drive for French control over Syria rapidly gave way to increasing opposition to French involvement there, particularly in the National Assembly. The Syrian mandate became a much-debated issue in French politics, and proposals for a reduction in the Syrian budget an annual phenomenon. There were still many deputies and senators who felt the need for a French presence in Syria and Lebanon, but increasing numbers of them, particularly those of the Left, who from the start had opposed France's involvement in the Levant, criticised the government's policy and the large expenditure it entailed. The opposition was centred in the Finance and Foreign Affairs Committees of both chambers; it eventually succeeded in exerting a strong influence on the government's Syrian policy.[10] Between 1920 and 1924 the civilian budget for Syria was cut from 185 million francs to only 8 million and the military budget from 560 million francs to 210 million. Over the same period the number of French soldiers in Syria and Lebanon was reduced from 70,000 to 20,000.[11]

Leygues, Briand and Poincaré, the three premiers who served before the rise to power of the Left in the summer of 1924, continued to advocate a French presence in Syria and Lebanon. They tried to counter criticism and prevent budget cuts by repeatedly declaring that the expenditure would only be for a transitional period, and that the mandated states would soon shoulder their own expenses. They argued that France's evacuation of the Levant would undermine its prestige as a great power, and have serious repercussions on its position in the North African colonies. They insisted that France did indeed have vital strategic, cultural and economic interests there. To weaken opposition from the Left and from liberal deputies, and to persuade the National Assembly to allocate the necessary administrative funds, Briand and Poincaré promised to adopt a liberal attitude in implementing the mandate, and to reduce direct French involvement in running Syria and Lebanon to a minimum.[12] Gouraud, who was held in high esteem by the French public, was summoned to Paris to help garner support at the end of 1920 and again the following year. He appeared before the influential Finance and Foreign Affairs Committees, where he emphasised the importance of France's presence in the area and its large agricultural and economic potential.[13] The High Commission, for its part, encouraged visits to the area by members of the National Assembly, journalists and public officials; in April 1921 it organised a trade fair, designed to encourage the expansion of French trade with Syria and to improve France's prestige there.[14] The High Commission was also involved in discreet contacts with French companies seeking to expand their interests in Syria and Lebanon.[15]

The drastic cuts in the Syrian budget and the continual criticism in France had a decided influence on French behaviour during the early years of the mandate. Policy fluctuated from one extreme to another: from a quest for complete domination over the region, the emphasis shifted to the maintenance of a limited presence there, or even to evacuation. Indeed, in October 1921 the French government decided to relinquish Cilicia to the Turkish nationalists despite strong opposition from rightist deputies and from Gouraud. Criticising this attitude, *L'Asie française* wrote:

> . . . nos embarras financiers, les récriminations du Parlement au sujet des crédits demandés pour la Syrie, l'indifférence d'une partie de l'opinion française, tout leur a fourni par la suite des motifs de croire que la France, au coeur vaillant, mais à la tête ardente, se lasserait des affaires lointaines, montrerait peu de persévérance dans ses desseins et renoncerait à la Syrie placée sous son mandat comme elle a déjà renoncé à la Palestine et à la Cilicie, pour concentrer tous ses efforts sur le seul Liban.[16]

The High Commission was particularly affected by the change in attitude in France. It no longer controlled sufficient military resources to impose its authority and to deter anti-French opposition. The drastic cut in its budget had left it without the necessary funds to secure the co-operation of various local groups and leaders, or to rebuild the economy, which was essential if France was to restore stability and gain the support of local residents for the mandate. Strong criticism in France of its policies and of the professional standards of its staff was often aired in the local press, further undermining its authority and prestige. Various groups and individuals in Syria and Lebanon knew that they could have High Commission decisions overruled by appealing to the government and National Assembly in Paris; both Christians and Muslims often did this. Many local leaders who had been prepared to co-operate with the French authorities immediately after Faisal's defeat were now less willing to do so. The evacuation of Cilicia was regarded by the Muslims as evidence that continued pressure might lead to a complete French evacuation of Syria. In Lebanon it made the Muslims even less willing to work together with the French authorities and the new Lebanese state, whose borders and independent status, they believed, might still be challenged if France evacuated the area.[17]

Increasing criticism and the need to cut administrative costs led the government to instruct the High Commission to adopt a more liberal attitude. The turning point came with the appointment of Briand at the end of 1920. On 9 January 1921 the new premier instructed de Caix, then acting high commissioner, to prepare a plan at once granting each state its own elected Council and establishing a Syrian federation in consultation with the local population. Briand stressed that each state should assume the expenses of government and administration '. . . because of the tendencies strongly manifested in the parliament as well as in the French public'. Following Briand's instructions, de Caix prepared a general programme for the reorganisation of the mandated territories, which he himself presented to Briand in Paris in July 1921. The programme was approved by the government and implemented the following year.[18]

The first problem faced by the High Commission in preparing this plan was the status of Lebanon. There was a general belief in France that the division of Syria into several regions linked in a federation would be the best answer to the country's regional, ethnic, religious and sectarian diversity. France had been pursuing this policy since 1920 despite strong opposition from the Muslim majority and the Arab nationalists. Such a division would help to weaken the Sunnis and the Arab nationalists, who formed the main opposition to the mandate. France decided to base its regime on the minority groups, the Lebanese Christians, 'Alawites and Druze who had shown themselves willing to co-operate. In de Caix's words:

Les groupes minoritaires sont un peu pour nous en Syrie, ce qu'est en Afrique la masse de plus d'un million d'Européens qui nous donnent un appui et une raison d'être durables. Ils ont l'avantage de se prêter à l'application du Mandat en même temps qu'à la constitution de Gouvernements indigènes dociles à notre direction, tandis que le Gouvernement d'une Syrie unitaire, constituée au profit des nationalistes, nous mettrait en présence du pouvoir indigène le moins maniable auquel nous pourrions avoir affaire.[19]

During the intensive discussions held in Beirut and Paris in the summer of 1920 the main questions which arose were the number of units into which Syria would be divided, and the nature of Lebanon's relations with the rest of Syria. De Caix suggested that Syria be carved into eight or nine small administrative provinces, including both ethnic regions and municipal districts, which would form a federation for economic and administrative purposes; it would be a system not unlike that of the Swiss cantons. His plan was intended for merely administrative purposes; he saw no need for any 'separate autonomous political entities'. Gouraud, in contrast, proposed a division into three or four large autonomous 'states', with political as well as administrative functions, to be linked together in a confederation. He argued that such a division would be more efficient and less costly for France; furthermore, France would be better able to exploit local differences if there were three or four large self-sufficient states, rather than eight or nine units whose small size would necessitate close co-operation.[20]

De Caix and Gouraud also disagreed on the question of Lebanon's links with the rest of Syria. De Caix suggested that Lebanon remain outside the Syrian federation and under direct French control, as the Christians considered themselves more advanced than the rest of the inhabitants and strongly opposed inclusion in a federation in which they would be a minority. De Caix was also concerned that the Lebanese Christians, who were more Westernised and difficult to govern, might become a source of trouble for France if they were incorporated in a federation. In his view:

> Il semble donc qu'il y ait intérêt pour notre action, à la fois au Liban et dans le reste de la Syrie à ne pas fondre notre vieille clientèle libanaise dans une Confédération syrienne dont l'évolution est encore douteuse; nous risquerions du même coup de perdre un élément qui nous est acquis et de rendre beaucoup plus difficile notre travail dans les autres régions syriennes.[21]

Gouraud on the other hand advocated the incorporation of Lebanon into a Syrian confederation, arguing that the two regions had common interests, particularly economic, which would inevitably lead to the establishment of close ties. Moreover, with its Christian majority and close links with France, Lebanon could serve 'as a balancing element *vis-à-vis* the Muslim states of the interior'. Gouraud also pointed out that France, as head of the confederation, would be able to guarantee Lebanese Christian rights. The federal council's authority would be limited to economic affairs, and important meetings would be presided over by the French secretary-general. Gouraud concluded that '. . . l'entrée actuelle du Grand Liban sous le régime du pouvoir fédéral exercé par la France permet de moins heurter le sentiment national syrien sans heurter en rien le sentiment libanais'.[22]

Despite the fact that de Caix's proposals on the administrative organisation of Syria and on Lebanon's position in the federation were supported by Premier Millerand, the plan ultimately implemented on 1 September 1920 was closer to Gouraud's proposals.

The mandated territories were divided into four large autonomous states: Greater Lebanon, Damascus, Aleppo and the 'Alawite region. A fifth autonomous region, Jabal Druze, was created the following year. No decision was made on the status of Lebanon, but it was assumed that it would have to maintain close economic ties with the rest of Syria.[23]

Although there was general agreement among the French on the eventual need for a Syrian federation, there was at first no sense of urgency. But the partition of Syria into autonomous 'states' aroused criticism in the National Assembly and the press. It was claimed that the majority of the local population opposed the move. Furthermore, partition was said to entail a larger and more expensive French administration; the creation of a Syrian federation or even a united Syria would relieve France of much of its obligations and expenditures. This criticism was in part inspired by the Arab natonalist groups in Syria and abroad who had embarked on an anti-French campaign and were demanding a united and independent Syria. Their activities, in particular at the League of Nations and in Paris, caused much embarrassment to the French government and the High Commission. Moreover, the upsurge of anti-Arab feeling among the public and many officials following the dramatic events of the summer of 1920 had already subsided. It began to be clear that if France was to remain in Syria and still drastically cut its military and budgetary expenditure there, some agreement had to be reached with the Muslim majority.[24]

Developments in the British mandate also helped prod France into a more conciliatory attitude. In 1921 the British appointed Faisal as king in Iraq and his brother 'Abdullah as emir in Transjordan. The installation of two anti-French Hashemite princes on Syria's doorstep greatly alarmed the French, who had unsuccessfully tried to dissuade the British from such a move. They feared that Iraq and Transjordan might become centres for anti-French activities among the Muslims in Syria and Lebanon. They now saw that a strong and united Syrian state would be better able to resist the attraction of Arab nationalism and the call for Arab unity from the neighbouring areas. The creation of a federation and the strengthening of the 'Syrian' entity against the 'Arab' entity supported by the British, was seen as the best way to counter the threat. According to de Caix:

> . . . la Fédération était pour nous un moyen de créer un certain équilibre entre les minoritaires et les nationalistes et de donner un

certain appaisement à ces derniers. En présence de l'attraction des Etats arabes de la zone britannique et de la Turquie kémaliste qui devait un grand prestige à ses succès, il fallait chercher, même dans le cadre d'une politique qui tendait à consolider les particularismes minoritaires à créer une institution, un symbole autour desquels pourrait naître, au moins chez les musulmans, un certain sentiment national syrien.[25]

There was general agreement among French officials that Lebanon should be closely linked with the rest of Syria in economic and financial matters, but there were differences of opinion concerning political ties. Some wanted to satisfy Muslim aspirations by including Lebanon, or at least some of the annexed areas, within a united Syria. Others, briefly including Gouraud, went so far as to propose the creation of a Syrian monarchy with a Turkish prince or the former Egyptian khedive on the throne.[26] Many French officials in both Beirut and Paris supported either the direct inclusion of Lebanon in the federation, or the creation of a confederation comprised of Lebanon and a Syrian federation. The latter proposal was intended to improve Lebanon's position *vis-à-vis* the states in the interior. Gouraud still believed in the need for incorporation, but increasing opposition from the Lebanese Christians made him reconsider this idea. De Caix, in contrast, continued to advocate the separation of Lebanon from the Syrian federation; he proposed that the common interests of the two regions be regulated by an agreement between them. Briand took a similar stand; he wrote to de Caix:

L'indépendance du Grand Liban que nous avons nous-mêmes proclamée l'an dernier (et que nous devons scrupuleusement respecter) est une première démonstration de notre politique. Ce pays chrétien est susceptible d'être amené complètement à notre culture et de s'appuyer plus tard sans arrière pensée sur nous, en même temps qu'il représente traditionellement notre influence en Orient. Nous ne devons en aucun cas noyer cet élément chrétien au milieu de l'élément arabe plus important numériquement. Dans l'organisation du mandat, le Liban doit donc conserver vis-à-vis de la Syrie, malgré la petitesse de son territoire, une position d'égalité.[27]

The debates among the French led to much discussion, rumour

and uncertainty among the inhabitants of Syria and Lebanon. In 1921 and 1922 the question of relations with the Syrian federation was the main political issue in Lebanon. It heightened tensions between the Christians and the French authorities and deepened the rift between Christians and Muslims, with profound consequences for internal political development. The issue has confronted Lebanon ever since, involving its very existence as an independent Christian entity, as well as its territorial integrity.[28]

The Lebanese Christians first became aware of a possible change in French policy at the end of January 1921, when a decree was published creating a common budget for Syria and Lebanon. The decree was submitted for approval by the Administrative Council; the latter firmly rejected it, claiming it violated Lebanon's independence and sovereignty, which the French themselves had proclaimed only a few months before. They demanded a separate budget for Lebanon. 'Common interests' such as customs and postal and telegraphic services would have to be regulated in an agreement between Lebanon and the federation, as between one state and another; in the meantime they should be placed under the supervision of the High Commission.[29]

The Lebanese Christians, especially the Maronites, were determined not to risk even the slightest possibility of losing the independence they had just gained. They feared a common budget would be the first step towards the incorporation of Lebanon into a Syrian federation and the loss of their political independence. They were alarmed by what they saw as a new French policy of appeasing the Muslims and by rumours that France intended to create a united Syria or even a monarchy. In the following months Lebanese Christians both in Lebanon and abroad waged an intensive campaign against the establishment of any ties between Lebanon and Syria. Telegrams of protest were sent to the High Commission and the French government and appeals were made to French supporters of the Lebanese cause. Christian newspapers published strongly worded attacks against any such move and against Muslims in Lebanon who supported Syrian unity. Once again it was the emigrants, particularly those in Egypt, who were the most vociferous. The Maronite Church also expressed its anxiety to the High Commission. The issue even caused an incident between Gouraud and the Maronite patriarch, when the latter declared at a reception on the first anniversary of the establishment of Greater Lebanon that he was prepared to mobilise all the Lebanese Christians and personally appear before the League of Nations to prevent incorporation.[30]

The Maronites' vehement opposition to any ties with Syria, even purely economic ones, arose from their deeply rooted fear of becoming a small Christian minority in a Muslim state. The establishment of an independent Lebanese state had not yet dispelled this fear. For them, independence primarily meant separation from Syria. They saw the creation of a Syrian federation as a possible first step in France's attempt to satisfy the demands of the Muslim majority. They preferred that Syria remain divided into separate states, believing that a united Syria would pose a serious threat to Lebanon.

Ties with Syria were also seen as a threat to Lebanon's territorial integrity. If the Lebanese accepted a common budget and economic union, it might be interpreted as recognition of Syrian rights to use the ports of Beirut and Tripoli, and hence even to participate in the administration of those cities. After all, the Muslim inhabitants in both places were already demanding union with the Syrian federation. A protest presented to the High Commission on 22 February 1921 by the Administrative Council, with the approval of all but two members, both Sunni deputies from Beirut, clearly expressed these fears:

L'Etat du Grand-Liban, indépendant de tout autre gouvernement, est seul qualifié pour administrer sur son propre territoire les divers services visés. Il en est ainsi, et en tout premier lieu, pour les villes-ports du Grand-Liban et les douanes qui en forment le légitime accessoire. Ces villes-ports, notamment Beyrouth capitale, forment partie intégrante du Grand-Liban et les Etats de l'Intérieur n'y peuvent légalement prétendre à aucun droit de propriété ou d'administration. De par le project, vouloir gérer ou administrer les ports et les douanes au nom d'une fédération ou même d'une association c'est implicitement reconnaître, sur ces ports et douanes, à l'Etat de l'Intérieur un droit, quoique lointain, de propriété ou de gérance qu'il n'a pas et que nous ne reconnaissons pas. En fait c'est violer les droits de l'indépendance du Grand-Liban. Certes l'Intérieur peut avoir un droit mais ce ne peut être ni un droit de propriété ni un droit d'administration. C'est tout simplement un droit de profit consistant en une part à déterminer sur les recettes douanières.[31]

The choice facing the French in 1921 and 1922 was familiar: to reach an agreement with the Muslim majority or to adhere to their traditional obligations to the Lebanese Christians. There were many French officials in Syria and Lebanon who leaned towards a policy favouring the Muslims, or at least sought to satisfy some of their aspirations; it was primarily the strong opposition of the Lebanese Christians which prevented France from pursuing this course. The Lebanese Christians were regarded as France's main allies in the Levant, and the High Commission was anxious not to antagonise them and their French supporters, especially now that many of its policies were under attack in France. At any rate some officials such as de Caix genuinely believed it was in France's interests to keep Lebanon out of the Syrian federation. Moreover, Lebanese Christian demands that the 'common interests' be placed under French control appealed to French officials seeking new revenue sources following the drastic cuts in the High Commission budget. The French authorities now moved to allay Lebanese Christian fears. Shortly after his return to Beirut in April 1921 Gouraud abolished the decree for a common budget. At the end of the year a separate budget was created for Lebanon, and it was decided that the income from the 'common interests' would be divided between Lebanon and the rest of Syria. When the Syrian federation was finally established in June 1922, Lebanon remained outside.[32]

The dispute over Lebanon's future relations with Syria led some Lebanese Christians to realise for the first time that there was a contradiction between their two ambitions for an independent Christian state and for extended borders. The theme was developed in a series of articles in *Correspondance d'Orient* by George Samné, its editor and the secretary-general of the Comité Central Syrien.[33] Samné, who still supported the CCS programme for an independent federal Syria including Lebanon, saw Lebanese Christian opposition to a federation as an obstacle not only to Syria's unity, but also to its independence, as the mandatory power would thus be obliged to retain its control over the whole region. He tried to persuade the Lebanese Christians to become part of the Syrian federation or at least to establish close economic links with it. Within its extended borders, Lebanon could no longer survive in isolation; the whole region had to be administered as one economic unit. Moreover, Syria was entitled to an outlet on the coast, vital to its economic survival. Samné warned the Lebanese Christians to take into account the internal pressure on the French government to reduce its involvement and expenditure in the Levant. France would be willing to remain in the area only if it could cut its expenses; this necessitated an agreement with the Muslim majority who opposed Lebanon's exclusion from the federation.

For Samné, the new demographic structure following territorial enlargement was another factor militating in favour of economic and political co-operation with Syria. Lebanon had been founded for religious motives: the desire to create an asylum for the Christians in the Levant. It was the main reason that the European powers had helped to create the autonomous Sanjak of Mount Lebanon in 1860, and that France had established Greater Lebanon in 1920. But in order to create a Christian homeland, there had to be an overwhelming majority of Christians. This was no longer the case:

> Comme en 1860 les Libanais réclament l'indépendance et le droit de faire chez eux ce qui leur plaît sans aucune ingérence extérieure, comme en 1860 ils veulent organiser un foyer chrétien, un refuge exempt de charges et de soucis. Mais le Liban de 1921 est un Grand Liban et ne répond plus aux données du problème. On compte dans sa population près de moitié de musulmans. Alors, où est le foyer chrétien, puisqu'un foyer chrétien, puisqu'un foyer est un endroit où l'on se groupe en famille? Qu'est ce qu'une famille où l'on trouve moitié d'étrangers?[34]

Lebanon had to choose between two alternatives: to remain independent with no links to Syria, in which case its territory had to be reduced, or to retain its enlarged borders, in which case it would have to co-operate with the rest of Syria and renounce its role as a 'foyer chrétien'. By striving to realise these two goals simultaneously, the Lebanese Christians were attempting to do the impossible: 'ils cherchent la quadrature du cercle'. But when the Lebanese Christians kept up their vehement opposition to any links with Syria and emigrant groups strongly criticised his articles, Samné became convinced by the end of 1921 that the only solution was to reduce Lebanon 'to the limits of a Christian homeland'.[35]

Samné was not alone in expressing such views. The results of the 1921 census and the deep division between Christians and Muslims over the question of relations with Syria made at least some French officials more aware of the serious difficulties involved in transforming the enlarged Lebanon into a viable state. It might be necessary, they thought, to revise Lebanon's borders by detaching some

of the heavily populated Muslim areas annexed in 1920. The driving
force behind this view was Robert de Caix; he promoted it first as
secretary-general in Beirut under Gouraud and Weygand, and later
in Paris as adviser on Syrian and Lebanese affairs to the Quai
d'Orsay, and as a French representative to the Permanent Mandates
Commission.[36] In the discussions preceding the creation of Greater
Lebanon, de Caix had opposed Gouraud's decision to comply with
the Maronite demand for borders which he regarded as over-
extended. Subsequent developments only strengthened his conviction. France had hoped that extended borders would strengthen the
position of the Lebanese Christians and at the same time create a
strong and permanent foothold for French influence in the area; in
reality, de Caix argued, they had weakened the Christians without
helping France to establish such a base. It would be in the interests of
both France and the Lebanese Christians to restore a clear Christian
majority by detaching some of the annexed areas, in particular those
with a large, compact Sunni population. By taking such a step
France would also weaken opposition to its mandate from the Muslims in both Syria and Lebanon. Six years after the creation of
Greater Lebanon de Caix wrote:

> Une erreur sérieuse, visible à l'époque même où elle fut
> commise, a consisté à créer un trop grand Liban. Il est certain
> que pour rendre possible la vie financière de cet Etat il était
> nécessaire de lui donner quelque chose de plus que les rochers
> où avait été contenu, malgré les efforts de notre diplomatie, le
> Liban de 1860. La France se devait à elle-même et devait à
> ses anciens clients une réparation de l'échec qu'elle avait subi
> alors. Mais les 'frontières géographiques' réclamées par les
> Libanais en 1860 et depuis étaient démesurées. Le Liban
> autonome a été viable en même temps qu'il était nécessaire
> parce-qu'il avait une population en grand majorité chrétienne,
> consciente d'elle-même et attachée à l'autonomie que lui avait
> assurée la France. Le Grand Liban de 1920 englobait au contraire
> beaucoup trop d'éléments non chrétiens dans les frontières
> beaucoup trop larges et aussi artificielles et déraisonnables, bien
> que 'géographiques' que celles qui avaient été infligées au
> Liban autonome de 1860. Une 'question du Grand Liban' n'a
> cessé d'exister depuis lors. Je n'irai pas jusqu'à dire qu'elle ne
> se serait pas manifestée si on s'était borné à donner au Liban
> des aggrandissements raisonnables. Lui eût-on   seulement

incorporé seulement Beyrout et Saida ou telle dépouille des vilayets turcs de Damas et de Beyrout enclavée par la Montagne que les nationalistes auraient peut être tout autant crié. Peut être même l'excès des largesses qui lui ont été faites pourrait-il faciliter une révision de frontières puis un appaisement des réclamations syriennes . . . Mais le fait est qu'il existe au Grand Liban un véritable irrédentisme et que l'on a rendu libanais de nombreux éléments musulmans qui ne veulent pas l'être et qui n'ont cessé de le dire avec une énergie qui variait seulement selon l'autorité qu'avait le Haut Commissariat sur le pays.[37]

It was particularly essential to detach the town of Tripoli and its environs. De Caix had opposed their annexation to Greater Lebanon from its very inception; during the next six years he proposed various plans for its separation. He argued that such a move would serve the interests of the Lebanese Christians, the inhabitants of the town and the rest of Syria. Lebanon would be rid of an irredentist Sunni Muslim centre whose inhabitants strongly opposed their incorporation in the Lebanese state, and the number of Sunnis in Lebanon would thus be significantly reduced. The town had close economic ties with the rest of Syria and served as its only natural port, whereas Lebanon already had the port of Beirut. Tripoli's annexation to Syria would remove one of the major sources of Syrian Muslim opposition to the mandatory power and the Lebanese state.[38]

At the beginning of 1921, while de Caix was serving as acting high commissioner in Gouraud's absence, he initiated a secret survey of Tripoli's population; he then proposed that the town be made an autonomous municipality independent from both Lebanon and Syria, and the seat of the High Commission. Transferring the High Commission from Beirut would remove its staff from the pressures and intrigues which were rife in that city while gaining the support of the Muslims, who would undoubtedly favour such a move. Tripoli would be a suitable site for the High Commission, as it was relatively close to Beirut and had easy access to the interior, in particular to Hama, which at one time was being considered as a capital for the future Syrian federation. The plan was briefly supported by Gouraud, who had by then returned from Paris, and also by Premier Briand, who himself stressed the need to detach Tripoli from Lebanon in order to secure a Christian majority in the Lebanese state. Briand proposed that Tripoli, Homs and Hama should together form one autonomous region as part of the Syrian federation. But de Caix's plan was never implemented, as it soon became clear that the Lebanese Christians vehemently opposed any move which might infringe on the territorial integrity of their state. In any case the overwhelming majority of the High Commission staff strongly objected to the move to Tripoli. They saw Beirut, with its large Christian population, as a part of France, and Tripoli as a hostile Arab Muslim town where they would be unable to pursue their way of life freely.[39]

De Caix also wanted to detach certain areas of the Beqa'a Valley, in particular the town of Ba'albek whose Mutawalli and Sunni inhabitants resented their annexation to Lebanon. He suggested that Lebanon's border with Syria in the Beqa'a Valley be defined according to Muslim or Christian ownership of the land. His border would have generally followed the Orontes River, although the Hermil area, which had been part of the autonomous Sanjak, would remain in Lebanon despite its Mutawalli population.[40]

The question of Tripoli became controversial once again early in 1923, following widespread agitation among the Muslims throughout Lebanon and especially in Tripoli. Petitions were sent to the French government and the presidents of the Senate and Chamber of Deputies demanding annexation to Syria. After the departure of Gouraud, who had fully identified with the Lebanese Christian cause, Muslims now felt they might be able to reverse France's previous policy. There was some basis for their belief, as de Caix, then acting high commissioner, was re-examining the possibility of detaching Tripoli from Lebanon. On 24 January, accompanied by the French governor of Lebanon, he visited Tripoli to investigate the grievances of its inhabitants. His visit gave rise to large-scale demonstrations in favour of annexation to Syria; his remark that Tripoli's annexation to Lebanon had been Gouraud's personal decision certainly did not help allay the unrest.[41]

The Lebanese Christians, already alarmed by the Muslim campaign, were further disturbed by de Caix's visit to Tripoli, as they were well aware of his views on the future of that town. 'Abdullah al-Khuri, the patriarchal vicar, complained that de Caix was more concerned for the fate of Tripoli than for that of the rest of Lebanon. The Christians consequently began their own campaign, vigorously led by the Maronite Church, to counter the Muslim demands. The Christian reaction illustrates well the basic principle underlying the relations between Christians and Muslims in Lebanon: to every action by one community there is a counter-reaction from the other. Faced with tension and unrest in both communities, de Caix promptly assured the Maronite patriarch that France had no intention of revising Lebanon's borders. Neverthe-less when Weygand, the new high commissioner, arrived in Lebanon in May de Caix tried to persuade him to detach Tripoli from Lebanon; but once again his policy was rejected.[42]

De Caix's failure to enlist the support of either Gouraud or Weygand can be attributed to the unwillingness of the two high commissioners to antagonise the Lebanese Christians. The imple-mentation of such plans would have been a drastic move, which both were reluctant to make. They also feared that any agreement to reduce Lebanon's territory would be regarded as a surrender to Muslim pressure and a sign of weakness that would undermine French prestige. The high commissioners who followed them, apart from Jouvenel, continued to support the preservation of the *status quo*, and as time went by it became increasingly difficult to consider any changes in Lebanon's borders.[43]

Considering the far-reaching consequences of Lebanon's territo-rial enlargement on its development as a Christian state, the ques-tion arises whether the Maronites were aware of its demographic significance, and if so, why they nevertheless continued to oppose all French attempts to revise the 1920 borders. It may be argued that before 1920 the Maronites had not been aware of the actual demo-graphic structure of the annexed areas or of the difficulties involved in incorporating a large Muslim population in a Lebanese Christian state. But following the census of 1921, and in light of vocal Muslim opposition to annexation, they should have had second thoughts about their demands for a Greater Lebanon. Their leaders had been warned by French officials, particularly by de Caix, of the possible danger entailed in an overexpanded Lebanese state. Nevertheless, they vehemently opposed every French attempt to reduce Lebanon's territory; their opposition was the main factor which prevented French authorities from pursuing such a policy between 1921 and 1926.[44]

The almost total Maronite disregard for these dangers may be explained through a combination of psychological, historical, eco-nomic and political factors. Memories of the War, when thousands of inhabitants of the Mountain had starved to death because of its inability to support them, were still fresh; Maronite leaders, particularly in the Church, were determined that Lebanon have sufficient lowlands to grow food, and ports to secure its ties with Europe. The Christian economic elites and entrepreneurs of Beirut and Mount Lebanon, who had been pressing for an extended Lebanon since the turn of the century, were not prepared to return to a smaller Lebanon in which their economic activities would be limited. The economic considerations were particularly strong in the case of Tripoli. With both Beirut and Tripoli within its boundaries, the Lebanese state was able to reap the economic benefits and the lion's share of the revenue from the trade of the whole of Syria. The detachment of Tripoli would not only have considerably reduced Lebanon's income, but would also have seriously undermined the prominent economic position of Beirut. The merchants of Beirut, already concerned about growing competition from the port of Haifa, regarded Tripoli's annexation to Syria as an even greater threat; with its easy access to the interior, Tripoli had a clear advantage over Beirut as a port and potential trading centre for the whole of Syria. As long as it remained in Lebanon it could be kept from endangering Beirut's position. Even the minority who were prepared to relinquish Tripoli feared that such a move might become a precedent for the other annexed regions and eventually lead to Lebanon's total disintegration.[45]

Although many of the Maronites had become aware of the presence of a large Muslim population in their newly-established state, they still did not regard it as a serious threat to the Christian character of Lebanon or to the pre-eminent position of their community. Their past experience under the Mutasarrifiya led them to believe that they would be able to retain their dominant position thanks to superior Western education, initiative, and the help of France. They thought the new groups could be incorporated into the Lebanese state without drastically changing its character or their own national goals. Their attitudes were reinforced by the activities and propaganda of Lebanese emigrants abroad. Far from their homeland, assimilated in a secular Western society, they tended to disregard the religious and sectarian differences which had arisen due to the expansion of Lebanon. These groups, who had played an important role from 1918 to 1920 in the establishment of Greater Lebanon, were still able to exert considerable influence on the Maronite Church and on Lebanese politicians during the early years of the mandate. They were the first to oppose French attempts to reduce Lebanon's territory; persistently suspicious of France's real motives in raising such proposals, they considered them as mere appeasement of the Muslims. French documents from this period, however, clearly show that politicians such as Millerand and Briand and officials such as de Caix supported these proposals primarily because they believed that the attainment of a clear Christian majority was in the best interests of the Lebanese Christians as well as of France.[46]

Behind all these factors was the deeply-rooted, almost mystical Maronite belief that these were the historical and natural borders of their homeland, a belief which was an integral part of Maronite nationalism. Since the early nineteenth century, and especially from mid-century on, the aspirations for historical-natural borders had been inseparable from the dream of an independent state. It was believed that only within such borders could a Lebanese state be economically viable and thus truly independent. The reduction of Lebanon's territory in 1860 in opposition to their demands added a feeling of injustice which further strengthened their claim for the return to historical borders. The actual creation of Greater Lebanon was thus regarded as the rectification of an injustice as well as the realisation of national goals. All these feelings lay behind their strong opposition to any modification of borders and their extreme stand in defence of territorial integrity. Having finally achieved their national goals after years of continuous effort, it was inconceivable to relinquish any part of the homeland because of some obscure danger which they believed they could overcome.

There were some Maronites who did understand that the change in demographic structure might indeed jeopardise the Christian character of their state, and who thus favoured the detachment of areas with a large Muslim population. The paucity of public support for such a move did not necessarily mean such support was lacking among the Maronite community as a whole. But those who advocated such a solution were aware of its unpopularity and feared the reactions of militant Maronite groups in Lebanon and abroad who might accuse them of treason. Hence they were extremely reluctant to back any French plans for territorial reduction; when they did so, it was discreetly, to the French authorities.[47] French documents testify that certain Maronites did indeed favour such a step at various periods. Immediately after the creation of Greater Lebanon residents of the Mountain had expressed their preference for a smaller Lebanon for fear of losing their privileged status. Later, their unwillingness to be linked to a Syrian federation led some Maronites, including members of the prominent al-Khazin family, to advocate territorial reduction. Even the Church's stand was not totally unanimous. Some clergymen, apprehensive about the annexation of heavily Muslim areas, had opposed the inclusion of Jabal 'Amel and demanded that the southern border of Lebanon follow the Litani. But this was a minority view; most of the Maronite Church and the overwhelming majority of the Maronite community opposed all attempts to modify the 1920 borders.[48]

Their opposition to territorial reduction meant that the Maronites more than ever would have to rely on France to guarantee the independent existence and territorial integrity of their country. Yet France's indecisive policy during the early years of the mandate left the Maronites in a state of perpetual anxiety over the fate of their national achievements. They knew about the growing opposition within France to intervention in the Levant, and about the demands to abandon the area altogether. They watched the French evacuate Cilicia despite their previous declarations about its economic value for France; the Armenians there, who had placed their trust in France, had to seek refuge in Syria and Lebanon. The victories of the Turkish nationalists in 1921 and 1922 amid persistent rumours that France intended to evacuate Syria and Lebanon added to their insecurity; indeed, in 1923 there was a general fear that the Turks might attempt to reoccupy the whole of Syria. Describing this atmosphere, Satow, the British consul-general in Beirut, wrote:

It is, in any case, surprising how widely the belief is held by many, including Europeans, that the French are not going to remain. Even the special message to the contrary recently sent by M. Poincaré and published in the local press has not availed to dispel this belief.[49]

Furthermore, the Maronites still feared that the French might reach an agreement with the Muslim majority at their expense. French attempts to link Lebanon with the Syrian federation were seen as a move in this direction. The continued hostility of the Muslims towards Lebanon, and their refusal to recognise its borders or its separate existence increased the Maronites' apprehensions.

Threatened from within and without, the Maronites felt compelled to defend their national achievement of 1920, and to establish Lebanon's independence and territorial integrity as irrevocable facts which neither the mandatory power nor the Muslims would be able to change. They were extremely sensitive and tended to over-react to any move by the French authorities which even suggested a modification of their policy towards Lebanon's borders or indepen-dence. They were anxious to gain international recognition for their new state, especially by the League of Nations. They made intensive efforts to ensure that Lebanon would be specifically mentioned alongside Syria in the mandate granted to France by the League of Nations; at San Remo and in the Treaty of Sèvres, Lebanon had not been mentioned. They enthusiastically celebrated 1 September, the anniversary of the proclamation of Greater Lebanon, as a national holiday.[50]

The behaviour of the new French administration and the limited Maronite role in running the newly established state gave the Maronites further cause to suspect France. Having played a crucial role in its creation, the Maronites considered Lebanon as their own country, designed to safeguard their political power and economic interests. They had hoped that with France's assistance they would attain prominent positions in the administration and thus gain con-trol over the country; they were disappointed when the French authorities did not hasten to fulfil these expectations. Most of them failed to comprehend that the Maronite connection was only part of France's overall policy, and that the French had their own interests and obligations in the region. They also failed to realise that the other communities in Lebanon, fearing Maronite domination, would not support the Lebanese state unless the French authorities adopted a strictly impartial position, any attempt by the French to do so aroused their opposition. They constantly tried to thwart France's efforts to establish closer relations with the other communities, especially the Muslims, for fear that their own relationship with the French might be affected. The French High Commission often criti-cised Maronite intransigence. Even Gouraud, who was known to sympathise with their objectives, described them on one occasion as 'difficult, spoilt and greedy' and criticised their attitude towards the Muslims in particular:

> En face de leurs adversaires, les Maronites s'inspirent malheureusement plutôt de leurs rancunes historiques que de leur intérêt politique. C'est ainsi qu'ils ont imprudemment et injustement attaqué dans leurs journaux la municipalité de Beyrouth dont le Président est musulman et ils donnent prise à leurs adversaires par l'ardeur avec laquelle ils défendent le

maintien des privilèges concédés au Liban par la charte de
1860 en matière d'impôts. . .[51]

The Maronite Church's continual interference in politics and in
the decisions of the High Commission aroused the indignation not
only of the Muslims, but also of other Christian communities as well
as French officials. Such intervention was especially apparent
during Gouraud's term in office. The many French missionaries in
Beirut also tried to influence the administration. The Maronite
Church had always played a major role in the political affairs of the
Mountain; it was now anxious to safeguard its position and influence in the new state it had helped to achieve. It saw itself as the
defender of Lebanon's political independence and territorial integrity and as the spokesman for Maronite interests, with every right to
intervene to further these interests. The Church was bitterly disappointed that Lebanon had not become the exclusively Maronite
Christian state it had envisaged, and that France failed to take a
consistent stand on Lebanon's independence and borders. This led
to some tension between the Church and the High Commission
which was to come into the open under Sarrail.[52]

Another cause of Maronite discontent was the shift of the
political and administrative centre from the Mountain, where they
comprised a majority, to Beirut, where they were only a minority
among other Christian and Muslim sects. The political and economic character of Lebanon would no longer be determined in the
Mountain, where Maronite nationalism had originated and developed, but in the town of Beirut which had been annexed to it. It was
the ideas that emerged in the pluralistic, secular and cosmopolitan
society of Beirut, with its merchants, financiers, entrepreneurs and
intellectuals, that guided the political development of Lebanon
from 1920 onwards, rather than the traditional concepts shaped in
the compact rural Maronite community in the Mountain. Only the
dualism between what can be termed the ideology of the 'Mountain'
and the ideology of the 'city' can explain many aspects of the
political development of modern Lebanon.[53]

This dualism resulted in two contrasting Christian attitudes
towards independence and the mandatory power, as expressed
throughout the mandate period. In spite of their discontent with
French policy, the Maronite Church and the Maronite peasantry in
the Mountain still regarded France as their traditional ally and protector. But this attitude was not always shared by the merchants,

intelligentsia and middle class of Beirut or by the emigrant groups. In those milieus, many believed that France had completed its task by establishing Greater Lebanon; as their interests were now no longer identical to those of France, they had to adopt an independent policy. France's wavering attitude towards Lebanon strengthened their conviction that they could no longer rely on the French to guarantee Lebanon's independence. Moreover, various commercial sectors in Beirut regarded French administration as a hindrance to economic activity. These sectors, educated in secular western values, held nationalistic ideas about self-determination, and wanted the immediate establishment of an independent state with its own sovereign institutions. At this stage, many inhabitants of the Mountain still regarded any government at all as something hostile and alien. Most often, it was the inhabitants of Beirut rather than those of the Mountain who determined the general attitude of the Lebanese Christians towards the mandatory authorities.[54]

Underlying these conflicting Christian positions on the French mandate were differences in the attitude towards the Muslims who had been annexed to Lebanon. To the Maronite Church and the inhabitants of the Mountain, the Muslims on the coast were still strangers to be feared and resented, who could not possibly be assimilated into the Lebanese state. As their loyalty lay with Syria and the Arab Muslim world, they were a threat to the independent existence and territorial integrity of Lebanon:

> . . . in fact in the 1920s and well into the 1930s the consensus among the Maronites, especially the inhabitants of the Mountain, was that 'the Moslems were strangers to the spirit of true Lebanonism . . . that their claim to being Lebanese was never to be trusted'.[55]

Such views naturally led to a complete reliance on France as guarantor and defender of Lebanon's independence and Christian character. Even when they were discontented with France's policy, and even while they were demanding a larger degree of self-government, these Maronites still favoured a French presence. Indeed, as Muslim opposition to the Lebanese state became more vociferous, so Maronite support for the French mandate increased despite their underlying grievances.

To the Christians in Beirut and in many of the emigrant groups, however, the Muslims did not appear so threatening. It would be possible to secure their acceptance of Lebanon by promising to safeguard their positions and interests in the new state. France would eventually evacuate the area; the Christians must therefore come to terms with the Muslims. It was partly in order to demonstrate to the Muslims, who opposed the French mandate, that Lebanon was no mere artificial creation, that some Christians sought a larger degree of independence from France and the establishment of sovereign national institutions. They regarded the French mandate as an obstacle to the Christian-Muslim co-operation which was essential to ensure Lebanon's independence; the Muslims would never recognise the country's separate existence or allow themselves to be integrated into it as long as it had to rely on France. These assumptions were to form the basis for co-operation between some Christians and Muslims in a common struggle against the French mandate which reached its peak during the Second World War in the fight for Lebanon's independence from France.[56]

The two Christian approaches differed not so much on goals as on the means to attain them: guarantee by a foreign power or agreement with the Arab Muslims. The Lebanese Christians had faced this dilemma even before the War, with the emergence of the Arab national movement. After the War the question became even more crucial, as France had taken over the coastal zone and Faisal's Arab government was in control of the interior. The attempt by seven members of the Administrative Council of Mount Lebanon to reach an agreement with Faisal's government in July 1920 showed that some Lebanese Christians wanted to seek a *modus vivendi* with the Muslims. Faisal's defeat and the occupation of all Syria by France did not resolve the dilemma. The Christians still had to find a solution to the problem of the Muslim population in the annexed areas.

Despite the incorporation of this large Muslim population, the Maronite Church along with many other Christians still regarded Lebanon primarily as a national home for the Christians in the Levant and as an asylum for persecuted Christian minorities in the East who rejected Muslim domination. In the words of Bishop 'Abdullah al-Khuri:

The Lebanon within its present boundaries was established with the approval of France in order to serve as a home for the Christians dwelling therein and to provide a refuge for the Christians in neighbouring Moslem countries in case they should be compelled to flee from the persecution of their neighbours. To be sure, it is regrettable that the recent events are evidence of a tendency to imperil the status of Lebanon, that last shield of Christianity in the Orient, and to place it under the Moslem yoke.[57]

The Maronites were alone in holding such views, which were emphatically rejected by Muslims and some non-Maronite Christians, as well as by people of all faiths who advocated a secular Lebanese nationalism cutting across religious and sectarian barriers. Some of the Maronites, however, attempted to broaden the narrow religious and sectarian basis of this doctrine. They argued that Lebanon was a place of refuge not only for Christians, but also for other sects who opposed Sunni domination, namely the Druze and Mutawallis.

Other historical and geographical theories were formulated to justify Lebanon's existence as an entity separate from the rest of the Arab world. Two intellectual movements which emerged during the 1920s, the 'Phoenicians' and the 'Mediterraneans' had a profound influence on Lebanese nationalism over the following two decades. Their ideas were primarily a response to the continuing challenge posed by the Arab national movement, whose influence was gaining ground among Lebanese Christians as well as Muslims.[58] Yet the basic concept of Lebanon as a predominantly Christian state remained unchanged, and by the early 1930s some Maronite leaders, such as Emile Eddé, had reached the only logical conclusion: areas with a large Muslim population had to be detached in order to safeguard the country's Christian character.[59]

But those Christians for whom territorial reduction was inconceivable, as they regarded extended borders to be essential for Lebanon's national survival, saw no alternative but to reach a *modus vivendi* with the Muslims. For them, the dream of Lebanon as an exclusively Christian entity had given way to a new concept: Lebanon would be a bridge between East and West and between Islam and Christianity. It would be a pluralistic state in which a multitude of different sects lived in harmony. Given time and stability, a new national identity could emerge, as had occurred during the half-century of the Mutasarrifya. The spokesman for this viewpoint was Michel Chiha, a Greek Catholic banker from Beirut who played an important role in the elaboration of the Lebanese constitution and who profoundly influenced political thinking in modern Lebanon.[60]

From the end of the 1920s these two approaches were embodied in the conflicting stands taken by two prominent Maronite politicians and their parties: Emile Eddé and the National Bloc, and Bishara al-Khuri and the Constitutionalist Bloc. The rivalry between them, which also involved considerations of personal ambition, dominated Lebanese politics throughout the mandate period. Emile Eddé represented the traditional Maronite view, while Bishara al-Khuri represented those who favoured a more practical attitude and sought to reach an agreement with the Muslims and the Arab nationalists. The fall of France in 1940 and the occupation of Syria and Lebanon by British forces led to the ultimate adoption of the second alternative, culminating in the National Pact of 1943.[61]

If the Maronites were the chief proponents of the idea of an independent Lebanese state, the Sunnis were its main opponents. Their refusal to recognise Lebanon's existence as a legitimate independent entity separate from Syria posed the most difficult problem in the political development of modern Lebanon. They resented their annexation to Lebanon, which they claimed had been carried out arbitrarily against their wishes, and they repeatedly insisted on being united with Syria. They regarded Lebanon as an artificial state created by a foreign power in order to dominate them; it was therefore unworthy of their allegiance. They never accepted Lebanese Christian claims that Lebanon had always been a distinct entity. Although they admitted that Mount Lebanon had its own special characteristics, they regarded the whole of Lebanon, in particular the annexed areas, as an integral part of Syria and the Arab world.[62]

Their incorporation in Lebanon involved, for the Sunnis, a grave religious, cultural, political and economic crisis and a powerful emotional blow. For the first time in their history they were a minority in a Christian state. Some of the factors contributing to their hostile attitude, especially during the period preceding the creation of the state, were described in previous chapters. To these were added basic considerations of religious beliefs and culture, and the more immediate problems involving their position in the new state. Contrary to the Western concept, Islam sees no separation between religion and state; it thus leaves little room for loyalty to a secular state, and certainly not to a Christian one. For Muslims, the role of the state is to implement and defend the shari'a (religious law). The Sunnis in Lebanon could therefore never fully identify with the Lebanese Christian state set up and guaranteed by a foreign Christian power; it was regarded as a challenge to their religion. Their religious and emotional crisis was compounded by the practical difficulties of defining their status in a non-Muslim state. Unlike the other sects in Lebanon, the Sunnis had never constituted a separate religious community; as an integral part of the Sunni Ottoman Empire, their laws had been the laws of the state.[63] Now they feared that in a state closely linked to France, which was known for its tendency to impose its culture and language on its colonies, their own Arab Muslim culture would suffer discrimination. The missionary orders, in particular the French ones, would now have a free hand to pursue their religious and educational activities; they might even try to convert Muslims to Christianity. The Sunnis thus became extremely vigilant in defending their culture and language.[64]

The loss of their former political pre-eminence was another important reason for the negative Sunni attitude towards the Lebanese state. Lebanese Sunnis had held privileged and influential positions alongside the Turks in the administration of the Ottoman Empire; their feelings of supremacy were reinforced by religious beliefs. Notables such as Salam and Bayhum had not only played prominent roles in the administration of the vilayet of Beirut; as members of the Ottoman parliament, they had felt involved in the affairs of the entire empire. Now their activities were restricted to the limited area of Lebanon, and even here they were being pushed aside by the Christians whom they had regarded as their inferiors. Their sense of under-representation in the political institutions and administration of the Lebanese state was one of their main grievances throughout the mandate period and even in independent Lebanon. Hence it was among the traditional Sunni notables of Beirut, Tripoli and Sidon that the main opposition to the Lebanese state arose; it was they who determined the negative attitude of their community towards Lebanon during the 1920s and early 1930s. Only in the late 1930s and 1940s, with the rise to power of a young generation of Sunni leaders who had grown up under the new Lebanese political system, was the way opened to a *modus vivendi* between these leaders and their Christian counterparts.[65]

The Sunni rejection of the Lebanese state, particularly during its first years, also reflected a concern over the economic consequences of separation from the rest of Syria, a concern that was shared by many Christians in the annexed areas. The coastal cities and the Beqa'a had close economic ties with the interior. Sunni merchants and financiers in Beirut and Tripoli, from whose ranks the community's political elite was largely drawn, were middlemen in the overseas trade of the interior. They feared that separation from the hinterland would seriously undermine their economic interests. The economic factor helps explain why Sunni attitudes in Beirut began to diverge from those in Tripoli during the 1930s. True, some of these difficulties can be attributed to geography and demography: Beirut was farther removed from the rest of Syria, and the Sunnis there constituted only a minority of the total population. But in the early years of the mandate the Sunni notables in Beirut were just as opposed to the Lebanese state as their co-religionists in the North. It was only following the rapid economic growth of the town that they adopted a more moderate stand, while Tripoli, badly affected by its annexation to Lebanon, remained a militant anti-Lebanese centre throughout the mandate.

The inequality in taxation rates between Mount Lebanon and the annexed areas was another source of discontent. Among the few steps that could indeed have been taken to weaken Sunni opposition to annexation would have been to reduce tax rates to the low level enjoyed by the inhabitants of the Mountain. But the previous tax rates were kept in force, while the inhabitants of Mount Lebanon opposed every French attempt to cancel their privileges. It took nearly 20 years for the tax systems of the two regions to be unified. This inequality roused frequent protests from the Muslims of the annexed areas, who complained that they were being exploited by the Maronites in the Mountain to finance the national budget, a disproportionate part of which was spent in Mount Lebanon.[66]

Christian attitudes towards them further increased the Sunnis' fear of becoming an inferior minority in a Lebanese Christian state. Having been under Muslim domination for centuries, the Christians intended to take full advantage of the prominent positions they now enjoyed. They never tired of repeating that Lebanon was their country, and they often adopted an offensive and even contemptuous attitude towards Muslims. For example, provocative articles against the Muslims frequently appeared in Christian newspapers, and the anniversary of the battle of Maisalun, which represented a humiliating defeat for the Muslims and the loss of their independence, was celebrated enthusiastically by some Christians.[67]

Sunni resentment of the French mandate was another major cause for their opposition to the Lebanese state. After the events of 1920 they regarded France more than ever before as their enemy, its mandate as a form of foreign rule imposed by force, and Lebanon itself as a permanent foothold for French domination over all of Syria. They saw the French presence as a guarantee of Christian supremacy, and they feared that even if France eventually evacuated Syria, it would still remain in Lebanon and continue to use its influence in favour of the Christians.

The Sunnis felt dominated by both the French and the local Christians. Any attempt to resist the French mandate was regarded by the Christians as a hostile act, while any opposition to annexation was considered as an anti-French move. But the situation also had its advantages, as it enabled the Sunnis to play one side off against the other. Thus Sunni leaders co-operated when the Lebanese Christians demanded greater independence from France, and were among the first to call for the establishment of sovereign institutions. This did not necessarily mean that they recognised the Lebanese state, but they did realise that only if Lebanon were independent from France could they achieve equality of status or even union with Syria. On the other hand, many Sunni notables collaborated with the French, in the belief that this was the only way to secure their positions and interests in Lebanon against the Christians. At the same time they repeatedly tried to convince the French that their request for separation from Lebanon and union with Syria was not an anti-French move.[68]

As they were now a minority in a Christian state, the Sunnis sought Muslim support from outside, and naturally turned to Syria. They did not drop their demand for union with Syria, a demand which remained a major factor in their conflict with the Christians and which dominated the Lebanese political scene throughout the mandate period and beyond. The Sunnis genuinely considered themselves to be an integral part of Syria torn off by the French. Syria, with its large Muslim population, symbolised a country with which they could identify religiously, culturally and nationally. The rise of Arab nationalism, which became a powerful political movement after 1920 was another important reason for their rejection of Lebanon and their insistence on union with Syria. After the partition of Syria by the French, Syrian unity and independence from France became the immediate national goals of the Arab nationalists. The Lebanese Sunnis, particularly the more educated younger generation, wholeheartedly pursued these goals, and many of them took an active part in the struggle of the Syrian nationalists in Syria, Lebanon and abroad. The Arab nationalist movement represented the values of Arabism, unity and independence, in complete contrast to what Lebanon stood for. These views held sway until the late 1930s, when some of the Sunnis became reconciled to their inclusion in Lebanon for the moment, while looking toward a more comprehensive Arab unity in the future. The Sunnis of Tripoli still tended to advocate immediate union with Syria, but it was the more moderate views generally held which finally prevailed, culminating under the leadership of Ri'ad al-Sulh in the National Pact of 1943.[69]

However, it took more than 20 years of coexistence with the Christians under one administration, and a change in the Christian stand, for this relatively moderate Sunni attitude to mature. In the early years of the mandate the Sunnis totally rejected the Lebanese state. The rapid succession of dramatic events in July and August 1920 had left them in a state of shock and confusion, and there was little organised opposition to the creation of Greater Lebanon. Some Sunni notables, including the mufti of Beirut and 'Umar Da'uq, the president of its Chamber of Commerce, even participated in the ceremony in which Gouraud proclaimed Lebanon's establishment.[70] It was only in the summer of 1921, when preparations were being made for the census as a first step towards a general election, that an organised Sunni opposition was manifested. The Sunnis refused to participate in the census on the grounds that they were being defined as citizens of 'Greater Lebanon', and that this could be interpreted as their recognition of the Lebanese state. They also denounced the census for distinguishing between the different Muslim sects, which they saw as a French-Christian device to sow discord among Muslims and undermine their political representation. In August a delegation of Sunni notables from Beirut, including Salam, Da'uq and Bayhum met with Gouraud to express their objections to the census and to French favouritism towards the Christians in the Lebanese administration. Gouraud, who was then trying to weaken Muslim opposition, took a conciliatory line and agreed that they would be defined as 'citizens of Beirut' in the census forms. With regard to their representation in the administration, he stressed that the French were maintaining total equality between Muslims and Christians. The High Commission also initiated a campaign in the local press to the effect that the census was intended purely for administrative purposes, and was necessary for the forthcoming elections. But despite pressure and sanctions by the French, some Muslims still refrained from participating.[71]

The forthcoming elections, the tension over future ties between Lebanon and the Syrian federation, and the campaign of the Arab nationalists in Syria and abroad led in late 1921 and early 1922 to growing Sunni opposition to annexation to Lebanon. Petitions and telegrams were sent by notables and organisations in Beirut and Tripoli to the High Commission, the French government and the League of Nations, and a campaign was waged in Muslim newspapers. The Sunnis began to celebrate the Muslim festivals with particular enthusiasm; on Fridays shops were closed and work ceased on a scale unknown before. This was a political demonstration in reaction to the religious and cultural challenge posed by annexation to a Christian state, as well as an expression of religious revival.[72] Sunni opposition was also manifested in the enthusiastic reception of the news of Turkish nationalist successes, such as the Franklin-Bouillon Agreement and the victories over the Greeks, which were seen as a Muslim triumph over Christians. Muslim organisations in Lebanon collected contributions in aid of the Turks, whose representatives were warmly received in Beirut.[73]

Some of the Sunnis resorted to more extreme measures. On 7 April 1922 As'ad Khurshid Pasha, a Muslim of Circassian origin who was serving as director of the interior, was assassinated in Beirut. The crime occurred at a time of widespread agitation throughout Syria and Lebanon over the forthcoming League of Nations discussions on the future of the mandate, which was further aggravated by the visit to Damascus and Beirut of Dr Crane, who had been a member of the American Commission of Inquiry. An extensive investigation by the French authorities revealed that a secret organisation, including Salim 'Ali Salam, had instigated the murder, which was intended to deter other Muslims from taking up positions in the Lebanese government. At the same time threatening letters were sent to Muslim and Christian officials. The assassination underlined the dilemma which the Sunnis faced in defining their attitude towards the Lebanese state. On the one hand their rejection of Lebanon made them reluctant to participate in the Lebanese administration, but on the other, the need to safeguard their interests led many to take up positions in it. Some attempted to solve this dilemma by continuing to express their opposition to the Lebanese state while serving in its administration and political institutions.[74]

The resort to such extremes showed how successful the French had been in enlisting Sunni co-operation. Although the authorities did not hesitate to take firm measures against anti-French elements when necessary, they usually preferred to secure the collaboration of Sunni leaders by offering tempting positions, and by demonstrating their impartiality towards the community as a whole. Their policy of appeasing the Sunnis was particularly evident in the summer of 1921 following the drastic cuts in the High Commission budget. A general amnesty was declared for the Arab nationalists, the Légion d'Honneur was bestowed upon Sunni notables and, in August, the autonomy promised to Beirut and Tripoli at the time of the proclamation of Greater Lebanon was granted. The High Commission also refrained from taking action against the manifestations of the Muslim religious revival, although it caused considerable economic difficulties. In November Gouraud visited the Grand Mosque of Beirut where he reiterated France's intention to maintain a strictly impartial attitude towards both Christians and Muslims. The French also gave wide publicity to their agreement with the Turkish nationalists, hoping thereby to demonstrate their willingness to co-operate with the Muslim world. In addition, the High Commission refrained from punishing the four Muslim notables accused of instigating the murder of As'ad Khurshid Pasha; they were simply banished from Beirut for a brief period. These measures achieved considerable success. During the following years, as it became apparent that France intended to stay in the area and that Lebanon was an established fact, increasing numbers of Sunnis became willing to co-operate with the French authorities.[75]

The attitude of the Maronites and the Sunnis towards the Lebanese state represented the two extreme stands. The other major communities in Lebanon, the Greek Orthodox, Druze and Mutawallis, adopted a more moderate position between these two extremes. They had become part of the Lebanese state by virtue of a French decree, without having been previously consulted. They lacked the passionate emotions and total identification of the Maronites towards Lebanon, and they felt less obliged to defend its independence and territorial integrity. On the other hand they did not adopt the hostile Sunni attitude and were willing to accept their inclusion in Lebanon as long as their vital interests were safeguarded. The fact that it was the French who had created Lebanon, and that France remained committed to its continued existence, was undoubtedly a major factor in their willingness to accept the new situation. The French and the Maronites, for their part, were anxious to prevent these communities from co-operating with the Sunnis and the Syrian nationalists. They attempted to gain their support for the Lebanese state, which was considered essential if Lebanon was to survive as an independent entity.

The attitude of the Greek Orthodox community continued to be ambivalent even after 1920. They resented the Maronites' possessive attitude towards the new state and their attempts to dominate it, but they also feared becoming a Christian minority in a large Syrian-Muslim state; the dilemma led many of them to adopt a neutral course between Maronites and Sunnis. Others, however, particularly among the clergy, disliked the Maronites and the French more than they feared the Muslims. As an urban community, the Greek Orthodox had closer ties with the Sunnis of Beirut and Tripoli than with the Maronites of Mount Lebanon. Trade with the Syrian interior was concentrated mainly in the hands of the wealthy Greek Orthodox merchants in Beirut, who were the first to fear the economic consequences of Lebanon's separation from Syria. Indeed, during 1921 and 1922, when the issue of the future links of Lebanon with the Syrian federation was raised, many Greek Orthodox, particularly those in Tripoli, supported the Sunni stand. The fact that the community was found not only in Lebanon but throughout Syria was another reason for their tendency to support closer links with the interior. As the Russian revolution had deprived them of the protection of a foreign power, they were more willing to reach an agreement with the Muslim majority, seeing this as the best way to safeguard their interests. Immediately after the War their patriarch concluded an agreement with Faisal, whose regime he continued to support until its defeat by the French. Finally, the Greek Orthodox were much more influenced by Arab nationalism than other Christians and were more prepared to support its national goals.[76]

The French were particularly anxious to gain the support of the Greek Orthodox, as they comprised the second largest and the most wealthy Christian community in Lebanon. Faisal's defeat and the cut-off of financial support from Russia and Greece had left their Church without the means to run its schools and institutions, a situation which the French authorities were quick to exploit. In early 1921 the High Commission concluded an agreement with Patriarch Haddad, in which it undertook to provide funds for Church activities. In April Gouraud held a reception for Greek Orthodox leaders and notables as a demonstration of France's intention to establish cordial relations with the community.[77] The French also worked with pro-French notables in Beirut, particularly Michel Twaini and Alfred Sursuk, to gain the group's support. In spite of these efforts there were still some members of the Greek Orthodox community, clergymen in particular, who continued to oppose both the Lebanese state and the French mandate. Messara, the anti-French bishop of Beirut, often threatened to collaborate with the Sunnis, using this

threat to try to extract more financial aid from the French authorities.[78] Najib Sursuk, a prominent notable from Beirut, continued to
argue that the creation of Greater Lebanon had been a mistake, and
to demand that Beirut be granted independent status. He co-operated
with Sunni notables in the city, who themselves were attempting to
gain the support of the Greek Orthodox for closer links with the rest
of Syria.[79] During the following years the attitude of the Greek
Orthodox community towards the French mandate and the Lebanese
state became less hostile, but a certain degree of reserve still
remained.

The stand of the Druze in Greater Lebanon differed from that of
the other non-Maronite communities as they were not newcomers;
they had always been an integral part of Mount Lebanon. They had
close historical ties with the Maronites and had a certain attachment
to the notion of Lebanon as an independent entity; but they also
feared Maronite domination over the new state and resented the
French mandate. Furthermore, they were concerned that in Greater
Lebanon they would be reduced to a small community with their
former prominent position undermined. These conflicting tendencies divided the community into two factions: those who pursued the
old tradition of ties with Lebanon and supported the French mandate, and those who adopted Arab nationalism with all its implications. The division was already apparent immediately after the War.
In the 1920s it was expressed in the stands of the two most prominent
families. The Junblats generally supported the Lebanese state and
co-operated with the French authorities, while the Arslans adopted
a more nationalist and anti-French attitude. In 1921 this factional-
ism manifested itself in acts of violence by armed bands in the Shuf
district, leading up to the murder of Fu'ad Junblat, the caimacam
there. The violence was probably instigated by anti-French Druze
leaders who were co-operating with Arab nationalists, in particular
Rashid Tali'a, a Lebanese who had served as wali of Aleppo under
Faisal and was now in exile in Transjordan.[80]

Since 1919 the High Commission had been trying to win support
for the French mandate among Druze both in Jabal Druze and in
Lebanon. After some setback, de Caix and Catroux, the French
delegate in Damascus, succeeded early in 1921 in concluding an
agreement with the former in which they undertook to recognise the
French mandate in return for a larger degree of local autonomy. The
tight feudal structure of the community made the French task easier
as it was sufficient to win over only a small number of prominent

notables to secure the co-operation of the whole community. In Lebanon the French tended to rely on the support of the Junblats, with whom they were on good terms, but they also attempted to win the support of other prominent families including the Arslans. They granted clemency to Amin Arslan and allowed him to return to Lebanon and renew his political activities despite objections from the Junblats. Many Druze resigned themselves to the French mandate and some even regarded it as a necessary guarantee for their interests against Maronite domination. They were willing to be equal partners in an independent Lebanese state, but not if it had a predominantly Maronite Christian orientation. Fear of Maronite domination led some of them to co-operate with the Sunnis, in part as a means to pressure the French authorities and the Maronites into granting them their share in the administration.[81]

The events of the summer of 1920 left the Mutawalli community deeply resentful of the French authorities. Many of their leaders and notables, as well as thousands of peasants, fled from their villages and found refuge in northern Palestine and in Transjordan. During the following months armed bands of Mutawallis continued to attack Christian villages, particularly in the Beqa'a Valley, prompting Gouraud to warn them that unless they ceased their activities French forces would have to take action. Local uprisings against the French continued well into 1921, when Kamal al-As'ad tried to instigate a rebellion in Jabal 'Amel. In June that year an attempt was made on Gouraud's life near Quneitra, apparently with the participation of some Mutawallis.[82]

However, with Faisal's defeat and France's occupation of all Syria the Mutawalli notables, like those of the other communities, became anxious to come to terms with the French authorities. Although from 1918 to 1920 they had co-operated with the Arab nationalists and had supported their struggle, they had not fully identified with their national goals. Their leaders now felt that in Lebanon, where they consituted a larger proportion of the population, they would be better able to retain their influential positions than in Syria, where they would be a small minority amidst masses of Sunnis, who had traditionally treated them as inferiors. These sentiments were particularly strong among the Mutawallis in Jabal 'Amel, who had always enjoyed a large measure of local autonomy and whose links with Damascus had never been close. On the other hand, the Mutawallis in the Beqa'a Valley did have close ties with Damascus, being part of the vilayet of Damascus; some of their notables had held positions in Faisal's government. This group adopted a more negative attitude towards Lebanon and the French, with opposition centred in Ba'albek, particularly among members of the Haider family.[83]

The French were still anxious to win the support of the Mutawallis, especially as the problem of the border with Palestine had not yet been settled; they feared that the British might attempt to gain Mutawalli support for annexation to Palestine.[84] They also strove to prevent the Mutawallis from co-operating with the Sunnis. The Christians, for their part, regarded the Mutawallis as potential partners in the Lebanese state despite the events of the previous year. Their past experience with the Mutawallis, who had successfully integrated into the autonomous Sanjak, led them to believe that it would be possible to integrate them into the Lebanese state as well. Moreover, in contrast to the Sunnis, this community existed solely in Lebanon. As with the Druze, the traditional nature of their feudal society facilitated the French task of enlisting their support. In an attempt to appease the Mutawalli notables, Kamal al-As'ad was granted clemency in April 1921; he was summoned to Beirut, where Gouraud presented him with the Légion d'Honneur despite the fact that he had previously been described as an enemy of the mandate. In a similar move the French appointed Ibrahim Haider as director of agriculture and later supported his election as a member of the Representative Council, hoping thereby to weaken his family's opposition. Indeed by the mid-1920s many Mutawallis in Jabal 'Amel had begun to realise the advantages of being annexed to Lebanon, and their main objective now became to achieve equality with Mount Lebanon in economic development, taxation and education, and recognition of their status as a community separate from the Sunnis.[85]

So far we have focused on the difficulties involved in transforming Lebanon into a viable state following its territorial enlargement. There were, however, certain objective factors which facilitated this task. The experience of the Mutasarrifiya, spanning over half a century, provided a precedent for effectively handling the political problems of a multi-confessional society, and the Administrative Council of Mount Lebanon was at hand as a model institution embodying the principle of sectarian representation and bringing the secular leaders of the various sects together. Indeed the political and administrative organisation of modern Lebanon was founded on this political tradition. In addition, the mere fact of living together in one country under one political and administrative system eventually had its effect, as even those who had completely rejected Lebanon's existence had to accommodate themselves to the new reality. Furthermore, in a country as small as Lebanon contacts between the various communities were inevitably close, particularly on the level of the political and economic elites. A new group of politicians gradually emerged, drawn from among all the communities, whose common interests and views were to determine the character of modern Lebanon. This process evolved mainly in Beirut, which became a melting pot and a crucible for ideas about the nature of the new state.

The economic prosperity Lebanon enjoyed under the French mandate was another factor which facilitated its consolidation and protected its political independence. It created the necessary climate for integrating the inhabitants of the annexed areas, especially their economic and political elites, thus enabling them to resist pressure and temptation from outside. Greater Lebanon was undoubtedly an economic success, realising many of the expectations of those economic circles which had continually striven for its establishment. With its new territories and ports and with Beirut, which became the economic and administrative centre for the whole of Syria, the country offered new economic opportunities which Lebanese entrepreneurs were quick to exploit. The fears of the merchants and financiers in Beirut of the possible repercussions of separation from Syria did not materialise, as no customs barriers between Lebanon and the interior were imposed in the mandate period. Moreover, Lebanon was favoured by the French in the allocation of financial aid and in development programmes.[86]

However, the political role played by the French mandate was probably the most important factor in the transformation of Greater Lebanon from an artificial entity into a relatively stable state with a political system under which the various communities could coexist. Although in one sense France's presence exacerbated the division between Christians and Muslims and increased the latter's hostility towards the Lebanese state, this was far outweighed by its positive contribution, particularly in the early years of the mandate when the country's political and administrative structure was being formed. It was France who held the country together in the face of strong Muslim opposition until the unifying forces could exert their influence. Large-scale French intervention in the Lebanese administration was essential, as only the French had both the vision and the power to impose the necessary political, administrative and legislative solutions on the various communities. Hence the High Commissioner, through his delegate in Lebanon, filled a role similar to that of the Ottoman governor during the Mutasarrifiya; the role of Gouraud and de Caix in shaping the political organisation of modern Lebanon resembled that of Da'ud Pasha in the formation of the autonomous Sanjak of Mount Lebanon over half a century before. The various sects in Lebanon would have been unable to reach a political settlement without the help of an external power.

Both the French and the Lebanese Christians realised that if Lebanon was to survive as an independent political entity it needed a sound political and administrative system. Only such a system could provide the stability which was essential in order to convince those who opposed the new state of the advantages of living there. The French faced enormous difficulties in trying to achieve this objective. The rift between Christians and Muslims was profound, while each of the two communities was further subdivided into sects, each striving to safeguard its own interests at the expense of the others. Every sect was further divided on a familial and personal basis. It was not easy for the French to appease everyone while antagonising no one. The French authorities had to contend with Sunni hostility towards the Lebanese state on the one hand, and the domineering attitude of the Maronites on the other. The traditional Lebanese approach to politics and government and the intrigues of ambitious politicians, so familiar to the country, made their task no easier. After having enjoyed local autonomy for centuries, many Lebanese, particularly those in the Mountain, were wary of any form of government. On the other hand there did exist a small but very active and vocal intelligentsia in Beirut who demanded a modern political organisation for their country, similar to that of the European states, whatever the gap between such aspirations and Lebanese political and social reality. Together with the emigrant groups, these intellectuals were always the first to criticise and oppose proposals or reforms made by the High Commission. They often aired their criticism in the numerous Lebanese newspapers which became an important forum for political debates.[87]

Despite these difficulties, the French and the Lebanese themselves succeeded during the early 1920s in establishing a sound political and administrative system which, for all its shortcomings, lasted for half a century. After the creation of Greater Lebanon, many

Lebanese were eager to build up their country. They were able to rely on a large group of Western-educated civil servants with rich administrative experience in Lebanon and Egypt, and on many French officials, who had a genuine desire to transform Lebanon into an exemplary state in accordance with French cultural values and liberal traditions. The Lebanese of that era, and writers and historians in later years, tended to over-criticise French policy and doubt French motives, failing to give due credit to France's very real contribution.[88]

One person who played a key role in shaping the political and administrative organisation of modern Lebanon was Robert de Caix. Some of the reforms and innovations he introduced between 1920 and 1923, such as the electoral laws, outlived the mandate. Describing de Caix's role in forming the Lebanese civil administration, Salibi wrote:

> From the time of his arrival until 1923, while he served under Gouraud and Weygand, de Caix laid the foundations of the new Lebanese administration, selecting among the graduates of the French and Roman Catholic missionary schools a number of assistants who became the first civil servants of modern Lebanon. Many of these civil servants continued to hold office throughout the mandatory period and the early years of independence. Some of them have remained in high positions to this day.[89]

De Caix had an ambivalent attitude towards the Lebanese Christians. He strongly objected to Maronite Church interference in High Commission decisions; he also considered the Lebanese Christians as ungrateful to France. At the same time he was fully aware that they were extremely sensitive concerning their autonomy, and he was the first to suggest that France conclude a treaty with Lebanon similar to the Anglo-Iraqi Treaty of 1922. He himself was not particularly popular with the Maronite Church or among Lebanese politicians. Describing the reaction in Lebanon to de Caix's forthcoming departure, Satow wrote:

> M. de Caix was not very popular even with his compatriots and his departure must be regarded with satisfaction by the native elements by whom he was not liked. Possibly this was because he had a keener grasp of their weaknesses and limitations than had General Gouraud.[90]

Indeed his appointment as the French representative to the Permanent Mandates Commission on Syrian and Lebanese Affairs in February 1924 aroused protests from Lebanese politicians, particularly from members of the Representative Council, one of whom described him as 'the French journalist . . . who has imposed on this country a constitution only fit for negroes, and has in general exposed Lebanese friendship for France to a severe strain'.[91]

This criticism largely reflected the indignation felt by many Lebanese over the limited degree of self-government granted by the French, for which they held de Caix mainly responsible. Their fears that the mandate would take the form of direct French control had already been expressed at the end of 1919 in Hawayik's memorandum to the Peace Conference and in the resolution adopted by the Administrative Council of Mount Lebanon. The critics wanted the Lebanese to run their own administration through their own elected and sovereign institutions; the mandatory power should merely assist and guide them towards full statehood.[92] But this was not how the French interpreted their role in Syria and Lebanon. Although the various premiers in Paris had given a very liberal interpretation to the new mandate concept, its actual implementation by the High Commission was far less liberal than had been intended. This contradiction was expressed in de Caix's own views on the mandate, which were to influence the conduct of the High Commission and help shape the political structure given to Syria and Lebanon in 1921 and 1922. De Caix argued that France's interests in Syria and Lebanon were compatible with its role as a mandatory power. The mandate convention had explicitly judged the inhabitants of the region to be not yet sufficiently mature for full independence, and had instructed the mandatory power to educate them for this objective. In order to fulfil this obligation, de Caix argued, France had to maintain sufficient authority to control and supervise the political development of the mandated states. He genuinely believed that the inhabitants of Syria and Lebanon were not ready for complete independence. In his dispatches and reports he often claimed that the demand for independence came from only a small educated and progressive minority in Syria and Lebanon, and from small groups abroad, and that the majority of the population was indifferent, concerned mainly with improving its standard of living. For this reason he also opposed any drastic changes in the administrative and political structure of the area; he preferred to retain the existing institutions, laws and customs while gradually introducing modifications to suit modern needs.[93]

Two issues which particularly agitated political life in this period, generating much tension between the Lebanese and the French authorities, were the nationality of the governor, and the powers and system of election of the future Representative Council. The question of whether the governor should be Lebanese or French had already risen in the summer of 1920. After an intensive period of debate and lobbying, a French governor, Trabaud, had been appointed.[94] Many Lebanese Christians, particularly within the Maronite Church, had hoped that a Maronite would be named to the position. Over the next six years the issue was repeatedly revived, fuelled by a genuine desire for self-rule, as well as by the intrigues of Maronite politicians seeking the office for themselves. The Lebanese Christians noted resentfully that the 'states' of Damascus and Aleppo had been allowed their own indigenous governors, while they, who were more 'advanced', had been placed under direct French administration like the less developed region of the 'Alawites. In fact, however, the French were acting largely in response to pressures from Muslims and non-Maronite Christians, who wanted a French governor as a guarantor of their interests and positions against Maronite domination.[95]

Lebanese concern over the question of autonomy was apparent in the relatively independent attitude adopted by the newly appointed Administrative Council. The old Administrative Council of Mount Lebanon had been dissolved in July 1920. On 22 September Gouraud appointed a new Council comprised of 17 members, which included representatives from the annexed areas and was based on confessional representation.[96] After its experience with the previous Council, the High Commission made sure to choose pro-French politicians to guarantee full support for its policies. In October it prevented the election of Habib Pasha al-Sa'd as president of the Council, favouring Da'ud 'Ammun, one of its most loyal supporters, instead; 'Ammun was subsequently elected. In reaction Sa'd resigned from the Council and accused the French of large-scale intervention in the Lebanese administration. But in spite of all the French precautionary measures, the new Council often took an independent stand, even opposing the High Commission on the question of the general budget and on relations with Syria. In these cases they were continuing the tradition of the Administrative Council under the Mutasarrifiya, which defended local interests against the Ottoman governor.[97]

In March 1922 the appointed Administrative Council was dissolved as the High Commission promulgated two decrees providing for a new Representative Council; they had been drawn up by de Caix, then acting high commissioner, in accordance with Briand's instructions. The decrees, No. 1307 which regulated the election of the Council, and No. 1304 *bis.* which defined the powers of the Council and of the governor, became organic laws; they were to have a profound influence on the political development of Lebanon. The first established the confessional character of the electoral system which, with some modification, still exists today, while the second largely determined the relations between the High Commission and the Lebanese parliament during the mandate.[98]

Decree No. 1307 stipulated that a Representative Council comprised of 30 deputies be elected for a period of four years by general suffrage, in two stages, based on confessional representation in proportion to the size of each community as recorded by the census of 1921.[99] The decree was based on the Organic Law of 1864 and on Ottoman and French electoral laws. Both the High Commission and the Lebanese themselves realised that in the prevailing circumstances only a system based on sectarian representation could lead to any form of coexistence between the various sects. It was the only way to allay the fears of the various communities about Maronite domination, and thus facilitate their integration in the Lebanese state. Such a system tended to minimise interconfessional conflict while ensuring interconfessional co-operation. It had been successfully used during the Mutasarrifiya, and in consultations between the High Commission and notables from the various sects it won almost unanimous support.[100]

As the system of sectarian representation was to determine the political development of modern Lebanon, it is appropriate to quote de Caix's own explanation for his decision:

Mais tout d'abord — et c'est là le point essentiel — nous nous sommes trouvés en présence de la vérité suivante, qui jamais ne s'était manifesté d'une façon aussi indiscutable: ce qui constitue la véritable nationalité du Liban, c'est le rite, c'est la communauté confessionelle. L'idée de Patrie, c'est à dire l'union de tous dans un même idéal temporel ou social, est incapable de prévaloir actuellement, contre les barrières séculaires qui séparent les multiples groupements religieux. Les deux grandes communautés chrétiennes et islamiques se subdivisent elles-mêmes en rites schismatiques divers, qui forment autant de nations nettement séparées. Or chaque nation se réclame de son droit propre aux fonctions gouvernementales et de la légitimité de son intervention dans les destinées du pays. Par suite la seule base d'une administration équitable devait être fournie par le dénombrement exact des ressortissants de ces différents groupements. Car avant que le temps n'ait fondu dans un intérêt commun les intérêts particuliers, le pays ne peut être conduit que par une politique de répartition justement proportionelle entre les éléments variés qui le composent.[101]

The decree also addressed the issue of the size of the electoral districts. There had been intensive discussions among French officials and Lebanese politicians on the matter, which would greatly influence the character of the future Council. The High Commission had to decide whether to adopt a large electoral district — the sanjak, or one based on the smaller caza. It wanted to ensure the election of a pro-French Council and at the same time secure the largest possible representation for the two Christian communities loyal to France: the Maronites and the Greek Catholics. As for the latter consideration, it was found that representation of the two communities would be the same in both systems. Yet de Caix argued that the sanjak electoral district was in the interests of the mandatory authority as well as of the two communities. In such a district the French could more easily prevent the election of hostile deputies, whereas in a smaller district deputies with strong local support could be elected despite French opposition. Furthermore, the larger the electoral district, the greater was the need for co-operation between the politicians of the various communities. True, the law stipulated that every district would choose a specific number of deputies from each of the different communities living there, but every deputy would be elected not only by the members of his own community, but by the whole electorate. Hence the law encouraged moderation, as an extreme candidate would find it difficult to enlist support within the other communities. De Caix's proposals were adopted, and six districts were defined: four sanjaks and the municipalities of Beirut and Tripoli.[102]

In contrast to the electoral law, which received unanimous support, Decree No. 1304 *bis.* aroused loud protests both in Lebanon and among Lebanese emigrants abroad. Although the decree appeared at first glance to be liberal, in fact it granted very limited authority to the Representative Council while giving extensive power to the governor. The Council had almost no legislative power; it was merely an advisory body. On every essential matter effective control rested with the governor, who could bypass the decisions of the Representative Council. The governor (or the high commissioner) had the right to initiate legislation; he could decide on a budget by decree even if the Council did not approve it; he could declare null and void all deliberations on matters not under the Council's jurisdiction; and he could adjourn or dissolve the Council altogether.[103]

The publication of the decree in March 1922 roused much indignation among the Lebanese, many of whom had regarded the creation of a sovereign legislative assembly as an expression of Lebanon's independent existence. They accused France of treating Lebanon as a colony in violation of its obligations as a mandatory power and its pledges to assist in forming a national government. Many claimed that Lebanon had enjoyed greater autonomy under the Mutasarrifiya than it did now under the French mandate. Among the first to take action were the Lebanese in Egypt, who began a campaign demanding that the law be modified. In Lebanon itself petitions and telegrams of protest were addressed to the High Commission, the French government, the National Assembly and the French press.[104] Christians and Muslims began to co-operate. Some of the petitions demanding independence and accusing France of not fulfilling its promises to the Maronite patriarch were even signed by Sunni notables. A joint deputation of Christians and Muslims appealed to the Maronite patriarch and the Sunni kadi of Beirut to intervene in order to obtain greater power for the future Council. In part this was a Muslim attempt to exploit Christian dissatisfaction to gain support for the complete independence of both Syria and Lebanon.[105]

The criticism and protests placed the High Commission in a most difficult position at the very time a strong wave of anti-French feeling was spreading throughout Syria. The High Commission was particularly concerned over Lebanese appeals to the National Assembly and over the articles appearing in the French press, as the National Assembly was then debating the Syrian budget and the government's policy in Syria and Lebanon. It feared that criticism and unrest would strengthen opposition to its policy and lead to further reductions in the budget; Poincaré, the new premier, might even be prompted to instruct the High Commission to scrap the decree altogether. In repeated despatches to Paris, de Caix defended the decree as the best possible solution under the existing political and social conditions; any modifications would only hinder the High Commission's ability to carry out its task in accordance with the mandate. In any case, de Caix argued, the decree was much more liberal than its critics claimed; it granted extensive power to the Council, particularly in fiscal matters. The High Commission sent Ayub Thabet, a Lebanese Christian, to Paris to counter the influence of the protests from Lebanese and emigrant groups. To the Lebanese, de Caix stressed that the decree was only a first step; the French authorities were considering how to grant greater power to the Council and more self-government to Lebanon. Despite all these arguments, the question of the power of the Council continued to generate discontent among the Lebanese until the Lebanese Constitution was drafted several years later.[106]

In May 1922 the first general election for the Representative Council was held, based on the two decrees. Many of the characteristics which would later become an integral part of the Lebanese electioneering system were manifested, such as intervention by the High Commission and by the Maronite Church; lack of true political parties[107] and strong competitiveness along regional, sectarian and personal lines. The extensive intervention of the High Commission was intended to ensure the election of pro-French deputies, particularly in light of the strong opposition to the limited power granted to the Council. The High Commission itself was under constant pressure from candidates anxious to show their loyalty to France in order to secure French support for their election. The Maronite Church openly intervened on behalf of candidates whose election it sought to ensure. In contrast, the Sunnis largely boycotted the elections; the American consul estimated that in Beirut only one-third of the electorate actually voted. The boycott was intended to demonstrate opposition to both the Lebanese state and the French mandate. Consequently all of the six Sunni candidates who won election were pro-French, nearly all of them politically unknown. Describing the atmosphere in Lebanon after the elections, Satow wrote:

> The general attitude of the majority of the population is one of indignation at the management of the elections. It is believed that a correct surmise as to the procedure adopted is that only those

candidates which the High Commission wished to be elected, have been elected. In fact the general opinion is that the whole thing has been a farce.[108]

The Representative Council remained in office for two-and-a-half years, until it was dissolved by Sarrail in January 1925. Its first president was Habib al-Sa'd,[109] who was followed by Na'um Labaki and Emile Eddé; all three were Maronites. A Sunni was elected vice-president, and one Mutawalli and one Greek Orthodox were elected secretaries, as the future system of maintaining a balance between the various sects took root. In spite of its limited formal power the Council gradually began to expand its influence, particularly as the High Commission was anxious to demonstrate that it had in fact granted the Council a large measure of authority. Indeed the Council frequently adopted a more independent stand than the French would have liked. It became a forum for grievances and opposition to French policies. It opposed any Lebanese responsibility towards the Ottoman Public Debt; it demanded the end of the capitulations and of the special duties on tobacco; and it refused to grant concessions to foreign companies in Lebanon. The Council also attempted to define the status and power of the French advisers and officials serving in the Lebanese administration, a frequent subject for Lebanese complaint.[110]

However, the importance of this Council and of those which followed was not so much in their immediate decisions — the High Commission continued to hold the reins of power — as in the fact that the institution became the symbol of Lebanon's independence, sovereignty and territorial integrity. It was the training ground for the development of a political life in harmony with Western democratic ideas, thus preparing the ground for parliamentary government. It gave rise to a secular leadership whose visions and values would determine the political development of modern Lebanon. The Councils aided in the gradual political integration of the Muslim leaders who had refused to recognise the Lebanese state, and encouraged the development of the inter-confessional co-operation which was later to characterise Lebanese politics. Finally, the Council elected in July 1925 played an important part in drawing up the Lebanese Constitution of 1926, which with some modification is still in force today.

4 UPHEAVAL AND RECONSTRUCTION

On 23 November 1922, after persistent rumours of his pending departure, Gouraud finally resigned from his post as high commissioner and returned to Paris. His resignation had been expected since April, when Poincaré, the new premier, had informed him that the High Commission's civilian budget for 1923 would be reduced from the current 120 million francs to only 8.2 million. Gouraud regarded this drastic cut as a personal affront and completely contrary to what, on a recent visit to Paris, he had been led to believe. Disturbed by the possibility of a Turkish attack on Syria, he also opposed the reduction in French forces. He maintained that both actions, coming simultaneously, would seriously undermine France's prestige and its ability to fulfil its mandatory obligations; in these circumstances he could no longer remain in office. Moreover, he was reluctant to modify his policies, particularly concerning the administrative organisation of the mandated territories, which had come under sharp criticism in France as too complicated and costly and out of line with the aspirations of the local inhabitants.[1]

Gouraud's natural successor seemed to be Robert de Caix, his secretary-general since November 1919, who had acquired an intimate knowledge of the mandated territories and their inhabitants. And in fact, after Gouraud's resignation de Caix was promised the position. But as tension increased between France and the Turkish nationalists early in 1923, with Mustafa Kemal's forces concentrated along the Syrian border raising the spectre of an invasion, Poincaré decided that the time was not yet ripe for a civilian high commissioner. He chose instead General Maxime Weygand, a distinguished general and devout Catholic. Weygand's appointment marked the end of three years of intensive activity during which Syria and Lebanon had undergone a thorough political and administrative reorganisation. The mandated territories now needed a period of stability to allow for the consolidation of the radical changes which had taken place. During his 19 months in office Weygand proved to be, if not a flamboyant innovator, an able administrator who quickly grasped local conditions and attitudes and acted accordingly. One of the most successful high commissioners, he gained the respect and confidence of both Muslims and Christians.[2]

Weygand based his policies on three principles which he regarded as essential for the successful implementation of the mandate: security, economic development and equality and justice.[3] His foremost goal was the restoration of security and order, which had considerably deteriorated throughout the mandated territories in early 1923 due to the successes of the Turkish nationalists, the shortage of French forces and the uncertainty over France's intentions. In the north, bands of Turkish irregulars supported by Mustafa Kemal's forces made frequent incursions into Syrian territory, while in other regions, particularly in the Beqa'a Valley, there were widespread acts of brigandage. But the most immediate and difficult problem Weygand faced was a serious outbreak of hostilities between the Druze and Maronites in the Shuf district, which claimed scores of victims on both sides. The renewed violence could partly be attributed to the traditional feud between the two communities, in which local incidents could spark off a chain of murder and revenge. But the political intrigues of local notables, particularly Druze, also played a role; these leaders encouraged such violence to demonstrate their resentment at having been displaced from influential and lucrative positions by Maronites and by other Druze supported by the French authorities. The French were convinced that outside elements were also involved in instigating these incidents; they suspected Rashid Tali'a and other exiled Lebanese Druze leaders of being responsible.[4]

Weygand was determined to suppress these activities, which were seriously undermining France's prestige in Lebanon and badly affecting the economy, especially summer tourism from Egypt, by now an important source of revenue. Moreover, he saw the disorders as an opportunity to dispel any doubts as to France's intention of retaining the mandate, and to demonstrate that he himself would not tolerate any activities which might undermine public security. Consequently he set up a special tribunal with summary powers; it did not balk at sentencing criminals to death. Druze notables were arrested and detained as hostages to prevent further murders and acts of brigandage, and heavy fines were imposed on vilages whose inhabitants were suspected of having participated in the violence. The caimacams of the Shuf and two other neighbouring districts were replaced by French military governors, and a new force of Lebanese gendarmerie, under the command of French officers, was organised to help maintain law and order. The French also began a large-scale operation to disarm the population in Lebanon, which continued throughout 1924 despite the strong resentment it aroused. These measures were largely successful, and by the end of 1923 law and order had been restored to most of the mandated territories. Nevertheless, tension persisted between the Maronites and the Druze in the Shuf. The latter claimed that they had been punished far more severely than the Maronites, a grievance which would contribute to another outbreak of inter-confessional hostilities in the Shuf during the Druze revolt in the spring of 1926.[5]

Weygand believed that economic prosperity was essential if the inhabitants of the mandated territories were to accept the French mandate. But his efforts in this direction were continually hampered by a lack of the financial resources necessary to revive the economy, which had been seriously affected by the War. He had, nevertheless, learnt from Gouraud's experience, and he tried to increase efficiency in the High Commission by reducing expenses and by putting to maximum use the small budget at his disposal. He strove to minimise the need for financial support from Paris, and by 1924 he succeeded in balancing the local budgets. He worked to reduce the share of the mandated territories in the Ottoman Public Debt (OPD) and in the Tobacco Régie, two issues which had generated strong local resentment. The OPD absorbed revenues which could otherwise have been used to stimulate economic growth in Syria and Lebanon and initiate new development projects. Weygand asked his government's permission to use some of this revenue to finance the High Commission programmes. He also tried to lower the high cost of rail transport, which was monopolised by French companies, arguing that it severely hampered the development of local trade. At the same time he repeatedly called on the government to end the uncertainty concerning France's intentions, so that French entrepreneurs would be more willing to invest in the mandated territories, which he believed had large economic potential.[6]

Gouraud's departure had understandably fuelled Maronite anxiety, and Hawayik had written to Poincaré asking that the high commissioner be kept in office. The Maronites feared a change in French policy; a new high commissioner might lack Gouraud's deep personal sympathy for their cause. Reports that de Caix might succeed Gouraud increased their apprehension, as they were well aware of his attitude on the question of Lebanon's borders. Weygand's appointment was therefore welcomed as a sign that the French government intended to continue its traditional support for the

Christians. Weygand himself quickly dispelled Maronite fears when, a few days after his arrival, he visited Hawayik and assured him that:

> L'indépendance du Grand-Liban n'a pas été proclamée par un homme en son nom personnel. Cette indépendance a été proclamée par la France entière, puissance forte. La France défendra de toutes ses forces, sa politique en Orient. L'indépendance du Grand-Liban est à la tête de son programme.[7]

Yet one of the main reasons for Weygand's success was his immediate understanding that religious and sectarian differences were a basic factor in the life of the region, especially in Lebanon, and that a strictly impartial policy towards the various communities was essential if accusations of favouritism were to be prevented. He saw France's main task in Lebanon as the bridging of the gap between Muslims and Christians; therefore, unlike Gouraud, he refrained from fully identifying with the Maronites. During his term in office the direct involvement and influence of the Maronite Church and the French missionaries in the decisions of the High Commission were considerably reduced.[8]

Nevertheless, Weygand's reassuring words were especially encouraging for the Maronites as the Sunnis were still waging an intensive campaign for their separation from the Lebanese state, in hopes of persuading the new high commissioner to change the status of the annexed areas and attach them to Syria. Turkish nationalist successes and the activities of their supporters added to the general unrest among the Muslims in Lebanon throughout 1923, as did the establishment of the Syrian federation in July 1922 and the formation of Syrian governmental institutions. Lebanese Muslim demands drew support from Syrian-Arab nationalist leaders on the coast, who had close ties with the Syrian nationalists in the interior and abroad. One of the most active of these was Ri'ad al-Sulh, who had returned to Lebanon from exile. The Muslim campaign for separation from Lebanon took on an increasingly organised nature during 1923, as notables from Beirut, Tripoli, Sidon and Ba'albek pooled their efforts. Petitions to the French government requesting separation from Lebanon were sent simultaneously from all these centres. In July, Muslim leaders from Tripoli and Beirut agreed to step up their activities and to send representatives to Europe, particularly to

France and to the League of Nations in Geneva to publicise their demands.[9]

This co-ordinated campaign included a renewed effort to gain the support of the Christians, as well as of other Muslim communities in Lebanon, for union with the Syrian federation. As in 1919 and 1920 the Greek Orthodox community was one of the main targets. The Muslims in Beirut, for example, used the Christian and Muslim festivals to demonstrate fraternity between the two communities. Commenting on this phenomenon Smart, the British acting consul-general in Beirut, wrote:

> It would seem that these demonstrations, which were carefully organised, are part of the Muslim Arab movement against the inclusion in the 'Grand Liban' of the territories not in the pre-War Lebanon, and, more generally, against the division of Syria into a number of states. The Muslims wish to win over Christians to the cause of Syrian unity.[10]

Muslim leaders from Beirut and Tripoli frequently held meetings in which members of the other communities were invited to take part. In their campaign against a separate multi-confessional Lebanese state, they exploited the general fear of Maronite domination among the other sects, the hostility between the Maronites and the Druze in the Shuf, and the resentment generated among the Mutawallis in south Lebanon and the Beqa'a Valley by the disarming carried out by the French authorities. They also sought the support of the Freemasons, whose activities intensified during 1923 and 1924 as they too strove for a secular Lebanon and a united and independent Syria. Most active was the Democratic Party for Union, which comprised both Christian and Muslim Freemasons.[11]

In spite of this organised activity and the general demand for separation from Lebanon, the Muslims were not always in full agreement about their objectives. Those in Tripoli and Ba'albek continued to seek immediate annexation to Syria, but among Beirut Muslims other ideas were discussed. Some proposed that Beirut become an independent city, while others advocated the creation of an independent coastal zone. The first proposal was supported by many members of the Greek Orthodox community and by the Muslim commercial sector. But a Muslim committee appointed at the beginning of 1923 recommended that the community continue to demand incorporation in the Syrian federation; if Beirut became independent, the increased settlement of Christians there might reduce the Muslims to a small minority.[12]

Faced with a Muslim campaign for annexation to Syria, Weygand immediately made it clear to its leaders and to the Syrian nationalists that France had no intention of altering the *status quo* or of evacuating the mandated territories. Then, in July 1923, the signing of the Treaty of Lausanne dampened Muslim hopes that a Franco-Turkish conflict might force France to abandon the area; two months later the mandate over Syria and Lebanon officially went into force, thus confirming Weygand's message. The High Commission took steps to suppress separatist manifestations and to warn Muslim leaders against instigating such activities. Consequently, Muslim separatist activities had largely abated by the end of 1923. Weygand had been working to gain the Muslims' confidence, showing far more understanding of their political, administrative, cultural and educational needs than had his predecessors; an increasing number of Muslim notables became willing to co-operate with the French authorities. Weygand's appreciation of Muslim and Syrian nationalist aspirations was one of the reasons he announced in June 1924 that he intended to create a Syrian state comprising the 'states' of Damascus and Aleppo. This move, however, only served to intensify the Syrian nationalist demand for a united Syria which would also include the 'Alawite state, Jabal Druze and the areas annexed to Lebanon in 1920; they now believed that constant pressure and persuasion could influence French decisions. In Lebanon the announcement made the Christians nervous, while encouraging the Muslims to keep up their demands for annexation to Syria.[13]

The most controversial issue in Lebanese politics continued to be that of the nationality of the governor. In May 1923, after a prolonged campaign led by Habib al-Sa'd, president of the Representative Council, in which Trabaud was accused of inefficiency and corruption, the latter finally resigned from his post and was replaced provisionally by Privat-Aubouard. But the uncertainty created by the lack of a permanent governor led to further rivalry and intrigue and the renewal of demands for an indigenous governor. Like Gouraud and de Caix, Weygand realised that a native governor would inevitably be a Maronite, and that this would increase resentment and fear of Maronite domination among the other communities, thereby strengthening Muslim separatist tendencies. He therefore asked the premier to approve the appointment of a permanent French governor until the organic law was completed. In June 1924 General

Vandenberg was appointed governor, and although a devout Catholic, he succeeded in maintaining an impartial position *vis-à-vis* the various communities.[14]

Weygand considered his work during his first 18 months in office as a foundation for the comprehensive administrative and economic programmes he hoped to implement now that security and stability had been restored. During his visit to Paris in summer 1924 he began preparations for drafting an organic law for the mandated territories, which France, as the mandatory power, was obliged to conclude within three years of the date the mandate officially came into force. Upon his return to Beirut he announced the appointment of Vandenberg to the members of the Representative Council. The new governor would serve for a transitional period during which the most liberal possible organic law would be drawn up. Weygand declared that the constitution would extend the powers of the Council and would provide that the head of the Lebanese state be appointed from a short list of candidates presented by the Council. On 29 November 1924, however, Weygand received a telegram from the minister of war informing him that General Sarrail was to supersede him as high commissioner and that he himself had to return immediately to his duties on the Supreme War Council. This unexpected step, and the manner in which Weygand was removed, antagonised both Muslims and Christians. Opposition was voiced to the frequent changes of high commissioner. The Lebanese Representative Council passed a resolution expressing gratitude to Weygand, and before his departure for Paris deputations and individuals from all the communities came to express their sympathy and support. Satow reflected the general dismay when he wrote: '. . . in order to satisfy the exigencies of French political intrigue at home, an administration which was becoming daily more efficient is to be broken up. The result can hardly be favourable to real French interests.'[15]

The appointment of Sarrail as high commissioner was indeed the outcome of French internal political intrigue, and had little to do with the merits of Weygand's administration. Following the success of the 'Cartel des Gauches' in the election of May 1924, Edouard Herriot, the new premier was increasingly pressed by Sarrail's supporters to rehabilitate him and return him to active duty despite his controversial role in the War. The appointment of this authoritarian and impatient 68-year-old general, who possessed neither the experience nor the inclination to deal with administrative affairs, was a serious mistake which proved most unfortunate for all concerned. During his ten months in office Sarrail undermined many of his predecessors' achievements and led his administration from one catastrophe to another, culminating in the outbreak of the revolt of the Druze and Syrian nationalists.[16]

The news of Sarrail's appointment stirred up uncertainty and unrest throughout the mandated territories. It aroused hope among Muslims and Syrian nationalists and fear among the Maronites, who were apprehensive about a high commissioner who, unlike his two predecessors, was an atheist and a reputed Freemason. They feared his appointment would mark a departure from the traditional French policy of reliance on the Christians, especially the Maronites, and inaugurate a new policy based on secular principles more receptive to the aspirations of the Muslim majority. For precisely these reasons the Muslims welcomed Sarrail's appointment. They hoped the new leftist French government would modify France's previous policy and implement the liberal declarations of the French Left, which sought to fulfil the aspirations of the inhabitants of Syria. On the eve of Sarrail's arrival in Beirut there were rumours and reports in the Muslim press that the new high commissioner intended to change the existing political organisation radically by creating a united Syria and returning Lebanon to its pre-war borders. The official establishment of the Syrian state on 5 December 1924, in accordance with the decree issued by Weygand on the day of his departure for Paris, was seen as the first step in this direction.[17]

The resulting anxiety among the Christians prompted some of their leaders to write to Shukri Ghanem in Paris, asking him to examine the truth of these rumours and to ask for the French government's reassurance as to the independence and territorial integrity of Lebanon. In reply to Ghanem's request, the Quai d'Orsay issued a statement on 3 January 1925 stressing that the French government had no intention of undermining 'the independence of Greater Lebanon, which had been proclaimed in 1920 and which has been confirmed several times since'.[18] For the same purpose Hawayik hastened to Beirut shortly after the arrival of the new high commissioner to learn in detail of his intentions. Hawayik's arrival in Beirut was seized by thousands of Maronites as an opportunity to stage large-scale demonstrations aimed at impressing upon Sarrail and the Muslims their strong opposition to any change in the *status quo*. At their meeting, Sarrail assured Hawayik: 'Le Grand-Liban ne peut pas être inquiété. La question de son indépendance, de son intégrité, encore une fois, ne peut plus se poser: c'est une affaire faite: un fait décidé, certain, sur lequel il n'y a plus à revenir.'[19] But at the same time Sarrail revealed his tactlessness and ignorance of local conditions when he declared to the Maronite patriarch that he would oppose any intervention by the Church in political affairs.

The impulsiveness which was to characterise many of Sarrail's decisions was demonstrated on the very day of his arrival in Beirut when, at a reception for the Lebanese Representative Council attended by General Vandenberg, he announced, to the surprise of the deputies and of the governor himself, that the latter was to be replaced by a native governor. Some non-Maronite deputies attempted to convince Sarrail that the country was not yet ready for this sudden change, and proposed that a French governor, preferably Vandenberg, retain this post until the organic law was elaborated; but their efforts were fruitless. On 5 January Decree No. 3023 was published, laying down the procedure for the election of a native governor. The Council was instructed to convene on 12 January to nominate three candidates, either Lebanese or French. After their approval by the high commissioner, the Council itself would proceed to elect one of them as the new governor for a period of three years. This was, in fact, the very procedure Weygand had proposed six months before. Sarrail's objective in this sudden move was twofold: to gain the support of the Lebanese by demonstrating his desire to implement a liberal policy, and at the same time to remove Vandenberg, who represented the previous French policy which he himself detested.[20]

Sarrail's sudden declaration caused confusion, rivalry and intrigue. Politicians who had been seeking this position since 1920 embarked upon intensive campaigns to gain support for their candidacies. Tension mounted between the various communities, particularly among those who feared that the election of a Maronite governor might lead to complete Maronite domination. The candidate who seemed most likely to be elected was Emile Eddé, president of the Representative Council. Other contenders were Habib al-Sa'd and Najib Sursuk. Eddé's candidacy received considerable political and financial support from the Maronite Church and the Jesuits, who were anxious that a politician they could trust be elected as the first native governor of Lebanon. Sarrail, however, had little desire to see as governor someone who would, in his words, be 'in the hands of the clerical party which is systematically hostile to all I do'.[21] He made it clear to Eddé and his supporters that he would oppose their campaign; if the Council insisted on Eddé's election, he would dissolve it. Sarrail now realised that his initiative had been premature and that a French governor would be preferable. He decided on Léon Cayla, governor of the 'Alawite state, as the best choice for governor of Lebanon. The High Commission launched a campaign, using intimidation and pressure, to ensure Cayla's election. The French authorities went so far as to instruct the Council to transfer the ballot box to the High Commission after the elections, although Decree No. 3023 had stipulated that the elections would be secret. Habib al-Sa'd took an active part in this campaign. Since he himself had no chance of being elected, he strove to prevent Eddé's election even though he had been leading the campaign for a native Lebanese governor since 1920. Faced with the high commissioner's determined opposition, anxious to avoid either strain in their personal relations or the dissolution of the Council, Eddé proposed to Sarrail that he appoint a governor of his own choice. Sarrail refused, insisting that the Council proceed with the elections.[22]

Sarrail's veto of Eddé's candidacy, and the procedure he laid down for the elections, roused strong resentment in the Council. Its members regarded these steps as an encroachment on their power and status as a sovereign elected body and a breach of Gouraud's May 1922 pledge that the Council could freely discuss all issues concerning Lebanon. In reaction to the high commissioner's crude attempt to impose his will, the majority of the deputies came out in support of Eddé's nomination. The Council meeting of 12 January became a showdown between the high commissioner and the deputies, who were under pressure to demonstrate their independence to the large crowd gathered outside. At the beginning of the meeting Eddé announced the withdrawal of his candidacy for 'known reasons'. The deputies then demanded the right to discuss Decree No. 3023, but the French delegate insisted that they proceed immediately to the nomination of three candidates. When the deputies refused to accept his ruling, he left the meeting, on Sarrail's instructions, amidst great commotion. The following day Sarrail dissolved the Council, officially relieved Vandenberg of his duties, appointed Cayla as provisional governor of Lebanon and fixed elections for a new Representative Council in six months' time. As a reward for his support, Sa'd was appointed by Cayla a few days later as secretary-general of the Council of Directors (that is, ministers of state), the chief local executive position. He replaced Auguste Adib Pasha, who had filled the post very successfully.[23]

The summary dismissal of General Vandenberg and the dissolution of the Lebanese Council exposed Sarrail to tough criticism both in the National Assembly and the Quai d'Orsay. Premier Herriot, who also served as minister of foreign affairs, asked Sarrail for an explanation of his failure to consult Paris before taking this hasty action. Sarrail's report to the premier about the whole affair was far from complete. He claimed he had dissolved the Council because it would not agree on the candidates and because of the 'scandalous corruption' which had accompanied the campaign. He accused the Maronite Church and the Jesuits of depositing 240,000 francs in a bank in Beirut to ensure the necessary support for Eddé's election. He claimed that Najib Sursuk had also offered large sums of money to any deputy who would support his candidacy. He argued that there had been no need for him to consult Paris, as he had acted within his rights in accordance with Decree No. 1304 *bis*. But the Quai d'Orsay maintained that the procedures laid down in Decree No. 3023 had been a departure from the existing organic law; it consequently recommended to the premier that Sarrail be requested to refrain from making any modifications in the existing electoral system until the new Council was elected. On 13 February Herriot instructed Sarrail: 'Veuillez ne procéder à aucune modification du régime électoral du Grand Liban, n'engagez en aucune manière, le Haut Commissariat en ce qui concerne les modifications à apporter à ce régime, sans mon assentiment préalable.' Two days later Sarrail acknowledged these instructions and undertook to abide by them. Nevertheless, a month later he was trying to introduce radical reforms in the Lebanese political system, again without informing the premier.[24]

The whole controversy put a severe strain on relations between Sarrail on the one hand and the Maronites, particularly the Church, and the French religious orders on the other. Their mutual suspicion and hostility continued throughout Sarrail's term in office. The Church regarded his veto of Eddé as a hostile act against the whole Maronite community, which had been striving to obtain a Maronite governor for many years. It was proof of his reputed anti-clericalism and his intention to restrict the role of the Church in the political life of Lebanon. It also confirmed their fears that his appointment marked a turning point in France's policy and a departure from the close relations that had existed between the Church and previous high commissioners. Commenting on the atmosphere created by Sarrail's actions, Satow wrote:

> Thus within eight days of his arrival, General Sarrail has removed one French Governor of Lebanon and replaced him, albeit temporarily, by another, has held out hopes of the appointment of a native Governor which can only be realised later and has dissolved the Representative Council. He must also have antagonised the Maronites and many of the French clergy. Further, confessional rivalries and jealousies must undoubtedly have been stimulated. It is clearly in the best interests of the country that clerical influence should be confined to its proper sphere and the jealousies between Maronites, Druzes, Moslems and other elements which form the population should disappear. But it is impossible that within a few years a situation which has existed for centuries should disappear, and after all French influence in this country is largely based upon their traditional relations with the Maronites and is largely due to the scholastic and other institutions directed by French priests and nuns.[25]

One of the long-standing principles of French policy in the Levant was to refrain from importing the secularism and anti-clericalism which had characterised much of the Third Republic. Thus, while in France a continual campaign was being waged against the Church, in the Levant France was recognised as the main defender of the Catholics. Successive French governments had been fully aware of the importance of this role in the advancement of French interests in the Levant, and had refrained from any acts which might have undermined France's status as the chief Catholic power. Sarrail's appointment did in fact mark a departure. Under his administration a conflict developed between clerical and anti-clerical forces, and the Lebanese found themselves increasingly involved in internal French ideological and political rivalries. The change stemmed from the fact that Sarrail's appointment had been a political act. Sarrail had close ties with the radical Left; the Right, now in opposition, seized every opportunity to criticise the government on the way it had replaced Weygand, and on Sarrail's own inadequacies. Sarrail's controversial policies gave frequent cause for such criticism. His moves against the Catholic sectors, whether local or French, roused strong criticism in the French National Assembly and press. It must be stressed, though, that the initiative in this conflict was often taken not by Sarrail, but by the powerful Catholic circles in Lebanon, especially the Jesuits and their supporters, who detested all that Sarrail represented. They waged a continuous campaign against him both in Lebanon and in France. The ranks of his opponents were swelled by the many French officers and officials he dismissed and sent back to Paris for various reasons during his term in office.[26]

A mere one week after his arrival, Sarrail managed to offend the Catholic clergy by tactlessly declining an invitation from the head of the Capuchins to attend a ceremony traditionally held in honour of French representatives in the Levant and symbolising recognition of France as protector of the area's Catholics. Sarrail's refusal brought immediate criticism from Catholics in Lebanon as well as from Paris. His claim that the ceremony was a private mass which did not require his attendance was rejected by Giannini, the apostolic delegate in Beirut, who warned him that his action would undermine France's traditional position in the area. Giannini's strong reaction should be seen in light of the growing tension between the Vatican and Herriot's government. Following the latter's hostile declarations and threats to break off diplomatic relations, the Holy See sought to warn the French government and public that a continued strain in relations could jeopardise France's interests in the East. This warning carried considerable weight as Italy, under Mussolini, was challenging France as the main Catholic power in the area.[27]

Faced with these threats and with charges in the National Assembly that Sarrail was improperly implementing his personal anti-clerical views in the mandated territories, Herriot promptly moved to reassure the deputies. He attached great importance, he told them, to France's traditional position as protector of the Christians in the Levant. The high commissioner, as representative of the French government, should not be under the control of any particular party in France; he was expected to respect the Catholic religion and to take into account the services rendered by Catholic institutions and individuals in Lebanon. Herriot repeated these assurances in a letter to Giannini on 4 March in which he stated that the French government had 'no intention of renouncing in the East either the duties or the rights which it [derived] from a long tradition sanctioned by international treaties and recognised by the Holy See'.[28] After receiving Herriot's instructions, Sarrail attended a special Easter mass at which an address was delivered by Giannini himself.

The new high commissioner's problems with the Catholic orders naturally affected his relations with the Maronites and their Church. For their part some Church figures, including Hawayik, tried to avoid direct involvement in internal French political and ideological rivalries, aware as they were of the possible consequences for their ties with France. At his meeting with Sarrail on 7 January Hawayik had already assured him that the Maronite Church and the Lebanese Christians had no desire to become involved in inter-party affairs in France. There was only one France on whom they could rely, and they wished to maintain as good relations with the present government and High Commission as they had with their predecessors. He expressed the same views in a letter to Herriot two months later:

> Etrangers aux luttes intérieures de la politique française, nous n'avons jamais voulu connaître, derrière les partis, comme je l'ai rappelé en toute occurrence, que la France amie et immortelle. Ce même sentiment a inspiré mon attitude à l'égard de Monsieur le Général Sarrail désigné comme Haut Commissaire au Liban. Sans m'arrêter au caractère tendancieux que certaines dépêches voulaient attribuer à cette nomination, j'ai considéré comme un devoir très simple de lui faire l'accueil et de lui rendre les honneurs qu'avaient reçus ses prédécesseurs.[29]

But these assurances did little to alter Sarrail's attitude. He still regarded the Maronite Church and the Jesuits as hostile towards him and his policies. Some members of the Maronite clergy, such as Bishop Mubarak, did indeed take an active part in the campaign against him, while Lebanese Christian newspapers, some of whose editors and journalists were graduates of Jesuit schools, levelled bitter personal attacks against him and Cayla, the new governor.[30]

In reaction to this campaign, Sarrail refrained from returning Hawayik's visit. This was in stark contrast to the practice of his two predecessors, who had paid courtesy visits to the patriarch upon arriving in Lebanon, out of respect for him and as an expression of the close ties beween France and the Maronites. Such behaviour was regarded by the Maronite Church and community as a serious affront, especially as Sarrail had paid official visits to the patriarchs of the Syrian and Greek Orthodox communities. These feelings were clearly expressed in the letter sent by Hawayik to Herriot on 7 March, in which he condemned Sarrail's attitude as harmful to the traditional relations between France and the Maronites. Only after criticism was aired in the National Assembly and instructions received from the premier did Sarrail pay an official visit to the Maronite patriarch in Bkerki on 30 March. But this did little to improve relations between the Church and the high commissioner.[31]

Sarrail's cold attitude towards the Maronite Church and the Catholic orders was not merely a product of his personal beliefs, or a reaction to their own hostility; it also reflected a general policy which he and Herriot were trying to implement in the mandated territories. Ever since the War the Left in France had been criticising the government's Syrian policy for relying exclusively on the Catholic elements and thus stirring up Muslim and Syrian-Arab resentment. The Left believed that if France adopted a liberal policy that adhered strictly to the principles of the League of Nations, and if it refrained from favouring the Catholics, it could reach an understanding with the Muslim majority. During his first six months in office Sarrail conducted a far more liberal policy towards the Muslims and Syrian nationalists than his predecessors had, in an attempt to gain their confidence. This hope proved to be naïve and short-sighted. France succeeded only in antagonising its most loyal supporters, without persuading the Syrian-Arab nationalists to moderate their stand, which became all too apparent in the summer of 1925 when they joined the Druze revolt against the French.[32]

The Maronites were deeply disturbed by Sarrail's attitude towards the Syrian-Arab nationalists. They watched him receive a steady stream of local and foreign-based nationalist delegations whose members had hitherto been banned as anti-French. Muslims in Lebanon were freely expressing their demands for union with Syria, and improving their relations with the French authorities at the same time. Leaflets calling for separation from Lebanon, which the French authorities did little to suppress, were distributed in Beirut. Reports and declarations by various French politicians further aggravated Maronite apprehensions. In a Chamber of Deputies debate of 31 January 1925 Henri Simon, rapporteur for the budget of the Ministry for Foreign Affairs, declared that it was a mistake to consider Greater Lebanon as being populated entirely by Maronites and to pursue a policy tending to favour the interests of the Maronites at the expense of the other elements.[33]

The Maronite Church made repeated attempts to steer the French back to their traditional policy. In all his contacts Hawayik never ceased to remind French officials of the historical ties between France and the Maronites, to emphasise to them how important Maronite support was for the continued presence of France in the region, and to warn them of the growing doubts and suspicions the new policies were awakening among France's supporters. By weakening the Maronites and strengthening the Muslims and Syrian nationalists, France was undermining its own position and interests. The letter to Herriot expressed these views clearly:

> Or la politique de M. le Haut-Commissaire, moins rassurante que ses paroles, risque de faire sombrer la cause du Liban au bénéfice de la cause qui fut vaincue à Meissaloun. Et c'est du sang français qui avait affermi pour toujours, pensions nous, la cause du Liban. Le plus vieil ami de la France en ce pays, j'estime que la politique du Haut-Commissaire, contrairement sans doute aux intentions de son ardent patriotisme, fait courir de sérieux dangers aux intérêts permanents de la France. Elle peut paraître grouper autour de sa personne d'anciens adversaires de la France. Permettez à un vieillard qui connaît son pays, de vous dire que ces adversaires se groupent non autour du mandat, mais contre les amis vrais du mandat.[34]

Despite Sarrail's reserved attitude towards the Maronites and the emphasis he laid on improving relations with the Muslims and Syrian nationalists, neither he nor Herriot intended to impair Lebanon's separate status or territorial integrity. On the contrary, Sarrail hoped to rapidly transform Lebanon from a divided sectarian country into a united and modern state, by introducing radical reforms based on secularist principles. During the first half of 1925 Sarrail and the energetic Cayla, to whom he gave a free hand in administrative matters, embarked upon an ambitious reform programme aimed at imposing Western secular political notions. Some of these reforms were no doubt specifically designed to weaken the influence of the Maronite clergy; but most of them simply aimed, however mistakenly, at transforming Lebanon into a viable state whose inhabitants would see themselves as citizens of a country rather than members of a particular Church or creed. Attempts to unify the tax systems of Mount Lebanon and the annexed areas and to involve the Muslims more in running the country were, in the long run, to Lebanon's advantage. But other reforms, such as those in the educational system, the administration and the electoral law, were far too radical for their time and further alienated the Maronites, who regarded them as a threat to their dominant position.[35]

Convinced of the need to weaken the influence of the clergy and to strengthen secularism as the basis for the Lebanese state, Cayla proposed to introduce a secular state educational system. As Lebanon was one country, he argued, it should have one unified system of education. Such a system would also improve educational opportunities for the Muslims, who had few schools of their own and resented having to send their children to Christian schools run by clergymen or missionaries. The Maronite Church, which had always been very sensitive to attempts to introduce secular education, strongly opposed Cayla's plan, regarding it as a fundamental threat to its influence and to the very existence of its community. The establishment of a state school system, it felt, might also cut into the financial support it was receiving for its own schools from the French authorities and from the Lebanese budget. The Church, together with the Catholic missionaries, launched a rigorous campaign against Cayla; it was led by Mubarak, bishop of Beirut, who actually refused to invite Cayla to High Mass on Easter Monday. Hawayik himself raised the issue at a meeting with Sarrail on 30 March, pointing out the importance of religious education in Lebanon and emphasising that by introducing secular education, France would merely weaken the Catholic elements, its most loyal supporters and the basis of its influence in the area. He raised the issue again at a meeting on 28 April with Cayla and de Reffye, the French secretary-general. Hawayik refused to accept Cayla's explanations and demanded a written commitment that he would avoid implementing his plan. Cayla vehemently refused, but Hawayik did succeed in obtaining a promise from de Reffye that financial support for the religious schools would not be affected by the introduction of state schools. As a result of all this opposition, very few of the educational reforms were actually put into practice.[36]

The project for radical administrative reform worked out by the governor in February and March 1925 had the same goal: to integrate the old and new regions of Lebanon. The existing administrative framework had been laid down in Decree No. 336 of 1 September 1920, which divided Lebanon into the Sanjaks of North Lebanon, Mount Lebanon, South Lebanon and the Beqa'a and the autonomous municipalities of Beirut and Tripoli. These boundaries maintained the existing confessional division between Mount Lebanon and the annexed areas and reflected de Caix's policy of avoiding fundamental changes. Cayla's new scheme proposed to divide Lebanon into eleven districts that cut across the old regional and sectarian lines. The reform was not limited to administration alone; it also applied to other areas such as the judicial and taxation systems, which were to be similarly readjusted. One objective was to cut administrative staff and expenditure. Describing the aims of the reform, Sarrail later wrote:

Des mesures préparatoires semblaient nécessaires pour amener le Grand Liban à sentir ce que le terme même de 'Mandat' signifait. Une des plus urgentes consistait à ne pas laisser face à face les anciennes circonscriptions administratives, qui dressaient le vieux Mont Liban maronite devant l'ancien municipe cosmopolite de Beyrouth, ou les régions essentiellement musulmanes de Tripoli et de la Bekaa. Une organisation administrative fusionnant une partie des populations des anciennes circonscriptions ottomanes fut, par suite, etudiée puis proposée par le Gouverneur de Grand Liban et finalement approuvée par le Haut Commissaire. Elle permettait en outre de faire coïncider l'organisation judiciaire nouvelle avec l'organisation administrative, ce qui jetait, pour l'amalgame, dans le même creuset, les populations des divers rites ayant chacune des charges et des privilèges spéciaux.[37]

But many Lebanese complained that comprehensive changes were being introduced without prior consultation with a properly elected body. The only body consulted was the Council of Directors, whose members had been appointed by the High Commission itself. There was also an outcry from officials who stood to lose their positions as the result of the new scheme. The strongest resistance came from the Maronite community and Church. Seeking to maintain the predominantly Christian character of Mount Lebanon, the Church opposed the incorporation of Christian areas of the Mountain with Muslim areas on the coast or in the Beqa'a Valley. At his meeting with Sarrail, Hawayik argued that this scheme, too, would weaken France's most loyal supporters. Nevertheless, the High Commission went ahead and on 9 April, in Decree No. 3066, the new administrative system was implemented.[38]

Maronite opposition during the following months centred mainly in Zghorta. This Maronite town had been the 'chef-lieu' of the Sanjak of North Lebanon; it was now to be united in one district with the Muslim town of Tripoli, which was to become the new administrative centre. Fearing the new plan would seriously affect the administrative and economic position of their own town, the

Maronite inhabitants filed repeated protests with the High Commission and the Quai d'Orsay; in mid-May they travelled in a convoy of 50 vehicles to Beirut, where they demanded to see Cayla; the governor refused to meet them. When questioned by the Quai d'Orsay, which had not been consulted on the reform, the high commissioner explained that Tripoli was better suited to be the administrative centre for the district, as it was larger and economically more important than Zghorta. He accused the Maronite clergy, particularly Bishop 'Abdullah al-Khuri, of instigating opposition among the inhabitants of the town. In the end, the French authorities were able to transfer the local administrative archives from Zghorta to Tripoli only after resorting to military force to overcome the opposition of the inhabitants.[39]

In their most ambitious step toward the removal of sectarian barriers and the introduction of a modern political system, Sarrail and Cayla proposed to modify the electoral law by abolishing confessional representation and replacing it by direct general representation. They argued that the existing arrangement increased religious and sectarian differences, giving rise to Muslim complaints of under-representation and Christian demands that a quarter of a million emigrants be included in the allocation of seats in parliament; the new Armenian group was not represented at all. The scheme would also do away with two-stage elections, in order to minimise bribery and corruption. Under the existing system, the small number of delegates in the second stage electoral colleges were open to influence by the various candidates. To forestall accusations that the Lebanese people were not consulted, a draft of the decree was published in local newspapers on 25 March, and the public was invited to comment. At the same time Cayla embarked on an intensive campaign to enlist Lebanese support for the reforms.[40]

The proposed electoral law was far too radical a revision of a basic and long-standing principle in the political life of Lebanon. It was received with strong reservations by both Christians and Muslims. Although some communities disputed the allocation of seats in the Representative Council, all of them supported confessional representation as the only way to guarantee that their voice would be heard and their interests preserved. The Maronites were the loudest in their opposition; fearing not only that their numbers on the Council might fall, but also that those opposed to the Lebanese state might win a majority and thus endanger Lebanon's independence and territorial integrity. The Maronite patriarch probably expressed the feelings of many when he accused the High Commission of introducing new laws too hastily and of treating Lebanon as a 'field for experiment', adding that 'by declaring a law one could not change the mentality of the people'.[41]

Over the following months the Quai d'Orsay and the French premier received many protests from Lebanon against the proposed electoral law. Neither Herriot nor the Foreign Ministry had been informed by Sarrail of his intention to introduce these reforms. They learned of them at the beginning of April when the issue was raised by a deputy following reports in the Lebanese and French press. Only after receiving an urgent dispatch from Paris demanding an explanation did Sarrail send details of his scheme and request the premier's approval. His initiative was criticised in the Quai d'Orsay as being contrary to Herriot's instructions of 13 February. In deliberations at the Quai d'Orsay, in which de Caix participated, it was argued that the previous law had enjoyed the full support of the Lebanese; instead of reducing inter-confessional conflict, the proposed system might have the opposite effect, as each community strove to protect its own interests and representation. It was also argued that the reforms might antagonise France's loyal supporters. It would be preferable to wait until the organic law was prepared and a Representative Council elected; the Council could then discuss any needed changes. The Quai d'Orsay's stand was accepted by the premier. Despite Sarrail's repeated attempts to persuade him to change his mind, Herriot firmly instructed the high commissioner to hold the elections according to the existing electoral laws.[42]

On 28 June the first stage of the elections for the Representative Council took place, followed two weeks later by the second stage. Although the French authorities had announced their intention to maintain a completely neutral stand, the elections were in fact manipulated by the High Commission, just as the previous elections had been three years before. The High Commission was anxious to secure a Council sympathetic to its policies, especially as it faced the important task of drafting an organic law, which would help define future relations between the mandatory power and the mandated territories. Cayla had his own reasons for seeking to ensure the election of sympathetic deputies, as he was anxious to secure his re-election as governor of Lebanon. He entrusted this task to Secretary-General Habib al-Sa'd, a reputed expert in arranging such matters. The activities of Cayla and Sa'd were conducted in such a controversial fashion that de Reffye complained in a private letter to

Berthelot that 'official pressure has never been greater'. De Reffye requested Berthelot's immediate intervention to put an end to 'this disgraceful conduct', warning that 'it will be with this discredited Council, elected without any freedom, from which the principal leaders of the country will be excluded as dangerous rivals, that we will have to form the organic law'.[43] Only 13 deputies from the former Council held on to their seats, as prominent Maronite politicians such as Emile Eddé failed to secure election. On the other hand, certain influential Sunni notables took a much more active role than they had in the previous elections; among those elected were 'Umar Da'uq and 'Umar Bayhum from Beirut and Khair a-Din 'Adra from Tripoli. These leaders were willing to co-operate with Sarrail's administration; they also realised that a Sunni boycott of the elections would be detrimental to their own and their community's interests.[44]

At its first meeting on 16 July the new Council elected Mussa Nammur, a Maronite from Zahle, as president, and 'Umar Da'uq as vice president. Shibl Dammus, a Greek Orthodox, and Yusuf al-Zein, a Mutawalli, were elected secretaries. One of the first resolutions expressed unanimous support for Sarrail and the French mandate. The Council had been expected to elect a native governor at once in accordance with Sarrail's declaration of six months before, but its members 'spontaneously' adopted a motion requesting that Cayla remain as governor until the organic law was prepared. Sarrail willingly complied with this request, a move which was criticised by the Quai d'Orsay.[45]

By the summer of 1925, relations between Sarrail and the Maronite Church and community had deteriorated into an open rift. The Maronites lacked any confidence in Sarrail's policies and reforms, which they regarded as pro-Muslim. On the other hand his relations with the Muslims in Lebanon and the Syrian nationalists had considerably improved. The Lebanese Sunnis were pleased to observe the strained relations between the high commissioner and the Maronites; they hoped to regain some of the positions and influence they had lost under the previous high commissioners. Sarrail's liberal attitude towards the Syrian nationalists encouraged them to feel that he might react more favourably to their own demands for union with Syria. They were therefore more willing to co-operate with the French administration than in the past, although their resentment of the Lebanese state remained undiminished.[46] Stability and security had considerably improved throughout the mandated territories. The High Commission was engaged in preparing the organic law, which it expected to complete by the following year in accordance with the terms of the mandate convention.

Within less than a month this apparently stable situation was shattered, as Syria and Lebanon were engulfed by a Druze revolt that shook the French mandate to its foundations and forced France into a thorough reconsideration of its policies. A description and analysis of the rebellion and its causes are outside the scope of this study, but the event had far-reaching consequences for France's policy in Syria and Lebanon, for relations between Lebanon and Syria, and for the final shape of the Lebanese Constitution of 1926. The revolt renewed the controversy over Lebanon's existence as an independent entity separate from the rest of Syria and revived French plans for the territorial reduction of Greater Lebanon. The revolt also confirmed a basic fact which remained valid throughout the mandate and after: the close link between Lebanese politics and the situation inside Syria.[47]

The events leading up to the Druze revolt exposed all the short-comings of Sarrail's policies, and bore the marks of his authoritarian character and tactlessness. Immediately after their arrival in Syria and Lebanon the French had recognised the need to gain the support of the Druze in Jabal Druze, one of the most warlike communities in Syria, and to separate them from the Syrian nationalists. On 4 March 1921 de Caix and Catroux had succeeded in concluding an agreement granting them a large measure of local autonomy with a minimum of French intervention in their affairs. But the death in September 1923 of Druze governor Salim al-Atrash and growing rivalry between local notables, led to the provisional appointment as governor of Captain Carbillet, the French adviser. Over the following 20 months the young officer tried to transform this backward feudal region into a modern developed society by imposing radical administrative, political, social and economic reforms, with little regard for the area's traditionally conservative character. In the course of his activities he antagonised many local notables, particularly the prominent Turshan family, by undermining their prestige and influence.[48]

During the first half of 1925 several delegations of notables from Jabal Druze went to Beirut to present Sarrail with their grievances against his delegate Carbillet, and to request his replacement by a native governor in accordance with the agreement of March 1921. Sarrail bluntly refused to see them, and even declared that the High

Commission had no record of any such understanding. When presented with a copy of the agreement, he stated that it was of historical value only and was in practical terms null and void. As Druze opposition to Carbillet and the French administration mounted Sarrail, in July, instructed his delegate to invite hostile notables to Damascus on the pretext of hearing their grievances. Upon their arrival they were arrested and imprisoned. This act sparked off the rebellion, which was declared in mid-July by Sultan al-Atrash, a young notable who had close ties with Syrian nationalists in Damascus. At this stage the uprising was still a local affair, as only a small faction of the Druze community rallied behind Sultan. But at the beginning of August Sarrail compounded his grave political mistake with a military blunder no less serious, when he sent an insufficiently prepared force commanded by General Michaud to advance on Suwaida, the region's capital. The defeat of this force on 3 August by Sultan al-Atrash greatly increased his prestige and transformed the rebellion at a stroke into a general uprising. It also prompted the Syrian nationalists to join the revolt, which they saw as an opportunity to drive the French out of Syria and to achieve by force the demands they had been unable to realise by political means.[49]

The revolt at first had little effect on Lebanon; if anything, it confirmed the feeling of particularism among Lebanese Christians and strengthened their determination not to get involved in the affairs of the rest of Syria. The anniversary of the establishment of the Lebanese state on 1 September was celebrated with exceptional enthusiasm as a demonstration of independence and loyalty to France. The Christians realised the benefits for their cause in the revolt, which would clearly put an end to Sarrail's attempts to reach an agreement with the Muslims. They enjoyed a certain feeling of satisfaction now that their warnings to the French about Muslim and Syrian nationalist unreliability had been borne out, and the Lebanese Christians had been shown to be the only loyal element on whom France could rely. The arrival in Beirut of wounded French soldiers, the publication of Sultan al-Atrash's national demands in the Egyptian press in August and the influx of Christian refugees from Damascus and the Houran caused some agitation; but it also served as proof that Lebanon was indeed the only secure refuge for Christians in the Levant.

In September, however, Christians in the Beqa'a Valley and in Wadi al-Taym in the south-east of Lebanon grew increasingly apprehensive about possible attacks by bands of rebels or by their own Druze neighbours. They appealed to the French for arms and for protective forces. Sarrail, who still regarded the revolt as a merely local affair, tried to calm them, sending a small force of French and Lebanese gendarmes to the region, and distributing a small quantity of arms among the Christian villages. By October, however, the defeats suffered by the French forces, the reports of a Druze advance towards Mount Hermon and Wadi al-Taym and the fear of a Druze uprising in Lebanon itself greatly alarmed the Lebanese Christians; they began to lose their confidence in the ability of the French forces to protect them.[50]

Early in November Lebanon became directly involved in the uprising. In his memoirs, Sultan al-Atrash claimed that from September he had been receiving appeals for assistance from the Druze of Mount Hermon and Wadi al-Taym, who reported that the French were disarming them and distributing their weapons to their Christian neighbours. Local French officers may in fact have taken such a step to deter the Druze from joining the rebels or attacking the Christians. The Druze leaders of Jabal Druze had always felt responsible for the fate of their brethren in Lebanon, but they now had additional political and military reasons for coming to their aid. By the beginning of October it was clear that the planned joint operation with Syrian nationalists to attack Damascus could not be carried out. This made it possible to concentrate the main Druze forces for an attack on Wadi al-'Ajam, Mount Hermon and south Lebanon. The occupation of these regions would have given the rebels control over important routes between Damascus, Quneitra and Marjayoun; they could then have advanced north in the Beqa'a Valley to cut off the main Beirut-Damascus road and railway, which were vital to the French. Moreover, by invading Lebanon and threatening the centre of French influence in Beirut, they would have obliged the French to divert forces from other areas in the interior. The occupation of Mount Hermon and Wadi al-Taym would have also enabled the rebels to fill out their ranks with local Druze, and would have brought them into direct contact with the Druze of Mount Lebanon and the Mutawallis in Jabal 'Amel and the Beqa'a Valley, thus enabling them to instigate a revolt in those areas. Sultan al-Atrash and other Druze leaders may have harboured ideas of establishing a large autonomous entity to encompass all the Druze centres from Jabal Druze, through Mount Hermon and Wadi al-Taym to the southern part of Mount

Lebanon. Whatever their ultimate objectives, a force of over 1,000 men, led by Zayd al-Atrash, Sultan's brother, advanced to Wadi al-'Ajam and Mount Hermon in October; by the end of the month they had taken over the whole region, including Majdal Shams, the main Druze centre in Mount Hermon, and were poised to attack south Lebanon.[51]

Both Sultan al-Atrash and the Syrian nationalist leaders headed by Shahbandar were aware of the potential danger in invading mixed Christian-Druze areas of Lebanon. They were anxious to forestall any outbreak of religious or sectarian conflict, as they aimed to present the rebellion to the League of Nations and to the public in Europe, particularly in France, as a national uprising against the mandate supported by the majority of the population. They also sought to discredit any claim that a French presence was necessary to protect the Christian minorities in Syria and Lebanon. After entering south Lebanon, Zayd issued a declaration to the Christians assuring them that his forces were engaged in a national and not a sectarian conflict, and that the attacks were directed only against the French and their supporters. He invited the Christians to join the common national cause, stressing that 'religion belongs to God, the motherland to all'.[52]

But the genuine desire of the Druze and the nationalist leaders to prevent a confrontation with the Lebanese Christians was to prove impossible to fulfil. Relations between the Christians and the Druze in Wadi al-Taym were already tense, and Zayd's forces consisted of irregular and ill-disciplined bands. Shortly after invading Lebanon, they and their local Druze supporters came into conflict with the Christians. On 10 November Zayd's forces occupied Hasbaya, the main Druze centre in the area, without opposition; they announced the formation of a provisional government there. The following day a Druze band led by Hamza Darwish, one of the rebel chiefs, attempted to take over the nearby Maronite village of Kawkaba. Its inhabitants opposed them. About 30 Christians were killed in the ensuing fight, and most of the houses were looted and set on fire after the women and children had been evacuated. This was precisely what Sultan al-Atrash and the nationalist leaders had sought to avoid. Zayd and local Druze notables attempted to calm the panic-stricken Christians; they delayed their advance on Marjayoun for five days at a crucial time for the French forces. When the town was finally occupied, the strictest precautions were taken to prevent a repetition of the Kawkaba incident, to avoid further sectarian conflict. Zayd even allowed the Lebanese gendarmerie to leave the town unharmed, and appointed a Christian as head of the local 'National Committee' which was formed to administer the liberated area.[53]

Zayd's efforts, however, had little effect on the Lebanese Christians, and within a short time the news of the incident at Kawkaba had spread panic throughout Lebanon. It revived memories of the massacre in Hasbaya in 1860, when about 1,000 Christians were massacred by the Druze. Thousands of Christians fled from their villages in the region and sought refuge in Zahle, Sidon, Beirut and northern Palestine. The Christians in Mount Lebanon and Beirut were so frightened of a Druze invasion and of an uprising of the Druze in the Shuf that General Duport, the acting high commissioner, and General Gamelin, the commander of the French forces, met with Hawayik and other Maronite bishops in an attempt to calm them, assuring them that France would protect the Christians. A vivid description of Lebanese Christian fears during this period is given by 'Atiyah:

> At Suk-al-Garb the scare mounted from day to day. The Druses in arms, in spite of the lapse of sixty-five years, were the Druses of 1860. An atavistic state of mind sprang into being . . . stories of atrocities against Christians of the inland villages began to circulate, recalling the most hideous incidents of the great massacre. Wild rumours arrived at the village every day; the Druses were advancing, bands of them had been seen in the valley, armed and desperate; they might attack the village any night. The scare grew. Groups of villagers stood about the market place every evening and every morning discussing the news. Even the sophisticated people from Beirut grew alarmed. It became a brave thing to wander about the village at night. In every house, every evening, people talked of nothing else. The old men of the village came with harrowing tales, sat around and reminisced again about 1860. The sophisticated people from Beirut decided that the mountains had become too unsafe. The French did not have sufficient forces. The Druses were beating them everywhere. . . It was safer to move to Beirut. They began to move.[54]

The Druze invasion of south Lebanon placed the French in a very difficult position; reports from the High Commission for a few days in mid-November described the situation as 'grave' and even 'critical'. At this stage sufficient French reinforcements had not yet arrived. Most of the French forces were engaged in containing local uprisings in the interior, leaving the whole of south Lebanon practically devoid of troops. Thus when Zayd's forces threatened to advance northwards through the Beqa'a Valley towards Ryak or Mount Lebanon and Beirut, the French had only a very limited force to oppose them. Small forces were sent to Jezzine, Beit a-Din, Tyre and Nabatiya and the Litani bridges. Arms were distributed to the Christians in Jezzine, where the Druze rebels were expected to launch their attack. Defence posts were dug and cannons installed in the mountains around Beirut. At the same time two French gunboats were sent to Sidon to protect the Christians and to deter an uprising by the Mutawallis. Two American destroyers went to Beirut at the beginning of November to protect American citizens, but an Italian request to be allowed to do likewise was turned down by the French government.[55]

Lack of French forces and the increase in rebel activities led the French to distribute arms among the Christians and to enlist volunteers. In October and November a campaign was conducted in the Lebanese Christian press with the encouragement of the High Commission calling upon the Christians to volunteer for the defence of their country and of their brethren in the south. A force of a few hundred Christian auxiliaries was formed under the command of Butrus Karam, a Maronite from north Lebanon. After the Kawkaba incident these troops were sent to Marjayoun to defend the Christians there; in fact, they engaged mainly in harassing local Druze inhabitants, and after a few skirmishes with Zayd's forces they were forced to retreat. Later on the French used these irregulars against rebel bands in the Beqa'a Valley and Jabal 'Akrun to the east of Tripoli. Volunteers were enlisted from other minority groups, especially the Kurds, the Circassians and the Armenians, and formed into irregular units, often under direct French command. Their activities roused much controversy and they were frequently accused of being involved more in looting, brigandage and harassment of the local population than in fighting the rebels.[56]

The arming of Christian and other minority volunteers against the rebels increased Muslim-Christian tension and led to nationalist accusations that the French were deliberately exacerbating the religious and sectarian conflict as part of a policy of 'divide and rule'. The support given by many Lebanese Christians and Armenians to the French made them natural targets for nationalist and Muslim hostility.[57] In a letter to the British and American consuls shortly after the Kawkaba incident, Sultan al-Atrash denied attacking the Christians and accused the French of undermining Muslim-Christian relations:

> Their evil deeds have even harmed some of our Christian brethren by the fact that they (the French) distributed arms to some of these Christians that they might rise against us. These Christians became arrogant and started to oppose our armies who were advancing against the enemy. We have proved, in numerous places where our armies entered, that we do not attack any peaceful persons, because we are all brethren in humanity and Syria is for the Syrians, no matter of whatever religion or sect they may be.[58]

The Muslim communities in Lebanon, who feared attack by armed Christians, were also resentful and apprehensive. A deputation of Druze notables went to Beirut to protest to the French authorities. Growing criticism in Syria and Lebanon, and the unfavourable reaction of the Quai d'Orsay to reports in the French and foreign press, led the High Commission to cease arming the Christians, but the use of irregular forces from minority groups continued throughout the rebellion.[59]

The Druze in Lebanon were placed in a difficult position by the uprising in Jabal Druze. Their natural tendency to support their brethren was encouraged by some influential notables such as 'Adel Arslan and Rashid Tali'a, who took an active part in the revolt. Hundreds of young Druze did indeed leave their villages in Mount Lebanon to join the rebels. But many Druze notables feared that their own positions and their community's relations with both the French and the Christians would suffer if they identified completely with the rebels. Living near the centre of French influence, they were aware of France's strength and its ability to mobilise forces against the insurgents. Some, particularly the Junblats and certain members of the Arslan family, especially Fu'ad and Tawfik, cautiously refrained from openly supporting the revolt. They took note of French precautionary measures, which included warnings against supporting the rebels and the preparation of lists of those who had joined them. In an attempt to prevent outbreaks of sectarian violence between Druze and Christians in Mount Lebanon, the French were organising meetings and mediating between notables of the two groups. In fact, most Druze and Christian notables did try to ward off sectarian confrontation; despite increasing tension, they succeeded during the first few months in doing so.[60]

Sectarian conflict in Mount Lebanon would have been inevitable had the rebels invaded the area. Immediately after the attack on Kawkaba, Amin Arslan and two other notables went to Hasbaya to meet Zayd al-Atrash and learn details of the incident. They brought a letter from Fu'ad Arslan, a member of the Lebanese Representative Council, requesting Zayd to refrain from invading Mount Lebanon. It is not clear whether the Druze forces had indeed planned such an operation, although they would undoubtedly have liked to provoke an uprising in the Druze centres of Shuf and al-Matn, and strengthen their ranks with thousands of Druze from that area. However the Kawkaba incident, the wide publicity it received and the strong reaction of the Lebanese Christians illustrated the dangers implicit in any invasion of a mixed Christian-Druze area. Consequently, in his reply on 13 November Zayd al-Atrash assured Fu'ad Arslan that his forces would not advance on Mount Lebanon.[61]

After occupying Marjayoun on 16 November Zayd's forces moved northwards from Hasbaya, aiming to capture Rayak, cut off the road and railway between Beirut and Damascus, and eventually join up with rebel bands near Ba'albek and Nabk. The only real obstacle was the town of Rashaya; its citadel, originally a palace built by the Shihabi emirs, was defended by a garrison of a few hundred French soldiers, Lebanese gendarmerie and Christian inhabitants. From 20 to 24 November the town became the scene of one of the fiercest battles of the revolt. The Druze suffered heavy casualties and the town was almost completely destroyed. The French garrison was relieved by French reinforcements from Rayak and Nabatiya and the Druze were forced back to Hasbaya. This was the first major Druze defeat, and it marked a turning point in the whole rebellion. The threat to Lebanon and to the vital network of roads and railways in the Beqa'a Valley was removed, while the French gained the time they needed to ship reinforcements from France. At the beginning of December French forces opened their counter-offensive. On the 5th of the month they recaptured Hasbaya after prolonged shelling and a fierce battle which forced the insurgents and most of the town's Druze inhabitants to flee to Majdal Shams. Two days later Mutawalli notables in Jabal 'Amel declared their support for the mandate, and shortly afterwards a delegation of Lebanese Druze went to Beirut to express their allegiance to the French authorities.[62]

The Druze invasion of south Lebanon, and indeed the whole revolt, had serious repercussions on sectarian relations within Lebanon and on relations between Lebanese Christians and Syrian nationalists. The invasion, and the continued activities of rebel bands in the Beqa'a Valley during most of the following year, caused widespread destruction in the area from Marjayoun in the south to Ba'albek in the north. In all, 108 Christians were killed, nearly 1,200 Christian homes in various villages were destroyed or damaged (429 in Rashaya and 136 in Kawkaba) and about 10,000 Christians became refugees. The Lebanese Christians, encouraged by their press and by an organisation of refugees from Rashaya and Kawkaba, raised an outcry every time the French authorities talked about a general amnesty for the Druze rebels. They demanded their punishment and the imposition of heavy fines to compensate the Christians who had suffered. But the Druze inhabitants had also suffered greatly. As the region was being reoccupied by French forces, Druze villages were heavily shelled; there were cases of looting and acts of revenge by French colonial forces and returning Christians, despite strict orders from the high commissioner. Most of the Druze inhabitants fled to Mount Hermon or northern Palestine.[63]

The growing tension between Druze and Christians, fanned by instigation from outside, finally led at the end of March 1926 to an outbreak of hostilities in the Shuf and Matn districts; the disorders continued until the summer, leaving scores of victims on both sides. Only after much effort did the French authorities succeed in restoring law and order. At the same time, tension was rapidly building up between Maronites and Sunnis, as the latter renewed their campaign for union with Syria. Commenting on the repercussions of the Druze invasion of Lebanon, Mayers, the British acting consul-general in Beirut, wrote:

> Thus out of the far-off revolt in their mountain of the chieftains of the Druses has come the re-awakening of the ancient enmity between Christianity and Islam and a restatement in all its acuteness of the separate individuality of the Lebanon.[64]

The Druze revolt highlighted once more the basic political and cultural differences between the Lebanese Christians, who aspired to an independent Christian state under French protection with close ties with the West, and the Syrian-Arab nationalists who demanded a united Syrian state completely independent of foreign rule. As in the period between 1918 and 1920, Syrian nationalists regarded the Lebanese Christians as traitors who opposed the national aspirations of the majority of the inhabitants of the region; it was they who were chiefly responsible for the French presence and the consequent division of Syria. Nationalists resented both active Christian support of French forces against the rebels, and the declarations of Christian leaders like Hawayik that the uprising showed the need for an independent Greater Lebanon as a base for French influence. Their hostility was further provoked by the vociferous and often offensive campaign in the Christian press against the rebels and their demands, particularly the call for a united Syria. One newspaper, for example, described this demand as 'the goal of ignorant Syrian fanatics'; another declared that the Lebanese had no liking for Syrian unity because '. . . they are the apostles of Western culture, while Syrian union turns its step towards the East'; a third paper argued: 'What prevents the Lebanese from joining the Syrian Union is that most Syrians, however various their aspirations may be, grope in the darkness of a mortal ignorance and are more like Beduins than really civilised people.'[65]

The Lebanese Christians were convinced that the invasion of south Lebanon and the activities of the rebel bands in the Beqa‘a Valley and around Tripoli were directed not only against the French, but against Lebanon's very existence and territorial integrity. They pointed to the demands of the Syrian nationalist leaders during the rebellion that the areas annexed to Lebanon in 1920 be returned, and to the Lebanese Muslim campaign for union with Syria. A resolution adopted on 30 November 1925 by the Representative Council (with two Sunni and two Druze deputies dissenting) thanked France for defending the independence and territorial integrity of Lebanon against the rebels. The Council of Directors also expressed its gratitude to the 'heroes of Rashaya' for defending Lebanese territory against the 'foreign bands', while Hawayik wrote to Cayla requesting that medals be struck in honour of those who had defended the 'Lebanese fatherland' from outside aggression.[66]

The Lebanese Christians were not alone in making such accusations; many French officials, including General Duport, the acting high commissioner, General Gamelin, and Secretary-General de Reffye, were equally convinced that rebel activity on Lebanese soil was directed against Lebanon's independence and territorial integrity. A French official who had been sent by the Quai d'Orsay to Syria and Lebanon in November on a mission of inquiry wrote:

> En ce moment nous assistons à la guerre de la Syrie contre le Liban. Vous le savez, les Syriens demandent l'unité de la Syrie en y comprenant les territoires qui ont été rattachés par nous au Grand Liban. Ces territoires se trouvent dans le Liban Sud, dans la plaine de la Bekaa, entre le Liban et l'Anti-Liban, et au Nord du Liban, autour du Tripoli. Nous avons donc eu une triple offensive des bandes de Soltan Attrache. Dans le Liban Sud, attaque sur Merdjayoun, Hasbaya, Rachaya. Elle avait pour but de rallier les populations Chiites et Métoualis du Liban Sud; de marcher avec elles sur le Nord en entraînant tous les Druzes de la montagne et d'attaquer Beyrouth. En même temps une offensive se prononçait au Nord en direction de Baalbek terre 'irrédente' de la Syrie et au Sud de Homs pour attaquer la trouée de Homs à Tripoli habitée par des musulmans. Si elle avait réussi, le parti extrémiste syrien aurait pu se targuer de ce succès pour demander l'annexion à la Syrie des territoires que ses troupes auraient occupés. Vous voyez donc qu'il ne s'agit pas seulement de brigands et de pillards mais qu'il y a derrière les révoltes une intelligence qui les guide vers un but désigné d'avance et qui utilise à son profit les liens religieux et les habitudes de pillage des habitants.[67]

Such accusations, one might claim, were grossly exaggerated. The Lebanese Christians were always suspicious of the Syrian nationalists, and French officials were only too happy to attribute such motives to the rebels. But the fact remains that during the first half of 1926, Syrian territorial claims to the annexed areas were a major cause of Jouvenel's failure to reach an agreement on a peaceful end to the rebellion. By the summer of 1926 many Frenchmen, including Jouvenel, and many foreign observers, genuinely believed that the territorial issue was an important factor in the intensification of the uprising. Samné reflected this belief when he wrote:

> S'il n'est pas certain que la question des frontières ait été la cause dominante de l'insurrection druse, elle a probablement contribué à l'éterniser. Mais d'autre part, il est manifeste que cette question des frontières a été un des motifs essentiels de la

rébellion damasquine et de toutes les agitations qui se sont produites depuis un an au-delà du pays druse. Cette opinion n'est pas seulement la mienne; c'est encore celle de tous les Français, militaires et civils, fonctionnaires et simples particuliers, qui ont séjourné au Levant ces derniers mois et qui ont cherché à comprendre les événements donts ils ont été les témoins impartiaux, désintéressés et totalement dépourvus de passion et de préjugé.[68]

However, before determining whether the Syrian nationalist leaders did exploit the Druze rebellion to further their demands to the areas annexed to Lebanon in 1920, it is worth while to examine briefly the origin of the territorial dispute between Syria and Lebanon. As part of their campaign for a united Syria, the Syrian nationalists argued that if the Maronites did not wish to be part of a Syrian union, they should restore to Syria all the territories annexed to Mount Lebanon and return to their pre-war borders. They were particularly anxious for the restoration of the fertile Beqa'a Valley and the port of Tripoli. The former was regarded as an integral part of Syria, forcibly detached by the French and annexed to Lebanon after having been part of the vilayet of Damascus for centuries and of the Syrian state under Faisal from 1918 to 1920. Like Faisal before them, the Syrian nationalists considered access to the sea to be of vital importance for Syria, which had been cut off from the coast following the establishment of the Lebanese and 'Alawite states and the autonomous Sanjak of Alexandretta. They saw Tripoli as the natural port for the interior; throughout the mandate period they repeatedly demanded its annexation to Syria. To reinforce their demands they pointed out that the majority of the inhabitants of these areas themselves supported attachment to Syria. As for the coastal area and Jabal 'Amel, their future should be decided by a plebiscite among the inhabitants, who could choose whether to be part of Syria or of Lebanon.[69]

The Syrian nationalists faced a continual dilemma in pursuing these territorial demands, as they were also seeking to gain the support of the Lebanese Christians in a common struggle for the complete independence of all the mandated territories. They believed that France was exploiting the Lebanese Christian desire for French protection as a pretext for maintaining a base in Lebanon from which all of Syria could be dominated. They were well aware of the mounting pressure in France for the evacuation of Syria, but were concerned that the moral obligation felt by many Frenchmen toward the Lebanese Christians would keep the French government from bowing to that pressure and giving up its mandate. Throughout the mandate period they strove to persuade the Lebanese Christians to relinquish their demand for French protection and to seek complete independence. Toward that end, they followed a cautious approach on the territorial issue to avoid antagonising the Christians. This can be seen in the resolutions adopted by the Syro-Palestine Congress in Geneva in 1921 and 1922, which defined Arab national goals in the wake of the French occupation of Syria. The resolutions intentionally refrained from raising the issue of Lebanon's borders, preferring to stress the demand for complete independence from France for both Syria and Lebanon. Moreover, like Faisal before them, many Syrian nationalists realised that if the heavily Muslim areas were detached from Lebanon, the small, mainly Christian Lebanese state that remained would be closely linked to the West and would be completely lost to the Arab Muslim world. On various occasions nationalist leaders used the territorial issue as a bargaining point to pressure the Christians into severing their close ties with France. In the end, when the Lebanese Christians finally relinquished their demand for continued French protection and sought complete independence during the Second World War, the Syrians dropped their territorial demands and recognised Lebanon's existing borders, at least *de facto*, as part of the deal.[70]

However, it took more than 20 years of Greater Lebanon's separate existence, and a radical change in Christian attitudes towards France, before the Syrian nationalists relinquished their territorial claims. In the early years of the mandate, the status of the annexed areas generated strong resentment against the French and the Lebanese Christians among the Syrian nationalists, the commercial sectors and the Muslim masses in Syria. Syrian leaders repeatedly demanded the restoration of the Beqa'a Valley and Tripoli to the Syrian state. Early in 1923, during the agitation in Tripoli for union with Syria, Subhi Barakat, head of the Syrian federation, visited the town, while Syrian leaders threatened to raise the issue at the League of Nations. Syrian nationalists both in Syria and abroad continually encouraged the Muslims in Lebanon to request their attachment to Syria. In May 1923 Ibrahim Hananu, a prominent Syrian nationalist, visited Beirut and Tripoli to discuss with Sunni notables a co-ordinated campaign for a united Syria. Immediately after Sarrail's arrival, delegations from Damascus and Aleppo came to

Beirut to present their demands for a united Syria, to include all the areas annexed to Lebanon in 1920. The same demand appeared in the programme of the Hizb al-Sh'ab, which was formed by Shahbandar in February with the participation of Muslim delegates from Lebanon.[71]

On 23 August 1925, a month after the outbreak of the rebellion, Sultan al-Atrash issued a proclamation in his capacity as 'president of the provisional national government', demanding complete independence for Syria, the evacuation of foreign forces and the establishment of a united Syrian Arab state 'from the coast to the interior'. The Syrian nationalists saw the Druze revolt as an opportunity to instigate widespread uprisings against the French as a means of forcing them to either evacuate the mandated territories altogether or to make concessions to Arab national aspirations. By occupying the Beq'a Valley, or at least by creating trouble there and in the Tripoli area, they hoped to force the French to restore these regions to Syria. Like Faisal before them, they also hoped that such disorders, particularly within Lebanon, would demonstrate to the Christians that France was unable either to protect them or to guarantee their independence and territorial integrity. In this way, they would be persuaded to relinquish their request for French protection and reach an understanding with the Syrians.[72]

Apart from the invasion of South Lebanon by Zayd al-Atrash's forces, the tactics adopted by the rebels were similar to those used by Faisal and the Syrian extremists in the Western Zone in 1919 and 1920. They encouraged armed bands of local supporters, as well as other bands from the interior, to engage in guerrilla warfare against the French, who found it extremely difficult to deal with such activity. The bands operated mainly in three areas: the southern Beqa'a, the central and northern Beq'a around Ba'albek, and Jabal 'Akrun. Following the forced retreat of Zayd's forces, Druze bands continued to act against French forces in the south from bases in Majdal Shams and Mount Hermon. Even after these areas were occupied by French forces early in April 1926, Druze bands led by 'Adel Arslan and Shekib Wahab continued to harass the French. Only a large-scale French operation in July and August forced them to flee. In the area around Ba'albek rebel military and political activity was co-ordinated by the Haider family; Tawfik Haider headed one band which harassed the French in the Beqa'a and the Anti-Lebanon on into 1926. In Jabal 'Akrun and 'Akkar, a band under Zein Muhi Ja'far, a Mutawalli, was responsible for most of

the rebel activity, which extended in the summer of 1926 to the outskirts of Tripoli, undermining security throughout the region.[73]

In addition to this military pressure, Syrian nationalists in Syria
and abroad used every meeting with the French, particularly with
Jouvenel, the new high commissioner, to reiterate their demand for
the restoration of the annexed areas. Shortly after his appointment
in November 1925, Jouvenel invited Shekib Arslan to Paris in order
to hear the nationalists' conditions for ending the revolt and reaching an agreement with France. Among these conditions, he learned,
was complete independence for Syria and Lebanon and a plebiscite
in the areas annexed to Lebanon to determine whether the inhabitants wished to be part of the Syrian or of the Lebanese state. At a
meeting with Jouvenel in Cairo on 30 November, the Executive
Committee of the Syro-Palestine Congress, headed by Michel
Lutf'allah, demanded *inter alia* the return of Lebanon to its pre-war
borders. In December and January, during negotiations in Beirut
between Jouvenel and the Syrian nationalists over the formation of
a Syrian government, a similar demand was made by Sheikh Taj
a-Din Hasani, to whom Jouvenel offered the position of head of the
Syrian state. Toynbee, in fact, claims that the territorial issue was
'the most serious stumbling block' in the negotiations; he blames the
refusal to comply with this request as 'perhaps the principal cause of
M. de Jouvenel's failure to overcome the hostility of the Sunnis and
the Druzes'.[74]

During the uprising, the demand for union of the annexed areas to
Syria was raised not only by the Syrian nationalists, but also by
Muslim inhabitants of those areas, particularly the Sunnis. From
the end of 1925 until the summer of 1926 a wave of intensive pro-
Syrian activity, unprecedented since 1920, spread throughout the
coastal area. Petitions were sent to the High Commission, the
French government and the League of Nations, commercial strikes
were organised, numerous meetings of notables and leaders were
held and articles supporting union with Syria were published in the
Muslim press. This agitation was a direct consequence of the strong
nationalist feeling generated throughout the mandated territories by
the revolt. The Muslims on the coast, who did not take up arms to
demonstrate active resistance to the French mandate, saw these
political activities as their own contribution to the national uprising.
They were encouraged to raise the level of protest against the
Lebanese state by the changing of high commissioners and the
ongoing work on the Lebanese Constitution. As in the past, each

change of high commissioner was seen by the Muslims as an opportunity to present their aspirations for union with Syria, in the hope that the new high commissioner would be more receptive to their demands. Shortly after his arrival Jouvenel was greeted by a delegation of Sunni notables who presented him with a detailed memorandum specifying their grievances against the Lebanese state. Attached to the memorandum were petitions signed by notables and religious leaders from Beirut, Tripoli, Sidon, Tyre and Ba'albek requesting separation from Lebanon and union with the Syrian federation. The drawing up of the Lebanese Constitution, as we shall see, also generated strong resentment among the Muslims; during the first half of 1926 it became a main focus for their opposition to the Lebanese state.[75]

This agitation was not always spontaneous. Much of it was coordinated and encouraged by new national committees in the coastal towns and in Ba'albek. The committees maintained close ties with the rebel leaders in Jabal Druze, with the nationalists in Damascus and with groups outside Syria, particularly the Syro-Palestine Committees in Egypt and Palestine. The Syrian nationalists worked to encourage these activities, as they strengthened Syrian claims to the annexed areas and demonstrated to the French public and the League of Nations that the residents of these areas were totally opposed to the French mandate. France, the mandatory power, was, after all, obliged to act in accordance with the wishes of the local population. Muslim leaders and nationalists in Beirut, especially Ri'ad al-Sulh and Amin Arslan, urged the Syrian leaders not to compromise on the Lebanese issue, as they feared they were doing in the negotiations between Sheikh Taj a-Din and his fellow-delegates and Jouvenel in Beirut in December 1925 and January 1926. Their main fear was that Syria might be content to gain the Beqa'a Valley and Tripoli, thus leaving the Muslims of the coast in a weaker position *vis-à-vis* the French and the Lebanese Christians. The uncompromising stand of these Muslims often forced the Syrian nationalists to adopt a more extreme position than they might otherwise have done on the question of the annexed areas. The French delegate in Lebanon even warned Jouvenel that 'the Sunnis in Beirut are today . . . the secret leaders of the Syrian revolutionary movements'.[76] The charge was perhaps somewhat exaggerated, but it contained more than a grain of truth. Living near the centre of French power, the Sunni Muslims of Beirut were in an excellent position to gauge the policies and intentions of the high commissioner.

The information and advice they were able to offer the Syrian nationalists was of undoubted value and enabled them to exert an indirect influence on the nationalist position.

During the first two months of the revolt the French government and public failed to grasp the seriousness of the situation, as Sarrail's dispatches were vague and inaccurate. Sarrail regarded the revolt as a local uprising. He was determined to suppress it quickly in order to prevent further criticism in France of his administration. The gravity of the situation became known in France only through foreign (especially British) newspaper reports. By October 1925, when the rebellion had already engulfed Jabal Druze and a large part of Syria, Sarrail was sending urgent dispatches requesting reinforcements. As expected, the news of the events in Syria roused strong criticism of Sarrail and his policies in the National Assembly and the French press. After the shelling of Damascus in the middle of October and the ensuing outcry, Briand, the new premier, was forced to act quickly. On 30 October he recalled Sarrail to Paris.[77]

The revolt came as a surprise and a bitter disappointment to the French government and public. It had been hoped that after the efforts of the previous years a stable and acceptable *modus vivendi* had been established, and that French policy in the mandated territories had finally found the right path. Instead, France found itself once more involved in a large and costly military operation which coincided with an economic crisis so severe that it led to the downfall of three governments in 1925 and 1926. The renewed troubles in Syria and Lebanon and the large expenditure they necessitated, revived resentment and opposition in France to the Syrian mandate, and led to a growing demand that the area be abandoned and the mandate returned to the League of Nations. The wide publicity and controversy which the revolt generated in the French and international press was a constant source of embarrassment to the French government. Despite strong criticism within France, Briand, who had formed a new government in November, reaffirmed in a National Assembly debate that France had no intention of relinquishing the mandate over Syria and Lebanon and would continue to fulfil its obligations as the mandatory power. But the revolt did lead the French government to re-examine its whole Syrian policy. Briand, who was determined to end the rebellion speedily, adopted policies far more liberal than had prevailed in the past. He decided to appoint a civilian high commissioner, as he was convinced that the recent events demonstrated that 'military men are suited to a particular task, and it was wrong to involve them in civil administration'.[78]

For this difficult task Briand chose Henry de Jouvenel, senator, journalist, editor of *Le Matin*, member of the Senate Commission for Foreign Affairs and the 'Groupe de la Gauche Démocratique', and a former delegate to the League of Nations. Jouvenel served for only six months, but his term covered one of the most crucial periods of the French mandate, both militarily and politically. Jouvenel and his supporters would later point to his many achievements during this short time: the ending of the revolt, the holding of elections and establishment of local governments, the opening of a dialogue with the Syrian nationalists and the granting of a constitution to Lebanon. On the debit side, his critics accused him of being naïve and opportunistic; they claimed that despite his numerous actions he accomplished very little of lasting value, and that his successor had to modify many of his reforms and rulings. Jouvenel in fact faced an extremely difficult task, as Sarrail had left the mandated territories in total disarray. The rebellion had spread throughout the region as the French lost any trust they may have enjoyed among the Druze and Syrian nationalists. Jouvenel was under constant pressure from the French government to end this embarrassing situation and achieve immediate results. Pressure also came from the Mandates Commission, which met in February, June and November 1926 to examine the operation of the French mandate in Syria following the rebellion. In addition, the September 1926 deadline for the completion of the organic law was rapidly approaching. The new high commissioner used a combination of skilful diplomacy and military pressure in his efforts to restore France's credibility in the mandated territories. He himself was convinced that France should not renounce the mandate over Syria and Lebanon, but he believed that the only way to retain it was not through military force but by reaching an understanding with the Syrian nationalists and the Muslim majority. He advocated the conclusion of a treaty with Syria similar to the Anglo-Iraqi Treaty of 1922, the granting of self-government to Syria and the adoption of a more positive attitude towards the nationalist demands for Syrian unity. In a private letter on the question of whether to retain the mandate, Jouvenel wrote:

> Notre première et très grave erreur est de sousestimer ces élites et surtout leurs chefs. Le parti du peuple comprend des personnalités de très haute valeur qu'on a injustement qualifiées de pseudo-intellectuels et d'apprentis politiques.

Chabendhar, Kurd'ali, Emir Takr, les Arslan etc . . . ne méritent pas ce désobligeant qualificatif, Chabendhar en particulier qui serait peut-être le Mustapha Kemal ou le Zougloul de la Syrie.[79]

Faced with the repeated Syrian nationalist demands for the return of the annexed areas and with the vociferous opposition of the Muslims inside these areas to the Lebanese state, Jouvenel came to believe that a solution to the territorial issue acceptable to the Arab nationalists was essential if an overall agreement with the Muslims was to be achieved. Throughout 1926 various French plans were aired for the territorial reduction of Lebanon. As in 1921 and 1922 these plans roused strong resentment among the Lebanese Christians, and helped to create an atmosphere of tension and suspicion at the very time the constitution was being drawn up.

Like de Caix before him, Jouvenel saw the detachment of Tripoli from Lebanon and its annexation to Syria as the first priority. Shortly after his arrival in Beirut, French officials began to stress the need for such a move in their talks with the Christians. At a meeting in December with a Maronite delegation from Zghorta which had come to request the restoration of their town as the administrative centre of its district, Jouvenel declared that 'he himself was not at all opposed to the attachment of Tripoli to Syria and that he would willingly accept such a request if it came from the Maronite patriarch'.[80] Jouvenel, well aware of the Maronite Church's strong opposition to previous French attempts to detach Tripoli, was clearly hoping that the patriarch would reconsider his stand in light of the revolt and the agitation within that city.

At the beinning of January 1926 Jouvenel sent Privat-Aubouard, the former governor of Lebanon, on a mission to Tripoli

'. . . en vue de fixer la valeur du mouvement de l'opinion publique tendant d'une part au détachement de l'Etat du Grand Liban de la ville de Tripoli et de ses environs à majorité sunnite, d'autre part à l'annexation de ce territoire à l'Etat de Syrie.[81]

From 13 to 16 January Privat-Aubouard met with prominent notables and leaders in Tripoli, al-Mina and 'Akkar in order to find out what was behind the recent demonstrations and to determine the aspirations of the local inhabitants. He interviewed a small number of notables who advocated annexation to Syria, but refrained from meeting 'Abd al-Hamid Karami, the former kadi of Tripoli and the most influential proponent of union with Syria, in order 'not to enhance his prestige'.[82] But most of those he interviewed were pro-French personalities who were already integrated in the Lebanese administration and therefore inclined to maintain the *status quo*. Among them were two members of the Representative Council, Khair a-Din 'Adra and 'Abud 'Abd al-Razak; the president of the council of al-Mina; a Maronite deputy; various notables; and a French merchant. The supporters of union with Syria explained that their demands stemmed from national and religious aspirations similar to those of the inhabitants of the interior, as well as from economic factors. Those who supported the retention of Tripoli within Lebanon claimed that the call for union with Syria had been greatly exaggerated; it reflected no more than local instigation by small groups of pan-Arab extremists and some ambitious individuals, amplified by certain administrative and economic grievances which could be overcome. Following these meetings, Privat-Aubouard recommended that the French authorities not attach too great an importance to the separatist movement in Tripoli, as in his view it did not reflect the wishes of the majority of a basically indifferent population. 'As always in the East', he said, these activities 'were the work of individuals and not groups'. In conclusion he recommended that the town remain part of Lebanon, and warned the French authorities that their silence on the matter would only encourage the instigators.[83]

The way in which Privat-Aubouard conducted his mission angered the separatist elements in the town. In a telegram to Jouvenel, 34 notables, including 'Abd al-Hamid Karami, protested that 'the methods used by Privat-Aubouard, who consulted mainly government officials who gave only their personal opinions were fruitless and useless'. They reiterated their request for separation from Lebanon and invited the high commissioner to visit the town to see for himself that their demands represented the genuine aspirations of the majority of its inhabitants. The leaders of the separatist movement did indeed have cause for complaint. Not only were the individuals consulted unrepresentative of the aspirations of the town's inhabitants, but before and during the inquiry the local French authorities had conducted a campaign of pressure to prevent the free expression of demands for union with Syria. These authorities took strict precautionary measures to prevent a repetition of the demonstrations which had taken place during de Caix's visit to Tripoli three years before. When the separatists attempted to organise a commercial strike to demonstrate public support for their demands, Deleuze closed down the markets for three days.[84]

Privat-Aubouard's conduct during the inquiry illustrated the opposition of many veteran High Commission staff to the policies and attitude of the new high commissioner and the assistants he had brought with him from France. This phenomenon would characterise Jouvenel's term in office, and would be responsible for certain contradictions in High Commission policies towards the rebels and the Syrian nationalists. The old staff, who were mainly military men, resented Jouvenel's policy of reconciliation with the rebels. They argued that the only way to end the rebellion was to impose a solution by force. Many French officers in the Lebanese administration believed that the detachment of areas from Lebanon to appease Muslims and Syrian nationalists would be a sign of weakness that could seriously undermine France's prestige in the area. They argued that Lebanese Christian support during the rebellion was proof that Lebanon was a reliable base for French influence in the region; France should strengthen the Christians rather than weaken and antagonise them. They were convinced that the pro-Syrian campaign in Lebanon was directed not only against Lebanon's independence and territorial integrity, but also against France, the creator of Greater Lebanon. As Deleuze argued in one of his reports: 'Cette campagne n'est pas dirigée seulement contre le Grand Liban. Derrière l'idée Grand Libanaise c'est le Mandat Français qu'on cherche à atteindre et les décisions qu'il a prises au Levant.'[85]

When Muslim opposition to the Lebanese state and demands for union with Syria intensified in December and January, these French officials advised the high commissioner to adopt a firmer stand towards the separatists. They warned him that unless stricter measures were taken law and order in Lebanon would rapidly deteriorate. In a letter to Jouvenel on 12 January 1926, Solomiac, the French delegate in Lebanon, proposed that urgent steps be taken against the separatist elements in Lebanon, that Sheikh Taj a-Din and other nationalist leaders who were in Beirut for the negotiations be sent back to Damascus, and that ties between the nationalists on the coast and those in the interior be blocked by every means. He also recommended stricter censorship of Muslim newspapers and suggested that officials who were serving in the Lebanese administration be forbidden to participate in political activities against the

Lebanese state. Similar recommendations were made by Cayla, Deleuze and Privat-Aubouard.[86]

At this stage Jouvenel himself became convinced of the need to act forcefully against separatist agitation, which was getting out of hand and alarming the Christians. On 17 January he announced that any petitions for or against the detachment of certain regions from Greater Lebanon would be useless, and suggested that the best way for the inhabitants of Syria and Lebanon to express their aspiration freely was by participating in the elections and the constitution-drafting process. He warned that

> A l'heure où la guerre n'est pas encore terminée, et où l'armée française vient à peine de sauver le Liban de l'invasion, chacun doit éviter scrupuleusement toute attitude qui pourrait le faire suspecter de connivence avec les bandes qui s'efforcent de mettre en péril la sécurite de l'armée et de l'Etat.[87]

In the following weeks pressure was brought to bear on Ri'ad al-Sulh and other leaders of the separatist movement on the coast to stop stirring up opposition to the Lebanese state; simultaneously Cayla warned officials in the Lebanese administration that

> Il n'est pas admissible que ceux qui participent à l'exercice de la puissance publique puissent mettre en question l'intégrité terri-toriale de l'Etat dont ils doivent être les premiers serviteurs. Si leurs opinions ne concordent point avec le plus élémentaire de leurs devoirs, on ne saurait comprendre qu'ils ne mettent pas fin à cette proposition en résignant leurs fonctions.[88]

In his letter to Jouvenel, Solomiac also suggested that the High Commission adopt a more favourable policy towards the Mutawallis to keep them from co-operating with the Sunnis against the Lebanese state. Since the end of 1925 Sunni leaders had been trying to persuade Mutawalli notables to support their campaign for Syrian unity and to refuse to participate in drafting the constitution. Among those most active in this campaign was Ri'ad al-Sulh, whose family in Sidon had close ties with Mutawalli notables in Jabal 'Amel. Thanks to these efforts, 400 Mutawalli notables from south Lebanon signed petitions demanding separation from Lebanon, although many prominent notables and religious leaders refused to take part in these initiatives. In order to prevent more Mutawallis from joining the opposition, and also to reward the community for not taking part in the rebellion, Jouvenel announced on 25 January that the Mutawallis would now be officially recognised as a community separate from the Sunnis and would be granted their own religious tribunal, two goals for which they had been aspiring since before the War. The Mutawallis received this move enthusiastically. The following day their religious leaders and deputies went to Beirut to express their gratitude to Jouvenel and to declare their allegiance to the Lebanese state within its existing borders.[89]

Yet the majority of the Mutawallis in the Beqa'a Valley, under the leadership of the Haider family, continued to oppose the Lebanese state and the French mandate and to demand annexation to Syria. Their stand was expressed in a resolution adopted on 11 January by the municipal council of Ba'albek, refusing to participate in the consultations on the constitution, protesting against the inclusion of their town in Lebanon and demanding union with Syria. The French authorities reacted immediately by dissolving the Council, claiming that it had exceeded its authority by intervening in political affairs. The following month Cayla and Solomiac, accompanied by Mussa Nammur, president of the Lebanese Representative Council and a resident of Zahle, visited Ba'albek, Zahle and other villages in the Beqa'a Valley. The visit had several aims: to demonstrate that the region was an integral part of the Lebanese state; to allay the fears of the local Christians, who had become extremely concerned about the activities of the rebel bands in the area, and to persuade the leaders of the local tribes not to join the rebels. The French authorities tried, with little success, to use Ibrahim Haider, the director of agriculture, to influence members of his family to moderate their stand. In the summer of 1926, following one of the more serious attacks by Tawfik Haider's band, Ibrahim Haider, who had by then been appointed a senator, was dismissed and imprisoned together with his cousin Subhi Haider, a deputy in the Representative Council. From the end of 1925 the French began to rely increasingly on the Hamades, a Mutawalli family from Hermil and the Haiders' rivals for influence in the Beqa'a; they particularly relied on Sabri Hamade, a deputy in the Council. He and other members of his family used their influence to prevent members of their community from joining the rebels, and to protect Christian villages in the areas; the French authorities rewarded them with influential positions.[90]

Notwithstanding the measures taken by the High Commission to suppress the separatist tendencies among the Muslims in Lebanon,

Jouvenel was still convinced of the need to find a solution to the Lebanese problem which would satisfy some of the demands of the Muslims and Syrian nationalists. In January and February 1926 Jean Mélia, whom Jouvenel had brought from Paris to serve as a liaison officer and to help draw up the organic law, held intensive discussions with the Lebanese Muslim leaders, Syrian nationalists and Lebanese Christians to learn their views, aspirations and reactions to various plans. Among the ideas he discussed were that Lebanon join the Syrian federation, or that its territory be reduced, or that Mount Lebanon and the coastal area become autonomous zones with federal ties between them. He particularly attempted to win the support of the Lebanese Christians for territorial reduction; with this aim in mind he met Hawayik in mid-February. The patriarch reacted angrily to the proposal to detach certain areas from Lebanon and threatened to go to Europe to prevent such a move. When he protested to Jouvenel over Mélia's behaviour, the high commissioner claimed that the latter had been acting on purely a personal and informal basis; in fact, these talks had undoubtedly been conducted with the full knowledge of Jouvenel himself.[91]

The inconsistent approach of the new high commissioner towards Lebanon's independence and territorial integrity, and his somewhat appeasing attitude towards the Syrian nationalists, revived the suspicions and apprehensions of the Lebanese Christians, especially the Maronites and their Church. True, as soon as he arrived in Beirut at the beginning of December 1925 Jouvenel had declared his support for Lebanon's independence and praised the heroic defence of Lebanon's borders by French forces. He had participated in the Consular Mass, and a few days later had visited the Maronite patriarch in Bkerki where he acclaimed the historic ties between France and the Maronites. These declarations had been taken by the Maronite Church as proof that the close ties between the Maronite community and the high commissioner were now restored after the estrangement under Sarrail. His statement 'peace for those who seek peace and war for those who seek war', and the steps taken by the High Commission in January against Muslim separatist activity, had been interpreted as signs of a firm new policy and were received with much satisfaction. In a letter to Briand on 1 February 1926 Hawayik had praised the new high commissioner and thanked the premier for appointing him. He had also sent a letter to Cayla expressing satisfaction at the firm measures he had taken to 'maintain Lebanon's unity, which was a trust placed under France's protection'.[92]

But within two months of Jouvenel's declaration of support for an independent Greater Lebanon, the Lebanese Christians began to discern signs that the high commissioner was in fact contemplating the detachment of certain regions from Lebanon and their annexation to Syria to appease the Syrian nationalists. These signs included Privat-Aubouard's mission to Tripoli, Mélia's activities, Jouvenel's speech in Damascus in which he referred to the 'United States of Syria and Lebanon', and reports from Rome (where the Mandates Commission was then sitting) that the high commissioner intended to organise the mandated territories on a cantonal system. Now, as always, the Maronites were the first to counter any attempt to harm Lebanon's independence or its existing borders. At the beginning of February, Yusuf al-Sawda and other Maronite notables formed an association for the preservation of Lebanon and the defence of its territorial integrity. Lebanese emigrant groups were called upon to take action. The Christian press began to condemn the new policies of the high commissioner and launch scathing attacks on the demands for Syrian unity. On 18 February, Michel Chiha and seven other Maronite and Greek Catholic members of the Council questioned the French delegate on the meaning of Jouvenel's declaration in Damascus.[93]

As in the past, it was the Church which led this campaign. At a meeting in mid-February between Bishop Mubarak and Mughabghab, the new Greek Catholic patriarch, it was decided to offer a resolution in the Representative Council with the support of the Christian deputies, imposing penalties on anyone who acted against Lebanon's territorial integrity; Mughabghab agreed to go to Paris to rally support against Jouvenel's policies. A week later, Hawayik and other Christian communal leaders, including the Greek Catholic and Syrian Catholic patriarchs and the Greek Orthodox bishops of Beirut and of Tyre and Sidon, gathered in Bkerki. They reiterated their support for Lebanon's existing borders and warned the high commissioner and the Representative Council against any concession to separatist demands. Hawayik also threatened that if such concessions were made, he would go to Europe and request a return to the previous arrangement of an international guarantee by the six European powers for the existence of the Lebanese state. By including the Council in their warning, they showed their lack of confidence in that body and their anxiety that a constitutional government not dominated by the Maronites might compromise Lebanon's independence and territorial integrity.[94]

Like all the high commissioners who had preceded him, Jouvenel faced a dilemma: whether to continue the traditional French support for the Lebanese Christians or to pursue an understanding with the Muslim majority. As before, the strong reaction of the Lebanese Christians and their French supporters, and the threat by the Maronite Church to act directly in France, brought immediate results. Jouvenel certainly did not want Hawayik or his representatives to go to Paris while the Syrian question was still a controversial issue in the National Assembly and the French press. Moreover, Hawayik's mention of the six powers who had guaranteed the autonomous Sanjak of Mount Lebanon was clear indication that the Maronites would not hesitate to turn to other European powers, including Italy, the second largest Catholic power, to defend their rights. Jouvenel immediately sent de Reffye to Bkerki in an attempt to appease the Maronite patriarch and the other Christian leaders. De Reffye reassured the assembled clerics that the high commissioner had no intention of harming Lebanon's independence or changing its borders; he took with him a copy of the French report to the Mandates Commission to prove that the statements attributed to Jouvenel were unfounded. This quick move calmed Hawayik and the other religious leaders, who sent letters to Jouvenel and Briand thanking them for these assurances and declaring the support of their communities for France and its mandate.[95]

These events confirmed Jouvenel in his belief that the dispute was not between France and the mandated territories, but between the inhabitants of the areas themselves, particularly the Syrian Muslims and the Lebanese Christians. As the date drew near for his return to Paris at the end of May and his appearance before the Mandates Commission in June, he became increasingly anxious to renew negotiations with the Syrian nationalist leaders, and to form a native government in Syria. This would demonstrate to the French government and public and to the Mandates Commission that the rebellion was nearing its end, and that a political solution to the Syrian problem had largely been achieved. He offered the position of head of the Syrian state to Damad Ahmad Nami, whom he encouraged to include Syrian nationalist leaders in his cabinet, realising that no other government would be accepted by the population or be able to remain in power. But personnel changes were not enough. As in the previous negotiations with Sheikh Taj a-Din, the

Syrian nationalists insisted on the annexation of Tripoli and the Beqa'a Valley. By this time Jouvenel had decided that an agreement with the Syrian nationalists and the Muslim majority had to be reached even at the price of antagonising the Christians. In the negotiations on the formation of a Syrian government he secretly assured Ahmad Nami and the other nationalist leaders that the French would leave the question of borders to the two states themselves and would try to persuade the Christians to accept the Syrian position. In return Ahmad Nami and the nationalist leaders participating in the talks undertook not to use force to achieve their territorial aims. Amin Sa'id gives further details of this secret agreement. He claims that Jouvenel sent Ahmad Nami two handwritten letters in April recognising Syria's rights to a seaport and undertaking to annex Tripoli and the 'Akkar and Ba'albek regions to Syria, so that the Damascus-Tripoli railway would not have to pass through Lebanese territory. According to Sa'id, certain Maronite leaders, including Hawayik and Emile Eddé, knew of the plan. Eddé even promised to try to gain his community's support, and signed one of Jouvenel's letters as proof of his intentions. Jouvenel gave his approval to the programme of 28 April in which Ahmad Nami's government called for the securing by peaceful means of access to the sea as one of its three main national goals. When the Lebanese Representative Council insisted on enshrining the existing borders in the Lebanese Constitution along with a prohibition on territorial concessions (articles 1 and 2), Jouvenel insisted on another provision (article 93) stipulating that Lebanon had to submit for arbitration by the mandatory power any conflict with its neighbours or other countries which might disturb peace and security.[96]

By pursuing this line Jouvenel provoked opposition from members of his own staff, as he had in January. In a May 5 memorandum to Jouvenel and to the Quai d'Orsay Cayla rejected the claim that Tripoli was the natural port for Damascus. Rather than deprive Lebanon of Tripoli and a large part of 'Akkar and the Beqa'a, he proposed that an economic agreement be sought that would meet the genuine needs of Syria and still guarantee the territorial integrity of Lebanon. The following month, under pressure from members of the Representative Council, Solomiac declared that France had not abandoned its support for Lebanon's territorial integrity. By promulgating the Constitution, he said, the high commissioner had reaffirmed France's guarantee of the borders of Greater Lebanon. His declaration brought sharp criticism from Jouvenel, but de

Reffye, whom Jouvenel had charged with the difficult task of arranging the negotiations between the two states, showed little enthusiasm for the job and on one occasion remarked to the British military liaison officer in Beirut that he was acting not from personal conviction but only in accordance with Jouvenel's instructions from Paris.[97]

Jouvenel's efforts to satisfy both parties proved counter-productive. The dispute emerged into the open on 13 June, when in a speech before graduates of the Jesuit University Charles Dabbas, the new president of the Lebanese Republic, declared amidst great enthusiasm that as long as he remained president he would defend Lebanon's territorial integrity as he had sworn to do under the Constitution, and proclaimed that every square inch of its territory was inviolable and inalienable. This declaration, and an article that appeared in *La Syrie*, the semi-official organ of the High Commission, reaffirming Lebanon's existing borders, led Ahmad Nami to threaten resignation; the statements went against his government's basic programme, and he demanded that the French publicly confirm the pledges they had given him. Only after de Reffye assured him that Dabbas had merely expressed his personal views was he persuaded not to resign. On 18 June, in the presence of de Reffye, the head of the Syrian state declared that the Lebanese president had no right to speak of the integrity of Lebanon when the wish of the whole people was that Syria and Lebanon be united. The British liaison officer in Beirut was correct in blaming the French for the growing tension between the two states; he remarked that

> . . . while they have promised Lebanon that the integrity of her frontiers shall be preserved, they have also approved the policy of the new Government of Syria, which claims an outlet to the sea, other than Alexandretta. This must be Tripoli, which is in Lebanon's territory. The French have consequently committed themselves to two promises which cannot be reconciled.[98]

In order to press the French into complying with their territorial demands and demonstrate their resentment of the Lebanese Constitution and of the establishment of the Lebanese Republic, the nationalist leaders in May and June encouraged armed bands to step up their activities in the Beqa'a Valley and in the region surrounding Tripoli. This led to a complete deterioration in public security. A band led by Tawfik Haider cut the railway between Ba'albek and

Homs, and on one occasion entered Ba'albek and set fire to the main administrative centre. In Jabal 'Akrun the rebel bands cut the railway between Tripoli and Homs and reached the outskirts of Tripoli itself, forcing the French to install machine guns and erect barbed wire to defend the city against their attacks. French officials were convinced that nationalist members of the Syrian government were behind these activities. Both de Reffye and Gamelin, the commander of the French army, made repeated requests to Paris to let them use force to restore law and order. At the beginning of June de Reffye was instructed by the Quai d'Orsay to warn the Syrian government that if it continued to encourage these activities or tried to take over the area by force, the negotiations with Lebanon on the territorial issue could not proceed. When this warning went unheeded, French forces in late June opened an extensive military offensive against the rebel bands in the Beqa'a and Jabal 'Akrun. French gunboats shelled Muslim villages in the area surrounding Tripoli, and in the town itself four nationalist leaders, including 'Abd al-Hamid Karami, were arrested. French troops, assisted by Lebanese gendarmerie, Armenian and Circassian auxiliaries and Maronite volunteers from Zghorta, began a large-scale operation against the rebels and their bases; villages whose inhabitants were suspected of helping the rebels were heavily fined. These measures later led to Muslim accusations of atrocities and pillaging by the irregular forces.[99]

At the same time, in June and July, the High Commission discreetly worked to obtain Christian support, especially in the Lebanese parliament, for Jouvenel's plan to detach Tripoli, 'Akkar and the Beqa'a Valley. Some Lebanese Christian notables and deputies, including Emile Eddé, secretly supported this move. However, the overwhelming majority of Lebanese Christians, led by the Maronite Church, strongly opposed the new French initiatives. For them, the rebellion had only proved that a loyal, intact Greater Lebanon was essential if France was to retain its influence in the region. It was foolish for France, as Hawayik put it, to weaken 'Christian Lebanon', which had remained loyal, and strengthen 'Muslim Syria', which had rebelled against the mandate. The Druze invasion of south-east Lebanon demonstrated the crucial value of the expanded borders. Without the Anti-Lebanon and the Beqa'a Valley, the rebels would have invaded Mount Lebanon directly and caused an outbreak of religious and sectarian conflict there. Hawayik's disappointment and anger showed up in a speech he made when de Reffye visited him later in the year:

Au cours de notre voyage à Paris, nous avons visité le Président de la République, M. Poincaré, et le Président du Conseil, M. Clemenceau; ils m'ont assuré qu'ils veilleraient au maintien des anciennes traditions et de l'indépendance du Liban dans ses frontières actuelles. D'où vient aujourd'hui ce tumulte que l'on répand autour du démembrement du Grand-Liban, par la cession de telle ville, Tripoli, par exemple, à l'unité Syrienne? Paix et bonheur à la Syrie, mais nous tenons par ailleurs à sauvegarder nos droits. Tripoli fait partie intégrante des territoires libanais. L'atmosphère qu'elle respire, ses eaux, ses richesses sont libanaises. Comment veut-on en priver le Liban au profit de la Syrie, alors que même du temps des Turcs, cette ville faisait partie du vilayet de Beyrouth.

Le Liban n'a point attiré la rébellion pour qu'il soit réduit à en faire aujourd'hui les frais. La France, nous le savons, ne peut pas manquer à sa parole. Elle nous a fait une promesse, elle doit la tenir. Ce n'est pas un privilège que nous demandons, mais justice et égalité par le maintien du Liban dans ses frontières actuelles. Dans ce maintien la France trouve en premier lieu son propre intérêt. Ce qu'elle cherche en effet c'est d'avoir un pied en terre ferme en Orient. Si elle croit le trouver ailleurs cela pourrait à la rigueur justifier son attitude. Le Liban est en mesure de provoquer des troubles, d'inquiéter le Gouvernement et de lui faire une systématique opposition. Mais, fidèle et sincère à ses sentiments et à ses traditions, il aime avant tout la paix et la tranquillité.[100]

Not only did the Maronite Church strongly oppose any attempt to modify Lebanon's borders, but Hawayik and other Christian religious leaders, along with the organisation formed by the refugees from Rashaya, proposed to the French government in the summer of 1926 that a population exchange take place in the area of Hasbaya-Rashaya, so that it be inhabited solely by Christians. Most of the Druze and Christian inhabitants of the region had fled following the hostilities; the Christians refused to return to their villages without securing compensation for themselves and punishment for the Druze who had attacked them. Some French officials saw the advantage of settling the area by Christians loyal to France, as this would separate the large Druze centres of Jabal Druze and Mount Hermon from the Druze in Mount Lebanon. Indeed, de Reffye, the acting high commissioner, requested a large sum of money to help the Christian inhabitants return, and even proposed settling Armenian refugees in the area. De Caix, too, later declared that the opportunity should have been taken to settle Christians in the region after most of the Druze had fled.[101]

The annexation of certain areas of Lebanon to Syria was only part of a comprehensive plan by which Jouvenel hoped to reach an agreement with the Syrian nationalists. Other major elements in this plan were the conclusion of a 30-year treaty and the formation of a Syrian federation to include, in addition to the Syrian state, Jabal Druze, the 'Alawite state and the Sanjak of Alexandretta. While in Paris Jouvenel attempted to enlist governmental support for his proposals. He met with much opposition from the Quai d'Orsay and the Right in the National Assembly. On the other hand, his initiative was supported by leftist deputies and by a number of liberal groups. Despite certain misgivings, Briand finally gave his consent for negotiations to be held between Jouvenel and the Syrian nationalists.[102]

Once the rebellion was suppressed, its leaders, along with other Syrian nationalists, were willing to negotiate, hoping to gain by political means what they had failed to achieve by force. Shahbandar, the chief rebel leader, told a Dutch journalist whom Jouvenel had sent to him as a mediator several months before, that the Syrians would be willing to drop their demand for the Beqa'a Valley if Tripoli were annexed to Syria. In July, Jouvenel held negotiations with Syrian Arab nationalist leaders; he invited three of them to Paris: Michel Lutf'allah, Shekib Arslan and Ihsan al-Jabiri. The nationalists later claimed that an agreement was almost reached at that time. However, the fall of Briand's government following the prolonged economic crisis and the formation of a new government by Poincaré in July put an end to Jouvenel's initiative. Poincaré, a conservative politician who favoured the traditional French policy of supporting the Christians, was unwilling to implement Jouvenel's liberal policies, particularly as the revolt had already been subdued and France's authority in the mandated territories restored. Moreover, the adoption of such controversial policies would undoubtedly have met with strong opposition from the Right and would have caused much controversy and conflict in the government and the National Assembly, which Poincaré was anxious to avoid lest his efforts to end the economic crisis be undermined. He thus rejected the proposals raised by Jouvenel, who subsequently resigned from his post as high commissioner in August 1926.[103]

Jouvenel's resignation ended the last serious French attempt to detach part of the territories annexed to Lebanon in 1920. Yet the idea retained the support of some French officials in the High Commission and the Quai d'Orsay. Indeed, in October 1926, upon the departure for Beirut of Henri Ponsot, the new high commissioner, de Caix included in a memorandum to the Quai d'Orsay a detailed plan for territorial reduction, in which he again proposed to annex Tripoli and part of the Beqa'a Valley to Syria. He also suggested that a railway line be constructed from Beirut to Tripoli in order to minimise the possible detrimental effect on Beirut's position and on France's extensive interests there if Tripoli became a modern port for Syria. Ponsot himself saw the value of accepting some of the territorial demands of the Syrian nationalists, but when faced with the strong opposition of the Lebanese Christians he, too, preferred to drop the whole idea, particularly as Paris was now disinclined to adopt such a policy. Thus the Lebanese Christians and the Maronite Church achieved their final victory in preventing any modification of the borders granted to Lebanon in 1920.[104]

The Syrian revolt of 1925-6 and its repercussions in Lebanon created particularly unfavourable conditions for the elaboration of the organic law for the mandated territories, the main task which France, as the mandatory power, had to accomplish in 1926. Nevertheless the promulgation of the Lebanese Constitution on 23 May 1926 was a most important political event; together with the establishment of Greater Lebanon in 1920 and the signing of the National Pact of 1943, it largely determined the character of modern Lebanon. The Constitution provided Lebanon with a parliamentary democracy. Its unique political system of confessional representation allowed the various sects, particularly the Muslims, to become integrated into the Lebanese state. Once adopted, the Constitution was cherished by the Lebanese and became a symbol of their independence, although the role of the French in drafting it generated much controversy. Many Christians and Muslims at the time, and later historians such as Rabbath, declared it to be mainly the work of the Quai d'Orsay, and claimed it had been imposed on Lebanon. On the other hand, some Lebanese, backed by historians such as Salibi and Rondot, asserted that it was prepared mainly by the Lebanese themselves, and that it genuinely expressed the wishes of the Lebanese people. French archival sources suggest that it was actually the joint work of both the Lebanese and the French; although it was modelled largely on the French Constitution of 1875, in many respects it reflected the specific needs of Lebanon.[105]

The Lebanese Constitution was part of the organic law which France, as the mandatory power, was obliged to prepare in accordance with the Mandate Act. The first article of the mandate for Syria and Lebanon stated that:

> The Mandatory shall frame, within a period of three years from the coming into force of this mandate, an organic law for Syria and the Lebanon. This organic law shall be framed in agreement with the native authorities and shall take into account the rights, interests and wishes of all the population inhabiting the said territory. The Mandatory shall further enact measures to facilitate the progressive development of Syria and the Lebanon as independent states. Pending the coming into effect of the organic law, the Government of Syria and the Lebanon shall be conducted in accordance with the spirit of this mandate. The Mandatory shall, as far as circumstances permit, encourage local autonomy.[106]

Thus the Mandate Act clearly vested in France the responsibility for drafting the organic law. This was, indeed, one of its main tasks in preparing the mandated territories for full independence. Any criticism of France for its participation in drawing up the Constitution was therefore unjustified. The controversy centred mainly on the interpretation of the provision that the organic law should be framed 'in agreement with the native authorities and shall take into account the rights, interests and wishes of all the population. . .' The Lebanese and Syrians took the term 'native authorities' to mean elected representatives, and therefore demanded the formation of constituent assemblies to participate fully in the elaboration of their respective constitutions. On the other hand, the French, at least until the end of 1925, opposed any form of 'collective' consultations. For their own reasons, they preferred a system of 'individual' consultations.

One important factor which must be taken into account when examining the origins of the Lebanese Constitution is the frequent change of high commissioners and French governments. From September 1923, when the mandate came into force, until May 1926, when the Lebanese Constitution was promulgated, there were three changes of high commissioner and four changes of government. The resulting uncertainty and inconsistency in French policy helps explain the different interpretations of France's role in the elaboration of the organic law. The various governments and high commissioners genuinely believed that the mandated territories should be granted liberal and modern institutions and that their inhabitants should be consulted in accordance with the terms of the mandate. But at the same time they were anxious that the organic law, which was to transform the mandated territories, at least nominally, into independent states, would safeguard France's interests and allow the high commissioner to retain effective control in administering these areas. It was the latter consideration which largely determined the French stand until the end of 1925, leading the Quai d'Orsay and the various high commissioners to oppose either the formation of native constituent assemblies or the participation of the existing Representative Councils in the elaboration of the organic law. The French were well aware that the Councils might voice strong opposition to the inclusion in the organic law of provisions safeguarding France's position and interests. One must also bear in mind that the Lebanese Constitution was merely one part of the organic law for all the mandated territories. The French could not allow the Lebanese greater freedom than the rest of Syria without causing similar demands to be raised by the Syrian nationalists.[107]

While in Paris in the summer of 1924, Weygand, together with a committee in the Quai d'Orsay, had prepared the first draft of an organic law for the mandated territories in accordance with Poincaré's instructions of December 1923. His intention had been to hold only limited individual consultations with leading local personalities, including some members of the Representative Councils, before completing the final draft. But his replacement by Sarrail in December 1924 led to a new French policy. Both Sarrail and Herriot advocated a more liberal organic law and more extensive consultations with the inhabitants of the mandated territories. Nevertheless, they were not prepared to allow the formation of constituent assemblies, or the participation of the existing Representative Councils in drafting the Constitution. The conflict with the Lebanese Council in January 1925 over the election of a governor could only increase Sarrail's reluctance to accept any form of collective consultation. Instead, the French formed a series of local commissions, which served merely as advisory bodies; their members were appointed by the high commissioner and were consulted on an individual basis only. At the end of February Sarrail appointed such a commission for Lebanon, comprised of representatives of the various communities and population sectors, and including prominent notables and politicians, traders, industrialists, lawyers and journalists — but not religious leaders.[108]

However, the controversy and criticism Sarrail's policies generated in the mandated territories and in France led some members of the National Assembly to doubt his ability to prepare an organic law in the spirit of the mandate and in accordance with the aspirations of the local population. Furthermore, as members of parliament themselves, they were inclined to react favourably towards the many protests and petitions they received from the Lebanese and the Syrian nationalists opposing individual consultations and demanding the formation of constituent assemblies. In a memorandum to the premier on 4 March 1925, Henri Simon criticised the lack of broader consultation with the inhabitants of the mandated territories; he proposed that a delegation including members of the National Assembly and constitutional experts go to Syria and Lebanon to assist in drawing up the organic law. Such a proposal could hardly have appealed to Herriot or Painlevé, who replaced him as premier in May; it was certainly not welcome to the Quai d'Orsay or to Sarrail. None of them was prepared for intervention by French politicians who had little knowledge of local conditions and who might adopt an attitude far more liberal than they themselves desired. The very arrival of such a delegation in Syria and Lebanon would undoubtedly have caused considerable political agitation. It would also have dealt a serious blow to Sarrail's prestige, as it could have been interpreted as a lack of confidence in his policies, which were already under sharp criticism. Nevertheless, following continued pressure from the National Assembly the French government sent Auguste Brunet, a deputy and a close friend of Sarrail, to the mandated territories to learn the views and aspirations of the local inhabitants concerning the organic law. Brunet arrived in Beirut on 19 May. After extensive meetings over the following month with various deputies and other prominent leaders, he recommended that the system of individual consultations as advocated by Sarrail and the Quai d'Orsay be continued.[109]

Even though they rejected Henri Simon's proposal, neither Painlevé nor Briand, the minister for foreign affairs, had full confidence in Sarrail's policies or in his ability to draw up an organic law. These doubts, and the pressure from members of the National Assembly, led Briand on 15 June to set up a commission comprised of members of the National Assembly, representatives of the Quai d'Orsay (including Robert de Caix) and constitutional experts, and chaired by Joseph Paul-Boncour, to draft an organic law. From the start Paul-Boncour and the representatives of the Quai d'Orsay differed over the form that consultations with the inhabitants of the mandated territories should take. The chairman advocated a policy far more liberal than that being followed by Sarrail and the Quai d'Orsay. After deliberations for more than a month, with Brunet's participation, the commission adopted the Quai d'Orsay's approach, and decided that individual consultations be continued. Yet under continual pressure from Paul-Boncour the list of those to be consulted was considerably enlarged. In Lebanon, it included, in addition to the original 35 members chosen by Sarrail in February, religious leaders from the various communities, leading professional men and members of the Lebanese administration. The commission decided to invite these representatives to send letters to Paris through the high commissioner expressing their views on the organic law. This form of consultation would be carefully controlled by the High Commission; not only did Sarrail choose those to be consulted, but the very knowledge that their letters to the drafting commission were to pass through his hands undoubtedly made some of them hesitate to express their views openly.[110]

The letters from the mandated territories were received by the Boncour Commission between August and October 1925. In Lebanon, those consulted represented a cross section of society, including prominent members of all the communities. Among them were the president and vice president of the Representative Council, deputies, religious leaders, professional men, heads of municipalities and high officials in the Lebanese administration. They were all asked to give their opinion on the form the Constitution should take and on relations between Lebanon and the rest of the mandated territories. Some sent detailed plans for the Constitution, while others offered general recommendations. Several of those consulted (such as Hawayik, Fu'ad Arslan, 'Umar Da'uq and the mufti of Beirut) called for the formation of a constituent assembly. There was almost unanimous support for the establishment of a republic and a parliamentary regime based on two houses with extensive legislative power. Some proposed that the parliament be elected by direct proportional representation, while others (for example, Shibl Dammus and the Druze Sheikh 'Aqal) supported a system based on confessional representation. There were those (mainly Muslims) who asked that the Constitution refrain from specifying the religion of the state, and that it be based on secular democratic principles.

There was a clear difference of opinion between Muslims and Christians over relations with Syria; most Muslims (for example, Sami al-Sulh and Muhammad Makhzumi) advocated that Lebanon be part of a Syrian federation, while most Christians (for example, Hawayik, Auguste Adib Pasha, Shibl Dammus and Emile Eddé) demanded complete political independence from Syria. But the division between the two communities was not clear-cut: some Muslims (such as Sheikh Muhammad al-Jisr from Tripoli) supported an independent Lebanon, while some Christians (such as Najib Sursuk) advocated close links with the Syrian federation.[111]

The election of the Representative Council and the outbreak of the Druze revolt in July 1925 had intensified the demands of the Lebanese for full participation in drafting the organic law. The members of the new Council strongly resented the fact that the Lebanese Constitution was being drafted in Paris and that they were not being consulted as a body. The affair revived their suspicions about French motives; they were determined to exercise their power on this matter as the true representatives of Lebanon. At the first session of the Council on 16 July, Yusuf al-Khazin, a Maronite deputy from Mount Lebanon and owner of the newspaper *al-Arz*, put forward a motion requesting that the organic law be prepared as soon as possible. On 4 August he submitted a written question to the high commissioner asking that the organic law be elaborated according to the Mandate Charter and the liberal principles of the mandatory power. In reply Solomiac, the French delegate, stated that the organic law was being prepared in consultation with the 'native authorities', with full consideration for the rights, interests and wishes of all the inhabitants of Greater Lebanon; those consulted, he said, included many high officials in the Lebanese administration and other prominent personalities.[112]

The Druze revolt and the criticism of Sarrail it evoked in France, the Mandates Commission and in Syria and Lebanon led to radical changes in French policy on drafting the organic law. In Lebanon, insecurity and the spread of nationalist feelings led Christians and Muslims alike to give greater voice to their demands for a constituent assembly, while newspapers of the two communities conducted a campaign against the method of individual consultations. But the two communities were in agreement for different reasons; the Christians, particularly the Maronites, who lacked any confidence in Sarrail, were anxious to see that the Constitution guaranteed Lebanon's existence as an independent Christian state, while the Muslims, whose nationalist and anti-French feelings had been intensified by the rebellion, were seeking to satisfy one of the main demands of their brethren in Syria, who had long advocated the convening of a constituent assembly. Thus when the Representative Council reconvened on 17 October, Maronite and Sunni deputies joined in adopting a resolution expressing the wish of the Council to take over the drafting of the Constitution. The resolution was sent by the Council's president, Mussa Nammur, to the Boncour Commission in Paris.[113]

The Commission, too, was shaken by the rebellion. Paul-Boncour himself strongly criticised the way Sarrail and the Quai d'Orsay were dealing with the organic law issue. Arguing that this had been one of the main causes for the uprising, he continually pressed the Quai d'Orsay to adopt a more liberal attitude in accordance with the spirit of the mandate. In a letter to the premier on 21 September, he recommended that local constituent assemblies or special commissions be formed to take part in drawing up the organic law. He later rejected various proposals of Sarrail and the Quai d'Orsay, including a suggestion that all members of the Representative Councils be consulted individually, and insisted that Sarrail come personally to Paris to explain his policies and plans.[114]

After the recall of Sarrail at the end of October Paul-Boncour made it clear to Briand that he was no longer prepared to preside over the Commission unless additional members of parliament were brought on and unless its procedures were changed. He repeated his request that local constituent assemblies or special commissions be formed, or that the existing Representative Councils be permitted to participate in the drafting of the constitutions. He asked that Council members be allowed to express freely the aspirations of the population, and that his Commission decide on the organisation of the mandated territories only after hearing the wishes of the people. Finally, he requested that the whole procedure be speeded up. Paul-Boncour was not alone in making such proposals. Following the uprising even some Quai d'Orsay and High Commission personnel began to argue that apart from certain provisions relating to France's authority as the mandatory power, it would be preferable to allow the local representatives of each state to decide on their own form of political organisation. At this stage Briand himself realised that in order to undo the effects of Sarrail's mistakes, France would have to adopt policies far more liberal than it would otherwise have contemplated. Adopting Paul-Boncour's recommendations, he appointed him as head of a new commission to draft an organic law, and agreed to allow the inhabitants of each of the two states to frame their own constitution. This was one of his chief instructions to Jouvenel before the latter left for the mandated territories.[115]

Thus it was largely due to the Syrian uprising that the French government adopted a more liberal attitude towards the participation of the inhabitants of the mandated territories in the elaboration of their own constitutions. Paradoxically, it was the Lebanese who were to benefit most from this new policy. Jouvenel had his own reasons for granting the Lebanese a large degree of freedom in this matter. He was trying to project a liberal stance before the Mandates Commission, where French policy in Syria and Lebanon was under strong criticism, and also induce the Syrian rebels to lay down their arms by the promise of similar liberal treatment. On 4 December, two days after his arrival in Beirut, Jouvenel announced in a speech to the Lebanese Representative Council that the period of individual consultations had passed. Wherever order had been secured — and only there — the era of constitutional activity could begin. He went on to say:

Puisque le Conseil Représentatif a prouvé, par son attitude, comme toute la Nation libanaise, le ferme volonté et le noble souci de maintenir un régime de paix sous le mandat français, il doit pouvoir doter le peuple libanais des bienfaits que cette paix et ce mandat comportent.

Votre Conseil a été élu en juillet dernier, et nous ne saurions, sans perdre le temps du pays, ajourner ses espérances jusqu'à des élections nouvelles. Je demanderai donc à M. le Gouverneur Cayla de convoquer en réunion extraordinaire le Conseil Représentatif du Grand Liban afin de lui remettre le soin de délibérer sur la Constitution. Le Conseil trouvera sans doute avantage à appeler à travailler avec lui, dans des commissions mixtes, les notabilités du Grand Liban et, en particulier, les représentants des diverses professions, afin de s'entourer de tous les avis autorisés et de toutes les obligations qui découlent pour la France des engagements qu'elle a pris envers la Société des Nations, lorsqu'elle a accepté avec le Mandat, sur les peuples de la Syrie et du Liban, un ensemble de droits et de devoirs. Quand vous aurez enregistré ce préambule nécessaire des constitutions, vous pourrez vous mettre à l'oeuvre, déterminer suivant les aspirations du suffrage universel qui vous a envoyés ici la répartition et la responsabilité des pouvoirs et le mode d'élection des représentants du peuple et du chef de l'Etat. Ainsi aurez-vous consacré l'indépendance nationale du Grand Liban.[116]

Over the following six months the Lebanese Representative Council set down to the task Jouvenel had outlined. On 10 December it met in extraordinary session; the French delegate opened the meeting with a reply to Fu'ad Arslan, who had asked for confirmation of the Council's power to prepare a Constitution: 'Except for the authority of the mandatory power, which will be defined by the high commissioner, I declare that the Representative Council has complete freedom in preparing the Constitution of the state.' The Council proceeded to elect twelve of its members, on a confessional and regional basis, to form a committee to draft the Constitution. Shibl Dammus, a Greek Orthodox from the Beqa'a who had received the votes of most of the members, was chosen to head the committee; he, Petro Trad and Michel Chiha were to be the main architects of the Constitution. The drafting committee appointed five of its members (Da'uq, Dammus, Haider, Chiha and Abu Nader) to a subcommittee, which in line with Jouvenel's declaration would determine the views of the people. The subcommittee decided that consultations would be carried out by means of questionnaires to be sent to representatives of the different communities, prominent notables, leading professional men, heads of departments and officials from the various districts. Because of the controversy surrounding the role of the Dammus committee, it is worthwhile quoting the questionnaire:[117]

1. What do you consider should be the type of government: constitutional monarchy or republic, and why?
2. Should the parliament be of one house or two, and why?
3. Should the head of the state be responsible, and to whom?
4. Should the government (i.e. the cabinet) be responsible to the head of the state or to the parliament, and why?
5. Should the responsibility of the cabinet be individual, or collective, or both, and why?
6. Should the representation of the people be on a confessional basis or not, and why?
7. Should the elections be direct, or should they be in two degrees? Should each elector have one vote, or should there

be plural voters, i.e. should persons of distinction have more than one vote?

8. How many electors should elect one deputy; how long should the mandate of the deputy last; and why?

9. If it is decided to create a senate, are the members to be elected, and in what way? Or will they be nominated, and by whom? Or will some be elected and some nominated, and in what proportion? How many senators should there be, and why?

10. If a senate is formed, for how long will the senators hold their seats, and why?

11. How should the electoral colleges be formed, and how will elections take place, and why?

12. Should government appointments, and more especially ministries in the government, be distributed on a confessional basis, and why?

13. Remarks.

The first and most difficult task faced by the drafting commission was to decide who should receive questionnaires, and in particular, how many people should be queried in each community and sector. Although the committee rejected demands from various groups, such as lawyers and journalists, that they be granted the formal right to vote for and approve the Constitution, the views expressed by those consulted would carry considerable weight. The various communities and sectors therefore had a clear interest in having as many of their own members queried as possible. The Maronites were resentful of the whole procedure, as they felt that their interests and views were not adequately represented either in the Council or in the drafting committee; they demanded the election of a new constituent assembly. This campaign was led by Emile Eddé and Yusuf al-Sawda, who tried to gain the endorsement of the Maronite Church. The Church was unhappy that only two religious leaders from each community were to be consulted, and it asked that the number of its own representatives be increased. In order to appease the Maronite Church and to keep it from supporting Eddé's and Sawda's campaign, Mussa Nammur and the drafting committee agreed to increase the number of consultees by granting every sect two representatives from each of its dioceses; the decision was received with satisfaction by the Maronite Church. The Muslims, who lacked any diocese-like structure, were to have their total number of representatives proportionately increased.[118]

During the last week of December the drafting committee sent out 210 questionnaires instead of the 111 it had originally intended to send. Those consulted included representatives of the Maronite Church (16), the Greek Catholic Patriarchate (14) and the Greek Orthodox Patriarchate (14); Muslim religious leaders (14); Mutawalli notables (11); Druze notables (6); former deputies (17); representatives of agricultural councils (24); the Association of Lawyers (11); the Association of Journalists (5) and municipalities (12); directors of administrative departments (11); representatives from associations of doctors and chemists, traders and property-owners and from the Chambers of Commerce of Beirut and Tripoli and officials in the Lebanese administration. The questionnaires were to be returned by 15 January 1926, but by 18 January the committee had received only 44 positive replies along with 18 unanswered questionnaires. Another 100 consultees requested that the deadline be postponed until the end of the month. The committee granted the extension; in all it received 132 positive replies. Most of those who refused to participate were Muslims, mainly Sunnis.[119]

While their brethren in Syria were fighting the French and voicing their opposition to an independent Lebanese state, the Sunnis could hardly have been expected to take part in drafting a Constitution that would symbolise the independent existence of that state. Their participation would have amounted to recognition of the legitimacy of Lebanon's existence within its existing borders, and acceptance that they were part of this state, both of which they totally rejected. The drafting of the Constitution thus became another opportunity to demonstrate their opposition to annexation to Lebanon and their aspiration to be part of the Syrian state. At a meeting on 5 January 1926, 37 of the most prominent Sunni notables and religious leaders of Beirut, including their two Council deputies, adopted a motion expressing these views. The resolution was sent by both the kadi and the mufti of Beirut to Mussa Nammur. The text was as follows:

Nous, présents à la délibération relative aux réponses à fournir aux dix questions posées par la Commission chargée d'élaborer le Statut Organique libanais et en vue d'accréditer des délégués pour assister à ses séances, avons décidé à l'unanimité le refus de participer à la préparation du dit Statut conformément aux voeux de tous les musulmans étant donné qu'il ne s'accorde pas avec les désiderata de la communauté musulmane qui forme la majorité écrasante dans les territoires annexés à l'ancienne province du Liban, lors de la proclamation du Grand Liban, en 1920, et que ces désiderata constituent le refus de l'annexion et la demande de rattachement à l'Union Syrienne sur la base de la Décentralisation.

La communauté musulmane a dans maintes circonstances élevé ses protestations contre cette annexion effectuée malgré sa volonté et sans plebiscite, protestations présentées à plusieurs reprises au Haut-Commissariat, à Paris et à la Société des Nations par une note imprimée renfermant les arguments décisifs et les causes évidentes et justes motivant le refus de cette annexion inventée qui a permis à la minorité de bénéficier au détriment de la majorité qui rejette cette annexion de plain droit.

La dernière protestation de la dite communauté a été récemment présentée à S.E. le Haut-Commissaire par l'intermédiaire d'une délégation composée de ses notables qui la lui a faite verbalement et lui a remis un mémorandum dont vous trouverez ci-joint une copie.

Pour ces motifs,

La communauté musulmane de Beyrouth a décidé à l'unanimité, profitant de l'occasion de la réception du questionnaire adressé à elle par la présidence de la commission du Statut Organique, de confirmer ses protestations contre l'annexion au Liban, le refus de participer à l'élaboration du Statut Organique et de répondre au questionnaire.

Elle maintient et réitère son désir de rattachement à l'union Syrienne sur la base de la Décentralisation pour la sauvegarde de ses droits légitimes et sacrés en tout temps et en toutes circonstances. Sur ce, elle considère inutile l'envoi de délégués de sa part.[120]

Over the following weeks most of the Sunni representatives, including religious leaders from Tripoli, 'Akkar, Sidon and Ba'albek, members of the municipal councils of Tripoli, Sidon and Ba'albek and of the Chambers of Commerce of Beirut and Tripoli, and other notables, returned their questionnaires unanswered. Nearly six years after their annexation to Lebanon, the Sunnis still resented being part of the Lebanese state. The drafting of the Lebanese Constitution, the most important political act in the shaping of the political structure of modern Lebanon, was carried out without their participation.[121]

It must be noted, though, that despite the almost total Sunni boycott of the constitutional consultations, the community was far from unanimous on the question of participation in the government of Lebanon. Many Sunni notables, politicians and officials were already integrated in the Lebanese administration, thinking it preferable to hold on to the influential positions they had already achieved than to play a smaller role in an expanded Syrian state whose main centre would inevitably be in the interior, at either Damascus or Aleppo. But those who wanted to participate in drawing up a Lebanese Constitution were unable to express their stand freely. The Syrian uprising aroused strong opposition among the wider Muslim public against collaboration with the French and the Lebanese state, and militant elements directly pressured and threatened those who were disinclined to support the demand for Syrian unity. Militant Sunni notables such as Karami, Jamil and 'Umar Bayhum, Dr Samih Fakhuri and Hassan al-Kadi pressured moderates like 'Abud 'Abd al-Razak and Khair a-Din 'Adra to go along with the negative stand of the majority. This pressure was very effective; nevertheless, some Sunnis, including Razak, Khair a-Din 'Adra and Muhammad al-Jisr, did take part in drafting the Constitution; a move which was obviously welcomed by the French authorities, who were encouraging the Muslims to participate.[122]

Some took a more equivocal stand. 'Umar Da'uq, for example, accepted an appointment on the drafting committee and initially participated in its workings, but later, under pressure from members of his community, adopted a negative attitude. Still, he was not inclined to support the general demand for union with Syria, and together with 'Abdullah Bayhum, members of the Chamber of Commerce of Beirut and Muslim and Christian traders, he tried to further the idea of making Beirut an independent city. With the co-operation of Subhi Haider he submitted a proposal to the drafting committee, which won the support of many Muslims, to divide Lebanon into two cantons — Mount Lebanon and the districts of the former vilayet of Beirut which had been annexed to it — with federal ties between them. They also argued that as the Muslims were not taking part in drafting the Constitution their representatives should be allowed to appear before the committee to present this plan, but their request was rejected.[123]

Despite the Sunni boycott, the drafting committee sought to open a dialogue with the Muslims in order to hear their views on the future political structure of Lebanon. The members of the committee were not alone in making such efforts. Increasing numbers of Christians, who were becoming disillusioned about France's ability to defend Lebanon's independence and borders, began to believe that the only way to secure the country's existence was to reach an agreement with the Muslims and grant them full participation in the running of the state.[124] Many Sunnis, for their part, were anxious to present the views and interests of their community, even if unofficially, before the Constitution was promulgated. This was the background for a meeting held on 3 March 1926 at Najib Sursuk's house, on the initiative of Faris Meshrek, who headed the Party for National Solidarity, in an attempt to find common ground between Christians and Muslims. The meeting was attended by more than 100 prominent notables and politicians from the various sects, including many members of the Representative Council. But the discussions, which were open and frank, produced no results. Sunni participants, especially Ri'ad al-Sulh, 'Umar Bayhum and Hassan Makhzumi, explained the reasons for their opposition to the Lebanese state and their request for links with Syria. Makhzumi expressed the feelings of many Sunnis when he declared:

> Je dois dire que le Grand Liban a été créé contre les musulmans. Il s'agissait de former un Etat chrétien. Quand l'autorité a créé le Grand Liban, nous autres musulmans, nous avons été sacrifiés, car notre pays est la Syrie. Si nous devions un jour rester grand libanais c'est qu'on l'aurait imposé. Nous demandons à être rattachés à la Syrie sous un régime fédéral.[125]

Other Sunnis, such as Yusuf al-Zein and 'Abud 'Abd al-Razak, together with Mutawalli representatives, pointed to the inequality in taxation and economic development between Mount Lebanon and the annexed areas, and demanded unification of the tax system and greater representation of their communities in governmental and administrative positions. The Maronites, for their part, rejected any attempt to impair Lebanon's independence and territorial integrity. Some of the Christians, including members of the drafting committee like Shibl Dammus, Petro Trad and Georges Thabet, did express their willingness to comply with some of the Muslim demands, but only within the framework of the Lebanese state.

Shibl Dammus pointed to the rational solution later adopted by his committee in order to allay the fears of the Muslim communities, when he stated:

> Il résulte de notre discussion qu'une minorité des habitants de ce pays craint d'être engloutie par la majorité. Etant donné que la loi règle les droits et les devoirs de tout citoyen et que d'autre part la constitution est en voie d'élaboration, je m'engage en qualité de Député et membre de la Commission du Statut à n'accorder mon vote qu'à tout projet de constitution sauvegardant les droits et intérêts de toute communauté dans ce pays.[126]

After analysing the replies to the questionnaires, the drafting committee found that the large majority of those consulted favoured a republican regime, a parliament comprised of two houses, ministers individually responsible to the parliament, and a political system based on sectarian representation; the latter provision was supported by 121 out of the 132 who replied. At the beginning of February the committee appointed two of its members to draft a Constitution based on these principles. On 22 March it met with those who had been consulted to inform them of the results of the consultations and to hear their demands and opinions on various issues. The delegates requested that when the draft of the Constitution was ready, they be reconvened to discuss it once more. The drafting committee maintained close contact with the French authorities, whose advice they sought on every sensitive issue; indeed, on one occasion Jouvenel remarked: 'Ever since I entrusted the Lebanese Representative Council to draft the Constitution by itself, it increasingly requested advice on how to proceed.' The drafting committee was particularly helped by Paul Souchier, who had been sent from Paris to assist in preparing the organic law. Nevertheless, its members enjoyed a large degree of freedom, as the French role was limited mainly to guidance and advice. Both Briand and the Quai d'Orsay considered the proposed Constitution, which Jouvenel had sent to Paris for approval, to be too liberal, but even so they were mainly concerned with the articles relating to the authority of the mandatory power and not the internal political organisation of Lebanon.[127]

If there is room for criticism of the role played by the French in drawing up the Constitution, it is in Jouvenel's haste to complete the process. He was anxious to promulgate the Constitution and have it approved before his return to Paris on 27 May, in order to present it to the Mandates Commission and the French government and public as the successful result of his liberal policies. The drafting committee came under continual pressure to complete the final draft and submit it to the Representative Council for approval before that date. On 18 May the Council was instructed to convene the following day as a constituent assembly. After hearing a report from Shibl Dammus on the workings of his committee, the Council debated the draft Constitution for four days, approving it on 22 May together with provisions relating to the authority of the mandatory power and the relations between Lebanon and the rest of the mandated territories, which had been appended by the French authorities.[128] On the following day, a Sunday, a special meeting of the Representative Council was held at which Jouvenel announced his approval of the new Constitution, which was then officially promulgated.[129]

This undue haste explains some of the Constitution's shortcomings. It was too complicated, and the governmental structure it provided too costly for a country as small as Lebanon; indeed, during the following years it was considerably amended. The Lebanese public and press, and the Maronite Church, were suspicious of the motives behind the high commissioner's haste, which led to increased accusations that the whole document was a French creation imposed upon the Lebanese.[130]

According to the new Constitution the Lebanese had to elect their own head of state. As in the past, the issue led to intense political activity and intrigue. The Maronites and their Church were determined that a Maronite should be president; the Church conducted a campaign for the nomination of Najib Melhame, a Maronite notable from Mount Lebanon, who had close ties with Habib al-Sa'd. But the prospect of a Maronite head of state roused opposition from the other communities, who feared Maronite domination of the government. Various deputies and notables proposed that a Frenchman continue to head the Lebanese state, and suggested that Cayla remain in office. But Jouvenel felt that under the new Constitution Lebanon should have a native head of state, and after Cayla resigned on 18 May 1926, the high commissioner chose as his replacement Charles Dabbas, a member of the Greek Orthodox community who was serving as director of justice and had proved his loyalty to France. The French knew that as a member of a minority community his appointment did not raise the opposition which would have been inevitable had the head of state been a Maronite, and they were certain that Dabbas would follow the advice and instructions of the High Commission. On 24 May Jouvenel named the 16 members of the Senate on a confessional basis. Two days later the Representative Council, which now became known as the Chamber of Deputies, held a joint meeting with the Senate, at which Charles Dabbas was officially elected president of the Lebanese Republic. On 31 May a cabinet was formed under Auguste Adib Pasha, and Lebanon entered a new phase in its political development.[131]

CONCLUSION

At the beginning of this work we sought an answer to the question whether the Lebanese state arose out of a genuine national movement with its own goals and aspirations or whether it was created artificially to serve French colonial interests, as claimed by the Muslims and the Arab nationalists, and we attempted to determine the respective roles of the French and the Lebanese Christians in the establishment of Greater Lebanon. Lebanon has indeed had a long history as a separate entity. The founding of Greater Lebanon in 1920 was the product of an historical process during which one community, the Maronites, concentrated in Mount Lebanon alongside the Druze, successfully resisted assimilation into the surrounding Muslim society, first under the Imarah and later under the Mutasarrifiya. In essence, Lebanese nationalism was a continuation of Maronite nationalism, and the emergence of modern Lebanon was the culmination of centuries of Maronite endeavours. It is therefore impossible to separate Maronite history from that of the country itself. The help the Maronites received from France in the formation of their independent state and the definition of its borders does not detract from the legitimacy of their national movement, which paralleled the efforts of other ethnic groups in the area — Armenians, Kurds, Jews and Arab Muslims themselves — to realise their own national aspirations with the help of friendly powers. One could even argue from this point of view that the Lebanese state is no more an artificial creation than are some of the present Arab states: Syria was formed by France from portions of the Ottoman vilayets of Aleppo, Damascus and Beirut, while Britain created Iraq from the vilayets of Basra, Baghdad and Mosul, and what became the Kingdom of Jordan from still other Ottoman lands.

For the Lebanese Christians, and the Maronites in particular, the appeal to France for help in realising their national aspirations was the natural outcome of their close historical, religious and cultural ties. France had been protecting them for centuries while advancing its own political, economic and cultural interests in the Levant. Yet the establishment of a politically independent Greater Lebanon was neither the inevitable outcome of this close relationship nor the only way to protect French interests in the area. French archival sources show clearly that between 1918 and 1920 a merely autonomous Lebanese entity with close political, administrative and economic ties with a Syrian federation was not an unacceptable solution for the French decision-makers and pressure groups, particularly those with economic interests in the Levant. Such a solution was supported at various stages by Picot, Gouraud and Jouvenel, as well as by the Comité Central Syrien. Moreover, there were those who realised that it was in France's interests to reach an agreement with the Muslim majority, even if this was contrary to the aspirations of the Lebanese Christians. This partly explains Clemenceau's attempts to reach an agreement with Faisal in April 1919 and January 1920, and Sarrail's and Jouvenel's pursuit of an understanding with the Syrian nationalists. The same concern explains the even more striking French reluctance to comply with all the Christian border demands, as evidenced first when Millerand and de Caix sought to establish a smaller, more viable Lebanese state with a clear Christian majority, and later when de Caix and Jouvenel made several attempts to revise the borders of Greater Lebanon and to detach some of the areas with predominantly Muslim populations.

The success of the Lebanese Christians in realising their national aspirations for an independent state with extended borders, did owe a great deal to external developments which took place during and after the War, particularly the growing pressure and sympathy they succeeded in mobilising in France. The strong rivalry which developed in the Levant immediately after the War between France on the one hand, and Britain, Faisal and the Arab nationalist movement on the other, created particularly favourable conditions for the realisation of Lebanese Christian aspirations. With its traditional position in the region contested by Britain and the Arab nationalists, France was forced to rely on Lebanese Christian support to strengthen its claims. The Christians fully exploited this situation, realising that in any agreement between France and the Muslims in Syria, their own interests would be the first to be compromised. As it transpired, the Christians had little to fear on that score. Clemenceau's failure in the elections, the rise to power of Millerand's more conservative government and Gouraud's appointment as high commissioner on the one hand, and the growing militancy of the Arab extremists in Damascus on the other, culminating in the unilateral declaration of independence of March 1920, made a conflict between the French and the Arab nationalists inevitable; a conflict from which the Lebanese Christians were to benefit the most. These events undoubtedly paved the way for the establishment of Greater Lebanon, but without the constant pressure and lobbying of the Christians in Lebanon, Lebanese emigrant groups and French supporters, it is doubtful whether a separate, completely independent Lebanese state would have been established; certainly not within the expanded borders of 1920. Indeed, it can be claimed that from 1918 to 1926 the various French governments were constantly being manipulated by the Lebanese Christians who succeeded in persuading them to establish an independent Greater Lebanon and to repel any assault against its independence or its borders.

Why then, was the belief so widespread that Greater Lebanon had been deliberately established by France to protect its own interests? Indeed, the French did regard the Lebanese state, once established, as a loyal base from which to influence and dominate all of Syria. The Christians encouraged this belief in support of their initial appeal to France to take over the region and, after 1920, in countering France's wavering official policy and domestic French demands for withdrawal. Christian leaders repeatedly emphasised the importance of an independent Christian Greater Lebanon as the only really reliable base for French interests in the region, although they themselves were primarily motivated by their recognition that only a constant French presence could protect the independence, territorial integrity and Christian character of the state against strong Muslim opposition within its borders and in Syria. Further support for the general belief that Lebanon was an artificial creation came from the fact that four other 'states' were also created by the French in Syria in 1920 and that they indeed were essentially artificial in nature. The Muslims and the Syrian Arab nationalists, who were involved in a bitter conflict with the French between the two World Wars in an attempt to realise the independence and unity of their state, including the areas annexed to Lebanon, naturally preferred to portray the Lebanese state as an artificial entity and the creation of a colonial power rather than as the expression of a genuine national movement.

After 1920 the Lebanese problem took on a new dimension. A Christian minority which had traditionally feared political and cultural assimilation and the loss of its national identity in an Arab Muslim society had succeeded in realising its aspirations for an independent state. But in the process it had created the new problem of a large Muslim minority which itself feared the loss of its national identity and culture in an essentially Christian state. The Lebanese

Christians, particularly the Maronites, can only regret the mistake they made in the 1920s by over-extending the borders of their country and opposing French attempts to revise them. They could have established a smaller, more compact and more viable state with a clear Christian majority had they divested themselves of Tripoli, 'Akkar and a large part of the Beqa'a Valley. Such a state might still have faced some Muslim opposition, but it would probably have had a greater chance of becoming cohesive and homogeneous. Instead, various historical, psychological and economic factors, combined with the sheer avidity of a few and the overconfidence of others in their ability to dominate the new state, led Maronite leaders, headed by their Church, to establish and maintain an expanded Greater Lebanon. The result was a deeply divided society that endangered the very survival of Maronite national achievements.

During the 1930s, particularly after the 1932 census, some Maronite politicians became more aware of the contradiction between the reality of Greater Lebanon in which half the population was Muslim and the concept of a Christian state; a situation which Samné aptly described as 'trying to square the circle'. The most prominent among them was Emile Eddé, who went one step further and arrived at the only possible logical conclusion when he advocated the detachment of areas with large Muslim populations as the only way for Lebanon to retain its Christian character. However, the overwhelming majority of the Maronite community, including their Church, failed to realise the possible consequences of such a situation; they remained adamant about retaining the existing borders at any price.

The course Lebanon finally took to solve this dilemma can be defined as a 'pragmatic approach'. Its main proponents and spokesmen during the 1930s and 1940s were Bishara al-Khuri and Michel Chiha; the latter profoundly influenced political thinking in modern Lebanon. Those who advocated this solution believed that given time and stability it would be possible to create a new Lebanese identity comprising all the sects, in a pluralistic state as had existed under the autonomous Sanjak. In the meantime they sought to achieve an equilibrium by pursuing an essentially confessional system as the basis for the political and administrative structure of the state.

In retrospect this conception proved to be mistaken, as it underestimated the latent strength of the religious, social and cultural barriers between the various sects, especially between Christians and Muslims. The assumption that Lebanon could retain its Western Christian character and still be accepted as a legitimate entity by the Muslims in Lebanon and elsewhere in the Arab world, proved false as well. The experience of the autonomous Sanjak of Mount Lebanon as an example of the successful achievement of an equilibrium between the various sects and of the formation of a special Lebanese identity was not relevant after all, as there were basic differences between the old Sanjak and Greater Lebanon. In the former there had been a clear Christian majority, with the Maronites comprising more than half the population; the Sanjak's Christian character and its domination by the Maronites had never been seriously contested by the other communities. In contrast, the Christians made up only half the population in Greater Lebanon, while the Maronites comprised less than a third. Now, more than 60 years later, demographic changes have given the Muslims a clear majority, with the Mutawallis emerging as the largest single community.[1] In the autonomous Sanjak harmony between the various sects had been guaranteed by an external authority, the Ottoman-Christian governor, who acted as arbiter. This situation continued during the mandate, with the French high commissioner filling the role of arbiter while also guaranteeing the Christian character of the state. However, the end of the French mandate removed the external authority and the various communities were left face to face.[2]

If there was any similarity between the autonomous Sanjak and Greater Lebanon, it was in the concept behind their formation and the way they were established. Each was created as a national home and refuge for the Christians in the Levant; the autonomous Sanjak after the massacres of 1860 and Greater Lebanon after the suffering of the Lebanese Christians during the First World War. Both entities were imposed through the military intervention of France without the agreement of the Muslims. Their continued existence was secured by external guarantors: the Sanjak by the six European powers and Greater Lebanon, between the two World Wars, by France.

The defeat of France, the Maronites' traditional protector, and the occupation of Syria and Lebanon by the British forces during the Second World War created the conditions which finally led to the adoption of the 'pragmatic approach'. The British representatives in the Middle East, whose country had occupied the Levant during the First World War and had then handed it to France, were determined not to repeat such a mistake. Furthermore, at the time, Britain was backing the concept of Arab unity in the form of the Arab League through which it hoped to secure its influence and interests in the Middle East after the War. France's presence in Syria and Lebanon was certainly not compatible with such a policy. British officers led by General Spears, head of the British Mission in Syria and Lebanon during the War, strove to oust France from the region under the pretext of obtaining complete independence for the two states. In Lebanon, the British found their main allies in Bishara al-Khuri and Kamil Sham'un. Khuri's collaboration with the British was undoubtedly motivated by his personal ambition to attain the presidency, for which he was competing with his sworn rival, Emile Eddé, who was supported by 'Free France'. Khuri's victory over Eddé in the 1943 parliamentary elections in which British and French officers were surreptitiously involved, marked the victory of those Christian leaders who advocated the severing of the historical ties with France and the linking of Lebanon to the Arab world, while retaining its independence and special identity. The National Pact concluded after the 1943 elections between Maronite President Khuri and Sunni Prime Minister Ri'ad al-Sulh, with the backing of the British representatives and the governments of Syria and Egypt, was the culmination of this process.

The National Pact was essentially an attempt to bridge the gap between the two contradictory conceptions of the national identity of the Lebanese state, namely Lebanese Christian or Arab Muslim. At the same time it was an agreement on the distribution of political power among the various sects in the independent state, based on the system of proportional confessional representation, which had already been adopted in the Lebanese Constitution of May 1926. This Christian-Muslim compromise not only enabled Lebanon to demand and receive its independence from France, but created later the general belief in a unique Lebanese political system which had succeeded in finding an effective solution for a multi-confessional society within the framework of a liberal Western democracy.

It soon became clear, however, that the gap which had existed between the Lebanese Christians and the Arab Muslims since the turn of the century was far more difficult to bridge than had been supposed. The mutual suspicions, fears, prejudices and centuries-old hostility were so deeply rooted that they could not be overcome by a compromise between a limited number of bourgeois political and economic elites from the various sects, since they did not necessarily reflect the stand of their communities as a whole. Many Muslims, particularly the Sunnis, continued to regard the Lebanese state as an illegitimate entity unworthy of their allegiance, and while they strove to achieve political, economic and social equality, they sought to transform Lebanon into a truly Arab state, indissolubly linked to the Arab world. Most of the neighbouring Arab states still regarded Lebanon, with its predominantly Christian character and close links with the West, as alien to the ideals of Arabism. On the other hand, many Christians, particularly Maronites, still deeply feared being engulfed by the Arab Muslim world and losing their national identity. They continued to believe that Lebanon was primarily a Christian state, a refuge for persecuted minorities, linked more to the Christian West than to the Muslim East. Others feared a change in the character of the Lebanese state and the loss of Christian control if the Muslims became a majority. These fears led the Lebanese Christians to continue to seek allies outside the Arab Muslim world, even after independence. Thus after Lebanon joined the Arab League in 1945, circles close to Emile Eddé and the Maronite Church, who opposed Khuri's policy, attempted to reach an agreement with the Zionist Jews in Palestine, believing in a common stand of two minority groups, each striving to realise its national aspirations in the midst of a hostile Arab Muslim world. Again in 1958, when faced with a strong wave of Arab nationalism generated by Nasser, the Maronites turned to the West, to the United States, to defend them. In 1975/6, when they found themselves isolated and abandoned by the West, the Maronites turned to Israel. After Bashir Jumayel's assassination in September 1982 and the election of his brother Amin as president, the United States again filled this role for a short period. This has further strengthened the belief in the Arab world that Lebanon in its present form is not really faithful to the tenets of Arab nationalism.

Today, more than 60 years after the establishment of Greater Lebanon, the wheel of history has turned full circle. In 1920 it was Syria and the Muslims of the annexed areas who sought to cut back the territory of Greater Lebanon. By the 1970s it was the Maronite Christians who were seeking to establish a smaller Christian state based on the original core of their homeland in Mount Lebanon,[3] while the Muslims, backed by Syria, were opposing partition. In the 1920s it was the Sunnis who proposed the establishment of two autonomous zones of Mount Lebanon and the coast, and the Christians who opposed the idea. Now, a solution based on a principle of geographical separation between the various religious communities is being advocated by the Maronites and the Druze, but is opposed by the Sunnis and Mutawallis. From 1918 to 1926 the Maronites could still have had a smaller Lebanon with a clear Christian majority, or a political system of autonomous cantons, but they preferred a Greater Lebanon. Today, Lebanon as a whole and the Maronites in particular, find themselves at a similar cross-roads, but this time isolated and lacking either the freedom of choice or the support of a strong Western power. The plan for partition of Lebanon and the creation of a smaller independent Christian state has little chance of being implemented as it is generating strong opposition from the Lebanese Muslims and the Arab states, particularly Syria, who had intervened in 1976 to prevent such a move. Furthermore, it is impossible to ignore the political, social and economic developments of the past 60 years in Lebanon. The lesson of Lebanon's historical past would seem to indicate that the best solution might well be the creation of a new decentralised political system based on sectarian cantons as once advocated by de Caix.

ABBREVIATIONS

AE	Archives du Ministère des Affaires Etrangères
AF	*L'Asie Française*
CHEAM	Centre de Hautes Etudes sur l'Afrique et l'Asie Modernes
CO	*Correspondance d'Orient*
FHJ	Fonds Henry de Jouvenel
FO	Foreign Office Papers
RDM	*Revue des Deux Mondes*
SHA	Service Historique de l'Armée (Section Outre-Mer)

NOTES

Chapter One

1. Geographical Syria is defined as the territory bordered by the Taurus range in the north, Sinai in the south, the Mediterranean in the west and the Syrian desert in the east.

2. For a statement of Arab Muslim aspirations for unity and independence, see memorandum from Muhammad Rashid Rida to Lloyd George, FO 371/4232, no. 105317, 25 June 1919.

3. FO 141/581, Faisal's interview with the American Commission of Inquiry, Damascus, 5 July 1919, Major Clayton to GHQ.

4. Hourani, A.H., *Arabic Thought in the Liberal Age 1798-1939* (Oxford, 1970), p. 290; and Husri, Sati al-, *Yawm Maisalun* (Beirut, 1964), pp. 263-4.

5. For example, see Rabbath, E., *Unité syrienne et devenir arabe* (Paris, 1939), Chapter II. On Rabbath, see Hourani, *Arabic Thought*, pp. 310-11.

6. Syria has never agreed to Lebanon's request to officially exchange ambassadors, claiming that as the two states have a special relationship, there is no such need.

7. See Appendix A: 'Revendication du Liban: Mémoire de la Délégation Libanaise à la Conférence de la Paix', submitted by Patriarch Elias Hawayik, Paris, 25 October 1919; Resolution approved on 9 December 1918 by the Administrative Council of Mount Lebanon before the departure of the first Lebanese delegation to the Paris Peace Conference in Muzhir, Yusuf, *Ta'rikh Lubnan al-'Amm* (Beirut, 1957), vol. II, pp. 873-5; and 'Mémorandum sur les Aspirations des Libanais', Alliance Libanaise, Cairo, 8 January 1918, FO 371/3398 25575/25575, no. 13, 26 January 1918, The Residency, Cairo to Balfour.

8. Salibi, K.S., *The Modern History of Lebanon* (London, 1968), p. xiii.

9. On the Imarah and the Maronites, see: Salibi, *the Modern History of Lebanon*; Harik, I.F., *Politics and Change in a Traditional Society, Lebanon 1711-1845* (Princeton, 1968); and Hourani, A.H., 'Lebanon: The Development of a Political Society' in Binder, L. (ed.), *Politics in Lebanon* (New York, 1965), pp. 13-29.

10. Harik, *Politics and Change*, p. 128.

11. The Mardaites were a warrior group who resisted the Arab invasion of Syria in the seventh century. The Maronite claim of being descendants of the Mardaites was to become an important national tradition.

12. Hourani, A.H., *Syria and Lebanon* (Oxford, 1954), p. 130.

13. Salibi K.S., 'The Traditional Historiography of the Maronites' in Lewis, B. and Holt, P.N., *Historians of the Middle East* (London, 1962), p. 215. See also: Hourani, A.H., 'Historians of Lebanon' ibid., pp. 226-45; Harik, *Politics and Change*, pp. 127-66; and Salibi, K.S., *Maronite Historians of Mediaeval Lebanon* (Beirut, 1959).

14. Harik, *Politics and Change*, Appendix I, The Maronite Imarah: The Church Plan for the Political Reorganization of Lebanon, pp. 294-5.

15. For studies on economic and social change in Lebanon, see: Polk, W.R., *The Opening of South Lebanon, 1788-1840* (Harvard University, 1963); and Chevalier, D., *La Société du Mont Liban à l'Epoque de la Révolution Industrielle en Europe* (Paris, 1971).

16. Hourani, A.H., 'Lebanon from Feudalism to Modern State', *Middle Eastern Studies* (April 1966), pp. 256-63. See also: Kerr, M.H., *Lebanon in the Last Years of Feudalism, 1840-1868: A Contemporary Account by Antun Dahir al-Aqiqi and*

Other Documents (Beirut, 1959); Porat, Y., 'The Peasant Revolt of 1858–1861 in Kisrawan', *Hamizrah Hehadash*, vol. XV, no. 4 (1965), pp. 379–400, and vol. XVI, no. 1 (1966), pp. 31–57.

17. Hourani, 'Lebanon from Feudalism to Modern State', p. 257; and 'Atiyah, E., *An Arab Tells His Story* (London, 1946), p. 10.

18. The 'Double Caimacamia' regime was imposed on Mount Lebanon in 1845 after repeated clashes between Maronites and Druze. The Mountain was divided into two administrative districts roughly along the Beirut-Damascus highway, with the Maronites to the north and the Druze to the south.

19. For the Règlement Organique see Hurewitz, J.C., *Diplomacy in the Near and the Middle East* (Princeton, 1956), vol. I, pp. 165–8. For the preparation and analysis of the Règlement Organique see: Jouplain, M., *La Question du Liban* (Paris, 1908), pp. 386–437; Spagnolo, J.P., *France and Ottoman Lebanon 1861–1914* (St Antony's College Oxford, 1977), pp. 41–7 and Chapter 4; and 'Constitutional Change in Mount Lebanon: 1861–1864', *Middle Eastern Studies* (January 1971), pp. 25–48.

20. In 1867 Italy joined the other signatory powers.

21. Spagnolo, *France and Ottoman Lebanon*, pp. 36–41.

22. Salibi, K.S., 'The Lebanese Identity', *The Journal of Contemporary History*, vol. 6, no. 1 (1971), pp. 76–88. See also Tarbin, Ahmad, *Lubnan Mundhu 'Ahd al-Mutasirrifiya ila Bidayat al-Intidab* (Damascus, 1968).

23. In 1865 the population of Mount Lebanon was given as 266, 487 — comprised of 220,496 Christians and 45,991 Muslims. The distribution of the six main sects was: Maronites — 171,800; Greek Orthodox — 29,326; Druze — 28,560; Greek Catholics — 19,370; Mutawallis — 9,820; Sunnis — 7,611, Spagnolo, *France and Ottoman Lebanon*, p. 24, note 3. In 1896 Cuinet gave a total of 399,530 comprised of 319,296 Christians and 80,234 Muslims: Maronites — 229,680; Greek Orthodox — 54,208; Druze — 49,812; Greek Catholics — 34,472; Mutawallis — 16,846; Sunnis — 13,576, Cuinet, V., *Syrie, Liban et Palestine* (Paris, 1896), pp. 202–11. See also table on p. 98.

24. Samné, G., 'Le Liban Autonome de 1861 à Nos Jours' (Paris, 1919), p. 6; Spagnolo, *France and Ottoman Lebanon*, pp. 132, 141–2.

25. Harik, p. 149. On Bishop Niqula Murad, see pp. 139–47.

26. On the relations between Karam and the Church see Spagnolo, *France and Ottoman Lebanon*, Chapters 3 and 4. See also Harik, pp. 147–52.

27. On the revival of Maronite ideas of independence and autonomy after 1876, particularly after the Balkan insurrections, see Spagnolo, *France and Ottoman Lebanon*, pp. 151–5; and Deebs, J., 'Les Maronites du Liban, Appel aux Catholiques' (Paris, April 1875).

28. Khalaf, S., 'Primordial Ties and Politics in Lebanon', *Middle Eastern Studies* (April 1968), pp. 243–69; Hourani, 'Lebanon from Feudalism to Modern State', p. 259; and Spagnolo, *France and Ottoman Lebanon*, pp. 85–93.

29. Jouplain, *La Question du Liban*, pp. 469–70.

30. Salibi, *The Modern History of Lebanon*, p. xiii.

31. For a description of physical, social, economic and administrative aspects of Lebanon before the First World War, see: Samné, G., *La Syrie* (Paris, 1920), Chapters IX and X; and Great Britain, Admiralty, Naval Intelligence Division, *A Handbook of Syria, including Palestine* (London, 1920), Chapter XII.

32. Such arguments had already been raised by Da'ud Pasha, the first governor of Mount Lebanon. On his attempts to enlarge the boundaries of the Sanjak, see Spagnolo, *France and Ottoman Lebanon*, pp. 113–17.

33. Jouplain, *La Question du Liban*, pp. 563–75; *Handbook of Syria*, p. 175; Samné, *La Syrie*, p. 276; and Dahir, M., *Ta'rikh Lubnan al-Ijtima'i* (Beirut, 1974), pp. 45–50.

34. Saba, P., 'The Creation of the Lebanese Economy — Economic Growth in

the Nineteenth and Twentieth Centuries' in Owen, R., *Essays on the Crisis in Lebanon* (London, 1976), pp. 1–22; and Safa, E., *L'Emigration Libanaise* (Beirut, 1960), pp. 159–64.

35. Jouplain, pp. 555–60; and Spagnolo, *France and Ottoman Lebanon*, pp. 223–6.

36. Jouplain, pp. 469–70. Owing to its increasing importance, in 1888 Beirut became the capital of the new vilayet of Beirut which was formed from the sanjak of Beirut (comprising the cazas of Tyre, Sidon and Marjayoun) and the four sanjaks of Latakia, Tripoli, Acre and Nablus. It covered 30,500 sq. km and in the 1880s its estimated population was 533,554 of whom 230,173 were Muslims and 166,443 were Christians, Cuinet, pp. 13–14.Beirut's population increased from an estimated 15,000 in 1848 to 70,000 in 1863, to 120,000 in the 1880s, and to 180,000 in 1914. See: Porter, H., *The History of Beirut* (Beirut, 1912), pp. 89–92; Jessup, H., *Fifty-Three Years in Syria* (New York, 1910), vol. I, p. 265; *Handbook of Syria*, p. 175; and Cuinet, p. 53. Cuinet gives the following breakdown of the population of Beirut: Muslims — 36,000; Catholics — 39,400, of whom 28,000 were Maronites; non-Catholic Christians — 37,000; Jews — 2,500; Druze — 400; Foreigners — 4,320.

37. For various estimates on the extent of emigration see: Jouplain, pp. 563–8; *Handbook of Syria*, pp. 185–9; Safa, *L'Emigration Libanaise*, pp. 187–91; and Issawi, C. (ed.), *The Economic History of the Middle East 1800–1919* (Chicago, 1966), pp. 269–73.

38. Jouplain, M., *La Question du Liban* (Paris, 1908). On Jouplain, see Hourani, *Arabic Thought*, p. 275.

39. Jouplain, *La Question du Liban*, pp. 576, 582.

40. Ibid., pp. ix, 598.

41. On the Maronites' traditional attachment to France see: Ristelhueber, R., *Les Traditions Françaises au Liban* (Paris, 1925); Baudicour, L., *La France au Liban* (Paris, 1879); and Lamy, E., *La France du Levant* (Paris, 1900). On the legal aspects of the French Catholic protectorate, see a paper prepared by the Foreign Office, FO 608/102, no. 3962, 10 March 1919.

42. Baudicour, Chapter 6. For Bishop Murad's activities in Paris, see Spagnolo, *France and Ottoman Lebanon*, pp. 20–1.

43. Jouplain, *La Question du Liban*, p. 589.

44. In fact, Cumberbatch, the British consul-general in Beirut, suspected that this action was motivated mainly by personal interests and rivalry between Lebanese politicians, FO 195/2277, no. 65, Beirut, 18 September 1908, and no. 66, 25 September 1908, Cumberbatch to Lowther. For a detailed description of the affair, see Khairallah, K.T., *La Syrie* (Paris, 1912), pp. 130–40.

45. FO 195/2277, no. 51, Beirut, 1 August 1908; no. 64, 9 September 1908; and no. 69, 8 October 1908, Cumberbatch to Lowther; and Lohéac, L., *Daoud Ammoun et la Création de l'Etat Libanais* (Paris, 1978), pp. 43–7.

46. FO 371/561 42599/39567, no. 812, Beirut, 19 November 1908, Cumberbatch to Lowther.

47. FO 371/561 39810/39567, no. 752, Constantinople, 6 November 1908, Lowther to Grey.

48. FO 371/762 331/331, no. 895, Const., 29 December 1908, and 1231/331, no. 1, 2 January 1909, Lowther to Grey.

49. FO 371/1006 6669/6669, Beirut, 25 February 1910, letter from Philippe al-Khazin to the British government requesting its support in resisting the attempt of the Ottoman government to incorporate Lebanon as a province in the empire. Sawda, Y. al-, *Fi Sabil al-Istiqlal* (Beirut, 1967), pp. 22–3; and Samné, 'Le Liban Autonome', pp. 8–10.

50. FO 371/781 44346/44346, no. 921, Const., 20 November 1909, Marling to Grey; and *AF* no. 126 (September 1911), pp. 405–12.

51. In his opinion 'The two principle scourges of Lebanon are the universal corruption among officials high and low and the unremitting struggle for office in all ranks. Every functionary has personal enemies who seek every opportunity to do him harm with the object of getting him dismissed and securing his place for one of their members.' FO 195/2311, no. 16, Beirut, 15 February 1909. See also: FO 195/2342, no. 10, Beirut, 18 February 1910, Cumberbatch to Lowther; FO 371/1006 7785/7785, 25 February 1910; and 23955/6999, no. 435, 28 June 1910, Lowther to Grey.

52. FO 195/2312, no. 58, Beirut, 16 August 1909; no. 68, 5 October 1909; and FO 195/2342, no. 18, 28 March 1910, Cumberbatch to Lowther; FO 371/1006 6669, no. 213, Const., 9 April 1910, Lowther to Grey. The original petitions are included in the dispatch. For the opposition of French financiers who had interests in the port of Beirut, see Monicault, J., *Le Port de Beyrouth et l'Economie des Pays du Levant sous le Mandat Français* (Paris, 1936), pp. 22–3.

53. FO 371/1006 13043/6669, no. 214, Const., 9 April 1910, Lowther to Grey; and Lohéac, pp. 47–52.

54. For various reform programmes see: FO 424/231, no. 75, Const., 4 May 1912; no. 115, 22 May 1912; no. 131, 22 May 1912; and no. 137, Lowther to Grey. See also Lohéac, pp. 52–62. Details can be found in *AF* which followed closely the events leading to the appointment of the new governor. See: no. 134 (May 1912), pp. 179–90; no. 136 (July 1912), p. 286; no. 137 (August 1912), pp. 345–6; and no. 141 (December 1912), pp. 515–20.

55. FO 371/1522 54463/52330, no. 79, Beirut, 4 December 1912, Cumberbath to Lowther. The position of president of the Administrative Council was officially held by the Mutasarrif, but it was actually the vice-president who filled the role.

56. FO 424/233, no. 165, Const., 23 December 1912, Lowther to Grey.

57. FO 371/1507 50279/33672, no. 984, Const., 21 November 1912; and FO 371/1848 54142/52892, no. 947, 22 November 1913, Lowther to Grey. For a description of the visit of the battleship *Jules-Ferry* in January 1912 to the Lebanese coast, see *AF* no. 131 (February 1912), pp. 81–2; and Atiyah, p. 25.

58. Jamal Pasha, *La Vérité sur la Question Syrienne* (Constantinople, 1916), pp. 38–43. In 1910 Philippe al-Khazin published a book, *Perpetuelle indépendance legislative et judiciaire du Liban*. See his letter to the British parliament, FO 371/1006 6669/6669, Beirut, 25 February 1910. Samné, *La Syrie*, pp. 220–1. The two Khazin brothers were executed in 1916 by the Turks.

59. Rabbath, E., *La Formation Historique du Liban Politique et Constitutionnel* (Beirut, 1973), p. 281.

60. Sawda, pp. 11-58. The author was one of the leading members of the 'Alliance Libanaise' in Egypt during the War.

61. See the letter sent by six prominent Christian leaders in Beirut to the French consul-general, 12 March 1913, in Jamal Pasha, *La Vérité*, pp. 50–4.

62. Ibid. See also the appeal by Nahla Mutran, a Greek Catholic notable, from Ba'albek to the French consul-general in Damascus, 15 January 1913, pp. 41–3; and Dahir, p. 49. He quotes a memorandum entitled 'The Beqa'a for the Lebanese', presented by the municipal council of Zahle to Ohanes Pasha in 1913. The inhabitants of Zahle, which was part of the Mountain, sought annexation of the Beqa'a Valley to Mount Lebanon, as the town was the main economic centre of the valley and many of them had land and property there. See Hakim, Y. al-, *Bairut wa Lubnan fi al-'Ahd al-'Uthmani* (Beirut, 1964), pp. 90–1.

63. Hourani, A.H., *Minorities in the Arab World* (London, 1947), pp. 23–7; and Ma'oz, M., *Ottoman Reform in Syria and Palestine 1840-1861* (Oxford, 1968), Part V. See also: Jessup, *Fifty-Three Years in Syria;* and Bliss, F.J., *The Religions of Modern Syria and Palestine* (New York, 1910).

64. Jessup, *Fifty-Three Years in Syria*, vol. II, pp. 729–30. For the attitude of the Muslims of Beirut towards the Christians, see pp. 675 and 729; Bliss, *Modern Syria*

and Palestine, pp. 28-9; and 'Atiyah, pp. 10-14.

65. For the complaints of Christians in Beirut that the municipality was dominated by Muslims, and their demand for separate municipalities — Christian in the east and Muslim in the west, see: FO 371/766 16532/3119, no. 298, Const., 24 April 1909, Lowther to Grey; and *AF* no. 121 (April 1911), pp. 195-6.

66. Salibi, K.S., 'Beirut under the Young Turks as Depicted in the Political Memoirs of Salim 'Ali Salam', (Beirut, 1974). Salam was a leading member and one-time president of the Society. See also Johnson, M., 'Factional Politics in Lebanon: The Case of the "Islamic Society of Benevolent Intention" (Al-Maqasid) in Beirut', *Middle Eastern Studies* (January 1978), pp. 56-75.

67. FO 195/2277, no. 51, Beirut, 1 August 1908, and no. 72, 16 October 1908, Cumberbatch to Lowther. Shekib Arslan, a deputy in the Ottoman parliament, was a prominent Druze notable who became a Muslim.

68. FO 195/2311, no. 32, Beirut, 28 April 1909; no. 38, 14 May 1909, and 2312, no. 53, 15 July 1909, Cumberbatch to Lowther; FO 371/766 19532/3119, no. 298, Const., 23 April 1909, Lowther to Grey.

69. FO 371/1256 43727/30691, no. 767, Const., 31 October 1910; and FO 371/1258 47158/30691, no. 830, 18 November 1911, Lowther to Grey.

70. Sa'id, Amin, *al-Thawra al-'Arabiya al-Kubra* (Cairo, 1933), vol. I, pp. 13-14. For a description of the shelling of Beirut by Italian warships in February 1912, and the inhabitants' reactions, see Porter, pp. 93-8; and 'Atiyah, pp. 19-20.

71. FO 371/1256 43727/30691, no. 767, Const., 31 October 1911, Lowther to Grey.

72. FO 371/1522 54463/52330, no. 79, Beirut, 4 December 1912, Cumberbatch to Lowther.

73. FO 371/1507 50279/33672, no. 984, Const., 21 November 1912, Lowther to Grey; and FO 371/1522 54463/52330, no. 79, Beirut, 4 December 1912, Cumberbatch to Lowther.

74. Ibid.

75. Salibi, Salam-Memoirs, p. 19; and Sa'id, Amin, *al-Thawra* vol. I, pp. 18-24.

76. Zeine, N. Zeine, *The Emergence of Arab Nationalism* (Beirut, 1966), pp. 101-2.

77. Jamal Pasha, *La Vérité*, p. 53.

78. FO 371/1788 7281/3535, no. 104, Const., 7 February 1913, Lowther to Grey. Although no documentary evidence could be found, the establishment of the reform movement in Beirut was probably supported by Kamil Pasha as part of his campaign against the CUP.

79. FO 371/1775 17975/253, no. 311, Const., 15 April 1913; 18583/253, no. 320, 18 April 1913; and 20328/253, no. 357, 28 April 1913, Lowther to Grey. See also *AF* no. 146 (May 1913), pp. 223-9.

80. FO 371/1775 22581/253, no. 409, Const., 13 May 1913, Lowther to Grey.

81. FO 371/1775 24349/253, no. 455, Const., 24 May 1913, Lowther to Grey; and 29858/253, no. 349, Paris, 28 June 1913, Carnegie to Grey.

82. FO 371/1775 28573/253, no. 543, Const., 18 June 1913, Lowther to Grey.

83. Salibi, Salam-Memoirs, pp. 25-6; and Haim, S.G., *Arab Nationalism: An Anthology* (London, 1962), p. 33.

84. See note 60. Salam referred to a request by Ahmad Mukhtar Bayhum, one of the Muslim delegates from Beirut, at a meeting with a French official in the Quai d'Orsay, to quote publicly the latter's assurance that France had no intention of annexing Syria. The Christian delegates opposed his request. Salibi, Salam-Memoirs, pp. 29-30. See also Sa'id, Amin, *al-Thawra*, vol. I, pp. 30-1, 98-101.

85. Jamal Pasha claimed that he had changed his attitude towards the leaders of the reform movement after discovering an attempt by two of its members, 'Abd al-Karim al-Khalil and Rida al-Sulh, to organise a rebellion in the Sidon area: Jamal Pasha, *Memories of a Turkish Statesman 1913-1919* (New York, 1922), pp. 206-9;

and Salibi, Salam-Memoirs, pp. 34-6. For an expression of anti-Turkish feeling among Muslim notables in Lebanon, see letters from Ahmad Mukhtar al-Sulh in Cairo to various notables in Lebanon and Syria in August 1918. FO 371/3384 173437/747, 15 October 1918.

86. Sfer, 'Abdallah Pasha, *Le Mandat Français et les Traditions Françaises en Syrie et au Liban* (Paris, 1922), pp. 22-3; Sawda, pp. 65-7; and Hakim, *Bairut wa Lubnan*, pp. 150-1.

87. Muzhir, vol. II, pp. 854-5; and Hakim, *Bairut wa Lubnan*, pp. 153-4.

88. Jamal Pasha, *Memories*, p. 202.

89. Jamal Pasha, *La Vérité*, pp. 124-5; and FO 141/526, no. 11056, Report on Lebanon, 10 January 1915. Upon the outbreak of the War, Maronite emigrants in Egypt attempted to organise a force of volunteers, but they were discouraged by the British. They also sent representatives to Greece and obtained the agreement of the Greek government to sell them arms and ammunition and to ship them to Lebanon provided that safe conduct through the British blockade was assured. See Tibawi, A.L., *A Modern History of Syria* (London, 1969), pp. 213-14.

90. Rabbath, *La Formation Historique du Liban*, pp. 247-54. For a detailed description of the War period, see Hakim, *Bairut wa Lubnan*.

91. For correspondence between Hawayik and the Turkish authorities, see Muzhir, vol. II, pp. 854-62. See also intelligence reports in FO 141/664. During the War, clergymen, in particular Bulus Aql, smuggled money from Lebanese emigrants into Lebanon through the French-occupied island of Arwad opposite Tripoli, and distributed it among the Mountain's inhabitants. Muzhir, pp. 862-3. See also Ajay, N.Z., 'Political Intrigue and Suppression in Lebanon during World War I', *International Journal of Middle East Studies*, 5 (1974), pp. 140-60; and Hakim, *Bairut wa Lubnan*, pp. 172-4, 271, 277-82.

92. Such accusations had already been made during the War by Lebanese Christian agents, FO 141/664, Report no. 111, Cairo, 22 May 1916. See also appeals by Lebanese in Cairo to American consul-general for relief for the Mountain. For estimates of fatalities, see: Coury, A., 'Le Martyre du Liban', Chambre de Commerce de Marseille, *Congrès français de la Syrie, Janvier 1919: Séances et Travaux* (Marseilles, 1919), Fascicule II, pp. 62-75; Hitti, P.K., *Lebanon in History* (London, 1957), p. 486; Antonius, G., *The Arab Awakening* (London, 1951), p. 241; and Hakim, *Bairut wa Lubnan*, pp. 249-55.

Chapter Two

1. On French educational activities in the Levant before the War, see Pernot, M., *Rapport sur un voyage d'étude à Constantinople, en Egypte et en Turquie-d'Asie, Janvier-Août 1912* presented to the Comité de défense des intérêts français en Orient (Paris, 1912), pp. 277-308, tables, pp. 324-9; Cressaty, Count, 'Les intérêts de la France en Syrie. Conférence prononcée par le Comte Cressaty sous la Présidence de M. Paul Doumer et sous les auspices de l'Alliance française (Paris, 21 May 1913), pp. 27-32; and Marseille, *Congrès français de la Syrie*, Parts II and III.

2. On French economic interests in the Levant before the War, see: Marseille, *Congrès français de la Syrie*, part I; Pernot, *Rapport sur un voyage*; Cressaty, 'Les intérêts de la France'; and 'Les intérêts financiers de la France dans l'Empire ottoman', Report prepared by French companies with investments in the empire, in FO 371/4235, no. 120607, 26 August 1919.

3. Samné, *La Syrie*, p. 80; Spagnolo, *France and Ottoman Lebanon*, pp. 282-3.

4. Pichon, J., *Le Partage du Proche-Orient* (Paris, 1938), pp. 15-31; Cassar, G.H., *The French and the Dardanelles* (London, 1971), pp. 46 ff., 73-4, 220-4; and Kedourie, E., *In the Anglo-Arab Labyrinth* (London, 1976), pp. 53-5. On the

original instructions for the establishment of the Légion d'Orient, see Samné, *La Syrie*, pp. 520–2.

5. For the French stand on the Sykes-Picot agreement, see: Pichon, *Le Partage*, Chapter VI; Samné, *La Syrie*, Chapter XXII; Caix, R. de, 'Dans l'Est — Questions pour la guerre et pour la paix', *AF* no. 173 (May–September 1918), pp. 61–9; and 'La France, l'Angleterre et la Syrie', no. 176 (August–November 1919), pp. 243–9. See also: Kedourie, E., *England and the Middle East* (London, 1956), Chapter II; and Nevakivi, J., *Britain, France and the Arab Middle East, 1914–1920* (London, 1969), Chapter II.

6. Kedourie, *In the Anglo-Arab Labyrinth*, pp. 113–15, 178–82.

7. Pichon, *Le Partage*, p. 110; Gontaut-Biron, Comte R. de, *Comment la France s'est installée en Syrie (1918–1919)* (Paris, 1923), pp. 77, 278. The author had close ties with Picot and served with him in the Western Zone in 1919.

8. Nevakivi, *Britain, France and the Arab Middle East*, p. 33.

9. Tibawi, p. 239.

10. Jung, E., *La Révolte arabe* (Paris, 1925), vol. II, p. 38; Gautherot, G., *La France en Syrie et en Cilicie* (Paris, 1920), pp. 16, 209; Caix, R. de, 'Dans l'Est — Questions pour la guerre et pour la paix', *AF* no. 173 (May–September 1918), pp. 68–9; and 'La France et la Syrie — Notre oeuvre dans le Levant et son avenir', *RDM* (Paris, 15 February 1919), p. 771. See also contents of posters distributed in Paris, FO 371/5181 5171/443, Paris, 20 May 1920, Derby to Curzon.

11. Gontaut-Biron, *Comment la France s'est installée*, pp. 43–6; Gautherot, *La France en Syrie*, Chapter VIII; 'Les affaires d'Orient à la Chambre des députés', address by Pierre Lenail, 26 March 1920, *AF* no. 181 (April 1920), pp. 130–5; and Briand, *ibid*. See also Lenail's address on 26 June 1920, no. 184 (July–August 1920), pp. 253–5.

12. See Millerand's address to the Senate, 28 July 1920, *AF* no. 184 (July–August 1920), pp. 281–7; and Flandin's address to the Senate, 5 April 1921, no. 192 (May 1921), pp. 195–8. Marcel Cachin, a socialist deputy, was an outspoken critic of French intervention in the Levant. See his addresses, 6 February 1920, no. 179 (February 1920), pp. 60–1, and 26 March 1920, no. 181 (April 1920), pp. 121–2.

13. Memorandum by Sir M. Sykes to Mr Barnes on the Anglo-French agreement in regard to the Arab state (n.d.) in private papers collection, Faisal, miscellaneous documents, Middle East Centre, St Antony's College, and Yale Papers, Report no. 6, 3 December 1917, pp. 14–15, microfilm in St Antony's College. Captain William Yale was a special agent of the USA in 1917–18 and later served as adviser to the King-Crane Commission.

14. Marseille, *Congrès français de la Syrie*, part I; 'Bulletin de la Chambre de Commerce de Marseille: Correspondance et Documents' (Marseilles, October 1919). See also a detailed study on Syria prepared for the Comité de l'action française à l'étranger', FO 608/105, no. 1192, 30 January 1919, and 'Le coton en Cilicie et en Syrie', appendix to *AF* (1922).

15. Lamy, E. *La France du Levant* (Paris, 1900); Bérard, V., *Le Sultan, l'Islam et les Puissances* (Paris, 1907); and 'Conférence de M. V. Bérard sur la France dans le Levant', address he gave at a joint meeting of l'Asie Française and the Comité de l'Orient, 8 February 1912, *AF* no. 131 (February 1912), pp. 50–8. See the way Flandin used Bérard's book to criticise his stand after the War in his address to the Senate on 5 April 1921, *AF* no. 192 (May 1921), pp. 196–7. See also Bérard's address to the Senate, 28 July 1920, no. 184 (July–August 1920), pp. 272–81; and Barrès, M., *Une Enquête aux Pays du Levant* (Paris, 1923). His visit took place in 1914. For his meeting with Hawayik, see vol. I, pp. 117–22. See also Bruneau, A., *Traditions et Relations de la France au Levant* (Paris, 1932), pp. 305–6. For bibliography of French works on the Levant, see Masson, P., *Elément d'une bibliographie française de la Syrie* (Marseilles, 1919). This was prepared for the congress in Marseilles and includes 4,530 references.

16. For details of the activities of these religious orders, see Marseille, *Congrès français de la Syrie*, part III.

17. The Syrian question became involved in the conflict between the French Catholic Church and its supporters, and the anti-clericalists. The Church attempted to exploit French public sentiment over France's position in Syria to further its own prestige. The Syrian problem also arose in France's relations with the Holy See. Some argued that the lack of diplomatic relations with the latter, which had been severed in 1904, was harmful to French interests in Syria, and that they should be renewed. See: Pernot, pp. 291–3, 301–5; 'Le Parlement et l'influence française dans le Levant', *AF* no. 154 (January 1914), pp. 91–102; and 'Les missions françaises du Levant en péril', pp. 148–51. See also Cambon, P., *Correspondance (1870–1924)* (Paris, 1946), vol. III, p. 30.

18. Pernot, p. i. For list of members see pp. ii–iv.

19. Denys Cochin, a member of Briand's government which concluded the Sykes-Picot agreement, acted in defence of the Christians in the Levant during and after the War. *AF* no. 201 (April 1922) p. 144. See a letter he sent from Beirut to the Quai d'Orsay while on a special mission in Lebanon during the Inquiry of the King-Crane Commission in Lebanon in AE, Levant, vol. 17, Beirut, 10 September 1919, pp. 173-5. See also his article in *Le Figaro*, 20 July 1919.

20. Samné, G., 'Comité de l'Orient: La question syrienne, exposé — solution, statut politique' (Paris, August 1918). See in particular the resolution adopted by the Comité on 6 October 1918, pp. 36-7. See also a visit by members of the Comité including Barthou, General Bailloud and Admiral Fournier on 29 January 1920 to Deschanel, the new president, in Gautherot, *La France en Syrie*, p. 209.

21. In 1915 Flandin published a pamphlet 'Rapport sur la Syrie et la Palestine' in defence of France's interests in the Levant. For the pamphlet and other documents on his activities, see his papers in the Bibliothèque Nationale. See also his address to the Senate on 5 April 1921 in *AF* no. 192 (May 1921), pp. 196-7, and no. 205 (September–October 1922), pp. 324-5.

22. *AF* no. 185 (September–October 1920), p. 297. See there also a list of members. For composition and aims of the society, see its first bulletin, April 1901. Eugène Etienne played an important part in French colonial activities before the War and headed 'La Ligue Coloniale Française'. Leygues, a leading member of the 'Syrian Party' became minister of the navy in Clemenceau's government in December 1917 and was responsible for French naval operations in Syria and Lebanon. After the War he continually pressured the government to defend France's interests in the Levant against the British and the Arabs.

23. For de Caix's views, see his articles which were regularly published in *AF*, for example: 'La crise orientale et les relations entre la France et la Turquie', no. 141 (December 1912), pp. 515-18; and 'La France et l'aventure turque', no. 160 (July–December 1914), pp. 271-3. At this early stage de Caix was already calling for France's participation in an invasion of Alexandretta. On his role in formulating French Syrian policy, see: Bérard's address to the Senate, 28 July 1920, p. 279; Marseille, *Correspondance et Documents*, p. 902; Rabbath, E., *L'Evolution politique de la Syrie sous mandat* (Paris, 1928), pp. 266-8; and Husri, p.82.

24. 'Le Comité et la question du Levant', *AF* no. 161 (January–March 1915), pp. 40-1; and L'Opinion française et les intérêts nationaux dans le Levant', pp. 42-8.

25. Huvelin, P., 'Que veut le Syrie?', *AF* (December 1921) (supplement); Marseille, *Congrès français de la Syrie*, and *Correspondance et Documents*. See the latter for report on Huvelin's mission. The mission's secretary was Paul Ghanem, nephew of Shukri Ghanem. For British reports and French press-cuttings on the congress, see: FO 371/3386 207880/747, no. 69, Marseilles, 12 December 1918, and 3385 201278/747, no. 64, 2 December 1918; and FO 371/4181 146021/2117, no. 127, 24

October 1919, British consul-general to FO.

26. Mutran, N., *La Syrie de demain* (Paris, 1916); Cressaty, and Jung, vol. I, pp. 135-7.

27. FO 608/105, no. 918, 15 January 1919, Curzon to Balfour; Yale Papers, Report no. 6, p. 12; and Jung, vol. II, pp. 105-6.

28. 'La Syrie devant la Conférence de la Paix'. Report prepared by Shukri Ghanem for the Quai d'Orsay. AE, Levant, vol. 7, Paris, 19 January 1919, pp. 285-7. Ghanem's declaration to the Peace Conference, FO 608/105, no. 2785, 24 February 1919. In March 1919 the Quai d'Orsay gave instructions to establish a society to counter anti-French propaganda in Egypt. The 'Comité Lebano-Syrien' was subsequently formed. It had close ties with the CCS and was headed by 'Abdullah Sfer Pasha, a Maronite who held a high position in the Egyptian administration; vol. 7, note no. 5, 9 January 1919, pp. 159-66.

29. On the CCS's attitude towards Faisal, see: Samné, *La Syrie*, Chapter XIX; and CCS, 'La question syrienne exposée par les Syriens' (Paris, 1919), pp. 26-31. Samné and Ghanem served as advisers in the preparation of the report for the 'Comité de l'action française à l'étranger' in December 1918, on the future organisation of Syria, FO 608/105, no. 1192, 30 January 1919.

30. The official programme of the CCS can be found in *CO*, 10 January 1918, pp. 24-6. For its reply to criticism on its stand on the question of Lebanon's independence, see: 'La Renaissance Libanaise de Sao Paulo', 25 April 1918, pp. 250-3; and 'Les "Minoritaires" syriens', 10 March 1918, pp. 129-33. On opposition of French economic groups to a separate Lebanon, see address by Huvelin in Marseille, *Correspondance et Documents*, p. 915.

31. AE, Levant, vol. 7, Note no. 5, 9 January 1918, and note no. 179, 24 December 1918; and FO 371/4181 98129/2117, no. 311, 23 June 1919, Clayton to Curzon.

32. For manifesto published by 'Ammun in September 1917 and the CCS attitude, see *CO* 10 March 1918, p. 157; 'La question syrienne exposée par les Syriens', p. 11. For Picot's complaints on 'Ammun's activities, see AE, Levant, vol. 14, 'Propagande chérifienne dans la zone Ouest', no. 277, Beirut, 4 July 1919, Picot to Pichon. See also Lohéac, pp. 71-2.

33. On the activities of the Alliance Libanaise, see Sawda, *Fi Sabil al-Istiqlal*. See also Auguste Adib Pasha, *Le Liban après la Guerre* (Cairo, 1917). Further details in Yale Papers: 'Historical Review of the Alliance Libanaise', 7 February 1918, and Report no. 12, 28 January 1918.

34. On the activities of the 'Comité libanais de Paris', see AE, Levant, vol. 9, pp. 228-30. The society was under the constant surveillance of the French police, at Ghanem's request. 'Note pour M. Goût', 4 February 1919, pp. 187-8; no. 108, Paris, 7 February 1919, from the minister for foreign affairs to the minister of the interior.

35. AE, Levant, vol. 2, the Admiralty to base in Port Sa'id, Paris, 4 October 1918, p. 133. On the Beirut incident, see dispatches in the same volume, pp. 121 ff., and Zamir, M., 'Faisal and the Lebanese Question, 1918-1920' (to be published in *Middle Eastern Studies*).

36. On the ceremony in Ba'abda: FO 371/3384 178951/747, no. 141, 26 October 1918, Clayton to FO. Sa'd later claimed that he had agreed to his appointment by Ayubi only after receiving Admiral Varney's approval. Coulondre decided not to appoint him, but a French officer, as governor, with Hawayik's approval. AE, Levant, vol. 3, no. 469, Beirut, 17 October 1918; no. 471, 18 October 1918; no. 489, 22 October 1918, and no. 493, 24 October 1918, Coulondre to Pichon.

37. On the Beqa'a Valley issue, see Zamir, 'Faisal and the Lebanese Question'. In petitions to the French from the Christians in the district of Ba'albek demanding annexation to Lebanon, they claimed that 75 per cent of the land and property in the district belonged to them. AE, Levant, vol. 8, 6 December 1918, p. 25; vol. 9,

no. 42, 12 February 1919; and vol. 10, no. 54, 21 February 1919, Picot to Pichon.
38. The Anglo-French Declaration in Nevakivi, Appendix B. For Christian and Muslim reactions to it see: AE, Levant, vol. 4, no. 561, Beirut, 13 November 1918, Picot to Pichon; vol. 5, no. 682, 10 December 1918; and Service des informations de la Marine dans le Levant, note no. 156, 22 November 1918. Telegram of thanks from Da'uq and Muslim religious leaders of Beirut, vol. 5, 7 December 1918, pp. 136–7. See also FO 371/3385 189886/747, no. 185, 16 November 1918, Clayton to Curzon. On Faisal's visit to Beirut: vol. 5, note no. 157, 26 November 1918.
39. AE, Levant, vol. 5, no. 644, Beirut, 3 December 1918, and nos. 680 and 683, 10 December 1918, Picot to Pichon. Pichon's dispatch, vol. 6, no. 499, 14 December 1918.
40. The original resolution in Arabic and its French translation, AE, Levant, vol. 6, pp. 72–80, Picot to Goût. Picot's request to decorate Sa'd in recognition of his assistance, vol. II, no. 458, Beirut, 22 March 1919.
41. AE, Levant, vol. 6, no. 192, Port Sa'id, 26 December 1918, Laffon to Pichon; no. 193, 27 December 1918; and no. 194, 31 December 1918. Lebanese delegation's letter of protest, vol. 7, no. 1, 2 January 1919. For a British summary of the incident, FO 608/96, no. 1873, 12 February 1919. See also detailed French complaint against the attitude of the British and the Arabs in the Western Zone, and British reply, in FO 608/107, no. 4967, London, 19 March 1919.
42. The Administrative Council's resolution appointed seven members, but the delegation comprised only five: two Maronites — Da'ud 'Ammun and Emile Eddé; a Greek Orthodox — 'Abdullah Khuri-Sa'adeh; a Druze — Najib 'Abd al-Malek; and a Sunni — 'Abd al-Halim Hajjar, who was twenty-three years old. On rivalry between 'Ammun and Eddé, and between them and the Greek Orthodox representative, see: AE, Levant, vol. 9, note 4 February 1919, p. 51; and vol. 10, Note pour M. Goût, 21 January 1919. 'Ammun's and other members' speeches to the Council of Ten, USA, *Papers Related to the Foreign Relations of the United States. The Paris Peace Conference, 1919*, vol. IV, pp. 2–5.
43. AE, Levant, vol. 10, Délégation libanaise auprès de la Conférence de la Paix: Note sur les frontières du Grand Liban, dated 8 March 1918.
44. Protests against the delegation: FO 371/4144 10636/135, 18 December 1918; 16405/135, 26 January 1919; 21006/135, 12 January 1919; 24648/135, 29 January 1919; FO 371/4153 37058/275, 10 February 1919. Jung, vol. II, p. 115.
45. FO 608/96, no. 2552, Cairo, 5 January 1919, 'Protestation adressée par l'Alliance Libanaise aux membres du Conseil Administratif du Liban.' For protests and request by the Comité Libanais de Paris to appear before the Peace Conference, see: FO 608/96, Paris, 10 February 1919, pp. 113–14; and AE, Levant, vol. 9, 14 February 1919, pp. 228–30.
46. AE, Levant, vol. 2, no. 4141, Paris, 8 October 1918, Pichon to Cambon; and vol. 3, Paris, 16 October 1918, Picot to Pichon. See also Picot's speech to the Comité de l'Orient, 6 August 1918 in CO, 25 September 1918, pp. 129–34.
47. AE, Levant, vol. 4, nos. 559–60, 4 November 1918, Picot to Pichon; and Note pour le Ministre, Paris, 15 November 1918, pp. 151–2. See also Sykes memorandum, FO 608/105, no. 870, 22 January 1919.
48. Brémond, E., *Le Hedjaz dans la guerre mondiale* (Paris, 1931), p. 308. For Allenby's opposition to French reinforcement, see his interview with the Council of Four, 20 March 1919, USA, *The Paris Peace Conference*, vol. V, pp. 8–11; and WO 106/189, 13 March 1919, WO to Allenby. See also AE, Levant, Vol. 7, no. 95, Beirut, 19 January 1919, Picot to Pichon.
49. For description of French administrative organisation of the Western Zone and criticism of lack of funds and staff, see: Gontaut-Biron, *Comment la France s'est installée*, Chapter VI; and Gautherot, *La France en Syrie*, Chapter VI. For comparison between the organisation of the British administration in Palestine and that of the French in Lebanon immediately after the occupation, see Presland, J., *Deedes*

Bey (London, 1942), pp. 296–9.

50. AE, Levant, vol. 4, no. 575, 16 November 1918, Picot to Pichon.

51. For the propaganda war between the French and the Arab government in the Western Zone, see Zamir, 'Faisal and the Lebanese Question'. Before and during the Peace Conference Picot sent petitions from the Lebanese to the Quai d'Orsay requesting a French mandate. See collections in vols. 8, 9 and 12.

52. Detailed description of the column's visit to south Lebanon in: Gautherot, *La France en Syrie*, pp. 8–12, 80–100; AE, Levant, vol. 9, no. 43, Beirut, 14 February 1919; and no. 265, 19 February 1919, Picot to Pichon. For Picot's negotiations with the Druze and a list of their demands, see vol. 10, nos. 350–2, 4 March 1919, Picot to Pichon. See also FO 371/3384 184647/747, no. 7191/P, Cairo, 4 November 1918, Allenby to WO.

53. FO 800/221, London, 16 September 1918, Sykes to Picot, and private letter from Sykes to Clayton, 3 March 1918. See also: *CO*, 30 March 1919, pp. 264–5; and Gontaut-Biron, *Comment la France s'est installée*, pp. 231–2.

54. AE, Levant, vol. 3, no. 471, 18 October 1918, Coulondre to Pichon; vol. 8, no. 133, Beirut, 26 January 1919, Picot to Pichon. See also: FO 608/93, no. 2625, 6 February 1919, Clayton to FO; and protest presented to Faisal by the Syrian Congress, FO 371/4182 130304/2117, 16 September 1919.

55. AE, Levant, vol. 8, Damascus, 18 January 1919, p. 196, extract of report by Faisal's delegate in Beirut, obtained by the French; vol. 9, no. 168, Beirut, 1 February 1919, Picot on a meeting with 'Umar Da'uq and Ahmad Mukhtar Bayhum; and vol. 11, no. 110, Beirut, 25 March 1919, 23 petitions from Muslims in Beirut requesting a Syrian federation under a mandatory power, sent by Picot to the Quai d'Orsay.

56. For Muslim complaints of French favouritism towards the Maronites, see: USA, *The Paris Peace Conference, 1919, The King-Crane Commission*, vol. XII, p. 852; and Gontaut-Biron, *Comment la France s'est installée*, pp. 104–7. For descriptions of local inhabitants' reaction to France and Britain, see: AE, Levant, vol. 6, note 157, 26 November 1918; no. 713, 13 December 1918, Picot to Pichon; and FO 371/3385, no. 190, 18 November 1918, Clayton to FO.

57. Khuri, B. al-, *Haqa'iq Lubnaniyah* (Beirut, 1960), vol. I, pp. 86–93.

58. For analysis of Faisal's reasons for opposing an independent Lebanon, see Zamir, 'Faisal and the Lebanese Question'.

59. Pichon, pp. 164–5; Brémond, p. 221, note 3, and pp. 241–54; Cambon, vol. III, pp. 275–6, 319–21; Watson, D.R., *Georges Clemenceau: A Political Biography* (Plymouth, 1974), pp. 366–72; and Bérard's address to the Senate, 28 July 1920, pp. 276–80.

60. On pressure from French public and press: Bérard, ibid., p. 79. Resolution adopted by the Committee for External Affairs in the Senate on 27 January 1919 demanding the safeguarding of French interests in 'la Syrie intégrale' in AE, Levant, vol. 8, pp. 141–3. See also: FO 371/4239, no. 2248, Paris, 3 December 1919, Crewe to Curzon; Cambon, pp. 333–4, 354–5, 370–2; and Lloyd George, D., *The Truth about the Peace Treaties* (London, 1938), vol. I, pp. 578–82.

61. On Tardieu's involvement in a plan for the Homs-Baghdad railway before the War, see Binion, R., *Defeated Leaders: The Political Fate of Caillaux, Jouvenel and Tardieu* (New York, 1960), pp. 226–39.

62. For Lawrence's role in the negotiations, see his memorandum to the Quai d'Orsay, 7 April 1919, AE, Levant, vol. II, pp. 247–9. De Caix claimed later that it had been Lawrence who prevented Faisal from concluding an agreement with the French. See his memorandum 'L'organisation donnée à la Syrie et au Liban, de 1920 à 1923 et la crise actuelle', October 1926, in vol. 200, pp. 35–6.

63. Zamir, 'Faisal and the Lebanese Question'. For Picot's stand see Yale Papers, Note on conversation with M. Georges-Picot, 17 April 1919.

64. AE, Levant, vol. 200, de Caix's memorandum, pp. 37–8.

65. AE, Levant, vol. 13, no. 724, Beirut, 23 May 1919, Picot to Pichon; FO 371/4181 105815/2117, Cairo, 8 July 1919, GHQ to FO; 91483/2117, Beirut, 9 June 1919; and 98129/2117, no. 311, 23 June 1919, Clayton to Curzon.

66. AE, Levant, vol. 13, nos. 760-1, Beirut, 31 May 1919; no. 226, 'Situation politique en Syrie', 3 June 1919; and Sa'd's letter to Picot and a copy of the resolution: no. 234, 3 June 1919, Picot to Pichon. See also: vol. 15, no. 338, 'Situation politique au Liban durant le mois de mai 1919', 4 July 1919; and no. 254, 2 June 1919, telegrams of support for the resolution.

67. AE, Levant, vol. 13, no. 226, Beirut, 'Situation politique de 19 au 26 mai 1919', 3 June 1919; no. 829, 13 June 1919; vol. 14, no. 871, 22 June 1919, Picot to Pichon; and Sawda, pp. 179-81.

68. FO 371/4181 105815/2117, Cairo, 8 July 1919, GHQ to FO.

69. AE, Levant, vol. 14, no. 871, Beirut, 22 June 1919, Picot to Pichon.

70. AE, Levant, vol. 13, no. 724, Beirut, 23 May 1919; no. 226, 3 June 1919, Picot to Pichon; and FO 371/4181 98129/2117, no. 311, Cairo, 23 June 1919, Clayton to Curzon.

71. AE, Levant, vol. 13, no. 724, Beirut, 23 May 1919; and no. 226, 3 June 1919, Picot to Pichon.

72. Caix, R. de, 'L'état présent des questions orientales et l'intérêt français', *AF* no. 175 (February–July 1919), p. 176.

73. AE, Levant, vol. 13, no. 761, Beirut, 1 June 1919; and nos. 820-1, 12 June 1919, Picot to Pichon.

74. AE, Levant, vol. 14, no. 277, 'Propagande chérifienne dans la zone ouest', Beirut, 4 July 1919, Picot to Pichon. See also Hakim, Y. al-, *Suriya wa'l 'Ahd al-Faysali* (Beirut, 1966), pp. 99-100.

75. David, P., *Un gouvernement arabe à Damas* (Paris, 1923), pp. 58-9. See also AE, Levant, vol. 25, nos. 620-2, Beirut, 13 March 1920, Gouraud to Quai d'Orsay. For debate on Lebanon in the Syrian Congress, see *al Mufid*, Damascus, 12 August 1919, translation in vol. 17, no. 485, Beirut, 1 September 1919, Laforcade to Pichon.

76. USA, *The King-Crane Commission*, vol. XII, 'Confidential Appendix to the Report upon Syria', pp. 848-50.

77. AE, Levant, vol. 15, no. 338, Beirut, 4 July 1919, Picot to Pichon. In a letter of 28 January 1920 to Cambon, the French ambassador in London, Hawayik wrote: 'Les autorités françaises de Syrie se rendent parfaitement compte que malgré les sacrifices énormes qu'elles s'imposent vis-à-vis des non-chrétiens, elles n'ont pas avancé beaucoup, et que plus on agrandira le Liban, plus la France sera chez elle et moins elle rencontrera de résistance ailleurs.' Vol. 125, pp. 141-2.

78. Sawda, p. 182.

79. USA, *The King-Crane Commission*, vol. XII, pp. 756-70, 848-50. See also Kedourie, *England and the Middle East*, pp. 145-6.

80. There were also several deputations representing professional groups such as lawyers, doctors and journalists, organised mainly by the French authorities. The analysis of the stand of the various communities is based on USA, *The King-Crane Commission*, vol. XII; Yale Papers, 'Recommendations as to the future disposition of Palestine, Syria and Mount Lebanon' and 'A report on Syria, Palestine and Mount Lebanon for the American commissioners', Constantinople, 26 July 1919; CO, 'La commission d'enquête americaine dans le Levant', 30 July–15 August 1919, pp. 70-6; *Journal du Caire*, Cairo, 21 July 1919; Howard, H.N., *The King-Crane Commission* (Beirut, 1963); and detailed reports prepared by French officers in each region of the Western Zone in AE, Levant, vols. 15, 16.

81. AE, Levant, vol. 14, nos. 982-4, Beirut, 9 July 1919, Picot to Pichon; vol. 16, no. 410, 'Opérations des commissionnaires américaines à Tripoli', 16 August 1919, Laforcade to Pichon; and *Journal du Caire*, Cairo, 21 July 1919. See also Muzhir, vol. II, pp. 882-4.

82. AE, Levant, vol. 14, no. 277, Beirut, 4 July 1919, Picot to Pichon; vol. 16,

no. 410, Beirut, 16 August 1919, Laforcade to Pichon; *CO* 30 July–15 August 1919, pp. 72–3; and Hakim, *Suriya wa'l 'Ahd al-Faysali*, pp. 61–5, 101–2.

83. AE, Levant, vol. 15, no. 338, Beirut, 21 July 1919, Picot to Pichon; FO 371/4184 14591/2117, 'General Report on Western Syria Completed by General Staff Intelligence.' July 1919, Chapter 15 — the Druze; and Hakim, *Suriya wa'l 'Ahd al-Faysali*, pp. 81–2.

84. FO 371/4184 145791/2117, General Staff intelligence report, Chapter 16 — the Mutawallis; and AE, Levant, vol. 16, no. 368, 'Opérations des Commissaires américains dans le sanjak de Saïda', Beirut, 8 August 1919, Laforcade to Pichon.

85. USA, *The King-Crane Commission*, vol. XII, pp. 857–8.

86. Ibid., 'Arab Feeling towards the French', pp. 852–3. See also Yale Papers, 'A report on Syria, Palestine and Mount Lebanon for the American commissioners', 26 July 1919.

87. Ibid.; and 'Recommendations as to the Future Disposition of Palestine, Syria and Mount Lebanon', 26 July 1919. See also Howard, p. 131.

88. Arslan, S., 'La mort du Patriarche Maronite' in *Nation arabe*, Geneva, November–December 1931, p. 50.

89. For the resolution, see *L'Asie arabe*, Paris, 5 October 1919. See also Hawayik's address before departing from Junieh in *CO*, 'Le départ du Patriarche Maronite pour la France', 15 September 1919, pp. 136–7.

90. AE, Levant, vol. 16, nos. 1875–6, Rome, 9 August 1919; nos. 1843–5, 5 August 1919; and nos. 1848, 1850–1, 6 August 1919, Barrère to Pichon. See Hawayik's letter of thanks to Barrère for his help for the Lebanese cause, vol. 126, 8 September 1920, pp. 14–15. See also Khuri, *Haqa'iq Lubnaniyah*, vol. I, p. 96.

91. *CO*, 'Le Patriarche Maronite en France', 15 September 1919, pp. 125–30. See also Feghali's interview in *Le Gaulois*, Paris, 14 September 1919 in FO 371/4182 131244/2117, Paris, 14 September 1919, Grahame to Curzon.

92. Muzhir, vol. II, p. 887. See also Hawayik's interview with Forbes-Adam, a member of the British delegation to the Peace Conference, in FO 371/4182 136086/2117, Minute by Mr Forbes-Adam, Paris, 26 September 1919.

93. For the memorandum, see Appendix A. 'Le Liban et la France: Documents publiés par le Patriarche Maronite' (Bkerki, 23 February 1936), pp. 8–9. There is some basis for 'Arida's claim, as the original draft of Clemenceau's letter to Hawayik was dated 27 October 1919, but was sent only on 10 November. See AE, Levant, vol. 19, p. 40.

94. Appendix B. On the same day Clemenceau sent a declaration to Picot for the Muslims in Syria and Lebanon, in which he stressed France's liberal policy towards them. To some extent this contradicted his letter to Hawayik. AE, Levant, vol. 19, nos. 921–3, Paris, 10 November 1919, Clemenceau to Picot.

95. Watson, p. 384; Jung, vol. II, pp. 126–7; and Bérard's address to the Senate, 28 July 1920, p. 279.

96. FO 371/5033 E1696/2, 7 March 1920, Negotiations between Faisal and the French government.

97. For an analysis of the negotiations, see Zamir, 'Faisal and the Lebanese Question'.

98. Butler, R. and Woodward, E. (eds), *Documents on British Foreign Policy, 1919–1939* (London, 1952), 1st. Ser., vol. IV, no. 310, Paris, 9 October 1919, Derby to Curzon. See also Lyautey, P., *Gouraud* (Paris, 1949), p. 219. General Lyautey, who established the French protectorate in Morocco before the War, greatly influenced French colonial policy. For a comparison between French policy in Morocco and in Syria, see Burke, E., 'A Comparative View of French Native Policy in Morocco and Syria, 1912–1925' in *Middle Eastern Studies*, vol. 9, no. 2 (May 1973), pp. 175–86. See also Bidwell, R., *Morocco under Colonial Rule, French Administration in Tribal Areas, 1912–1956* (London, 1973).

99. For Gouraud's stand on Syria, see: 'Réunion du Comité du 11 décembre, 1920 — Exposé verbal du général Gouraud' in *AF* no. 188 (January 1921), pp. 6–12; General Gouraud, 'La France en Syrie', extract from *Revue de la France*, 1 April 1920; 'L'Oeuvre de la France en Syrie'. *RDM* 15 February 1921, pp. 801–40; 'Le Général Gouraud en Syrie', *CO* 30 October 1919, pp. 247–51, 260–4; and Lyautey, *Gouraud*. The author served under Gouraud in Syria and Lebanon.

100. 'Exposé verbal du général Gouraud', p. 8. See also Picot's remark in FO 371/4185 156779/2117, no. 311, Cairo, 10 November 1919, Meinertzhagen to Curzon. On Gouraud's attempts to deploy French forces in the Beqa'a, see Zamir, 'Faisal and the Lebanese Question'. For criticism of Clemenceau's decision not to allow Gouraud to occupy the Beqa'a, see Lyautey, P., *Le Drame Oriental* (Paris, 1923), pp. 162–3. For de Caix's criticism of Gouraud's cautious policy towards Faisal, see Millerand's Papers, Bibliothèque Nationale, Box 60, letter from de Caix to Millerand, 4 May 1920.

101. Bérard's address to the Senate, 28 July 1920, p. 279. On de Caix's proposal to present Faisal with an ultimatum, see his letter in Millerand's Papers, 4 May 1920. For summary of his policy, see memoranda he presented to the Quai d'Orsay, AE, Levant, vol. 22, 'Note sur la politique de l'accord avec Faysal', 26 January 1920, pp. 50–77; vol. 31, 'Esquisse de l'organisation de la Syrie sous le Mandat français', 17 July 1920; and vol. 200, 'L'organisation donnée à la Syrie et au Liban de 1920 à 1923 et la crise actuelle', October 1926, pp. 22–141.

102. AE, Levant, vol. 126, Hawayik's letter to Barrère, Neo Kannobin, 8 September 1920, pp. 14–15. See Gouraud's attitude towards Hawayik in the official ceremony on 1 September 1920 of the proclamation of Greater Lebanon, FO 371/5040 11571/2, no. 77, Beirut, 2 September 1920, Fontana to the Secretary of State for Foreign Affairs.

103. Two people particularly active in Beirut at this time in defence of the Lebanese Christian cause were Giannini, the delegate of the Holy See and Father Catin, a Jesuit and former chancellor of the medical school at St Joseph University. See, for example, Giannini's dispatches to the Holy See in AE, Levant, vol. 26, no. 1171, Beirut, 15 March 1920, Giannini to Cardinal Gaspari, and dispatches transferred by the French chargé d'affaires in the Vatican, to Millerand, 20 April 1920, pp. 233–6. Father Catin participated in meetings of the Comité de l'Asie Française before and during the War. He also took an active part in the congress in Marseilles. On his influence in Beirut, see: Khuri, *Haqa'iq Lubnaniyah*, vol. I, p. 99; and Sawda, pp. 155–8. On Father Catin's role, Bruneau quoted the following: 'C'est au 'Père Catin que la France doit son mandat sur la Syrie et le Liban.' Bruneau, p. 304. See also visit by Cardinal Dubois, head of the Catholic Church in Paris, to Beirut at the beginning of 1920, and reaction of Christians and Muslims, in: vol. 19, nos. 1515–16, Beirut, 8 December 1919, Gouraud to Pichon; and FO 371/5032 1584/2, no. 8, Beirut, 20 February 1920, Wratislaw to FO.

104. AE, Levant, vol. 20, Note 13, 14 November 1919; vol. 21, Note on conversation with Faisal, Paris, 9 January 1920, pp. 141–2; and vol. 26, no. 1171, Beirut, 15 March 1920, Giannini to Cardinal Gaspari.

105. AE, Levant, vol. 200, de Caix's memorandum, p. 77. Both Lawrence and Sykes claimed that the Maronites constantly tried to hinder *rapprochement* between the French authorities and the inhabitants of Syria and Lebanon, particularly the Muslims; vol. 11, Lawrence's memorandum to the Quai d'Orsay, 7 April 1919; and Sykes' memorandum, FO 608/105, no. 870, 22 January 1919.

106. AE, Levant, vol. 200, de Caix's memorandum, pp. 71–8.

107. See Millerand's reply to Cachin in the Chamber of Deputies, 6 February 1920 *AF* no. 179 (February 1920), pp. 61–2; and his address to the Senate, 28 July 1920, no. 184 (July–August 1920), pp. 281–4. See also: Jung, vol. II, pp. 136–7, 143–5; and Cambon, vol. III, pp. 386–7.

108. On the formation of Millerand's Syrian policy, see his private papers, in

particular Box no. 60. See also: AE, Levant, vol. 22, nos. 98, 103, Paris, 31 January 1920; vol. 23, nos. 149-55, 10 February 1920; vol. 28, nos. 426-35, 455-63, 4 May 1920; and nos. 505-18, 27 May 1920, Millerand to Gouraud.

109. AE, Levant, vol. 19, nos. 1563-6, Beirut, 29 November 1919, Gouraud to Clemenceau; vol. 21, note 20, 12 December 1919 and note 23, 19 December 1919. See also Hawayik's letter to Cambon, vol. 125, 28 January 1920, pp. 141-2. On the publication of the Clemenceau-Faisal agreement in *al-Barq*, Beirut, 21 January 1920, see Muzhir, vol. II, pp. 908-9.

110. The delegation was headed by Bishop 'Abdullah al-Khuri and included Emile Eddé, Joseph Gemayel, Alfred Sursuk and Tawfik Arslan. For Hawayik's letter to the Administrative Council and the latter's resolution of 28 February 1920 authorising the delegation, see AE, Levant, vol. 24, no. 81, Beirut, 2 March 1920, Gouraud to Millerand. See also vol. 32, 'Note pour M. de Peretti par R. de Caix', pp. 145-6, 14 August 1920. Criticism of the three Lebanese delegations and their members, in *L'Asie arabe*, Paris, 15 April 1920.

111. AE, Levant, vol. 125, 'Les revendications libanaises: Note de la troisième délégation libanaise', Paris, 21 February 1920, pp. 145-6. For other memoranda see: pp. 147-51, 20 March 1920; pp. 165-6, 26 April 1920; and pp. 174-5, 13 May 1920. Lebanese Christian pressure on French authorities to occupy the Beqa'a, vol. 20, Note no. 13, 14 November 1919. On Gouraud's and de Caix's stand on the Beqa'a, see Zamir, 'Faisal and the Lebanese Question'.

112. Copy of the resolution in Millerand Papers, Box 60.

113. See his addresses in the Chamber of Deputies, 26 March 1920, *AF* no. 181 (April 1920), pp. 130-5, and on 26 June 1920, no. 184 (July-August 1920), pp. 253-5. Two years later when he visited Hawayik, the Maronite Bishop Pierre Feghali described him as 'the eloquent defender of Lebanese independence in the Chamber of Deputies', Hobeika, P., *Discours, Allocutions, Articles: Mgr. Michel Feghali* (Junieh, 1938), pp. 106-10.

114. Millerand Papers, Box 60, 'Réponse au questionnaire dressé par M. Lenail, 1 March 1920'; AE, Levant, vol. 26, nos. 788-97, Beirut, 7 April 1920, Gouraud to Millerand; and 'Note pour M. de Peretti de M. Bertrand', Paris, 10 April 1920, pp. 131-2.

115. AE, Levant, vol. 10, no. 356, Beirut, 4 March 1919, and no. 360, 6 March 1919, Picot to Pichon.

116. Yale Papers, 'A report on Syria, Palestine and Mount Lebanon for the American Commissioners', 26 July 1919, p. 15.

117. FO 371/4186 163275/2117, no. 92, Cairo, 2 December 1919 in Meinertzhagen's dispatch to Curzon. See also his dispatch no. 311, 10 November 1919 in FO 371/5185 156779/2117. For Muslim reaction to the agreement, see protests by the Arab liaison officer to Picot in AE, Levant, vol. 18, no. 537, Beirut, 18 October 1919, Picot to Pichon. On the rise of the extremists and increasing pan-Islamic and anti-European sentiment, see: vol. 18, note 4, 26 September 1919; vol. 21, report 24, 15 December 1919; and note 21, 2 January 1920. For a draft of a proposed treaty between the Arab government and the Turkish nationalists against the French, found in 'Adel Arslan's papers which were seized by the French, see vol. 35, no. 25, Beirut, 19 January 1921, de Caix to Millerand. On Rashid Rida's disappointment with Arab *rapprochement* with the Turks, see his interview with Picot in vol. 18, no. 1276, Beirut, 8 October 1919, Picot to Pichon. See also Sa'id, Amin, vol. II, pp. 92-104.

118. AE, Levant, vol. 18, nos. 1276-8, Beirut, 26 September 1919, Laforcade to Pichon; no. 1412, 25 October 1919, Picot to Pichon; and vol. 19, Bulletin de renseignements hebdomadaires, no. 4, 15-22 December 1919. See also: FO 371/4186 174490/2117, 13 January 1920, Meinertzhagen to Curzon; and FO 371/5032 1198/2, 8 March 1920, report attached from 3 January 1920.

119. Detailed descriptions of attacks are to be found in volumes of these months in

AE. For summary see two memoranda which Gouraud handed to Faisal in January upon the latter's return from Paris, in vol. 22, 15 January 1920, pp. 168–76. See comprehensive report prepared by the high commissioner after the occupation of Damascus, including documents seized by the French, in vol. 33, 'Note au sujet des rapports entre le Haut Commissaire de la République Française en Syrie-Cilicie et l'Emir Fayçal', 22 September 1920. See also Sa'id, Amin, vol. II, pp. 105–17.

120. After the declaration of independence, Gouraud claimed that upon his return from Paris, Faisal himself had informed him that he had provoked the troubles in the Beqa'a in order to improve his position in the negotiations: AE, Levant, vol. 25, no. 652, Beirut, 17 March 1920; vol. 26, no. 795, 7 April 1920, Gouraud to Millerand; and Gouraud's letter to Allenby in FO 371/5036 6994/2, 9 June 1920. Gouraud repeated this accusation on 7 August in a speech at a reception for Syrian notables in Damascus, *al-Barq* Beirut, 9–11 August 1920. Translation in 'Arabic Press Extracts' prepared by the Arab Bureau in FO 371/5189 10972/499, 25 August 1920. Gouraud's accusations are verified by a letter Faisal sent from London quoted in Qasimiya, Khayriya, *al-Hukuma al-'Arabiya fi Dimashq bayna 1918–1920* (Beirut, 1971), p. 151, note 4. See also vol. 21, Note on conversation with Faisal, Paris, 9 January 1920, pp. 141–2.

121. FO 371/5035 5690/2, no. 35, Beirut, 13 May 1920, Wratislaw to FO; and Lyautey, *Le Drame Oriental*, p. 167. It is impossible to ascertain the exact number of people killed, but it was probably over 200.

122. AE, Levant, vol. 18, note 6, 10 October 1919; Private letter from Kamal al-As'ad to Na'if Soubeh, 18 May 1920, in FO 371/5120 7727/85, Jerusalem, 10 June 1920, General Bols to FO; *al-Mufid* Damascus, 2 July 1920, in 'Arabic Press Extracts', FO 371/5188 9334/499, 19 July 1920; and *al-Kinana* Damascus, 'The French in Jabal 'Amel', 26 May 1920, 7808/499, 14 June 1920.

123. For Gouraud's request for 20,000 rifles to arm the Christians: AE, Levant, vol. 125, no. 1652, Paris, 26 March 1920, War Minister to Foreign Minister; and no. 905, 3 April 1920. Faisal's complaint to Lloyd George, FO 371/5035 5904/2, no. 541, 4 June 1920. Complaint by the Muslims on the coast to Gouraud, *al-Kinana* Damascus, 22 May 1920, in FO 371/5188 6497/499, 7 June 1920. On the Christians' provocative behaviour see: *L'Asie arabe* Paris, 20 August 1919; vol. 18, note 4, 26 September 1919; and Zayd's letter to Allenby, 3 January 1920, in FO 371/4187 176608/2117, no. 2, Damascus, 3 January 1920, WO to Under Secretary of State of FO.

124. AE, Levant, vol. 16, Beirut, 20 August 1919, p. 202, Laforcade to Pichon; vol. 18, no. 308/S, Rapport politique mensuel (Août 1919); no. 1278, 26 September 1919, Laforcade to Pichon; and note 6, 10 October 1919. The report claimed that a committee of Druze leaders including Amin and 'Adel Arslan, was established in Damascus and was attempting to provoke sectarian hostility in Mount Lebanon for political reasons. The report also gives the reasons for the Druze attack on Sa'd. See also vol. 19, note 4, 15–22 October 1919; and FO 371/4233 109428/109425, 28 July 1919.

125. AE, Levant, vol. 19, note 4, 15–22 October 1919; vol. 20, note 13, 14 November 1919; and note 14, 21 November 1919. See also FO 371/4185 156779/2117, no. 311, Cairo, 10 November 1919, Meinertzhagen to Curzon.

126. AE, Levant, vol. 20, note 19, 5 December 1919; vol. 20, no. 1658; and vol. 22, no. 224, Beirut, 30 January 1920, Gouraud to Pichon. Autonomy for the Druze was included in Clemenceau's agreement with Faisal, 6 January 1920. See also *al-Mufid* Damascus, 2 July 1920 in FO 371/5188 9334/499, 19 July 1920. The newspaper stated that it was Major Clayton who persuaded the Druze leaders in the Houran to refrain from invading Lebanon. On the selection of Druze as bodyguards for Gouraud, see FO 371/5032 1584/2, no. 8, Beirut, 20 February 1920, Wratislaw to FO. For detailed description of relations between the Druze and France, see Abu Rashid, H., *Jabal al Duruze* (Cairo, 1925).

127. AE, Levant, vol. 21, note 25, 26 December 1919 and note, 26 February 1920; vol. 26, Rapport Hebdomadaire no. 11, 16 April 1920; vol. 28, Greek Catholic Metropolite of Tyre to Gouraud, 15 May 1920, pp. 5–14; and FO 371/5036 8101/2, Cairo, 26 June 1920, Allenby to Curzon.

128. AE, Levant, vol. 22, de Caix's memorandum, 30 January 1920, p. 141; see also p. 75; vol. 24, nos. 589–90, Beirut, 10 March 1920, and nos. 992–6 in vol. 27, 10 May 1920, Gouraud to Millerand. Faisal received reports from Paris on de Caix's intentions: vol. 29, nos. 1162–3, Beirut, 6 June 1920, Gouraud to Millerand. See also Kamal al-As'ad's letter to Na'if Subeh, 18 May 1920 in FO 371/5120 7727/85.

129. AE, Levant, vol. 21, detailed report from the Greek Catholic Metropolite of Tyre to Gouraud, 15 May 1920, pp. 5–14. For a British report of the incident see FO 371/5120 6193/85, no. 576, Cairo, 1 June 1920, Allenby to Curzon. See also As'ad's private letter.

130. FO 371/5036 7737/2, no. 47, Beirut, 12 June 1920, Wratislaw to FO; and AE, Levant, vol. 28, nos. 1015–17, Beirut, 15 May 1920, Gouraud to Millerand. See also Safa, M.J. al-, *Ta'rikh Jabal 'Amil* (Beirut, n.d.) pp. 221–30.

131. Millerand Papers, Box 60, de Caix's letter, 4 May 1920; *AF* no. 183 (June 1920), p. 199; *The Times* London, 17 May 1920 in FO 371/5035 5097/2, 19 May 1920; and Question to the Foreign Minister in the parliament on the incident of 'Ain Ibel in FO 371/5119 5231/85, 10 May 1920. See also FO 371/5035 5691/2, no. 36, Beirut, 13 May 1920, Wratislaw to FO.

132. AE, Levant, vol. 24, note 48, 27 February 1920; and vol. 26, no. 1171, Beirut, 15 March 1920, Giannini to Cardinal Gaspari. For rumours that the French were leaving Lebanon, see: FO 371/5033 1773/2, no. 303, Const., 2 March 1920, high commissioner to Curzon, enclosure no. 1; and FO 371/5120 6487/85, no. 40, Beirut, 25 May 1920, Wratislaw to FO. On the massacre in Marrash, see Véou, P. du, *La passion de la Cilicie, 1919–1922* (Paris, 1954), pp. 122–9.

133. AE, Levant, vol. 26, Rapport hebdomadaire, no. 6, 19 March 1920. Reaction in Christian and Muslim press: vol. 25, pp. 280–2; and FO 371/5034 3500/2, no. 22, Beirut, 29 March 1920, Wratislaw to FO. Protests against declaration of independence in *CO*, 'Protestations syriennes contre les décisions du "Congrès syrien" ', 15 April 1920, pp. 314–16.

134. AE, Levant, vol. 25, nos. 623–4, Beirut, 13 March 1920, Gouraud to Millerand, and no. 278, Paris, 25 March 1920. 'Abdullah al-Khuri transferred Millerand's letter to Hawayik and Sa'd; nos. 704–5, 25 March 1920, Gouraud to Millerand; and vol. 26, report no. 7, 26 March 1920. See also: FO 371/5034 3500/2, no. 22, Beirut, 29 March 1920, Wratislaw to FO; and *CO* 15 April 1920, p. 324, and 15 May 1920, p. 413.

135. AE, Levant, vol. 26, Report no. 7, 26 March 1920; vol. 33, 'Difficultés économiques provoqués entravers au commerce', pp. 208–10; SHA, Box 2B1, Rapport Hebdomadaire, 3 May 1920; and Box 4B2, nos. 929–30, 30 April 1920, protest of Chamber of Commerce of Beirut sent to Gouraud by 'Umar Da'uq. For detailed description of economic situation in the Western Zone, see reports compiled by General Staff Intelligence, July 1919 in FO 371/4184 145791/2117. See also: FO 371/5034 2539/2, no. 18, Beirut, 17 March 1920, Wratislaw to FO; and *The Near East* London, 4 March 1920, p. 317, and 25 March 1920, pp. 424–5.

136. FO 371/5032 1584/2, no. 8, Beirut, 20 February 1920; and FO 371/5032 3500/2, no. 22, 29 March 1920, Wratislaw to FO.

137. Appendix C. On the deterioration in relations between the French authorities and Sa'd and other members of the Administrative Council, see Khuri, *Haqa'iq Lubnaniyah*, vol. I, pp. 99–105.

138. Gouraud had a secret 'political fund' from which money was given to various individuals and organisations for furthering French interests. Among the recipients were the Dutch consul in Beirut and the Spanish consul in Jerusalem. One Lebanese who received money was Michel Twaini, a Greek Orthodox notable from Beirut who

headed a group of Christians who supported France. For details, see: SHA, Box 5B2, no. 70, Paris, 17 January 1920, Pichon to Gouraud; Box 4B2, no. 697, 24 March 1920; no. 171, 30 December 1919; no. 773, 5 April 1920; and no. 822. On the special attitude of the French towards Michel Twaini, see Khuri, *Haqa'iq Lubnaniyah*, vol. I, pp. 104–5.

139. The request for a constitution had already been included in the Administrative Council's resolution of 20 May 1919. For Gouraud's letter to Habib al-Sa'd and the names of the 14 members, one of whom was Paul Nujaim, see *CO* 15–30 July 1920, pp. 32–3. For public statements by Habib al-Sa'd and Da'ud 'Ammun on the future form of the Lebanese government, see *al-Barq* Beirut, 22 June 1920. See also: FO 371/5036 7737/2, no. 47, Beirut, 12 June 1920; and 5037 8502/2, no. 49, 2 July 1920, Wratislaw to FO.

140. AE, Levant, vol. 125, Hawayik to Gouraud, 29 May 1920, p. 179. On activities of Faisal's representatives among the Lebanese Christians, see: vol. 24, note 48, 27 February 1920; vol. 25, Report no. 2, 8 March 1920, pp. 268–70; and in particular SHA, Box 2B1, weekly intelligence reports of 8 June 1920, 22 June 1920, 29 June 1920 and 5 July 1920. See also FO 371/5037 8502/2, no. 49, Beirut, 2 July 1920, Wratislaw to FO.

141. For rumours of French agreement with Faisal, see *Lissan al-Hal* Beirut, 6 June 1920, 12 June 1920 and 17 June 1920. AE, Levant, vol. 37, no. 207, Beirut, 18 October 1921, Gouraud to Briand; SHA, Box 4B2, nos. 1403–6, Beirut, 12 July 1920, Gouraud to Millerand; no. 1044, 26 July 1921; and nos. 1364–7, 18 October 1921, Gouraud to Briand. The affair of the Administrative Council has been extensively discussed by Lebanese historians. Details which emerge from French documents, including intelligence reports in Boxes 2B1 and 12B3 are similar to descriptions given by Muzhir, vol. II, pp. 920–9. See also *CO* 30 October 1920, pp. 258–65.

142. Appendix D.

143. Sawda, pp. 293–4; Khuri, *Haqa'iq Lubnaniyah*, vol. I, pp. 105–7.

144. Zamir, 'Faisal and the Lebanese Question'.

145. SHA, Box 2B1, Rapport Hebdomadaire, 15 June 1920 and Box 4B2, nos. 1403–8, Beirut, 12 July 1920, Gouraud to Millerand.

146. In a letter to Gouraud, Millerand pointed to the undesirable effect the affair of the Administrative Council would have on the French public and proposed to provoke incidents against Faisal in the Eastern Zone which would preoccupy the French press instead. In fact, Gouraud had sent his ultimatum to Faisal two days earlier. SHA, Box 5B2, no. 717, Paris, 16 July 1920, Millerand to Gouraud. See also: FO 371/5038 9644/2, no. 55, Beirut, 16 July 1920, Wratislaw to FO; and AE, Levant, vol. 37, no. 207, Beirut, 18 October 1921, Gouraud to Briand.

147. AE, Levant, vol. 126, Hawayik to Barrère, Neo Kannobin, 8 September 1920, pp. 14–15; and SHA, Box 4B2, nos. 1399–1400, Beirut, 10 July 1920, Gouraud to Millerand.

148. For the organisation of the mandated territories and Lebanon's relations with the rest of Syria, see Chapter 3.

149. AE, Levant, vol. 31, 'Esquisse de l'organisation de la Syrie sous le Mandat français', 17 July 1920, pp. 38–46. See also vol. 32, Note pour M. de Peretti par R. de Caix, 14 August 1920, pp. 145–6.

150. AE, Levant, vol. 125, nos. 796–818, Paris, 6 August 1920, Millerand to Gouraud. See also dispatch from the American consul-general in Beirut to the State Department on his conversation with de Caix: no. 170, Beirut, 15 September 1920, in Browne, W.L., *The Political History of Lebanon, 1920–1950* (Salisbury, NC, 1976), collection of documents on Lebanon in the State Department, vol. I, pp. 12–15.

151. CO, 'Discours du Général Gouraud à Zahlé', 15–30 November 1920, pp. 308–10; AE, Levant, vol. 32, no. 1256, Beirut, 4 August 1920, Gouraud to Millerand. For decree no. 299 concerning the annexation of the Beqa'a Valley to Lebanon, see Khuri, *Haqa'iq Lubnaniyah*, vol. I, p. 309.

152. SHA, Box 4B2, nos. 1577–84, Beirut, 13 August 1920, Gouraud to Millerand. See also: nos. 1623–4, Paris, 19 August 1920, Millerand to Gouraud; and AE, Levant, vol. 32, nos. 1628–31, Beirut, 20 August 1920, Gouraud to Millerand. De Caix argued that it was preferable for the High Commission to be situated in the interior rather than in Beirut. One of his reasons was that pressure from Lebanese Christians in Beirut would hinder the French authorities from pursuing an impartial policy in the mandated territories. See, for example, his memorandum in vol. 31, pp. 40–1.

153. SHA, Box 4B2, no. 848, Paris, 21 August 1920; and AE, Levant, vol. 125, nos. 862–70, 23 August 1920, Millerand to Gouraud. See also Millerand's letter to 'Abdullah al-Khuri confirming that he accepted Gouraud's stand on Lebanon's borders, in vol. 32, 24 August 1920, pp. 235–7; Khuri's reply, 9 September 1920, vol. 125, pp. 269–70.

154. AE, Levant, vol. 125, Decrees nos. 318–21, pp. 273–7. The proclamation of Greater Lebanon was delayed twice by Gouraud from 15 and 23 August. For the ceremony and Gouraud's speech, see nos. 1688–90, and pp. 260–5. See also FO 371/5040 1157/2, no. 77, Beirut, 2 September 1920, Fontana to FO. For Decree no. 318, 31 August 1920 which defined Lebanon's borders, and Decree no. 336, 1 September 1920 on the administrative organisation of Lebanon, see Khuri, *Haqa'iq Lubnaniyah*, vol. I, p. 310–12.

155. Lloyd George, vol. II, pp. 1101–3. Faisal believed that if Clemenceau had stayed in office, he could have reached a compromise with him, FO 141/439 4075/4, minutes of meeting with Faisal in Foreign Office, 6 April 1921.

Chapter Three

1. The figures for 1911 are based on a report by the mutasarrif of Mount Lebanon from 1918. See Rabbath, *La formation historique du Liban*, p. 4; the 1921 census in AE, Levant, vol. 39, p. 56; and *CO*, May 1922, pp. 280–1. The Muslims were underrepresented in this census; see pp. 253–4 for their attitude towards the census. For the 1932 census see 'Régie des Travaux du Cadastre et d'Amélioration Foncière: Statistiques Relatives', December 1934, in SHA, Box 13B2. This was the last official census held in Lebanon and is considered accurate. See also: Feriet, R., *L'Application d'un Mandat* (Beirut, 1926), pp. 20–1; Rondot, P., *Les Institutions Politiques du Liban* (Paris, 1947), pp. 28–9; and 'Le recensement de la Syrie de mandat français et la répartition des communautés confessionelles', *AF* no. 233 (June 1924), pp. 240–3.

2. These calculations are based on the geographical distribution of the various communities as given in the census.

3. Salmon, E., 'La communauté musulmane au Liban' in CHEAM, Document no. 291, tables on p. 10A (n.d.). For the figures for Beirut in 1943 see Rondot, *Les Institutions Politiques*, p. 32, and *Les Chrétiens d'Orient* (Beirut, 1955), pp. 27–9. In 1932 the population of Beirut was 161,947, of whom 87,872 (54.25 per cent) were Christians, including 22,989 Armenians, and 67,510 (41.68 per cent) were Muslims, *AF* no. 298 (March 1932), p. 112.

4. For a comprehensive study of Lebanese emigration prepared by the High Commission, see AE, Levant, vol. 262, Beirut, 29 July 1922, and Safa, *L'Emigration libanaise*, pp. 192–8. For French attempts to restrict emigration and the campaign against it in the Lebanese press, see SHA, Box 4B2, no. 1779, 26 September 1920, Gouraud to Hawayik; and Box 23B3, Bullet. de Rens. no. 564, 16 November 1923, and no. 568, 5 December 1923; FO 371/6453 630/117, no. 113, Beirut, 21 December 1920, Consul Fontana to Curzon; and *CO* 15–30 November 1920. On the Lebanese

emigrants' campaign for inclusion in the 1921 census see: Sawda, pp. 315–16, and Lohéac, pp. 121–4.

5. SHA, Box 23B3, Bullet. de Rens. no. 531, 2 August 1923; Rondot, *Les Institutions Politiques*, p. 55, and *Les Chrétiens d'Orient*, pp. 187–91; Jalbert, L., *Syrie et Liban — Réussite française?* (Paris, 1934), Chapter VI.

6. AE, Levant, vol. 200, de Caix's memorandum, pp. 75–6; and Rondot, P., 'Les structures socio-politiques de la nation libanaise', *Revue française du Science Politique* (Paris, 1953), pp. 80–104.

7. Hess, C.G., and Bodman, H.L., 'Confessionalism and Feudality in Lebanese Politics', *Middle East Journal*, 1954, pp. 10–26.

8. On the organisation of the High Commission, see documents in AE, Levant, vols. 47A and B, in particular Decree no. 824, 17 March 1921 in vol. 47A, pp. 173–9. On this subject and on the implementation of the French mandate in Syria and Lebanon, see: Feriet, *L'Application d'un Mandat*; O'Zoux, R., *Les Etats du Levant sous Mandat français* (Paris, 1931); Rondot, P., 'L'Expérience du Mandat français en Syrie et au Liban (1918–1945)' in *Revue Générale de Droit International Public* (Paris, 1948), pp. 387–409. Two basic works in English are: Hourani, *Syria and Lebanon*, and Longrigg, *Syria and Lebanon under the French Mandate*. See also two official publications of the High Commission: Haut-Commissariat de la République française en Syrie et au Liban, *La Syrie et le Liban en 1922* (Paris, 1922), and *La Syrie et le Liban sous l'Occupation et le Mandat Français 1919–1927* (Paris, 1927).

9. FO 371/9056 4055/4032, no. 42, Paris, 22 April 1923, Phipps to Curzon. Flandin's reaction to the prospect of the evacuation of Cilicia, in *AF* no. 192 (May 1921), pp. 195–8; Huvelin, P., 'Que veut la Syrie?', Supplement to *AF* (December 1921). This report, prepared by a mission to Syria in 1919 headed by the author, was probably published to counter claims that Syria had no important economic value for France. See also: Desjardins, M., *Le Problème syrien du point devue économique* (Lille, 1928); Monroe, E., *The Mediterranean in Politics* (Oxford, 1938), pp. 75–89; and Roberts, S.H., *A History of French Colonial Policy; 1870–1925* (London, 1929), vol. II. For a critical work on French involvement in Syria, see Mazière, P. La, *Partant pour la Syrie* (Paris, 1926).

10. For example, the following motion was passed on 21 December 1920: 'The Senatorial Committee on Foreign Affairs, anxious not to attack the prestige of the French flag or the duties of France in the East, but no less anxious to preserve for her her freedom of action, to ensure the defence of her frontiers and the strict execution of the Treaty of Versailles, is of opinion that as large and as speedy a reduction as possible should take place in the sacrifices of all kinds imposed on the country in Syria and Cilicia.', FO 371/5041 16025/2, no. 3786, Paris, 21 December 1920, Lord Hardinge to Curzon. See also: FO 371/7845 3622/266, no. 844, Paris, 4 April 1922, Hardinge to Curzon; and FO 371/7848 9298/274, 22 August 1922, Director of Military Operations and Intelligence WO to FO. For detailed coverage of the debates in the National Assembly on French Syrian policy, see *AF* 1921 and 1922, in particular Jonnart's speech in the Senate, 5 April 1921, no. 192 (May 1921), pp. 203–6, and Bérard's speech, 27 October 1922, no. 207 (December 1922), pp.464–70. Bérard proposed the motion requiring the government to request the National Assembly's approval of its Syrian budget every four months, thus enabling the latter to keep close watch on the government's policy in Syria and Lebanon. See also: 'La Syrie devant le Parlement français', *CO* January 1925, pp. 16–20; and Lyautey, *Le Drame Oriental*, pp. 199–201.

11. FO 371/7845 11908/266, no. 5923, Paris, 27 October 1922, Hardinge to Curzon; Rabbath, *L'Evolution politique de la Syrie sous Mandat*, pp. 100–1; and Hourani, *Syria and Lebanon*, p. 155.

12. FO 371/5041 15478/2, no. 3676, Paris, 10 December 1920, and 16025/2, no. 3786, 21 December 1920, Hardinge to Curzon; Briand's addresses to the Senate, 5 April 1921 and 12 July 1921, in *AF* no. 192 (May 1921), pp. 206–8, 378–80; and

Poincaré's address to the Chamber of Deputies, 1 June 1921, p. 268. See also: AE, Levant, vol. 197, 'Note sur les origines du Mandat français en Syrie', 9 March 1926, pp. 195–218; and Lyautey, *Le Drame Oriental*, p. 188.

13. Gouraud was in Paris from November 1920 to April 1921 and from December 1921 to April 1922. AE, Levant, vol. 39, no. 748, Paris, 2 April 1922, Gouraud to Poincaré; FO 371/5041 15478/2, no. 3676, Beirut, 10 December 1920, Hardinge to Curzon; and *CO* 15 January 1922, 'Gouraud en France', pp. 16–22.

14. AE, Levant, vol. 200, de Caix's memorandum, pp. 61–2; FO 371/6454 5798/117, no. 67, Beirut, 7 May 1921, Satow to FO; FO 371/7848 11367/274, no. 122, Aleppo, 4 October 1922, Morgan to FO; *CO* 15 March 1921, 'La Foire de Beyrouth', pp. 204–8; 'Une Mission française d'Etudes Economiques en Syrie', *Bulletin officiel du Comité France-Orient*, no. 29 (October–November 1922), p. 10. The mission, headed by Lenail, included members of the Chambers of Commerce of Paris, Marseilles and Lyons. See also *AF* no. 206 (November 1922), pp. 423–4.

15. For such contacts, see: FO 371/7847 7683/274, no. 218, Damascus, 23 August 1922, and 9566/274, no. 247, 23 August 1922, Palmer to FO; and FO 371/7848 11109/274, no. 2390, Paris, 13 October 1922, Hardinge to Curzon.

16. *AF* no. 211 (May 1923), p. 133.

17. For Gouraud's reaction to drastic cuts in the Syrian budget for 1923, see AE, Levant, vol. 39, nos. 334–45, Beirut, 26 April 1922, Gouraud to Poincaré; vol. 200, de Caix's memorandum, pp. 27–9, 60–2; FO 371/6453 630/117, no. 113, Beirut, 21 December 1920, Fontana to Curzon; FO 371/7848 12679/274, no. 165, Beirut, 31 October 1922, Satow to Curzon; 'L'Organisation de la Syrie sous le Mandat français', *RDM* 1 December 1921, pp. 633–63. The article was written anonymously by Robert de Caix. See in particular his reaction to criticism of the High Commission expenditure, pp. 651–7. Jonnart's address to the Senate, 5 April 1921, *AF* no. 192 (May 1921), pp. 203–6; Burckhard, C., *Le Mandat français en Syrie et au Liban* (Nimes, 1925), pp. 93–6; and Gontaut-Biron, Comte R. de, *Sur les routes de Syrie après neuf ans du Mandat* (Paris, 1928), pp. 146–7.

18. AE, Levant, vol. 47A, nos. 40–3, Paris, 9 January 1921, and nos. 317–20, 17 March 1921, Briand to the High Commission. For the programme for the organisation of Syria, and the government's approval, see: nos. 640–1, Paris, 23 June 1921, Briand to Gouraud; and vol. 126, no. 226, Beirut, 18 July 1921, Gouraud to Briand. See also *CO* 30 November 1921, pp. 853–5.

19. AE, Levant, vol. 200, de Caix's memorandum, p. 48.

20. AE, Levant, vol. 31, 'Esquisse de l'organisation de la Syrie sous le Mandat français', memorandum by de Caix, 17 July 1920, pp. 46ff., and vol. 125, nos. 1626–36, Beirut, 20 August 1920, Gouraud to Millerand. FO 608/105, no. 1192, 30 January 1919, 'French plans for organisation of Syria in the event of its becoming a French sphere'. This is a copy of a comprehensive report prepared by a French committee which fell into the hands of the British. The report proposed the division of Syria into eight to ten regions combined in a confederation.

21. AE, Levant, vol. 31, de Caix's memorandum, pp. 38–40.

22. AE, Levant, vol. 125, nos. 1626–36, Beirut, 20 August 1920, Gouraud to Millerand.

23. AE, Levant, vol. 125, nos. 796–818, Paris, 6 August 1920, and nos. 862–70, 23 August 1920, Millerand to Gouraud; 'Les Gouvernements autonomes de la Syrie', *AF* no. 190 (March 1921), pp. 94–8; and Longrigg, pp. 113–18, 123–32.

24. AE, Levant, vol. 35, nos. 317–20, Paris, 17 March 1921, Briand to the High Commission; vol. 38, Ihsan al-Jabari's letters to the French premier, Geneva, 23 December 1921 and 30 December 1921, pp. 37–9, 41–3. Petition from Syrian notables including Shahbandar, Sati al-Husri, Shukri al-Kuwatli and Sa'id Haider from Ba'albek to the British authorities, FO 371/6454 5732/117, 12 May 1921, Secret Intelligence Service to FO. For the general amnesty granted by the French to the Syrian nationalist leaders in June 1921, see FO 371/6461 9932/7255, no. 113, Beirut,

19 August 1921, Satow to Curzon; Samné, G., 'L'Organisation de la Syrie et le Statut du Liban', *CO* 15–30 September 1921, pp. 625–37. For description of Syrian nationalist activities in Europe, see Amin, Sa'id, vol. III, pp. 261–86.

25. AE, Levant, vol. 200, de Caix's memorandum, p. 53; vol. 35, nos. 317–20, Paris, 17 March 1921, Briand to the High Commission; vol. 36, nos. 1088–94, Beirut, 5 August 1921, Gouraud to Briand; vol. 39, nos. 334–45, Beirut, 26 April 1922, Gouraud to Poincaré. FO 371/6455 7234/117, no. 133, Jerusalem, 2 June 1921, Herbert Samuel to Churchill; FO 141/439 1090/4, no. 244, FO, 24 January 1921, Curzon to Hardinge; and FO 141/580 10855/9049, no. 137, Beirut, 24 October 1923, Acting Consul-General Smart to Curzon.

26. AE, Levant, vol. 200, de Caix's memorandum, pp. 27, 70; FO 371/6454 4938/117, no. 47, Beirut, 9 April 1921, Satow to Curzon; FO 371/7852 8483/802, Beirut, no. 124, 16 August 1922, Satow to FO; and Gontaut-Biron, *Sur les routes de Syrie*, pp. 64–5.

27. AE, Levant, vol. 35, nos. 317–20, Paris, 17 March 1921, Briand to the High Commission, and 'Résumé du rapport de M. de Caix sur l'organisation de la Syrie', 5 April 1921, pp. 234–9; vol. 126, 'Conseil Fédéral de la Syrie et du Liban', 11 February 1921, pp. 97–100, and no. 226, Beirut, 18 July 1921, Gouraud to Briand, pp. 210–12; vol. 208, 'A propos d'une conversation à Paris le 13 octobre 1922 avec le Comte Robert de Caix', pp. 58–66 (une conversation avec de Caix); and General Catroux, *Deux missions en Moyen-Orient (1919–1922)* (Paris, 1958), pp. 26–9.

28. For detailed coverage of this issue, see Lebanese press reviews prepared by the High Commission, and Intelligence Reports for 1921 and 1922 in SHA, Boxes 9B3 and 11B3. See, for example, Box 9B3, Bullet. de Rens. no. 124, 3 March 1921, no. 138, 23 March 1921, no. 139, 24 March 1921 and no. 141, 26 March 1921. They give details of articles published in the Muslim newspaper *al-Haqiqa*, which conducted a campaign for Syrian unity. See also: Dahdah, S. al-,'Lubnan al-Kabir wa Suriya', *al-Mashriq* 1923, pp. 454–62; Samné, G., 'Le Grand Liban et la Syrie', *CO* 30 April 1921, pp. 337–44; Rabbath, *Unité Syrienne et devenir arabe*, pp. 159–60; and Rondot, *Les Chrétiens d'Orient*, pp. 247–52.

29. AE, Levant, vol. 35, nos. 441–4, Beirut, 17 March 1921, de Caix to Briand, and no. 536, Beirut, 7 April 1921, Gouraud to Briand; and Lohéac, pp. 116–20.

30. AE, Levant, vol. 126, Petitions from the Alliance Libanaise to Briand, 24 February 1921, p. 126, and from Habib Bustani, leader of the Lebanese National Party to the Quai d'Orsay, 11 March 1921, p. 108. See also p. 152. Vol. 208, 'une conversation avec de Caix', pp. 58–66. SHA, Box 9B3, Bullet. de Rens. no. 124, 3 March 1921, and no. 141, 26 March 1921; FO 371/6457 11985/117, no. 139, Beirut, 15 October 1921, Satow to Curzon; and *CO* 15 January 1922, pp. 22–3. For Lebanese emigrant activities in Egypt, see: Sawda, pp. 315–19, 333–54 and 381–8; and Sfer Pasha, *Le Mandat français*, pp. 58–62. The latter headed an organisation in Egypt called 'La Ligue pour la défense des droits du Grand Liban'.

31. Lohéac, p. 118.

32. AE, Levant, vol. 35, nos. 533–6, Beirut, 7 April 1921, Gouraud to Briand; vol. 47A, Gouraud's speech to the Administrative Council, 20 April 1921, pp. 181–5. See also his speeches in Damascus, 20 June 1921, pp. 187–94, and in Aleppo, 28 June 1921, pp. 196–202; and vol. 47B, 'Projet d'organisation de la Syrie', 1 September 1921, pp. 1–5. In January 1923 a provisional agreement was signed between Lebanon and the Syrian federation on the division of the revenue from the 'common interests', according to which Lebanon received 47 per cent and the rest of Syria 53 per cent, an arrangement clearly to Lebanon's advantage. For a protest from Subhi Barakat, president of the Syrian federation against this arrangement, see FO 371/9053 4981/531, no. 85, Damascus, 28 April 1923, Palmer to FO.

33. Samné, G., 'Le Grand Liban et la Syrie', *CO* 30 April 1921, pp. 337–44; 'La Question du Liban ou la quadrature du cercle', 15 May 1921, p. 385–90; 'L'Organisation de la Syrie et le statut du Liban', 15–30 September 1921, pp. 625–37;

and 'La Fédération syrienne et le Mandat français', 15–30 August 1922, pp. 449–55. See also Sawda, p. 322.

34. Samné, 'La Question du Liban ou la quadrature du cercle', pp. 388–9.

35. Samné, 'L'Organisation de la Syrie et le statut du Liban', p. 633.

36. AE, Levant, vol. 35, 'Résumé du rapport de M. de Caix sur l'organisation de la Syrie', 5 April 1921, pp. 234–9; vol. 200, de Caix's memorandum, pp. 71–8, 106–18. For Jouvenel's attempts to bring about the territorial reduction of Lebanon, and de Caix's support, see next chapter. See also: Rabbath, *Unité syrienne et devenir arabe*, pp. 159–76; and Rondot, *Les Institutions politiques du Liban*, pp. 30–1.

37. AE, Levant, vol. 200, de Caix's memorandum, pp. 71–2. De Caix refers to the territorial dispute between Syrian nationalists and Lebanese Christians over Tripoli and the Beqa'a Valley in 1926. On this subject see next chapter.

38. AE, Levant, vol. 35, 'Résumé du rapport de M. de Caix sur l'organisation de la Syrie', 5 April 1921, pp. 234–9; vol. 200, de Caix's memorandum, pp. 110–17. It seems that de Caix saw Tripoli as a suitable place for establishing a French military base; see Weygand, M., *Mémoires: Mirages et Réalité* (Paris, 1957), pp. 290–1.

39. AE, Levant, vol. 35, 'Résumé du rapport de M. de Caix sur l'organisation de la Syrie', 5 April 1921, pp. 234–9; nos. 317–20, Paris, 17 March 1921, Briand to the High Commission; and vol. 200, de Caix's memorandum, pp. 110–11. SHA, Box 4B2, nos. 460–3, Beirut, 20 March 1921, de Caix to Briand.

40. AE, Levant, vol. 200, de Caix's memorandum, pp. 110–11.

41. SHA, Box 23B3, Bullet, de Rens. no. 415, 12–14 January 1923, and no. 419, 23–25 January 1923; FO 371/9055 1890/1890, no. 24, Beirut, 6 February 1923, Satow to Curzon; and *CO* April 1923, pp. 241–2.

42. AE, Levant, vol. 191, no. 66, Beirut, 10 February 1923, and no. 98, 22 February 1923, de Caix to Poincaré; vol. 262, Bishop 'Abdullah al-Khuri's letter to 'Abdullah Sfer Pasha, Bkerki, 23 March 1923, and the latter's letter to the director general of the Quai d'Orsay, Paris, 21 April 1923, pp. 94–5. FO 371/9056 2678/2678, Beirut, 21 February 1923, to which is attached press cutting from *La Syrie*, Beirut, 21 February 1923, informing of the establishment of 'La Ligue pour la défense de l'intégrité des territoires du Grand Liban' by the Lebanese National Party, headed by Habib Bustani. See also Rabbath, *Unité syrienne et devenir arabe*, p. 158.

43. AE, Levant, vol. 200, de Caix's memorandum, pp. 108, 111–12.

44. AE, Levant, vol. 35, nos. 441–4, Beirut, 17 March 1921, de Caix to Briand; vol. 191, no. 66, 10 February 1923, de Caix to Poincaré, to which is attached a letter from Habib al-Sa'd, president of the Representative Council, protesting that in the mandate for Syria and Lebanon, the word 'Lebanon' appeared, and not 'Greater Lebanon'. See also: vol. 200, de Caix's memorandum, p. 108; vol. 208, 'une conversation avec de Caix', pp. 58–66; and vol. 262, Bishop 'Abdullah al-Khuri's letter to 'Abdullah Sfer Pasha, 23 March 1923, pp. 94–5.

45. Ibid. On 1 October 1921 Gouraud officially opened the Tripoli-Homs railway. It had originally been built by a French company in 1911 but was dismantled by the Turks during the War. The Tripoli-Beirut railway was opened only in 1942. See: FO 371/6463 11509/11509, no. 134, Beirut, 7 October 1921, Satow to FO; and FO 371/9055 1890/1890, no. 24, Beirut, 6 February 1923, Satow to Curzon. See also Gulick, J., *Tripoli: A Modern Arab City* (Oxford, 1967), p. 90. French companies and financiers were reluctant to develop the port of Tripoli fearing it might affect their investments in the port of Beirut. See: Monicault, J., *Le Port de Beyrouth et l'économie des pays du Levant sous le Mandat français* (Paris, 1936), pp. 190–1; and *La Syrie et le Liban en 1922*, pp. 129–31.

46. AE, Levant, vol. 400, memorandum by the Comité Libanais de Paris to the French premier, 1 September 1926, pp. 4–13; Epstein, E., 'The Lebanon: Demographic and Political Survey' (Jerusalem, 1943), CHEAM, pp. 4–8. For details of activities of Lebanese emigrant groups see the books by Sawda and 'Abdullah Sfer Pasha.

47. Zamir, M., 'Emile Eddé and the Territorial Integrity of Lebanon', *Middle Eastern Studies* (May 1978), pp. 232–5. For example, Suleiman Kena'an, a Maronite and former member of the Administrative Council, who was exiled by the French in 1920, later co-operated with Syrian nationalists abroad and advocated Lebanon's return to its pre-war borders and complete independence from France. His activities angered the Lebanese Christians. See his pamphlets in FO 371/7846 188/274, London, 16 February 1922; and Sawda, pp. 359–64. See also Gontaut-Biron, *Sur les routes de Syrie*, p. 12.

48. AE, Levant, vol. 31, de Caix's memorandum, p. 43; vol. 32, nos. 1657–8, Rome, 10 August 1920, Barrère to the Quai d'Orsay, in which he quoted the Maronite Bishop 'Awad, who feared the Maronites might become a minority in Greater Lebanon; vol. 35, nos. 441–4, Beirut, 17 March 1921, de Caix to Briand; vol. 125, nos. 796–818, Paris, 6 August 1920, Millerand to Gouraud; and vol. 208, 'une conversation avec de Caix', pp. 58–66. The Maronite Church's attitude was undoubtedly influenced by the fact that Bishop 'Abdullah al-Khuri, who supported the idea of a Greater Lebanon, held a very influential position in the Church during the 1920s.

49. FO 371/9053 867/867, no. 7, Beirut, 10 January 1923, Satow to Curzon; FO 371/6453 630/117, no. 113, Beirut, 21 December 1920, Consul Fontana to Curzon; 1399/117, no. 5470, Cairo, 25 January 1921, GHQ Egypt, to WO; 906/117, no. 237, Paris, 17 January 1921, Hardinge to FO; FO 371/7846 2785/274, no. 44, Damascus, 23 February 1922, Palmer to FO; FO 371/7848 10961/274, no. 140, Beirut, 3 October 1922, Satow to Curzon; and AE, Levant, vol. 262, 'Notes sur la Syrie', Cairo, 25 April 1922, memorandum presented by 'Abdullah Sfer Pasha to the French representative in Egypt.

50. AE, Levant, vol. 125, Petitions from Lebanese Christians, pp. 180–4; vol. 190, no. 461, Beirut, 14 July 1922, Gouraud to Poincaré; vol. 191, no. 66, Beirut, 10 February 1933, de Caix to Poincaré, which includes a resolution passed by the Representative Council on 29 June 1922 in which the mandatory power was requested to officially inform the League of Nations of the establishment of an independent Lebanese state. See also: *CO* March 1923, pp. 176–7; and Sawda, pp. 340–2.

51. AE, Levant, vol. 37, no. 122, Beirut, 11 August 1921, Gouraud to Briand; vol. 34, a letter to Bishop 'Abdullah al-Khuri, 22 October 1920, pp. 179–86; and Sfer Pasha, *Le Mandat français*, Chapter VII ff.

52. For the role of the Maronite Church, see Kerr, D., *The Temporal Authority of the Maronite Patriarchate 1920–1958: A study in the relationship of religious and secular power*, thesis prepared at St Antony's College, 1973. The most influential of the Jesuits were Père Catin and Père Chanteur. The latter was rector of the University of St Joseph. See: FO 371/10165 11158/10588, no. 150, Beirut, 1 December 1924, Satow to Chamberlain; Sawda, p. 287; Catroux, pp. 57–67; and Weygand, pp. 235–6.

53. AE, Levant, vol. 200, de Caix's memorandum, pp. 72–6; Hourani, A., 'Ideologies of the Mountain and the City' in *Essays on the Crisis in Lebanon*, pp. 33–41; Hourani, 'Lebanon from Feudalism to Modern State' and 'Lebanon: the Development of a Political Society' in Binder (ed.), *Politics in Lebanon*, p. 27. See also: Rondot, *Les Chrétiens d'Orient*, pp. 27–9; and Tannous, A.I., 'The Village in the National Life of Lebanon' in *Middle East Journal*, January 1949, pp. 151–63.

54. AE, Levant, vol. 34, letter to Bishop 'Abdullah al-Khuri, 22 October 1920, pp. 179–86; vol. 208, 'une conversation avec de Caix', pp. 58–66; vol. 262, no. 396, Aley, 30 August 1923, Weygand to Poincaré; and Hourani, 'Lebanon from Feudalism to Modern State', pp. 262–3.

55. Yamak, L.Z., *The Syrian Social Nationalist Party, An Ideological Analysis* (Harvard, 1966), p. 34. The author quotes Riyashi, I., *al-'Ayyam al-Lubnaniyah* (Beirut, 1957), pp. 164–5. See also Khalaf, T., 'The Phalange and the Maronite

community' in *Essays on the Crisis in Lebanon*, pp. 43–57.

56. For example, some Maronite emigrants suggested that Hawayik support the appointment of a Druze or Muslim governor of Lebanon in order to gain the support of these communities for the Lebanese state. AE, Levant, vol. 34, letter to Bishop 'Abdullah al-Khuri, 22 October 1910, pp. 179–86; and vol. 208, 'une conversation avec de Caix', pp. 58–66. See also 'Une opinion chrétienne libanaise sur le rôle du Liban auprès des pays arabes' (Anon.) CHEAM (n.d.).

57. Epstein, 'The Lebanon', p. 10.

58. For Christian-Maronite ideology, see: Yamak, Chapter III; and Hourani, *Arabic Thought in the Liberal Age*, Chapter XI, and *Syria and Lebanon*, Chapter VII. For a recent study of Maronite ideology as expressed by the Phalange, see Entelis, J., *Pluralism and Party Transformation in Lebanon: al-Kata'ib 1936–1970* (Leiden, 1974).

59. Zamir, 'Emile Eddé and the Territorial Integrity of Lebanon'.

60. For Chiha's views, see his books: *Le Liban d'Aujourd'hui* (Beirut, 1942) and *Politique Intérieure* (Beirut, 1964). See also: Hourani, *Arabic Thought in the Liberal Age*, pp. 319–23; Salibi, *The Modern History of Lebanon*, p. 167; and Lohéac, pp. 76–8.

61. Epstein, 'The Lebanon', pp. 12–13; and Salibi, *The Modern History of Lebanon*, pp. 171–5.

62. For the Sunni attitude towards the Lebanese state see: Atiyah, N.W., *The Attitude of the Lebanese Sunnites towards the State of Lebanon*, thesis prepared in SOAS, 1973; Salmon, 'La Communauté musulmane au Liban'; Epstein, 'The Lebanon', pp. 16–20; Yamak, pp. 37–42; and 'Rapport sur la situation actuelle de la Syrie', presented by the Nakib al-Ashraf of Beirut to Jouvenel (n.d.), in FHJ. See also the books of Muhammad Jamil Bayhum, such as *Lubnan baina mushriq wa mughrib, 1920–1969* (Beirut, 1969) and *'Urubat Lubnan* (Beirut, 1969).

63. Rabbath, *La Formation Historique du Liban*, p. 159.

64. AE, Levant, vol. 200, de Caix's memorandum, pp. 33–4. For example, a society was established in the AUB in March by Muslim students in order to safeguard the Arabic language. In the same month Muslim notables in Beirut decided not to send Muslim pupils to Christian schools: vol. 191, no. 282, Beirut, 19 June 1923, Weygand to Poincaré; and SHA, Box 23B3, Bullet. de Rens. no. 440, 20–21 March 1923. See also: Salmon, pp. 26–34; Catroux, pp. 58–67; and Johnson, 'Factional Politics in Lebanon: The Case of the "Islamic Society of Benevolent Intentions" (Al-Maqasid) in Beirut'.

65. AE, Levant, vol. 200, de Caix's memorandum, pp. 72–5. Another source of Muslim opposition was the 'Young Muslims', a group formed in Beirut by sons of well-known Muslim notables. Its members included Ahmad Da'uq, Dr Samih Fakhuri, Jamil Bayhum, Muhammad 'Ali Bayhum and Najib Talhuk. See: vol. 190, nos. 580-2, Beirut, 21 July 1922, Gouraud to Poincaré; vol. 208, p. 173, and Intelligence Report no. 684, 6 September 1923; and SHA, Box 11B3, Bullet. de Rens. no. 226, 19 July 1921.

66. See Appendix E: and 'Le régime des impôts en Syrie et au Liban', in SHA; Box 11B3, Bullet. de Rens. no. 281, 27–30 November 1921 (annexe no. 61). See also Lohéac, pp. 103–6.

67. AE, Levant, vol. 37, no. 122, Beirut, 11 August 1921, Gouraud to Briand; vol. 426, 'Syrie et Liban, Rapport Mensuel d'Ensemble', June/July 1921; SHA, Box 11B3, Bullet. de Rens. no. 219, 9 July 1921; CO 15–30 August 1921, pp. 606–7; and Kautharani, W., *al-Ittijahat al-ijtima'iya as-Siyasiya fi Jabal Lubnan wal-mashriq al-'arabi, 1860–1920* (Beirut, 1978). The author quotes an article by Ayub Thabet acclaiming the French victory in Maisalun, pp. 348–9.

68. AE, Levant, vol. 262, 'Note d'un notable musulman', 25 April 1922, pp. 17–20; FO 371/6455 8376/117; no. 88, Beirut, 4 July 1921; and FO 371/6456 11510/117, no. 136, 7 October 1921, Satow to FO.

69. Sulh, K. al-, 'Mushkilat al Ittisal wal-infissal fi Lubnan' (Beirut, 1937), an important pamphlet describing the change in attitude of the Lebanese Muslims towards Syria and Lebanon, published following the 'Conference of the Coast'. See also: Salmon, pp. 37–42; Yamak, pp. 37–42; and Dawn, C.E., 'The Question of Nationalism in Syria and Lebanon' in *Tensions in the Middle East*, Middle East Institute, (Washington, 1956), pp. 11–17.

70. AE, Levant, vol. 37, no. 122, Beirut, 11 August 1921, Gouraud to Briand. Some Sunni notables sought to organise a movement against the establishment of Greater Lebanon, but Salam argued that this would be useless as the French had already made their decision: SHA, Box 12B3, Bulletin Quotidien no. 1318, 7 August 1920, and Box 9B3, Bullet. de Rens. no. 14, 28 September 1920.

71. AE, Levant, vol. 37, no. 122, Beirut, 11 August 1921, and no. 222, 28 October 1921, Gouraud to Briand; telegram from the 'inhabitants of the vilayet of Beirut' protesting against their annexation to Mount Lebanon, 25 August 1921, pp. 51–2. See also: SHA, Box 11B3, Bullet. de Rens. July/August 1921; and *CO* 30 January 1922, pp. 69–70. Following Gouraud's compliance with the Muslims' request, a group of Christians set up a committee to act against it. They met with Gouraud, who reassured them that Beirut's status remained unchanged: Bullet. de Rens. no. 250, 22–23 August 1921; and FO 371/6456 9989/117, no. 114, Beirut, 23 August 1921, Satow to FO.

72. AE, Levant, vol. 36, no. 932, Beirut, 4 July 1921, and vol. 37, no. 122, 11 August 1921, Gouraud to Briand; FO 371/6455 8376/117, no. 88, Beirut, 4 July 1921, Satow to Curzon. For a list of petitions from the Sunnis in Lebanon to the League of Nations, see FO 371/7852 7246/7084, no. C.460, Geneva, 12 July 1922.

73. AE, Levant, vol. 37, no. 122, Beirut, 11 August 1921, Gouraud to Briand; vol. 208, no. 705, Beirut, 13 September 1923, Weygand to Poincaré; SHA, Box 17B3, Bullet. de Rens. 14–15 September 1922; FO 371/7848 10961/274, no. 140, Beirut, 3 October 1922, and FO 371/7852 12759/12758, no. 166, 3 November 1922, Satow to FO; FO 371/7848 10967/274, no. 274, Damascus, 23 September 1922, Palmer to FO; and *CO* 30 January 1922, 'Manifestations turcophiles', pp. 67–9.

74. The other three Sunni notables were Hassan Kadi, Salah Bayhum and Salim Tayara. See de Caix's report to Poincaré after Berthon raised the issue in the Chamber of Deputies, in AE, Levant, vol. 422, Beirut, 2 February 1923, pp. 22–38; and vol. 208, no. 283, Beirut, 20 April 1922, de Caix to Poincaré. See also FO 371/7846 4201/274, no. 54, Beirut, 11 April 1922, Satow to Curzon.

75. FO 371/6461 9932/7255, no. 113, Beirut, 19 August 1921; FO 371/7849 13060/274, no. 168, 7 November 1922, Satow to Curzon; and *CO* 15 October 1921, pp. 698–701, and 15 December 1921, pp. 890–2.

76. AE, Levant, vol. 200, de Caix's memorandum, pp. 75–6; Rondot, *Les Chrétiens d'Orient*, Chapter X; Haddad, *Syrian Christians in a Muslim Society*, pp. 90–3; and Epstein, 'The Lebanon', pp. 30–5.

77. AE, Levant, vol. 37, no. 122, Beirut, 11 August 1921, Gouraud to Briand. For the draft of the agreement between Catroux and Patriarch Haddad, see: SHA, Box 7B3, no. 89, Damascus, 18 October 1920 Catroux to Gouraud; Box 9B3, Bullet. de Rens. no. 1, 13 September 1920; FO 371/6454 4931/117, no. 50, Beirut, 13 April 1921, Satow to Curzon; and Catroux, Chapter VIII.

78. AE, Levant, vol. 37, no. 122, Beirut, 11 August 1921, Gouraud to Briand; vol. 276, letter from Bishop Messara to Poincaré, Paris, 18 September 1923, pp. 14–16; 'Note pour Monsieur le Président du Conseil' (n.d.), pp. 20–1; no. 446, Beirut, 10 July 1922, Gouraud to Poincaré; and FO 371/9056 6081/4032, no. 42, Aleppo, 30 May 1923, Consul Smart to Curzon.

79. AE, Levant, vol. 38, nos. 181–3, Beirut, 22 February 1922, de Caix to Poincaré; vol. 200, de Caix's memorandum, pp. 75–6. Najib Sursuk's opposition can partly be attributed to his political ambitions. He was related to Georges Lutf'allah, one of the three Lutf'allah brothers, also a Greek Orthodox, who had his

own political ambitions in Lebanon. During the early years of the mandate, plans to make Lebanon a princedom were mooted several times, especially by Habib Bustani's party, and Georges Lutf'allah sought the position of monarch for himself. In 1929 he participated in the Lebanese presidential elections but was not elected.

80. AE, Levant, vol. 36, nos. 1088–94, Beirut, 5 August 1921, Gouraud to Briand; vol. 38, p. 40, and vol. 201, memorandum from 'Ali Junblat to Ponsot (n.d.), pp. 159–72. Fu'ad Junblat's widow, Sit Nazira, was influential among the Druze in Lebanon during the mandate and their son Kamal Junblat played an important role in Lebanese politics after independence. See Gordon, H.C., *Syria As It Is* (London, 1939), pp. 24–6.

81. For the draft of the agreement between the High Commission and the Druze in Jabal Druze see: SHA, Box 7B3, no. 167, Damascus, 24 January 1921, Catroux to de Caix; Box 23B3, Bullet. de Rens. no. 465, 13–14 May 1923; Epstein, 'The Lebanon', pp. 24–30; and Sa'id, Amin, vol. III, pp. 227–31.

82. For the attempt on Gouraud's life, see documents in AE, Levant, vols. 36–8. See also: SHA, Box 9B3, Revue de la presse de Beyrouth, 19–23 September 1921; and *CO* 15–30 November 1920, pp. 308–10.

83. For the position of the Mutawallis in Lebanon, see: AE, Levant, vol. 200, de Caix's memorandum, pp. 113–14; 'Les Chiites du Liban Sud' (Anon.), CHEAM; Salmon, 'La communauté musulmane au Liban'; and Epstein, 'The Lebanon', pp. 20–4.

84. Kamal al-As'ad proposed to Herbert Samuel that he would get the Mutawallis in Jabel 'Amel to sign petitions supporting annexation to Palestine: SHA, Box 9B3, Bullet. de Rens. no. 8, 22 September 1920. On 12 December 1920 the Administrative Council passed a resolution opposing the British and Zionists' demand for the area south of the Litani: AE, Levant, vol. 126, p. 42; and Lohéac, pp. 115–16. On Herbert Samuel's visit to Kamal al-As'ad at his home in Taibeh, and the French reaction, see FO 141/580 10855/9049, no. 137, Beirut, 24 October 1923, Smart to Curzon.

85. AE, Levant, vol. 190, Petition from the inhabitants of Jabal 'Amel to the high commissioner, 9 November 1922, pp. 251–5; SHA, Box 11B3, Bullet. de Rens. no. 173, 10 May 1921; FO 371/6461 9932/725, no. 113, Beirut, 19 August 1921; and FO 371/10160 5145/218, no. 72, 29 May 1924, Satow to FO.

86. Sorel, J.A., *Le Mandat Français et l'Expansion Economique de la Syrie et du Liban* (Paris, 1929); Himadeh, S.B. (ed.), *Economic Organisation of Syria* (Beirut, 1936); *La Syrie et le Liban sous l'occupation et le Mandat français*, 1919–1927; and Owen, R., 'The Political Economy of Grand Liban 1920–1970' in *Essays on the Crisis in Lebanon*, pp. 23–32.

87. For two detailed reports on the Lebanese press, see. AE, Levant, vol. 58, 'Note sur les journaux et les revues paraissant actuellement à Beyrouth et au Liban', 1 July 1921, pp. 69–101; and vol. 286, 'Etude sur la presse du Liban', 25 February 1924, pp. 45–149.

88. See, for example, the books by Edmond Rabbath, Muhammad Jamil Bayhum and Ziadeh, N., *Syria and Lebanon* (Beirut, 1968).

89. Salibi, *The Modern History of Lebanon*, pp. 165–6; Khuri, *Haqa'iq Lubnaniyah*, vol. I, pp. 121–2; Weygand, pp. 210–11; and FO 371/6457 11985/117, no. 139, Beirut, 15 October 1921, Satow to Curzon.

90. FO 371/10610 2177/218, no. 24, Beirut, 23 February 1924, Satow to FO. See also: AE, Levant, vol. 200, de Caix's memorandum, pp. 73–4; and Sawda, pp. 333–6.

91. FO 371/10160 2177/218, no. 24, Beirut, 23 February 1924, Satow to FO; AE, Levant, vol. 191, Fu'ad Arslan's address to the Representative Council, 18 February 1924, pp. 284–5; and a memorandum presented by Da'ud Barakat, president of the Alliance Libanaise to Henry de Jouvenel, Cairo, 30 November 1925, in FHJ.

92. See, for example, report prepared by a committee of members of the Repre-

sentative Council appointed on 8 August 1922 to examine various aspects of Lebanon's relations with the mandatory power: AE, Levant, vol. 217, pp. 151-70; FO 371/5040 13526/2, no. 89, Beirut, 12 October 1920, and FO 371/6453 630/117, no. 113, 21 December 1920, Fontana to Curzon; FO 371/7846 4800/274, no. 61, Beirut, 28 April 1922, Satow to Curzon; and Khuri, *Haqa'iq Lubnaniyah*, vol. I, pp. 108-13.

93. AE, Levant, vol. 47B, no. 69, Beirut, 30 January 1922, de Caix to Poincaré; vol. 200, de Caix's memorandum, pp. 22-43; vol. 208, 'une conversation avec de Caix', pp. 58-66; and vol. 224, memorandum by de Caix, Paris, 26 January 1926, pp. 92-4. See also his article in *RDM*, 1 December 1921, pp. 633-63; and Hourani, *Syria and Lebanon*, pp. 169-70.

94. From 1920 to 1926 there were four French governors in Lebanon: Trabaud (September 1920 to May 1923), Privat-Aubouard (May 1923 to June 1924), Vandenberg (June 1924 to January 1925) and Cayla (January 1925 to May 1926).

95. A main source of opposition to the appointment of a French governor was Habib al-Sa'd, who had his own ambitions for this office. From 1920 to 1923 he conducted an intensive campaign against Trabaud, which led to tension between him and the High Commission. AE, Levant, vol. 34, letter to Bishop 'Abdullah al-Khuri, 22 October 1920, pp. 179-86; vol. 208, 'une conversation avec de Caix', pp. 58-66; SHA, Box 9B3, Bullet. de Rens. no. 10, 4 October 1920, and no. 34, 22 October 1920; Box 17B3, Bullet. de Rens. no. 292, 3-5 January 1922; FO 371/5040 13526/2, no. 89, Beirut, 12 October 1920, Fontana to FO; FO 371/7848 8945/274, no. 125, Beirut, 23 August 1922, Satow to FO; Khuri, *Haqa'iq Lubnaniyah*, vol. I, pp. 114-15; and Lohéac, pp. 78-80.

96. The Council originally comprised 15 members: 6 Maronites, 3 Greek Orthodox, 1 Greek Catholic, 2 Sunnis, 2 Mutawallis and 1 Druze. After Sunni protests of being underrepresented, Gouraud added two more Sunnis.

97. The Maronite Church supported the election of Habib al-Sa'd and opposed Da'ud 'Ammun, whom it considered too secular and liberal. After his election 'Ammun met Hawayik in an attempt to seek his support. SHA, Box 9B3, Bullet. de Rens. no. 24, 10-11 October 1920; FO 371/5040 13526/2, no. 89, Beirut, Fontana to FO; Sawda, pp. 287-8; and Lohéac, pp. 96-9.

98. AE, Levant, vol. 47B, pp. 80-116; and *La Syrie*, Beirut, 24 March 1922.

99. The 30 deputies were divided as follows: 10 Maronites, 4 Greek Orthodox, 2 Greek Catholics, 6 Sunnis, 5 Mutawallis, 2 Druze and 1 Minorities.

100. AE, Levant, vol. 39, Bulletin Périodique no. 43, 1-20 March 1922; vol. 47B, no. 265, Beirut, 15 April 1922, de Caix to Poincaré. Numerous studies have been made on the Lebanese confessional political system. The basic work on this subject is Rondot's *Les Institutions Politiques du Liban*. For more recent works, see: Rizk, C., *Le Régime Politique Libanais* (Paris, 1966); and Hudson, M.C., *The Precarious Republic: Political Modernization in Lebanon* (New York, 1968).

101. AE, Levant, vol. 47B, no. 265, Beirut, 15 April 1922, de Caix to Poincaré.

102. Ibid., vol. 38, nos. 181-3, Beirut, 22 February 1922, de Caix to Poincaré. Manipulation of the size of the electoral districts and the number of deputies was often used by the High Commission and later by the Lebanese presidents to influence the results of the elections. See: Hess and Bodman, 'Confessionalism and Feudality in Lebanese Politics'; Landau, J.M., 'Elections in Lebanon', *The Western Political Quarterly* (University of Utah), March 1961, pp. 121-47; and Ziadeh, N., 'The Lebanese Elections, 1960', *Middle East Journal*, 1960, pp. 367-81.

103. AE, Levant, vol. 47B, no. 266, Beirut, 19 April 1922, de Caix to Poincaré; FO 371/7846 3857/274, no. 40, Beirut, 29 March 1920, Satow to Curzon; Browne, *The Political History of Lebanon*, vol. I, Document 5, no. 675, Beirut, 27 April 1922, the American consul-general in Beirut to the secretary of state; 'Le Conseil Représantatif et le Gouverneur du Liban', *CO* 15-30 July 1922, pp. 385-92; and Sfer, *Le Mandat français*, pp. 84-96.

104. AE, Levant, vol. 38, Telegrams of protest, pp. 37, 157, and vol. 39, pp. 126, 201, 286-7. See also: no. 64, Cairo, 10 April 1922 and no. 81, 28 April 1922, Gaillard to Poincaré; 'Association "Le Jeune Liban"', Mémoire sur la Questionne libanaise', Cairo, April 1922 (pamphlet).

105. Following a French press publication at the end of 1921 that France intended to grant only limited power to the Representative Council, 'Umar Da'uq proposed to the Administrative Council that it discuss the issue and present its views to Gouraud, who was about to leave for Paris. His proposal was supported by other Council members but was vetoed by the French representative. AE, Levant, vol. 38, Translation from *al-Basir*, Alexandria, 21 December 1921, p. 8; vol. 39, Telegram of protest signed by Christians such as Georges Thabet, Habib Bustani and Michel Zakur, and Muslims such as Salim 'Ali Salam and 'Umar Da'uq, 10 April 1922, p. 19; pp. 224-6; and Bulletin Périodique no. 39, 5 December 1921. See also: FO 371/7846 4201/274, no. 54, Beirut, 11 April 1922, Satow to Curzon; and *CO* 15 January 1922, pp. 23-9.

106. AE, Levant, vol. 39, nos. 286-7, Beirut, 3 April 1922, and nos. 297-8, 11 April 1922, de Caix to Poincaré; vol. 47B, no. 266, 19 April 1922, de Caix to Poincaré; SHA, Box 17B3, Bullet. de Rens. no. 323, 6-9 April 1922. See also *CO* 30 January 1922, 'L'Interview du Dr Tabet', pp. 62-4.

107. There were, in fact, two political parties, the Party for Democratic Union, and the Progress Party, but they were merely groups of notables and intellectuals formed for political discussion. The former was established at the end of 1920 by Muslims and some Christians and had close ties with the Freemasons. It sought complete independence and unity for Syria and opposed the French mandate and the Lebanese state. For its programme, see *CO* 28 February 1921, pp. 169-70. The Progress Party was established shortly afterwards to counter the activities of the Party for Democratic Union and Muslim opposition to Lebanon. It was the successor of an earlier group, the 'Comité du Groupement Chrétien', which had been formed a year before in support of a French mandate and a Greater Lebanon. The president of the Progress Party was Jean de Freij and its members included Emile Eddé, Bishara al-Khuri, Michel Chiha, Yusuf al-Jumayil and Alfred Naqash. For its programme, see *CO* 15 February 1921, p. 126, and 30 March 1921, pp. 277-8.

108. FO 371/7847 3994/274, no. 81, Beirut, 1 June 1922, Satow to FO. For details of the elections see press reviews for March-May 1922 in SHA, Box 9B3. For a list of the elected deputies and brief biographical notes, see Browne, *The Political History of Lebanon*, vol. I, document no. 8, no. 717, Beirut, 3 June 1922, the American consul-general to the secretary of state. See also *CO* 15-30 June 1922, pp. 339-41, and 15-30 July 1922, pp. 414-17.

109. In fact, three months before, de Caix had suggested the election of Sa'd as president of the future Representative Council as he enjoyed popular support and could therefore withstand increasing opposition to the mandate and the Lebanese state. AE, Levant, vol. 38, nos. 181-3, Beirut, 23 February 1922, de Caix to Poincaré; and FO 371/7847 5994/274, no. 81, Beirut, 1 June 1922, Satow to Curzon.

110. AE, Levant, vol. 191, Fu'ad Arslan's address to the Council, 24 March 1924, pp. 286-91; vol. 209, no. 724, 19 October 1924; and vol. 217, pp. 151-70, report by the committee of members of the Representative Council on Lebanon's relations with the mandatory power. FO 371/7850 14552/891, no. 186, Beirut, 12 December 1922; and FO 371/9056 4512/4032, no. 56, 24 April 1923, Satow to FO.

Chapter Four

1. AE, Levant, vol. 39, nos. 334-45, Beirut, 26 April 1922, Gouraud to Poincaré; vol. 200, de Caix's memorandum, pp. 27, 61; FO 371/7849 13830/274, no. 176,

Beirut, 25 November 1922, Satow to FO; FO 371/7852 13235/13235, no. 914, Cairo, 18 November 1922, Acting High Commissioner to Curzon; *CO* June 1923, p. 377; and Weygand, pp. 207, 222-3.

2. FO 371/9056 4055/4032, no. 42, Paris, 22 April 1923, Phipps to Curzon, and 4512/4032, no. 56, Beirut, 24 April 1923, Satow to FO; 'Le Général Weygand en Syrie', *AF* no. 211 (May 1923), pp. 132-5; and Weygand, pp. 209-10.

3. AE, Levant, vol. 191, no. 341, Aley, 24 July 1923, Weygand to Poincaré; vol. 200, pp. 295-6, article by Weygand in *Le Temps*, Paris, 25 November 1926; Weygand, Chapter III; 'Le nouveau Haut-Commissaire de France en Syrie', *CO* October 1923, pp. 257-60; and Giscard, R.V., 'La Syrie et le Liban sous le Mandat français, mai 1923 — novembre 1924', *RDM*, 15 April 1925, pp. 838-65. The author headed Weygand's cabinet.

4. AE, Levant, vol. 191, nos. 248-50, Beirut, 22 May 1923, Weygand to Poincaré; SHA, Box 23B2, Bullet. de Rens. no. 465, 13-14 May 1923. Detailed descriptions can be found in the dispatches of Satow, who followed closely these events. See, for example: FO 371/7849 14551/274, no. 185, Beirut, 7 December 1922; 371/9055 1223/1223, no. 17, 19 January 1923; 1891/1223, no. 47, 29 March 1923; 3641/1801, no. 57, 3 May 1923; 5288/2204, no. 61, 9 May 1923; 5554/2204, no. 67, 15 May 1923; 5555/2204, no. 68, 16 May 1923; and 6100/2204, no. 80, 29 May 1923, Satow to FO.

5. AE, Levant, vol. 191, no. 341, Aley, Weygand to Poincaré; vol. 192, no. 834, Beirut, 9 December 1924, Acting High Commissioner to the Quai d'Orsay. Further details can be found in various intelligence reports for 1923-4 in SHA, Box 23B3. See, for example: Bullet. de Rens. no. 485, 5 June 1923; no. 508, 4 July 1923; no. 525, 22-23 July 1923; and no. 554, 29 September 1923. On the organisation of the Lebanese gendarmerie, see *CO*, September 1923, pp. 551-2, and January 1925, p. 37. See also: Weygand, pp. 211-12; and Khuri, *Haqa'iq Lubnaniyah*, vol. I, pp. 122-3. The author was a member of the special tribunal.

6. AE, Levant, vol. 191, no. 341, Beirut, 24 July 1923, Weygand to Poincaré; Weygand, pp. 262-71; Weygand, 'L'Avenir de la Syrie', *Marche de France*, September 1924; FO 371/10160 3625/218, no. 45, Beirut, 8 April 1924; and 371/10850 451/357, no. 4, 9 January 1925, Satow to Chamberlain.

7. *CO*, June 1923, p. 376; AE, Levant, vol. 262, no. 396, Aley, 30 August 1923, Weygand to Poincaré; Weygand, pp. 235-6; and Hobeika, pp. 110-13, 123-8.

8. FO 371/10165 11158/10588, no. 150, Beirut, 1 December 1924; 11423/10588, no. 155, 8 December 1924, Satow to Chamberlain; Weygand, pp. 234-43; and Toynbee, A.J. (ed.), *Survey of International Affairs, 1925* (London, 1927), vol. I, p. 404.

9. SHA, Box 23B3, Bullet. de Rens. no. 452, 25-29 April 1923; no. 465, 13-14 May 1923; no. 485, 5 June 1923; no. 499, 23 June 1923; no. 564, 16 November 1923; Bulletin Hebdomadaire de Rens. no. 571, 22 March-5 April 1923; AE, Levant, vol. 262, p. 112; FO 371/7848 10961/274, no. 140, Beirut, 3 October 1922; 371/9053 867/867, no. 7, 10 January 1923, Satow to Curzon; and 9637/531, no. 93, Aleppo, 15 September 1923, Russel to FO. See also *CO*, April 1923, pp. 241-2, June 1923, p. 376, and October 1923, p. 612.

10. FO 371/9053 10856/867, no. 138, Beirut, 26 October 1923, Acting Consul-General Smart to Curzon. On Weygand's visit to the Greek Orthodox patriarch and the Muslims' reactions, see SHA, Box 23B3, Bullet. de Rens. no. 554, 29 September 1923. See also: no. 551, 22 September 1923; no. 562, 30 October 1923; and Bullet. Périodique, no. 64, 6-30 April 1923.

11. SHA, Box 23B3, Bullet. de Rens. no. 465, 13-14 May 1923, no. 511, 6 July 1923; no. 548, 16 September 1923; and no. 564, 16 November 1923. For activities of the Freemasons, see various intelligence reports in above Box. In November 1923 the Freemasons established their own newspaper, *al-'Ahrar*, edited by Gabriel Twaini.

12. SHA, Box 23B3, Bullet. de Rens. no. 415, 15 January 1923; no. 419, 27 January 1923.

13. AE, Levant, vol. 191, no. 341, Aley, 24 July 1923, Weygand to Poincaré; vol. 200, de Caix's memorandum, pp. 67–8; SHA, Box 23B3, Bullet. Périodique no. 64, 6–30 April 1923; Weygand, pp. 238–9; and *CO*, October 1923, pp. 607–11. Weygand persuaded Subhi Barakat, head of the Syrian federation, to come to Beirut and take part in the celebrations on the anniversary of Lebanon's independence on 1 September 1923. This was the first official visit by a Syrian leader. It was received with much satisfaction by the Christians and helped to calm the Muslims. See Hobeika, p. 122.

14. AE, Levant, vol. 191, no. 341, Aley, 24 July 1923; vol. 262, no. 396, 30 August 1923; and no. 525, 30 October 1923, Weygand to Poincaré; FO 371/9056 4512/4032, no. 56, Beirut, 24 April 1923; 371/10164 5460/5460, no. 77, 14 June 1924; and 371/10160 5883/218, no. 90, 25 June 1924, Satow to FO. See also: Weygand, pp. 241–2; Toynbee, p. 406; and *CO*, July 1924, pp. 429–31. From June 1924 the French governor ceased to fill the role of both governor and delegate of the high commissioner; a separate delegate was appointed to allow the governor greater freedom.

15. FO 371/10165 11158/10588, no. 150, Beirut, 1 December 1924; and 11423/10588, no. 155, 8 December 1924, Satow to Chamberlain. See also: Weygand, pp. 285–6, 295–8; Gautherot, G., *Le Général Sarrail Haut-Commissaire en Syrie* (Paris, 1925), pp. 4–5; Gaulis, B.G., *La Question arabe* (Paris, 1930), pp. 142–3; *AF* no. 228 (January 1925), pp. 31–2; no. 229 (February 1925), pp. 61–2; and *Bulletin Officiel du Comité 'France-Orient'*, January 1925, p. 6. After Sarrail was recalled, both Muslims and Christians requested the reappointment of Weygand. This idea received some support in France, but was opposed by the Left and by those who argued that the time had come for a civilian high commissioner.

16. *Journal des Débats* Paris, 29 November 1924, in FO 371/10165 10672/10588, Paris, 1 December 1924, Crewe to Chamberlain; Gautherot, *Le Général Sarrail*, pp. 24–5; Toynbee, pp. 404–5; and Herriot's declaration in a debate in the Chamber of Deputies, 31 January 1925, in *AF* no. 229 (February 1925), p. 64.

17. SHA, Box 23B3, Bullet. Hebd. de Rens. no. 586, 27 December 1924–3 January 1925; FO 371/10165 11423/10588, no. 155, Beirut, 8 December 1924; and 371/10160 11714/218, no. 158, 16 December 1924, Satow to FO. See also: *AF* no. 229 (February 1925), p. 63; and 'Le Général Sarrail en Syrie', *CO* December 1924, pp. 657–8.

18. Gautherot, *Le Général Sarrail*, p. 23; and AE, Levant, vol. 218, Paris, 19 December 1924, Ghanem's letter to Herriot. See also Ghanem's letter to the secretary-general of the Comité 'France Orient', 30 October 1925, in *Bulletin Officiel du Comité 'France Orient'*, November–December 1925, pp. 2–3.

19. For details of the conversation see Gautherot, *Le Général Sarrail*, pp. 8–10, 33–6. See also 'Abdullah al-Khuri's speech on 6 January 1925, pp. 31–2.

20. AE, Levant, vol. 262, a detailed memorandum from Vandenberg to Herriot, 31 January 1925, pp. 171–82; SHA, Box 23B3, Bullet. Hebd. de Rens. no. 586, 27 December 1924–3 January 1925; FO 371/10850 273/273, no. 1, Beirut, 5 January 1925; and 450/273, no. 3, 8 January 1925, Satow to FO; Gautherot, *Le Général Sarrail*, pp. 6–7; and *CO*, February 1925, pp. 49–51. As further demonstration of his liberal intentions, Sarrail abolished on 10 January the martial law which had been in force since the British occupation.

21. AE, Levant, vol. 262, nos. 22–3, Beirut, 26 January 1925, Sarrail to Herriot.

22. AE, Levant, vol. 262, Vandenberg's memorandum, pp. 171–82; no. 1/c.c., Beirut, 23 January 1925, Sarrail to Herriot; SHA, Box 3B1, Bullet. Hebd. de Rens. no. 589, 17–31 January 1925; FO 371/10850 494/357, Beirut, 16 January 1925, Satow to FO; and *CO*, February 1925, pp. 81–2.

23. AE, Levant, vol. 262, no. 16, Beirut, 16 January 1925; no. 1/c.c., 23 January

1925; and nos. 22–3, 26 January 1925, Sarrail to Herriot; FO 371/10850 494/357, no. 7, Beirut, 16 January 1925, Satow to FO; *CO*, February 1925, pp. 84–5; Gautherot, *Le Général Sarrail*, pp. 11–15; and Khuri, *Haqa'iq Lubnaniyah*, vol. I, pp. 126–9. Vandenberg refused to accept his dismissal by Sarrail and to return to Paris; he did so only after receiving Herriot's instructions. See also the debates in the Chamber of Deputies, January 1925, *AF* no. 229 (February 1925), pp. 59–62.

24. AE, Levant, vol. 262, no. 1/c.c., Beirut, 23 January 1925; nos. 22–3, 26 January 1925, and no. 52, 15 February 1925, Sarrail to Herriot; Note pour Monsieur le Président du Conseil, sur le Rapport du Général Sarrail en date du 23 janvier A.S. de la dissolution du Conseil Représentatif du Grand Liban, 10 February 1925, pp. 202–4; and no. 55, Paris, 13 February 1925, Herriot to Sarrail.

25. FO 371/10850 494/357, no. 7, Beirut, 16 January 1925, Satow to FO.

26. AE, Levant, vol. 218, no. 106, Beirut, 14 February 1925, Sarrail to Herriot. Under Sarrail the Sûreté Générale followed closely the activities of the Action Française in Lebanon. See reports for September and October 1925, in vol. 425. See also: FO 371/10852 6888/357, no. 136, Beirut, 27 October 1925, Mayers to Chamberlain; and the debates in the Chamber of Deputies 20–31 January 1925, *AF*, no. 229 (February 1925), pp. 48–72. For criticism of Sarrail's policies, see Gautherot, *Le Général Sarrail*, published one month after Sarrail's appointment. The author had close ties with the Catholic Church. For a critical account of French policy in Syria and Lebanon and of the role of the French religious orders and the Maronite Church, see Mazière, P. La, *Partant pour la Syrie* (Paris, 1926). The author was a journalist who went to Syria in November 1925 to report on the rebellion. See, for example, pp. 97–102.

27. AE, Levant, vol. 271, no. 22, Paris, 20 January 1925, Quai d'Orsay to Sarrail; and no. 18, Beirut, 22 January 1925, Sarrail to Quai d'Orsay. The incident was debated at length in the Chamber of Deputies in January 1925, *AF* no. 229 (February 1925), pp. 48–72. For Giannini's letter to Sarrail, 3 January 1925, see p. 57. On Franco-Italian rivalry in the Levant see: 'Sur Politique d'Abandon', no. 245 (December 1926), pp. 354–8; and Cole, S.M., *Italian Policy in the Eastern Mediterranean, 1912–1923*, PhD thesis (Cambridge, 1975). See also FO 371/10850 630/273, no. 9, Beirut, 21 September 1925, Satow to FO.

28. Toynbee, p. 418; AE, Levant, vol. 262, nos. 22–3, Beirut, 26 January 1925, Sarrail to Herriot; vol. 271, p. 67; FO 371/10850 476/273, no. 211, Paris, 27 January 1925; 705/357, no. 305, 5 February 1925, Crewe to Chamberlain; 2552/357, no. 49, Beirut, 21 April 1925, Mayers to FO; and Herriot's declaration, 31 January 1925, *AF*, no. 229 (February 1925), p. 64.

29. AE, Levant, vol. 274, Bkerki, 7 March 1925, Hawayik's letter to Herriot, pp. 32–4; and Gautherot, *Le Général Sarrail*, p. 33–6.

30. In reaction to the press campaign Sarrail and Cayla frequently suspended publication of newspapers and on 21 April promulgated a Decree (No. 3080) limiting the freedom of the press; this in turn led to further opposition. See: AE, Levant, vol. 192, no. 110, Beirut, 14 February 1925; no. 139, 28 February 1925; vol. 286, no. 149, 25 April 1925, Sarrail to Herriot, and pp. 184–6. See also a letter of 18 August 1925 defending Sarrail, sent by Emile Arabe, head of the Lebanese Association of Doctors and Chemists, to Kirilis, editor of *Echo de Paris*, which criticised Sarrail's policies, in vol. 192, pp. 196–210; *CO*, May 1925, pp. 223–4; and La Mazière, pp. 106–7.

31. AE, Levant, vol. 274, Bkerki, 7 March 1925, Hawayik's letter to Herriot, pp. 32–4; vol. 278, no. 129, Paris, 27 March 1925; no. 272, 13 May 1925, Quai d'Orsay to Sarrail; and no. 119, Beirut, 30 March 1925, Sarrail to Quai d'Orsay. For a report of the meeting between Hawayik and Sarrail, see 'Compte-rendu de l'entretien du Patriarche Maronite et du Général Sarrail, Haut-Commissaire, à Bekerké, le 30 mars 1925' in FHJ. See also: FO 371/10850 1764/357, no. 21, Beirut, 21 February 1925; and 2480/357, no. 45, 9 April 1925, Satow to FO.

32. FO 371/10850 849/357, no. 24, Damascus, 30 January 1925; and 371/10851 6390/357, no. 192, 4 October 1925, Smart to FO; 'Le Général Sarrail en Syrie', *CO* December 1924, pp. 657–8; Gautherot, *Le Général Sarrail*, pp. 22–3; Longrigg, p. 148; MacCallum, E.P., *The Nationalist Crusade in Syria* (New York, 1928), pp.18–19; and Majzoub, M., *Le Liban et l'Orient Arabe 1943–1956* (Aix-en-Provence, 1956), p. 159.

33. For Henri Simon's declaration, see: *AF* no. 229 (February 1925), p. 60; and FO 371/10850 705/357, no. 305, Paris, 5 February 1925, Crewe to Chamberlain. See also: 2480/357, no. 45, Beirut, 9 April 1925; 2552/357, no. 49, 21 April 1925, Satow to FO; Gautherot, *Le Général Sarrail*, p. 23; and *CO* May 1925, pp. 203–7.

34. AE, Levant, vol. 278, Hawayik's letter to Herriot, pp. 32–4. See also: Report of Hawayik's meeting with Sarrail on 30 March 1925; and 'Compte-rendu de l'entrevue du Patriarche Maronite avec M. de Reffye, Secrétaire Général du Haut-Commissariat et M. Cayla, délégué au Gouvernement du Grand Liban' (n.d.), the meeting was probably held on 28 April 1925, in FHJ.

35. For summary by Cayla of his policies, see pamphlet 'Anniversaire de la Proclamation de Grand-Liban: Discours prononcés le 1er Septembre 1925 par le Gouverneur de l'Etat et par le Président du Conseil Représentatif' (Beirut, 1925). See also an article by Samné in defence of Sarrail and Cayla in *CO* May 1925, pp. 203–7, and October 1925, pp. 155–9.

36. Hawayik's meetings with Sarrail, 30 March 1925, and with de Reffye and Cayla, 28 April 1925, in FHJ; FO 371/10850 2840/357, no. 45, Beirut, 9 April 1925, Satow to FO; *CO* May 1925, pp. 205–6; and Toynbee, pp. 420–1. Article 10 in the Lebanese Constitution, which was promulgated the following year, stated that: 'Education shall be free in so far as it is not contrary to public order and morals and does not affect the dignity of any of the religions or creeds (madhahib). There shall be no violation of the right of religious communities (tawa'if) to have their own schools, provided they follow the general rules issued by the state regulating public instruction.' *The Lebanese Constitution*, prepared by the AUB (Beirut, 1960).

37. 'Rapport du Général Sarrail: La situation dans les pays sous mandat pendant les 10 premiers mois de 1925'. Document no. 6 in a collection of documents in FHJ, which give Sarrail's version of the events during his term in office. See also: FO 371/10850 1463/357, no. 26, Beirut, 2 March 1925; and 1972/357, no. 36, 21 March 1925, Satow to FO; 'Le projet de réorganisation administrative du Grand Liban', *CO*, June 1925, pp. 259–64; and 'Les circonscriptions administratives nouvelles du Grand Liban', *AF*, no. 238 (February 1926), pp. 62–5. In March the French introduced reforms in the judicial system, which also led to strong opposition. See: FO 371/10850 2107/357, no. 38, Beirut, 26 March 1925; and 3590/357, no. 77, 8 June 1925, Satow to FO.

38. FHJ, Hawayik's meetings with Sarrail, 30 March 1925 and with de Reffye and Cayla, 28 April 1925; FO 371/10854 1463/357, no. 26, Beirut, 2 March 1925; and 1972/357, no. 36, 21 March 1925, Satow to FO. An attempt was made to weaken Maronite opposition by the creation of another district by granting autonomous status to Deir al-Kamar.

39. AE, Levant, vol. 192, no. 162, Beirut, 18 May 1925; and nos. 187–9, 22 May 1925, Sarrail to Quai d'Orsay; Note pour Monsieur le Directeur des Affaires Politiques et Commerciales, Paris, 27 May 1925, pp. 67–8; SHA, Box 3B1, Bullet. Hebd. de Rens. no. 593, 21–29 March 1925.

40. AE, Levant, vol. 262, no. 134, Beirut, 10 April 1925; and no. 140, 28 April 1925, Sarrail to Herriot; and FO 371/10850 2342/357, no. 46, Beirut, 9 April 1925, Satow to FO.

41. FHJ, Hawayik's meeting with Sarrail, 30 March 1925; FO 371/10850 2342/357, no. 46, Beirut, 9 April 1925, Satow to FO.; and *CO*, March 1925, p. 125.

42. AE, Levant, vol. 218, Note pour le Président du Conseil, 8 April 1925, pp. 171–2; vol. 262, no. 137, Paris, 9 April 1925, Herriot to Sarrail; Note pour

Monsieur le Directeur des Affaires Politiques et Commerciales, 25 May 1925, pp. 260-1; and de Caix's memorandum, 25 May 1925, pp. 262-4.

43. AE, Levant, vol. 263, de Reffye's letter to Berthelot, Beirut, 7 June 1925, pp. 2-5.

44. For further details of the elections, see: AE, Levant, vol. 192, no. 193, Beirut, 10 July 1925, Sarrail to Quai d'Orsay; vol. 258, Rapport Trimestriel, 21 October 1925, pp. 3-6; vol. 263, pp. 11, 37; FO 371/10850 3713/357, no. 79, Beirut, 11 June 1925; and 4210/357, no. 92, 8 July 1925, Satow to Chamberlain; *CO*, July 1925, pp. 13, 16-20; August 1925, pp. 49-51, 74; and Khuri, *Haqa'iq Lubnaniyah*, vol. I, pp. 129-31.

45. AE, Levant, vol. 263, no. 268, Beirut, 12 July 1925; nos. 270-1, 18 July 1925; nos. 273-4, 20 July 1925; and no. 392, 24 July 1925, Sarrail to Quai d'Orsay; no. 262, Paris, 16 July 1925; and nos. 265-6, 18 July 1925, Berthelot to Sarrail.

46. AE, Levant, vol. 221, no. 508, Beirut, 19 September 1925, Sarrail to Briand. See also extract from *Le Réveil*, 5 November 1925, in FO 371/10852 7052/357, Beirut, 6 November 1925, Mayers to FO.

47. For further studies of the Druze revolt, see: Carbillet, G. (Capt.), *Au Djébel Druse* (Paris, 1929); Andréa, C.J.E., *La Révolte Druse et l'Insurrection de Damas 1925-1926* (Paris, 1937); Toynbee, *Survey of International Affairs*; MacCallum, *The Nationalist Crusade in Syria*; and Sa'id, Amin, *al-Thawra al-'Arabiya al-Kubra*.

48. See, for example, Toynbee, pp. 406-39.

49. For Sarrail's version of the events leading to the revolt, see his report in FHJ. See also 'Rapport du Général Gamelin, Commandant Supérieur des Troupes du Levant, sur les Opérations Militaires depuis le Départ du Général Sarrail' Document no. 7 in the same collection. For criticism of Sarrail's policy towards the Druze, see AE, Levant, vol. 200, de Caix's memorandum, pp. 79ff.

50. AE, Levant, vol. 195, p. 147; vol. 258, Rapport Trimestriel, Beirut, 21 October 1925; FO 371/10850 4626/357, no. 130, Damascus, 27 July 1925, Smart to FO; and *CO*, September 1925, pp. 104-5.

51. Sultan al-Atrash's memoirs were published in the weekly magazine *Bairut al-Massa*, Beirut, from the end of 1975 to mid-1976, see no. 108, 24 February-1 March 1976; and Sa'id, Amin, vol. III, pp. 351-2. See also: FO 141/552 7446/357, no. 156, Beirut, 23 November 1925, Mayers to Chamberlain; 7471/357, no. 254, Damascus, 23 November 1925; and 371/11505 1481/12, no. 285, 28 December 1925, Smart to Chamberlain; and AE, Levant, vol. 195, nos. 498-509, Beirut, 10 November 1925, Duport to Quai d'Orsay.

52. Sultan al-Atrash's memoirs, *Bairut al-Massa*, no. 108, 24 February-1 March 1976; no. 109, 2-8 March 1976; and no. 111, 16-22 March 1976. See also: Sa'id, Amin, vol. III, pp. 351-63; MacCallum, pp. 139-43; and Toynbee, pp. 428-34. For political propaganda of the rebels in south Lebanon, see: AE, Levant, vol. 195, no. 511, Beirut, 11 November 1925; and nos. 649, 14 November 1925, Duport to Briand.

53. For Sultan al-Atrash's version of the incident, see *Bairut al-Massa* no. 108, 24 February-1 March 1976, and no. 109, 2-8 March 1976. See also: AE, Levant, vol. 195, nos. 408-9, Beirut, 10 November 1925; no. 414, 416, 16 November 1925, AFL (Armée Française du Levant), to Ministry of War; and FO 371/10852 7291/357, no. 150, Beirut, 15 November 1925, Mayers to Chamberlain.

54. 'Atiyah, *An Arab Tells His Story*, pp. 129-30; AE, Levant, vol. 195, no. 418, Beirut, 17 November 1925, AFL to Ministry of War; no. 672, 22 November 1925, Duport to Briand; and a special report to Berthelot, Beirut, 28 November 1925, pp. 250-5.

55. AE, Levant, vol. 195, no. 511, Beirut, 11 November 1925; nos. 515-17, 13 November 1925, Duport to Briand; special report to Berthelot, 28 November 1925, pp. 250-5; and no. 487, Beirut, 4 November 1925, High Commission to Quai d'Orsay. The volume also includes extensive correspondence between Paris and

Rome concerning the Italian request to send two destroyers to Lebanon. See also FO 371/10853 7412/357, no. 152, Beirut, 17 November 1925, Mayers to Chamberlain. General Gamelin later described the situation: 'Mais à ce moment surgit un danger très grave pour l'Etat du Grand Liban et pour les populations chrétiennes de sa partie méridionale. L'insurrection du Mont Hermon s'étendait brusquement aux Druzes de la Région de Rachaya et de Merdjayoun et ces deux localités tombaient aux mains des bandits. Le Chouf, théâtre des massacres de 1860 était menacé. La route de Beyrouth était ouverte, Rachaya où se trouvaient isolés deux escadrons était menacée.'

56. Sultan al-Atrash's memoirs, *Bairut al-Massa*, no. 109, 2–8 March 1976; AE, Levant, vol. 195, no. 413, Beirut, 13 November 1925; nos. 564–5, 27 November 1925; no. 530, 19 November 1925, Duport to Quai d'Orsay; and no. 482, Paris, 17 November 1925, Quai d'Orsay to Duport. See also: FO 371/10852 7291/357, no. 150, Beirut, 15 November 1925, Mayers to Chamberlain; and Toynbee, p. 437.

57. There had been strong hostility towards the Armenians before the revolt. For example, a Syrian nationalist deputation which met with Sarrail in Beirut in January 1925 demanded, *inter alia*, that immigration of Armenian refugees to Syria be stopped. Their participation in the French auxiliary forces brought this hostility to its peak. Armenian refugee camps in Damascus were attacked by rebels and many Armenians fled to the coast. The deterioration in Muslim-Christian relations in Syria and Lebanon was reported in detail by Smart, the British consul-general in Damascus, who frequently warned that French policy was exacerbating the hostilities between the two communities. See, for example: FO 371/11517 236/236, no. 290, Damascus, 30 December 1925; 1591/236, no. 79, 24 February 1926, Smart to Chamberlain; 1836/236, no. 35, Aleppo, 4 March 1926, the consul to FO; and Toynbee, pp. 435–6.

58. FO 371/10853 7765/357, no. 260, Damascus, 2 December 1925; FO 141/552 7471/357, no. 254, 23 November 1925, Smart to FO; Atrash's letter, 25 November 1925. See also: Sultan al-Atrash's memoirs, *Bairut al-Massa*, no. 108, 24 February–1 March 1976, and no. 109, 2–8 March 1976.

59. FO 141/552 7746/357, no 156, Beirut, 22 November 1925, Mayers to Chamberlain.

60. AE, Levant, vol. 195, no. 672, Beirut, 22 November 1925, Duport to Quai d'Orsay; and FO 371/11506 2650/12, no. 72, Beirut, 9 April 1926; 2734/12, no. 76, 19 April 1926, Satow to FO. See also daily summaries of Lebanese press prepared by the Service de la Presse in the High Commission, in FHJ, for example, no. 229, 8 October 1925. During the revolt Lebanese Druze notables, both on their own and on French initiative, attempted to mediate between their brethren in Jabal Druze and the French authorities. For example, in August 1925 Nazira Junblat was sent by Sarrail to Jabal Druze for this purpose, and in January 1926 Jouvenel sent Amin Arslan on a similar mission.

61. Sultan al-Atrash's memoirs, *Bairut al-Massa*, no. 109, 2–8 March 1976, including Zayd al-Atrash's letter to Fu'ad Arslan.

62. Ibid.; Sa'id, Amin, vol. III, pp. 359–63; AE, Levant, vol. 195, nos, 424–5, Beirut, 21 November 1925; no. 433; 24 November 1925, AFL to Ministry of War; no. 692, 28 November 1925, Duport to Quai d'Orsay; vol. 196, no. 464, 6 December 1925; nos. 592–606, 6 December 1925; no. 608, 7 December 1925 and no. 726, 12 December 1925, Jouvenel to Briand. See also: FO 371/10853 7620/357, no. 162, Beirut, 29 November 1925; 7791/357, no. 166, 6 December 1925; and FO 406/56, no. 360, 20 December 1925, Mayers to Chamberlain. In his report Gamelin remarked on the resistance of the French forces in Rashaya: 'Les deux escadrons de Rachaya reçurent l'ordre de tenir sur place: ils soutinrent un siège héroïque qui égale les plus beaux faits d'armes de l'Histoire.' See also Jouvenel's speech on 3 December 1925 at a military ceremony in honour of the defenders of Rashaya, in vol. 196, no. 726, Beirut, 12 December 1925, Jouvenel to Briand.

63. AE, Levant, vol. 198, no. 157, Cairo, 5 June 1926, copy of report sent by the Syro-Palestine Committee to the League of Nations; no. 334, Beirut, 17 May 1926, 'Révolte Druze: Les Crimes commis par les Insurgés', Jouvenel to Briand. For detailed reports on the refugee problem, see: vol. 203, 30 September 1927, pp. 107–19; and 'Mesures prises en faveur des réfugiés', Document no. 9, in a collection of documents in FHJ. See also: vol.195, pp. 241, 275–80; vol. 196 nos. 622–3, 9 December 1925; no. 740, 18 December 1925, Jouvenel to Briand; FO 371/10853 7620/357, no. 162, Beirut, 29 November 1925, FO 406/56, no. 360, 20 December 1925, Mayers to Chamberlain; and Sa'id, Amin, vol. III, pp. 362–3.

64. FO 371/10853 7791/357, no. 166, Beirut, 6 December 1925, Mayers to Chamberlain. French and British sources give many details of the deterioration in Maronite-Druze relations in the Shuf in the spring and summer of 1926. See, for example: AE, Levant, vol. 197, nos. 217–19, Beirut, 1 April 1926, AFL to Ministry of War; vol. 198, Bulletin d'Information de la Direction des Renseignements du Haut Commissariat, no. 3, Beirut, 1 May 1926; vol. 199, no. 531, Beirut, 3 August 1926, de Reffye to Quai d'Orsay; FO 371/11506 2650/12, no. 72, Beirut, 9 April 1926; 3615/12, no. 121, 2 June 1926; 2734/12, no. 76, 19 April 1926; 3055/12, no. 92, 6 May 1926; and 3152/12, no. 100, 12 May 1926, Satow to FO.

65. FO 371/11517 458/236, no. 18, Damascus, 12 January 1926; 236/236, no. 290, 30 December 1925, Smart to FO; FO 406/57, no. 176, Beirut, 30 December 1925; 371/11505 631/12, no. 13, 17 January 1926, Mayers to Chamberlain; Bonardi, P., *L'Imbroglio Syrien* (Paris, 1927), pp. 84–5. The author describes the strong Maronite support for Sarrail's firm measures against the rebels, including the shelling of Damascus. Hawayik was quoted as saying to Jouvenel: 'You don't do enough hanging.' Binion, p. 373, note 16.

66. For the resolution of 30 November 1925, see Appendix F. See also: AE, Levant, vol. 195, no. 578, Beirut, 1 December 1925, Duport to Briand; FHJ, Hawayik's letter to Cayla, Bkerki, 29 December 1925; and FO 371/11505 631/12, no. 13, Beirut, 17 January 1926; 866/12, no. 20, 25 January 1926, Mayers to Chamberlain. Zayd al-Atrash's declaration to the Christians on 22 November 1925, denying any intention of harming Lebanon's borders, did not detract from their conviction, as he also announced that the future of the Lebanese areas occupied by the rebels would be decided in negotiations between Syria and Lebanon after the expulsion of the French; a statement which could hardly have been reassuring to the Lebanese Christians. See Sa'id, Amin, vol. III, pp. 353–9.

67. AE, Levant, vol. 195, Special report to Berthelot, Beirut, 28 November 1925, pp. 250–5; nos. 551–4, Beirut, 22 November 1925, Duport to Jouvenel; and no. 649, 14 November 1925, Duport to Briand.

68. 'La Difficulté Libanaise', *CO* August 1926, pp. 57–61; Toynbee, pp. 449–50; and La Mazière, pp. 191–9.

69. Rabbath, *Unité syrienne et devenir arabe*, pp. 172–88; and Dawn, 'The Question of Nationalism in Syria and Lebanon'.

70. See two pamphlets published by the Syro-Palestine Congress: al-mu'atamar al-suri al-falastini, Nida ila al-mujtam'a al-'amm li-usmat al-'umam (Cairo, February 1922); Mudhakirat a'amal al-wafd al-suri al-falastini (Cairo, January 1923); and Sa'id, Amin, vol. III, pp. 271–80.

71. SHA, Box 23B3, Bullet. de Rens. no. 452, 25–29 April 1923; no. 484, 4 June 1923; FO 371/9053 9637/531, no. 93, Aleppo, 15 September 1923, Russel to FO; FO 371/10850 849/357, no. 24, Damascus, 30 January 1925, Smart to FO; Sa'id, Amin, vol. III, pp. 289–92; and MacCallum, pp. 17–19. See for example the strong reaction of the Syrian Representative Council to the adjustment of the borders of Syria and Lebanon when two villages in the district of Damascus were annexed to Greater Lebanon, FO 371/10850 2109/357, no. 56, Damascus, 25 March 1925, Smart to FO.

72. Sa'id, Amin, vol. III, pp. 311–12; and Toynbee, p. 426.

73. For the activities of the rebel bands in Lebanon, see reports in AE, Levant,

vols. 195-8. See also General Gamelin's report in FHJ; Toynbee, pp. 437-9; Sa'id, Amin, vol. III, pp. 459-70, 632-3, names of the bands and areas of their activities. FO 141/552 7471/357, no. 254, Damascus, 23 November 1925, Smart to Chamberlain; and FO 371/11507 4080/2, Beirut, 17 June 1926, Report from the British liaison officer, Beirut, on the political and military situation in Lebanon.

74. Toynbee, p. 450. See also: FO 371/11505 460/12, no. 7, Beirut, 9 January 1926; 886/12, no. 20, 25 January 1926; 371/11506 1924/12, no. 52, 8 March 1926, Mayers to Chamberlain; 371/11505 1481/12, no. 285, Damascus, 28 December 1925, Smart to FO; and MacCallum, pp. 173-81. For the Arab version of the negotiations between the Syrian nationalists and Jouvenel, see Sa'id, Amin, vol. III, pp. 370ff.

75. For the memorandum, see Appendix E. Detailed description of Lebanese Muslim opposition to the Lebanese state, and their demand for union with Syria, can be found in daily reports prepared by the French delegation in Lebanon, entitled 'Rapport Journalier sur la situation politique en Grand Liban', and files of petitions from Tripoli and Sidon in FHJ; and various intelligence reports in SHA, Box 26B3. See also: FO 371/11505 460/12, no. 7, Beirut, 9 January 1926; 631/12, no. 13, 17 January 1926, Mayers to Chamberlain; and Sa'id, Amin, vol. III, pp. 411-18. Muslim opposition was also expressed in *al-'Ahd al-Jadid*, a newspaper established in Beirut in March 1925 by Khair a-Din al-Ahdab. The French suspected it received financial support from the Syro-Palestine Committee in Cairo. See, for example, Rapport Journalier, 22-23 December 1925, 31 December 1925 and 26 February 1926.

76. FHJ, no. 109 S/D, Beirut, 12 January 1926, Solomiac to Jouvenel. See also: Rapport Journalier, 25 December 1925, 1 January 1926 and 5 January 1926; AE, Levant, vol. 196, nos. 58-9, Beirut, 15 January 1926, Jouvenel to Briand; SHA, Box 26B3, Bullet. de Rens. no. 133, 12 June 1926; FO 371/11505 866/12, no. 20, Beirut, 25 January 1926, Mayers to Chamberlain; and FO 371/11508 6952/12, no. 213, 8 December 1926, Satow to FO.

77. FHJ, 'Note pour le Ministre', prepared by 'Direction des Affaires Politiques et Commerciales — Asie', Paris, 23 October 1925; FO 371/10852 6888/357, no. 136, Beirut, 27 October 1925, Mayers to Chamberlain; 7121/357, no. 2448, Paris, 18 November 1925; and 371/10851 6841/357, no. 2359, 7 November 1925, Crewe to Chamberlain; 'Les Débats Parlementaires sur la Syrie', *AF* no. 237 (January 1926), pp. 9-31; and 'Les Evénements de Syrie et le Rappel du Général Sarrail', *CO*, November 1925, pp. 193-5.

78. *AF* no. 237 (January 1926), pp. 24-8. Briand also quoted the instructions he gave to Jouvenel before he left for Syria and Lebanon. See also: 'Sur une Politique d'Abandon', no. 245 (December 1926), pp. 354-8; AE, Levant, vol. 197, 'Note sur les origines du Mandat français en Syrie', 9 March 1926, pp. 195-218; and La Mazière, pp. 211-22.

79. FHJ, no. 1678, Beirut, 7 December 1925, note entitled 'Maintien ou abandon progressif du Mandat de la France en Syrie', attached to private letter from Jouvenel to M. Vaucher. See also AE, Levant, vol. 229, no. 12, Beirut, 9 January 1926, Jouvenel to Briand. Before appointing Jouvenel, Briand had offered the post to Paul-Boncour and Paul Doumer, both of whom turned it down. On Jouvenel's appointment and his policies, see: FO 371/10852 6954/357, no. 2376, Paris, 10 November 1925; 7121/357, no. 2448, 18 November 1925; 371/11515 2213/146, no. 59, Beirut, 21 March 1926, Mayers to Chamberlain; 371/11516 5013/146, no. 1617, 27 August 1926, Crewe to Chamberlain; *AF* no. 236 (December 1925), pp. 336-9; *CO* November 1925, pp. 257-60; Binion, Chapter 13; and Gaulis, pp. 143-50. On the question of French policy towards the Lebanese Christians and the Syrian Muslims, one of Jouvenel's assistants remarked: 'Il est deux parts dans ce mandat: une part qui est minime, elle appartient au Liban, qui est siège d'une féodalité religieuse véritable; le Liban, ce petit Liban, c'est pour nous toute la Syrie, et ses désirs s'expriment hautement. Pour interprètes nationaux, il y a les patri-

arches des divers rites et pour exécutants les congrégations. A côté, est la deuxième part: c'est l'Etat de Syrie, ce sont les musulmans. Ils sont le nombre deux millions. Ceux-là, on les connaît moins bien, et le Quai d'Orsay les a longtemps ignorés. Ils ont été par nous déçus, persuadés que nous demeurions puissance chrétienne, intégralement. Sarrail, sur ce point, avait vu juste.' Vol. 196, Beirut, 28 December 1925, pp. 102–4.

80. FHJ, Rapport Journalier, 18 January 1926; the report also stated that Maronites in Zghorta supported the detachment of Tripoli from Lebanon, as this would have enabled their town to regain its position as the main administrative centre of north Lebanon.

81. FHJ, 'Rapport de M. Privat-Aubouard, Inspecteur Général des affaires administratives sur sa mission à Tripoli (13–16 janvier, 1926).'

82. Ibid. On the eve of the mission Karami requested Sheikh Yusuf Stefan, a prominent Maronite notable from north Lebanon, to accompany him to visit Hawayik and ask him to support the annexation of Tripoli to Syria. After consulting Deleuze, an officer of the Service de Renseignements, Stefan declined Karami's proposal. Rapport Journalier, 18 January 1926. One of the arguments raised by separatist leaders during the enquiry was that the detachment of Tripoli would improve Christian-Muslim relations in Lebanon.

83. Privat-Aubouard's report.

84. FHJ, telegram no. 435, 16 January 1926, from the inhabitants of Tripoli to the high commissioner. See also: Rapport Journalier, 13 January 1926, and 19 January 1926; and no. 377, Beirut, 3 February 1926, the French delegate in Lebanon to the high commissioner.

85. FHJ, Rapport Journalier, 13 January 1926. See also: AE, Levant, vol. 229, no. 12, Beirut, 9 January 1926, Jouvenel to Briand, in which he criticised the methods used by the French intelligence officers; and FO 371/11505 866/12, no. 20, Beirut, 25 January 1926, Mayers to Chamberlain.

86. FHJ, no. 109 S/D, Beirut, 12 January 1926, Solomiac to Jouvenel; AE, Levant, vol. 196, nos. 58–9, Beirut, 15 January 1926, Jouvenel to Briand; and Bulletin d'Information du Cabinet du Haut-Commissaire, no. 3, Beirut, 4 February 1926, pp. 235–6.

87. FO 371/11505 631/12, no. 13, Beirut, 17 January 1926, Mayers to Chamberlain.

88. FHJ, 'Etat du Grand Liban, Cabinet: Note Circulaire no. 610', Beirut, 13 January 1926. See also: no. 143, Beirut, 18 January 1926, Solomiac to Jouvenel; Rapport Journalier, 19 January 1926; and SHA, Box 26B3, Bullet. de Rens. no. 33, 19 January 1926. The complete failure of the amnesty which Jouvenel had offered to the rebels if they surrendered by 8 January 1926 probably strengthened his conviction of the need to adopt a tougher stand. See FO 371/11505 74/12, no. 175, Beirut, 22 December 1925, Mayers to Chamberlain.

89. FHJ, no. 109 S/D, Beirut, 12 January 1926, Solomiac to Jouvenel; Rapport Journalier, 12 January 1926 and 16 January 1926; no. 5718, 7 December 1925, and no. 5837, 10 January 1926, petitions from Mutawalli notables; AE, Levant, vol. 196, no. 112, Beirut, 31 January 1926, Jouvenel to Briand. See also: CO, March 1926, p. 137; and Muzhir, vol. II, pp. 969–70.

90. FHJ, Rapport Journalier, 27 December 1925, 28 December 1925 and 13 January 1926. To the last report is attached the resolution adopted by the municipal council of Ba'albek, with four in favour and three abstentions. See also: no. 377, Beirut, 3 February 1926, and no. 573, 22 February 1926, Solomiac to Jouvenel; AE, Levant, vol. 199, no. 444, Beirut, 29 June 1926, de Reffye to Briand; and FO 371/11507 3918/12, no. 131, Beirut, 16 January 1926; 4273/12, no. 140, 5 July 1926, Satow to Chamberlain.

91. FO 371/11505 866/12, no. 20, Beirut, 25 January 1926; 371/11515 1209/146, no. 30, 7 February 1926; 1569/146, no. 40, 22 February 1926; 2213/146, no. 59,

21 March 1926, Mayers to Chamberlain; and Sa'id, Amin, vol. III, pp. 384, 387. While in Paris in summer 1926, Mélia attempted to promote a liberal policy towards the Syrian nationalists' demands, including Syrian unity and the territorial reduction of Lebanon. See, for example, his articles in *CO*: 'L'Unité syrienne: il faut réviser l'arrêté du Général Gouraud', August, 1926, pp. 64–7; and 'Les Chrétiens d'Orient et la protection française', September 1926, pp. 126–9. For reaction to his campaign by Syrian and Lebanese newspapers, see Revue de la Presse, 4 August 1926 and 7 August 1926 in FHJ. See also his book, *Chez les Chrétiens d'Orient* (Paris, 1929).

92. Hawayik's letter to Cayla, Bkerki, 19 January 1926, attached to Rapport Journalier, 20 January 1926. On the Maronite Church's stand on various issues such as Lebanon's independence, amnesty for the rebels, the organic law, the power of the Representative Council and religious education, see memorandum Hawayik presented to Jouvenel probably shortly after his arrival in Beirut, entitled 'Note confidentielle à Son Excellence M. de Jouvenel Haut-Commissaire de la République Française en Syrie et au Liban' (n.d.) in FHJ. See also: AE, Levant, vol. 196, no. 726, Beirut, 12 December 1925, including extracts of two speeches made by Jouvenel immediately after his arrival in Beirut; vol. 278, Bkerki, 1 February 1926, pp. 54–5, Hawayik's letter to Briand, and the latter's reply; FO 371/10853 7791/357, no. 166, Beirut, 6 December 1925; and 8139/357, no. 171, 14 December 1925, Mayers to Chamberlain. On the enthusiastic reception accorded to Jouvenel by the Maronites when he visited Hawayik, see La Mazière, pp. 54–63.

93. FHJ, 'Compte rendu succinct du Conseil Représentatif', 10 February 1926 and 18 February 1926, including Chiha's question and the French delegate's reply, Rapport Journalier, 1 February 1926; AE, Levant, vol. 258, pp. 167–9, Jouvenel's speech in Damascus, 6 February 1926; vol. 263, pp. 55–61, extracts from *Journal du Caire* 15 February 1926, *L'Orient* and *Le Réveil*, criticising Jouvenel's policy towards Lebanon. See also: FO 371/11515 1569/146, no. 40, Beirut, 21 February 1926; 1779/146, no. 51, 4 March 1926, Mayers to Chamberlain; and Khuri, *Haqa'iq Lubnaniyah*, vol. I, p. 132. Following Jouvenel's speech in Damascus, the Councils of Aleppo and Deir a-Zor passed resolutions demanding the creation of a 'United Syrian State' including Lebanon; see Toynbee, p. 447.

94. FHJ, Sûreté Générale, Renseignements no. 109 i/g, Beirut, 17 February 1926; and FO 371/11515 1779/146, no. 51, Beirut, 4 March 1926, Mayers to Chamberlain.

95. AE, Levant, vol. 229, no. 176, Beirut, 24 February 1926, Jouvenel to de Caix; vol. 263, pp. 68–70, letter from Christian religious leaders to Jouvenel, 15 March 1926, and to Briand, 24 March 1926; and FO 371/11515 1779/146, no. 51, Beirut, 4 March 1926, Mayers to Chamberlain.

96. AE, Levant, vol. 198, nos. 293–4, Beirut, 27 April 1926, Jouvenel to Briand; Bulletin d'Information des Renseignements du Haut Commissariat, no. 3, 1 May 1926; vol. 200, de Caix's memorandum, pp. 86–9; vol. 225, Ponsot's memorandum, 3 May 1927, pp. 1–11; vol. 263, nos. 420–2, Paris, 26 June 1926, Jouvenel to de Reffye; and Sa'id, Amin, vol. III, pp. 428–34. Sa'id's account of the episode is accurate and consistent with French documents.

97. FHJ, 'L'accès de Damas à la mer', memorandum by Cayla, Beirut, 5 May 1926; nos. 600–2, Beirut, 30 June 1926, Souchier to Jouvenel; AE, Levant, vol. 201, memorandum by de Reffye for the period 27 May–12 October 1926, while he served as acting high commissioner, pp. 117–53, in particular pp. 123–4; vol. 263, nos. 420–2, Paris, 26 June 1926, Jouvenel to de Reffye. See also: FO 371/11507 4268/12, serial no. 26, Beirut, 30 June 1926, British liaison officer in Beirut to General Staff Headquarters, Palestine Command; 371/11516 4157/146, no. 138, Beirut, 30 June 1926, Satow to FO.

98. FO 371/11507 4268/12, serial no. 26, Beirut, 30 June 1926, British liaison officer in Beirut to Palestine Command; and Sa'id, Amin, vol. III, p. 434. See also:

SHA, Box 32B3, Bullet. d'Information de la Direction de Rens. du Haut-Commissariat, no. 5, 16 June 1926; nos. 603–4, Beirut, 30 June 1926, de Reffye to Quai d'Orsay; AE, Levant, vol. 201, de Reffye's memorandum, pp. 117–53; and FO 371/11516 4957/146, no. 165, Beirut, 13 August 1926, Satow to FO. A few days after his speech, Dabbas visited the Grand Mosque in Beirut on the occasion of a Muslim festival. His speech there was rudely interrupted and the mufti and kadi were later asked by the French authorities to apologise to the Lebanese president.

99. AE, Levant, vol. 198, no. 374, Paris, 7 June 1926; and vol. 199, no. 405, 29 June 1926, Berthelot to de Reffye. Vol. 199 contains detailed reports on the French operations against the rebel bands in Lebanon in the summer of 1926. See for example: nos. 410–15, Beirut, 16 June 1926; no. 444, 29 June 1926; no. 531, 11 August 1926, de Reffye to Quai d'Orsay; nos. 474–6, 12 June 1926; nos. 488–93, 16 June 1926, AFL to Ministry of War; extracts of newspapers, pp. 108, 206; and vol. 201, de Reffye's memorandum, pp. 117–53. Satow and the British liaison officer in Beirut also sent detailed reports of these activities. See for example: FO 371/11506 3615/12, no. 121, Beirut, 2 June 1926; 371/11507 3918/12, no. 131, 16 June 1926; 4273/12, no. 140, 5 July 1926; 4403/12, no. 144, 13 July 1926; 371/11516 4157/146, no. 138, 30 June 1926, Satow to FO; and FO 371/11507 4268/12, no. 26, 30 June 1926; report from the British liaison officer. See also Sa'id, Amin, vol. III, pp. 459–70, which gives detailed descriptions of the bands' activities including exchange of letters between the rebels and the Maronites of Zghorta.

100. AE, Levant, vol. 200, pp. 226–7, extract from *Le Réveil*, 8 October 1926. See also: Appendix G, a letter from Hawayik to Briand, 15 July 1926; vol. 263, pp. 123–5, letter from the Greek Catholic patriarch to Briand, 30 July 1926; no. 451, Paris, 23 June 1926, Jouvenel to Briand; vol. 400, pp. 4–13, memorandum from the Lebanese Committee of Paris to the French premier, 1 September 1926; and FHJ, 'Note confidentielle' from Hawayik to Jouvenel (n.d.). For French efforts to enlist Lebanese Christian support for the relinquishment of Tripoli and the Beqa'a Valley to Syria, see: nos. 600–2, Beirut, 30 June 1926, Souchier to Jouvenel; and nos. 707–9, 19 July 1926, de Reffye to Quai d'Orsay. See also: FO 371/10853 8139/357, no. 171, Beirut, 14 December 1925, Mayers to Chamberlain; speech by 'Abdullah Sfer Pasha, 6 November 1926, at a conference held by the 'Comité France-Orient' in *Bulletin officiel du Comité France-Orient*, November 1926, pp. 12–18; and La Mazière, pp. 196–9.

101. Appendix G. See also: AE, Levant, vol. 199, pp. 9–13, memorandum to Briand from the 'Délégation Permanente des Sinistrés de Rachaya', 12 June 1926; nos. 605–13, Beirut, 4 September 1926; no. 582, 15 September 1926; and vol. 200, no. 632, 11 October 1926, de Reffye to Quai d'Orsay; de Caix's memorandum, pp. 113–14; and vol. 263, pp. 123–5, letter from the Greek Catholic patriarch to Briand, 30 July 1926. After their first proposal to prevent the Druze from returning to Rashaya was turned down, its Christian inhabitants, who refused to return to the town, demanded that a new town for Christians only should be built in the Beqa'a near Shtura. See FO 371/12301 174/5189, no. 219, Beirut, 20 December 1926, Satow to FO.

102. FO 371/11516 4957/146, no. 165, Beirut, 13 August 1926, Satow to FO; 6713/146, no. 2319, Paris, 6 December 1926, Crewe to Chamberlain; Sa'id, Amin, vol. III, pp. 511–13; MacCallum, pp. 193–4; and Binion, pp. 161–2.

103. AE, Levant, vol. 200, de Caix's memorandum, p. 110; vol. 225, nos. 18–21, Beirut, 7 January 1928, Ponsot to Quai d'Orsay; FO 371/11516 5013/146, no. 1617, Paris, 27 August 1926, Crewe to Chamberlain; Binion, pp. 161–2; and Rabbath, *Unité syrienne et devenir arabe*, pp. 26–7. On Samné's support of Jouvenel's attempts to revise Lebanon's borders, see: *CO* August 1926, 'La difficulté libanaise', pp. 57–61; September 1926, 'Vers le Petit Liban', p. 100; and October 1926, 'La tâche du nouveau Haut-Commissaire de France en Syrie', pp. 145–50.

104. AE, Levant, vol. 200, de Caix's memorandum, pp 107–20; vol. 225,

pp. 1–11, Ponsot's memorandum, 3 May 1927; and vol. 201, pp. 113–14, Beirut, 12 January 1927, letter from Dabbas to Poincaré, thanking him for the support he had expressed for Lebanon's territorial integrity when he met the Lebanese premier, Auguste Adib Pasha, in Paris.

105. Rabbath, *La Formation Historique du Liban*, pp. 360–1; Ziadeh, *Syria and Lebanon*, p. 50; MacCallum, pp. 190–3; Salibi, *The Modern History of Lebanon*, pp. 167–8; Rondot, *Les Institutions Politiques*, pp. 11, 79–81; and Rondot, 'The Political Institutions of Lebanese Democracy', in Binder, *Politics in Lebanon*, pp. 127–41.

106. Hourani, *Syria and Lebanon*, pp. 308–14.

107. AE, Levant, vol. 217, pp. 151–70, report by the committee of members of the Representative Council on Lebanon's relations with the mandatory power, April 1924; and pp. 215–16, note no. 801/C, Beirut, 19 February 1924, by Privat-Aubouard.

108. For various projects for the organic law prepared under Weygand and Sarrail, see AE, Levant, vols. 217–18. See also vol. 218, no. 8, Beirut, 12 January 1925; no. 32, 19 January 1925; no. 104, 14 February 1925; and no. 138, 28 February 1925, Sarrail to Herriot; and no. 37, Paris, 7 February 1925, Herriot to Sarrail. Among the 35 members of the commission were Habib al-Sa'd, Emile Eddé, Shibl Dammus, Petro Trad, Charles Dabbas, Auguste Adib Pasha, Najib Sursuk, Ayub Thabet, 'Umar Da'uq, Muhammad al-Jisr, Sami al-Sulh, Fu'ad Arslan, Yusuf al-Zein and Ibrahim Haider.

109. AE, Levant, vol. 218, Note pour Monsieur le Président du Conseil, 8 February 1925, pp. 171–2; *Le Temps*, 16 April 1925, p. 173; no. 243, Beirut, 22 April 1925, Sarrail to the prime minister; letter to Henri Simon, pp. 185–8, 27 May 1925; and *CO*, January 1925, pp. 16–20. On Brunet's mission, see: vol. 207, memorandum to Brunet from Gabriel Kabbaz, editor of *L'Orient* criticising Sarrail's policies, 27 May 1925, pp. 4–12; FO 371/10850 3713/357, no. 79, Beirut, 11 June 1925, Satow to Chamberlain; *AF*, no. 235 (October 1925), p. 230; Muzhir, vol. II, p. 958; Sa'id, Amin, vol. III, p. 293; and Stein, L., *Syria* (London, 1926), pp. 79–80.

110. Detailed reports of the workings of the Commission, including minutes of its meetings can be found in AE, Levant, vols. 218–19. For example, see vol. 218, memorandum on pp. 197–200; note of 4 July 1925, p. 203; minutes of its first meeting, 3 July 1925, pp. 208ff; vol. 219, minutes of its second meeting, 10 July 1925, pp. 22–90, including an appendix prepared by de Caix; and third meeting, 21 July 1925, pp. 203–25. See also: vol. 218, no. 263, Paris, 16 July 1925, and vol. 223, nos. 269–70, 23 July 1925, Briand to Sarrail; and memorandum, 29 October 1925, pp. 164–6.

111. The original letters can be found in AE, Levant, vols. 218–25. See also: vol. 223, 'Analyse: consultation de notables', 15 October 1925, pp. 85–101; and vol. 224, 'Consultations individuelles', 1 December 1925, pp. 16–42.

112. AE, Levant, vol. 219, no. 353, Beirut, 25 August 1925; no. 473, 7 September 1925, Sarrail to Briand; and no. 319, Paris, 28 August 1925, Briand to Sarrail. See also Rabbath, *La Formation Historique du Liban*, pp. 365–7.

113. For criticism of the form of individual consultations in the Lebanese press, see FHJ, daily press review prepared by the High Commission, in particular no. 238, 19 October 1925; no. 240, 21 October 1925; no. 241, 22 October 1925; and no. 247, 29 October 1925. See also: Rabbath, *La Formation Historique du Liban*, p. 367; and Rondot, *Les Institutions Politiques*, p. 11.

114. AE, Levant, vol. 221, Paul-Boncour's letter to the prime minister, 21 September 1925, pp. 259–61; nos. 365–7, Paris, 23 September 1925, Briand to Sarrail; vol. 222, nos. 420–2, Beirut, 30 September 1925, Sarrail to Briand; note, p. 243; vol. 223, memorandum, 25 October 1925, pp. 1–3; Note pour Monsieur le Secrétaire Général, 14 October 1925, pp. 83–4; and vol. 224, memorandum for Jouvenel, 21 November 1925, pp. 2–9. See also Paul-Boncour's speech in the debates

in the Chamber of Deputies, 20 December 1925, in *AF* no. 237 (January 1926), pp. 16–18.

115. AE, Levant, vol. 223, Paul-Boncour's letter to Briand, 2 November 1925, pp. 167–71; memorandum to the Quai d'Orsay, pp. 184–5, 190–3; vol. 224, memorandum for Jouvenel, 21 November 1925, pp. 2–9; and FHJ, 'Le Statut Organique: Note de M. de Reffye', 9 November 1925. See also speeches by Paul-Boncour and Briand in the debates in the Chamber of Deputies, 20 December 1925, *AF* no. 237 (January 1926), pp. 16–18, 24–8. See in particular p. 27, in which Briand quotes his instructions to Jouvenel upon the latter's departure for the mandated territories.

116. AE, Levant, vol. 196, pp. 44–7. See also: no. 745, Beirut, 21 December 1925; vol. 224, no. 12, 9 January 1926, Jouvenel to Briand; and Grousset, P., *La Constitution Libanaise du 23 Mai 1926, Révisée le 17 Octobre 1927* (Toulouse, 1928), pp. 68–70.

117. FHJ, 'Procès-verbal de la Séance du Conseil Représentatif du Jeudi 10 Décembre 1925'. The twelve members of the committee were Shibl Dammus and Petro Trad (Greek Orthodox); Georges Thabet, Georges Zua'in and Roukhus Abu Nader (Maronites); Joseph Salem (Greek Catholic); Michel Chiha (Roman Catholic); 'Umar Da'uq and 'Abud 'Abd al-Razak (Sunnis); Yusuf al-Zein and Subhi Haider (Mutawallis); and Fu'ad Arslan (Druze). On 25 January 1925 Arslan resigned because of illness and was replaced by Dr Jamil Talhuk; see Rapport Journalier, 14 December 1925, 16 December 1925, and 'Compte rendu succinct de la séance du Conseil Représentatif en date du 25 janvier 1926'. For the questionnaire see: Rapport Journalier, 21 December 1925; and FO 371/11515 481/146, Beirut, 6 January 1926, Mayers to FO. As president of the Representative Council, Nammur was also officially the president of the drafting committee.

118. FHJ, Rapport Journalier, 21 December 1925, 12 January 1926 and 19 January 1926; SHA, Box 26B3, Bullet. de Rens. no. 19, 2 January 1926; Box 32B3, Bulletin d'Information du Cabinet du Haut Commissaire, no. 1, 28 December 1925; FO 371/11505 234/12, no. 177, Beirut, 30 December 1925; 371/11515 481/146, 6 January 1926; and 1209/146, no. 30, 7 February 1926, Mayers to Chamberlain.

119. FHJ, see supplement to Rapport Journalier, 19 January 1926, which gives the division of the 210 delegates. See also Rondot, *Les Institutions Politiques*, p. 80.

120. FHJ, resolution attached to letter no. 109 S/D, Beirut, 12 January 1926, from Solomiac to Jouvenel. The memorandum mentioned in the resolution is reproduced in Appendix E.

121. The Muslim refusal to participate in drawing up the Constitution is described in detail in FHJ, Rapport Journalier, particularly for January 1926. See for example reports from 13 January 1926 and 16 January 1926. See also: Rabbath, *La Formation Historique du Liban*, pp. 378–9; and Rondot, *Les Institutions Politiques*, p. 48.

122. The French used moderate and pro-French Sunni notables in their attempts to persuade the Muslims to participate. For example, they sent Muhammad al-Jisr on a mission to Tripoli, but their efforts met with little success. See FHJ, letter no. 143, Beirut, 18 January 1926, Solomiac to Jouvenel.

123. FHJ, Rapport Journalier, 12 December 1925, 18 December 1925, 4 January 1926, 15 January 1926, 20 January 1926, 1 February 1926, and 2 February 1926. See also Gaulis, pp. 165–6. One of the reasons for Christian opposition to division into two cantons was their fear that the Muslims, who comprised the majority in the coastal area, would dominate this canton, which was economically more important. See FO 371/11515 1779/146, no. 51, Beirut, 4 March 1926, Mayers to Chamberlain.

124. AE, Levant, vol. 263, letter from Abdullah Sfer Pasha to Hawayik, Heliopolis, 2 March 1926, pp. 62–7; FO 371/11515 1209/146, no. 30, Beirut, 7 February 1926, Mayers to Chamberlain; *CO*, April 1926, pp. 154–5; and Gaulis, pp. 181–2. The author reports that a Maronite committee, with Sheikh Dahdah as president, was formed to create closer links between Syria and Lebanon and to end

the misunderstanding between the Maronites and Syrians of the interior. See also FO, 141/552 7446/357, no. 156, Beirut, 22 November 1925, Mayers to Chamberlain.

125. For report of the meeting at Najib Sursuk's house, see FHJ, Rapport Journalier, 4 March 1926.

126. Ibid. See also AE, Levant, vol. 222, Shibl Dammus' letter to the Boncour Commission, Beirut, 24 September 1925, pp. 118–23; and Rondot, *Les Institutions Politiques*, p. 80.

127. FHJ, Rapport Journalier, 6 February 1926; 'Séance tenue le lundi, 22 mars 1926 à 10 heures par la Commission du Statut Organique'; AE, Levant, vol. 196, no. 81, Beirut, 9 February 1926, Jouvenel to Briand; vol. 295–306, Paris, 19 May 1926, Briand to Jouvenel. SHA, Box 32B3, Bullet. d'Information de Rens. no. 4, 15 February 1926; FO 371/11516 2974/146, no. 89, Beirut, 1 May 1926; and 371/12303 471/44, no. 11, 17 January 1927, Satow to FO; and *CO*, February 1926, pp. 61–2. See also: Khuri, *Haqa'iq Lubnaniyah*, vol. I, pp. 132–3; and Rondot, *Les Institutions Politiques*, pp. 80–1. Some Lebanese deputies opposed the inclusion of articles relating to the authority of the mandatory power in the Constitution. But Briand insisted that these articles be included in the Constitution of Lebanon as well as in those of the Alawites and of Alexandretta, which were being prepared at the same time.

128. There is some uncertainty concerning the vote of the Muslim deputies. Jouvenel informed Briand that the Constitution was approved unanimously. See: AE, Levant, vol. 263, no. 363, Beirut, 23 May 1926, Jouvenel to Briand; and Rabbath, *La Formation Historique du Liban*, p. 374. This may have been because the final vote was made on the Constitution as a whole. In fact during the debate some Muslim deputies opposed Articles 1 and 2, which determined the inviolability of Lebanon's territory, and Article 4, which declared Beirut to be the capital of the Lebanese Republic. See: Sa'id, Amin, vol. III, pp. 417–18; Rondot, *Les Institutions Politiques*, p. 48; and Mélia, *Chez les Chrétiens d'Orient*, pp. 180–1. The latter quotes the following resolution opposing Article 1 adopted by the Muslim deputies on 19 May 1926; 'Nous, représentants des territoires annexés au Mont-Liban, sans la consultation de leurs habitants, protestons contre le chapitre premier de la Constitution et réclamons le détachement de ses territoires, en les dotant d'une autonomie administrative, économique et politique, à condition de s'unir au Liban et à la Syrie.' According to Mélia, the result of the voting on this Article was: 14 in favour, all Christians; 11 against, 10 of whom were Sunnis and Mutawallis, while three Muslims were absent. See also FO 371/11516 2974/146, no. 89, Beirut, 1 May 1926; and 5616/146, no. 192, 21 September 1926, Satow to FO.

129. The Lebanese Constitution has been analysed and described in numerous studies. See, for example: Grousset, *La Constitution Libanaise*; Rabbath, *La Formation Historique du Liban*, pp. 374–402, and al-*Wasit fi'l Qanun al-dustur al-Lubnani* (Beirut, 1970); Hassan, Hassanal-, *al-Qanun a-dusturi wal-dustur fi Lubnan* (Beirut, 1963); Khateeb, Anwar al-, *al-'Usul al-barlamaniyah fi lubnan wa sa'ir a-duwal al-'arabiyah* (Beirut, 1961) and 'Uwaidat, 'Abdu, *al-Nuzum al-dusturiyah fi Lubnan wal-bilad al-'arabiyah wal-'alam* (Beirut, 1961).

130. FO 371/11516 3306/146, no. 107, Beirut, 18 May 1926; 3496/146, no. 113, 25 May 1926; 3634/146, no. 117, 27 May 1926; 5616/146, no. 192, 21 September 1926; and 6334/146, no. 199, 22 October 1926, Satow to FO. See also Browne, *The Political History of Lebanon*, vol. I, pp. 56–7, Beirut, 27 May 1926, the American consul-general Knabenschue to the secretary of state.

131. FHJ, Rapport Journalier, 10 May 1926, 17 May 1926, and 21 May 1926; no. 338, Beirut, 18 May 1926, Jouvenel to Briand; AE, Levant, vol. 224, nos. 360–2, Paris, 1 June 1926, Berthelot to Jouvenel; and vol. 263, no. 376, Beirut, 27 May 1926, Jouvenel to Briand, informing him of Dabbas' election by a majority of 44 in favour and 1 against. See also: FO 371/11516 3306/146, no. 107, Beirut, 18 May

1926; 3634/146, no. 117, 27 May 1926; 3805/146, no. 125, 8 June 1926, Satow to FO; *CO*, June 1926, pp. 272–3; and Khuri, *Haqa'iq Lubnaniyah*, vol. I, pp. 134–5.

Conclusion

1. It is estimated that the Muslims now comprise over 60 per cent of Lebanon's population. Unofficial figures published in *al-Nahar* of 5 November 1975 estimated a Muslim population of over 2 million (970,000 Mutawallis, 690,000 Sunnis and 348,000 Druze) and 1,250,000 resident Christians (496,000 Maronites, 260,000 Armenians, 230,000 Greek Orthodox and 213,000 non-Maronite Catholics).

2. The attempts of the Lebanese presidents to fulfil this role after independence completely failed, with serious repercussions on the stability of the state. Contrary to that of the Ottoman governor and the French high commissioner, the president's authority evolved from the Lebanese people and not from an external power. Moreover, the president had to fill two contradictory roles simultaneously: that of an objective arbiter between the various communities, while as a Maronite Christian, defender of Christian interests and the Christian character of the state. It was no coincidence that the most serious crises in the history of independent Lebanon were linked to the institution of the presidency, particularly to the election of a new president, as in 1952, 1958, 1975/6 and 1982.

3. See a pamphlet entitled *Greater Lebanon — Half a Century's Tragedy* published by the Maronite University of Kaslik in October 1975, in Zamir, M., 'Smaller and Greater Lebanon — The Squaring of a Circle?', *The Jerusalem Quarterly*, no. 23 (Spring 1982), pp. 34–53.

APPENDIX A MEMORANDUM PRESENTED BY THE MARONITE PATRIARCH HAWAYIK TO THE PARIS PEACE CONFERENCE, 25 OCTOBER 1919

LES REVENDICATIONS DU LIBAN
MEMOIRE DE LA DELEGATION LIBANAISE A LA CONFERENCE DE LA PAIX

Le Patriarche Maronite, président de la Délégation Libanaise à la Conférence de la Paix, agissant au nom du Gouvernement et òu Conseil Administratif du Liban, dont il a mandat, ainsi qu'au nom des populations des villes et campagnes libanaises qui demandent leur rattachement au Liban, et ce sans distinction de rites ou de confessions, populations dont il est dûment mandaté et dont les mandats ont été déposés, par les soins du Ministère des Affaires Etrangères de la République Française, au Secrétariat général de la Conférence de la Paix, a l'honneur de solliciter de la haute justice de LL. EE. les Plénipotentiaires des Puissances alliées et associées siégeant en Conseil suprême, à la Conférence de la Paix.

1. La reconnaissance de l'Indépendance du Liban proclamée par le Gouvernement et le peuple libanais, le 20 mai 1919.

2. La Restauration du Liban dans ses limites historiques et naturelles, par le retour à lui des territoires qui lui ont été arrachés par la Turquie.

3. Les sanctions contre les auteurs ou les instigateurs des atrocités et des exécutions commises au Liban par les autorités turco-allemandes; les réparations à exiger de la Turquie, réparations nécessaires à la reconstitution et au repeuplement du Liban, décimé par un affamement systématique organisé par l'ennemi.

4. Le principe du mandat étant posé par le Traité de Paix de Versailles du 28 juin 1919, et sans que cela aliène les droits du Liban à la souveraineté, la remise de ce mandat au Gouvernement de la République Française qui, conformément à l'article 22 du pacte de la Société des Nations, voudra bien accorder au Liban son aide et ses conseils.

269

Le Patriarche, président de la Délégation Libanaise a l'honneur
d'apporter aux revendications de son pays, les explications et justifi-
cations suivantes:

I. Indépendance du Liban

L'Indépendance du Liban, telle qu'elle a été proclamée et telle
qu'elle est conçue par la presque unanimité des Libanais, n'est
point simplement l'indépendance de fait qui résulte de l'effondre-
ment de la puissance ottomane, c'est encore et surtout une indéen-
dance complète vis-à-vis de tout état arabe qui se constituerait
en Syrie. Par une conception abusive de la notion de la langue, on
a voulu confondre le Liban et la Syrie ou, plutôt, fondre le Liban
dans la Syrie. C'est là une erreur. Sans remonter à leurs
ancêtres Phéniciens, les Libanais ont toujours constitué une
entité nationale distincte des groupements voisins par sa langue, ses
moeurs, ses affinités, sa culture occidentale. Et si, après
seulement 400 ans d'occupation arabe de la Syrie, la langue du
vainqueur finit jadis par s'infiltrer au Liban, de nombreuses
localités de celui-ci ont conservé depuis et conservent jusqu'à ce
jour un accent et un idiome particuliers, qui, à eux seuls, et sans
parler des langues liturgiques du pays, suffiraient à enlever à la
langue arabe toute valeur comme attribut de la nationalité.
D'ailleurs, l'exemple de l'Amérique du Nord, des Etats de
l'Amérique du Sud, de la Belgique wallonne et, plus récemment, de
l'Autriche allemande, ramène à ses justes proportions la valeur
nationalitaire de la langue.

Cette indépendance du Liban vis-à-vis de tout gouvernement
syrien, arabe ou autre, se justifie par d'autres considérations dont
l'importance n'échappera pas à la Conférence de la Paix.

1 Considérations Historiques

Quiconque a étudié l'histoire de ce pays sait, à n'en pas douter, et
les documents abondent, que le Liban a conservé, au milieu de la
sujétion absolue des populations voisines au vainqueur arabe ou
turc, souvent une complète indépendance, toujours une autonomie que le règlement organique, élaboré par les grandes puissances en 1860, tout en la restreignant, n'a fait que confirmer. Cette
indépendance qui consacrait l'exonération du Liban de tout
impôt, de tout service militaire vis-à-vis de la Turquie et lui

laissait son administration indigène, constituait une doctrine gouvernementale telle que la Turquie elle-même qui, en pleine guerre, ne recula ni devant la suppression des capitulations, ni devant les massacres, ni devant l'affamement des populations libanaises, se garda néanmoins, au plus forte de ses succès, d'en modifier le principe et ne chercha à aucun moment à fusionner le Liban avec les vilayets voisins.

Les puissances alliées et associées pour lesquelles le Liban a tant souffert feront-elles moins pour ce pays que la Turquie elle-même?

2 Considérations Politiques

Cette situation indépendante du Liban s'appuyait sur une organisation politique, puis parlementaire, qui jusqu'à 1908, date à laquelle fut promulguée la constitution ottomane, resta sur tout le territoire de l'Empire la seule de ce genre. Alors que la Syrie voisine subissait le sort de toutes les provinces turques et paraissait ignorer tout ce qui constitue la vie politique d'un pays, le Liban, en dépit du resserrement de ses frontières, imposé par les machinations des diplomates turcs aux auteurs du règlement organique de 1860, jouissait d'un régime représentatif que, jusqu'à la veille de la guerre, il a encore cherché à améliorer. L'activité politique du Liban alla plus loin. Il ne cessa de réclamer à la Turquie le versement des arriérés de sa dette et fit souvent appel dans ses revendications financières et territoriales aux puissances protectrices. Le Conseil administratif du Liban, les nombreux comités libanais, au Liban et à l'étranger, se firent les ardents défenseurs de ces revendications. Y a-t-il rien de comparable au point de vue de l'évolution politique entre le Liban et la Syrie? Et ne serait-il pas d'une justice élémentaire de respecter l'indépendance complète du Liban vis-à-vis de la Syrie, alors que rien n'unit ces deux pays, ni leur passé, ni leurs aspirations, ni leur évolution intellectuelle, ni leur évolution politique?

Les puissances alliées et associées peuvent-elles, à cet égard, faire moins aujourd'hui que ne fit l'Europe en 1860, en consacrant solonnellement, par un acte diplomatique, les nécessités politiques et ethniques ayant de tout temps séparé le Liban de la Syrie voisine?

3 Considérations de Culture

A ces considérations historiques et politiques, tres sommairement exposées, ne se bornent pas les différences essentielles qui existent entre le Liban et la Syrie.

Alors que l'instruction et la culture européenne sont, les grandes villes exceptées, peu répandues en Syrie où l'élément nomade forme une partie importante de la population, le Liban, au contraire, constitue en Orient le principal foyer de la culture occidentale. Sans parler des écoles de Beyrouth, où une nombreuse jeunesse venue de toutes les parties de l'Orient reçoit une instruction solide, il n'est point de petite ville ou de village libanais qui n'ait son collège ou son école.

La Délégation Libanaise se permet, à cet égard, de rappeler sans vouloir citer des noms, que ce sont surtout des Libanais qui, sous la désignation générique et impropre de Syriens, tant en Egypte qu'en Amérique ou ailleurs, distingués dans l'administration publique et les différentes branches de l'activité scientifique, littéraire et économique.

Le degré de culture qu'a atteint le Liban constitue ainsi pour ce pays, à morphologie si précise et si distincte, un des titres les plus indiscutables à l'indépendance.

4 Considérations de Fait et de Droit

Il est enfin trois considérations d'importance capitale qui, la Délégation Libanaise en a l'intime conviction, assureront au Liban l'indépendance complète qu'il réclame et à laquelle il a pleinement droit:

1. Bien qu'au point de vue légal et international, le Liban n'ait pas été en état de guerre avec les empires centraux, cet état de guerre a existé en fait. Dès le mois d'août 1914, et malgré des difficultés de tous ordres, des contingents libanais accourus du Liban et des pays d'émigration s'enrôlèrent sous les drapeaux alliés; nombreux sont ceux qui sur les fronts de France, des Dardanelles, de Salonique et de Palestine payèrent de leur sang leurs sympathies alliées et leur amour de la liberté. D'autres, aussi nombreux, apportèrent à la Croix-Rouge alliée, tant en Egypte, lors de l'expédition des Dardanelles, qu'en France même, leurs concours dévoués. Enfin et surtout, le Liban paya, durant la guerre, le plus formidable, le plus sanglant tribut qu'un peuple ait jamais eu à payer pour la défense d'une cause. Les plénipotentiaires alliés et associés savent que l'affamement du Liban ordonné par les autorités turco-allemandes, en représailles des sympathies libanaises pour la France, entraîna la mort de plus du tiers de la population du pays dont un grand nombre de localités sont

actuellement complètement désertes et en ruines.

Il n'est point de bataille, si sanglante qu'elle ait été, qui ait donné ce pourcentage de mortalité.

2. A la date du 20 mai 1919, le parlement libanais, élu par le peuple et obéissant à la volonté unanime des habitants, proclama l'indépendance du Liban, dont, par ses mandataires, il a l'honneur aujourd'hui de solliciter la reconnaissance. La Délégation Libanaise espère fermement que les puissances alliées et associées qui ont proclamé solonnellement le droit des peuples de disposer d'eux-mêmes et ont fait de ce principe la base de l'organisation de l'humanité nouvelle, voudront consacrer ce droit dont la volonté nationale libanaise a usé et pour lequel fut versé tant de sang libanais.

3. Sans remonter à la déclaration du Gouvernement de la République Française du 28 décembre 1917, au sujet de l'indépendance du Liban, la Délégation Libanaise rappelle respectueusement que le principe de cette indépendance a été formellement reconnu dans l'article 22 du Pacte de la Société des Nations du Traité de Paix du 28 juin 1919. Cette indépendance que s'engagent à reconnaître les puissances alliées et associées est devenue un fait depuis la ratification du Traité de Versailles, et n'a nullement besoin pour avoir toute sa force juridique et exécutoire de la conclusion de la paix avec la Turquie.

II Restauration du Liban

En réclamant son agrandissement le Liban ne réclame, en réalité, que sa restauration territoriale dont font foi l'histoire et la carte de l'Etat-Major français de 1860–1862.

Cette restauration territoriale du Liban dans ses limites historiques limites marquées: à l'O. par la Méditerranée; au N. par le Nahr-el-Kébir (Eleutherus); au N.-E. par une ligne partant de celui-ci contournant la plaine d'El-Bukeia et la rive orientale du lac d'Homs; à l'E. par les crêtes du Djebel-el-Charki (Anti-Liban) et celles du Djebel-el-Cheikh (mont Hermon); au S.-E. par une ligne partant des derniers contreforts du mont Hermon et contournant le bassin de Houleh (Samachonitis); au S. par une ligne partant des montagnes à l'est de ce lac et contournant celui-ci pour aboutir, à l'Ouest, au cap dit Ras-el-Nakoura; répond à une entité géographique qui fut, jadis, la Phénicie et qui, dans les temps modernes jusqu'à 1840, constitua le territoire libanais.

Elle constitue la réparation d'une série d'injustices et de spoliations dont le Liban fut victime de la part de la Turquie. Elle répond à une nécessité vitale pour un pays qui, privé des plaines du Nord (Akkar), de celles de l'Est (Bâalbek, Bekaa) serait une chaîne de montagnes improductives et incapables d'assurer l'existence de leurs habitants. L'expérience de la guerre l'a démontré d'une façon péremptoire et douloureuse. Alors que les vilayets voisins, ont pu, durant toute la guerre produire des quantités considérables de blé qui, sur place, ont assuré la vie et une relative aisance des populations, le Liban, bloqué et livré systématiquement à ses propres ressources, sans possibilité d'importer du blé des régions voisines, vit mourir de faim le tiers environ de sa population. C'est là une preuve décisive de la nécessité, pour le Liban, de récupérer, pour subsister, l'intégralité des territoires qui, autrefois, lui ont appartenu. De ces territoires certains lui fourniront le blé nécessaire à son existence et d'autres (Tyr, Saïda, Beyrouth, Tripoli) constitueront les débouchés naturels absolument indispensables à sa vie économique.

Indépendamment des raisons de justice et d'humanité qui imposent la restauration du Liban dans ses limites mentionnées, il est une considération à laquelle LL. EE. les Plénipotentiaires alliés et associés voudront bien, nous l'espérons, accorder toute l'importance qu'elle mérite. C'est que l'immense majorité des populations occupant les territoires revendiqués par le Liban s'est prononcée pour le rattachement de ces territoires au Liban et a opté pour la nationalité libanaise qui fut toujours l'idéal de ces populations presque toutes libanaises d'origine.

Cet idéal, le principe de droit des peuples à disposer d'eux-mêmes, solonnellement proclamé par les Alliés, leur permet aujourd'hui de le réaliser. Les mandats déposés au Secrétariat de la Conférence de la Paix expriment nettement et énergiquement le voeu de ces populations.

III Sanctions, Reparations

La Délégation Libanaise n'abusera pas de la bienveillante attention de LL. EE. les Plénipotentiaires alliés et associés en leur retraçant le tableau des déportations, des exécutions, des atrocités dont les Libanais furent victimes de la part des autorités militaires et civiles turco-allemandes. Elle ne dira pas les circonstances dans lesquelles ces autorités imposèrent et développèrent cet horrible affamement du Liban qui enleva plus du tiers de la population de ce pays; procédé d'extermination sans exemple dans l'histoire et qui, au milieu même de l'horrible boucherie, a révolté la conscience universelle. Seuls, l'attachement des Libanais à la cause de Alliés et leur fidélité à la France provoquèrent ces mesures de sauvage répression. A ces représailles cruelles, portant sur les personnalités et sur la collectivité libanaises, les turco-allemands ajoutèrent différents procédés de persécution: extorsions, impositions, déboisement, non seulement des forêts mais encore des champs de mûriers, seule ressource du pays.

De pareilles mesures que condamne le droit des gens et qu'à aucun moment n'a justifié la moindre nécessité militaire, la Délégation Libanaise les porte à la connaissance de la Conférence de la Paix et sollicite:

1. Des sanctions contre les auteurs et les instigateurs de ces atrocités, Turcs ou Allemands, à quelque degré de la hiérarchie civile ou militaire qu'ils appartiennent.

2. Des réparations aux familles des victimes et des déportés ainsi que des indemnités devant permettre la reconstitution, le reboisement et le repeuplement du Liban. Ce dernier ayant perdu, par la famine organisée par l'ennemi, une grande partie de sa population, les indemnités, en améliorant ses conditions économiques, permettront à ses émigrés d'y revenir et de le repeupler.

IV Mandat

Les conjonctures présentes et le désir de faciliter à la Conférence de la Paix sa tâche, déjà si laborieuse, font à la Délégation Libanaise un devoir de ne point soulever la question de déterminer si l'article 22 du Pacte de la Société des Nations du traité de Versailles vise le Liban, pays déjà depuis longtemps indépendant et dont l'indépendance, quoique restreinte en la forme, a été en principe confirmée par le règlement organique de 1860–1861.

Quoiqu'il en soit de cette question préjudicielle que la Délégation Libanaise entend réserver, si, conformément à la lettre et à l'esprit de l'article 22 du Pacte sus-mentionné, le principe du mandat a pour but de favoriser et de hâter l'accession à la souveraineté nationale des peuples auxquels il est appliqué — le Liban, placé depuis 60 ans sous le régime du mandat international et ayant depuis longtemps fait son éducation politique, mériterait d'être aujourd'hui un État souverain. Néanmoins et tout en maintenant ses droits à cette souveraineté, le Liban s'incline devant la décision de la Conférence de la Paix concernant le Régime des mandats. Il s'incline d'autant plus volontiers que dans la double crise politique et économique que traverse le monde il a besoin du concours et de l'aide d'une grande puissance occidentale.

Cette puissance, dans le choix de laquelle l'article 22 fait intervenir au premier chef la volonté des populations intéressées, le Liban, dans sa partie ancienne et ses parties revendiquées, l'a déjà choisie d'enthousiasme. C'EST LA FRANCE.

Des raisons d'ordre divers justifient ce libre choix:

1. Ce sont d'abord des RAISONS DE SENTIMENT, D'AFFINITÉ ET DE CULTURE: Les Libanais ne sauraient oublier les bienfaits dont, à travers les siècles, ils furent l'objet de la part de la France. La reconnaissance qu'ils en éprouvent est une de leurs traditions nationales. Ils tiennent à le proclamer solennellement à la Conférence de la Paix.

Des relations politiques et commerciales plusieurs fois séculaires, l'établissement au Liban de nombreux chevaliers francs dont, jusqu'aujourd'hui, on retrouve en ce pays le nom et le souvenir, un attrait atavique puissant qui, légué par leurs ancêtres Phéniciens, fondateurs des grandes villes du littoral français méditerranéen, a toujours poussé les Libanais vers la France, tout cela créa entre les deux pays des affinités comme on en voit rarement dans l'histoire des peuples. Le terrain de la culture française était ainsi tout préparé. Au-delà des frontières françaises, il n'est point de pays où cette culture soit plus répandue et plus intense.

2. Les raisons de sentiment auxquelles il est plus haut fait allusion prennent leur source dans des CONSIDÉRATIONS HISTORIQUES.

Ces dernières remontent aux premières expéditions françaises en Orient, expéditions au cours desquelles la France, tant en Syrie qu'en Egypte, sut apprécier le dévouement des Libanais. Depuis, en échange de ce dévouement et des services rendus, elle ne cessa de leur accorder toute sa protection. La protection des Libanais, tant au Liban qu'à l'Étranger, fut en France, pendant des siècles, et reste jusqu'à ce jour, une doctrine gouvernementale dont jamais les différents régimes ne se départirent. Ce fut plus qu'une doctrine gouvernementale, ce fut une doctrine nationale. Alors que durant la première moitié du XIXe siècle, le Liban traversait une des crises les plus douloureuses de son histoire, seul de tous les peuples, le peuple français, par la voix de son Parlement, sut défendre la cause de ce petit peuple lointain et ami. Durant la guerre qui vient de finir, la France fit tout pour venir en aide aux malheureuses populations libanaises persécutées, bloquées et affamées. Enfin, fait qui a, à leurs yeux, une importance capitale: la première déclaration de l'indépendance du Liban eut lieu du haut de la tribune de la Chambre française, le 27 décembre 1917.

3. A ces considérations historiques et de sentiment s'ajoutent des RAISONS D'INTÉRÊT ET DE DIGNITÉ.

En demandant le mandat français, les Libanais sont profondément convaincus que la France libérale et généreuse saura non seulement respecter leur indépendance, mais l'affermir, la garantir, la défendre.

Ils sont convaincus qu'elle saura aussi respecter leur dignité, leur gouvernement et leur administration qu'ils désiront conserver essentiellement libanaise; qu'elle viendra au Liban en conseillère et amie; que durant la période du mandat qui préparera le Liban à la souveraineté, elle développera le sentiment national en laissant aux mains des Libanais l'organisation, l'administration et la justice de leur pays. A cet égard l'expérience est faite. Partout où ils ont passé les Libanais ont pu donner la mesure de leurs capacités. L'exemple de l'Égypte à laquelle ils ont apporté, dans l'oeuvre de son relèvement intellectuel et politique, leur concours si hautement apprécié, est une preuve démonstrative de leurs aptitudes administratives et éducatrices. Les Libanais sont enfin convaincus que, loin de diviser, la France mandataire fera tout pour cimenter l'unité nationale des différentes communautés du Liban; que dans un régime démocratique où la Chambre élue aura toutes les attributions des Parlements des pays occidentaux, elle aidera au respect de toutes les libertés, et, par la représentation proportionnelle, à la sauvegarde du droit des minorités; qu'elle augmentera les ressources du pays auquel elle s'est déjà tant intéressée; qu'elle y créera des institutions et des Écoles Nationales; et qu'enfin, fidèle à ses traditions et à son histoire, dans une loyale et généreuse collaboration avec le peuple et le Gouvernement libanais, elle saura y défendre, développer, intensifier de toutes façons et sous toutes les formes, le sentiment nationale qui ayant résisté à toutes les oppressions et à tous les malheurs, sort grandi des suprêmes épreuves.

Le Président de la Délégation Libanaise
ELIAS PIERRE HOYEK
Patriarche Maronite d'Antioche et de tout l'Orient
Paris, 25 octobre 1919
Pamphlet in AE, Levant, vol. 266.

APPENDIX B LETTER FROM CLEMENCEAU, THE FRENCH PRIME MINISTER, TO THE PATRIARCH HAWAYIK, 10 NOVEMBER 1919

Présidence du Conseil   Paris, le 10 Novembre 1919

Monseigneur,

Les entretiens que, depuis votre arrivée à Paris, vous avez eus avec M. le Ministre des Affaires Étrangères et avec moi-même vous auront confirmé dans la conviction que le Gouvernement de la République demeurait invariablement attaché aux traditions de mutuel dévouement, établies depuis des siècles entre la France et le Liban.

Ces entretiens vous auront également donné la certitude que les solutions que nous poursuivons à la Conférence de la Paix sont, dans leur ensemble, conformes aux aspirations des populations dont vous êtes le Haut Représentant.

Le désir des Libanais de conserver un Gouvernement autonome et un Statut national indépendant s'accorde parfaitement avec les traditions libérales de la France.

Avec le soutien et l'aide de la France, indépendants de tout autre groupement nationale, les Libanais sont assurés de conserver leurs traditions, de développer leurs institutions politiques et administratives, de hâter eux-mêmes la mise en valeur complète de leur pays, de voir enfin leurs enfants se préparer dans leurs propres écoles aux fonctions publiques du Liban.

Les limites dans lesquelles s'exercera cette indépendance ne peuvent être arrêtées avant que le Mandat sur la Syrie ait été attribué et défini. Mais la France qui a tout fait en 1860 pour assurer au Liban un territoire plus étendu, n'oublie pas que le resserrement des limites actuelles résulte de la longue oppression dont a souffert le Liban. Désireuse de favoriser le plus possible les relations économiques entre tous les pays confiés à son mandat, elle tiendra également le plus grand compte, dans la délimitation du Liban, de la nécessité de réserver à la 'Montagne' des territoires de plaine et l'accès à la mer indispensable à sa prospérité.

Je suis certain, en vous donnant ces assurances, de répondre aux sentiments qui ont déterminé les populations du Liban à demander une fois de plus le mandat de la France pour leur pays et je veux espérer que la solution définitive donnée par la Conférence à la question syrienne permettra au Gouvernement français d'accomplir dans la plus large mesure les voeux de ces vaillantes populations.

Veuillez agréer, Monseigneur, les assurances de ma haute considération.

Signé: Clemenceau

Sa Béatitude
Monseigneur Hoyek
Patriarche Maronite

AE, Levant, vol. 19, p. 40.

UNE RÉSOLUTION DU 'CONSEIL ADMINISTRATIF'

Le 29 novembre 1919, au cours d'une importante réunion tenue à Bé'abda par le Conseil Administratif libanais, la résolution suivante a été votée:

Le Conseil Administratif du Liban;

Considérant que le Liban jouit de son autonomie administrative le distinguant des autres provinces ottomanes faisant partie des territoires occupés par les Alliés, et cela en vertu d'un Protocole garanti par les grandes Puissances européennes et établi, après une étude approfondie de la question, en harmonie avec les moeurs et les traditions libanaises;

Considérant que le Conseil, qui représente le peuple libanais, a mission de sauvegarder ladite autonomie jusqu'à ce qu'il soit statué définitivement sur les demandes du Liban;

Considérant, d'autre part, que ce Conseil et le peuple libanais sont absolument convaincus des bonnes intentions des autorités françaises d'occupation, et ont pleinement confiance dans les promesses réitérées de leurs hauts représentants au sujet de l'aide réelle, désintéressée et éloignée de toute idée de domination ou de colonisation que lesdites autorités entendent prêter à ce pays;

En conséquence, et dans le but de faciliter la bonne marche d'administration militaire d'occupation au Liban et de la mettre plus en harmonie avec son indépendance et ses privilèges;

Le Conseil croit de son devoir de formuler les observations suivantes:

1. Il est nécessaire de bien déterminer les pouvoirs des contrôleurs, inspecteurs et agents nommés de la part les autorités d'occupation, afin que ces pouvoirs ne dépassent pas les limites du contrôle, de la surveillance et de la transmission de leurs observations ou instructions au Gouvernement central exclusivement, lequel fera le nécessaire. Il ne devrait pas leur être permis d'exercer une autorité directe quelconque sur les fonctionnaires libanais, de

crainte de porter atteinte au prestige du gouvernement libanais et de paralyser l'action desdits fonctionnaires dans le libre exercice de leurs fonctions, ce qui amènerait la perturbation dans l'administration, irait à l'encontre du but poursuivi et porterait gravement atteinte à notre régime d'autonomie intérieure. Il convient, en outre, que la correspondance continue, comme par le passé, à avoir lieu directement entre le gouvernement central et les Kaïmakams (chefs de district) sans l'intermédiaire des contrôleurs, étant donné que le Kaïmakam représente le gouvernement central dans son district et qu'il ne lui sera pas possible de remplir convenablement ses fonctions ni d'en assumer les responsabilités si l'on multiplie les autorités supérieurs ou si l'on paralyse ses communications avec l'autorité officielle compétente.

2. De même qu'il n'est pas permis aux fonctionnaires administratifs d'intervenir pour quelque prétexte que ce soit dans les affaires judiciaires, ni d'exercer n'importe quelle pression sur les magistrats, à plus forte raison une intervention de ce genre ne doit-elle pas être permise aux contrôleurs ou aux représentants de l'autorité militaire, d'autant moins que dans tous les pays du monde, même en Turquie et dans les provinces ottomanes, de telles interventions sont formellement prohibées.

3. Considérant que les divers Protocoles internationaux publiés successivement depuis 1892 garantissent l'inamovibilité des magistrats libanais et interdisent la révocation ou le déplacement d'un juge quelconque sans une enquête préalable faite par les soins et sous la surveillance du Conseil Administratif de la Montagne, ce dernier attire l'attention des autorités d'occupation sur la nécessité de respecter minutieusement les dispositions desdits Protocoles sur ce point.

4. De même que les fonctionnaires civils et les magistrats libanais doivent être laissés libres de remplir leurs fonctions dans les conditions précitées, il faut également que les chefs de la Milice libanaise et des conseils militaires libanais demeurent indépendants dans l'exercice de leurs fonctions. Il ne doit pas être permis aux inspecteurs d'exercer sur eux une autorité directe. Ils doivent remettre leurs observations au commandant de la milice qui agira conformément aux règles. Dans le cas où ces observations concerneraient le commandant lui-même, il y aurait lieu de les soumettre au Gouverneur de la Montagne qui y donnera les suites qu'il convient. Certes, le Conseil Administratif n'ignore pas la nécessité de la présence de quelques officiers français pour aider

à l'instruction et au contrôle de la milice libanaise. Mais il estime que leur action ne doit pas dépasser ces mêmes limites et qu'il est indispensable d'abord que les grades hiérarchiques entre eux et les officiers libanais soient respectés, et ensuite que le conseil militaire libanais continue à être formé exclusivement d'officiers libanais agissant en toute liberté dans l'exercice de leurs légitimes fonctions.

5. Le Conseil Administratif a pris connaissance de la décision générale No. 361 relative aux mesures temporaires prises quant à la nomination des fonctionnaires et à l'acceptation des candidats aux postes vacants au moyen de concours publics sans tenir compte des distinctions religieuses et, tout en désirant le maintien de ces concours pour l'admission à de tels postes, il estime néanmoins que la méthode adoptée par ladite circulaire n'étant pas conforme aux règles suivies jusqu'à présent dans l'administration de la Montagne, spécialement en ce qui concerne les droits des diverses communautés, il conviendrait de s'en tenir aux dites règles en attendant que le statut du Liban et la forme de son Gouvernement soient définitivement arrêtés.

6. Il est parvenu à la connaissance de ce conseil que M. Gobran Boutros, de Beyrouth, a été nommé Président du Tribunal d'el-Koura. Ce fait est sans précédent depuis l'établissement du Protocole Libanais, car la règle suivie depuis lors est que les magistrats et fonctionnaires libanais sont nommés uniquement par le Gouvernement libanais, au point que le Gouvernement turc lui-même n'intervenait pas dans la nomination du personnel de l'administration du Liban.

7. Le Conseil observe, d'après ce qui se passe, parfois, que l'on a une trop grande tendance à révoquer les fonctionnaires pour des fautes légères ne méritant pas une aussi sévère mesure. Or, considérant que la plupart des fonctionnaires libanais n'ont d'autres moyens de vivre et d'entretenir leurs familles en dehors de leurs traitements; que plusieurs d'entre eux sont entrés dans cette carrière dès leur jeune âge et qu'ils ne peuvent pas, après une longue période de service, changer d'occupation; considérant d'autre part le préjudice moral qu'une révocation est de nature à causer à celui qui en est victime; ce Conseil appelle l'attention des autorités sur ce point très important afin que la plus grande circonspection possible soit observée à cet égard.

Ces remarques du Conseil Administratif sont dictées du point de vue du régime d'autonomie dont le Liban jouissait par le passé. Maintenant toutefois que notre complète indépendance a été décidée — suivant la communication qui nous en a été faite par M. Georges Picot, ex-Haut-Commissaire; et par le général Gouraud, son successeur — avec l'aide de la France, il est évident que nous ne pouvons être moins bien traités ni avoir moins de liberté que par le passé. Il est bien certain que le Conseil qui, au nom des Libanais, a demandé avec force l'aide de la France ne saurait refuser le concours qu'elle veut bien lui prêter, d'autant moins qu'il fonde sur elle de grands espoirs. Il espère toutefois que l'on apportera grand soin à ce que ce concours soit une aide réelle augmentant les droits et les prérogatives des Libanais, donnant plus d'autorité et de prestige à leurs fonctions, et ne se transformant pas en une domination qui paralyserait leur action et affaiblirait la dignité du Gouvernement libanais.

Telles sont les observations que le Conseil Administratif libanais croit devoir formuler en vue de faciliter la bonne marche de l'administration et de mettre les actes des autorités d'occupation en harmonie avec les intérêts et l'indépendance des Libanais. Il prie Monsieur le Gouverneur Militaire du Liban de bien vouloir les soumettre aux hautes autorités compétentes.

Correspondance d'Orient, 15 February 1920, pp. 117–19.

APPENDIX D   RESOLUTION ADOPTED BY SEVEN MEMBERS OF THE LEBANESE ADMINISTRATIVE COUNCIL, 10 JULY 1920

LE 'MEMORANDUM DES SEPT'

Le Conseil administratif du Liban, parlement composé, d'après le statut, de treize membres, et aujourd'hui de douze membres actifs seulement, par suite de la démission d'un des deux représentants du caza de Kisrawâne — a pris le samedi 10 juillet 1920, à la grande majorité de ses membres, la décision suivante:

Attendu que les Libanais (depuis que les grandes puissances ont proclamé le droit des peuples de ces pays à constituer un gouvernement national) ont demandé et demandent sans cesse la confirmation de leurs droits à la constitution d'un gouvernement national indépendant;

Attendu que l'indépendance du Liban est prouvée historique-ment et établie depuis de longs siècles; que la situation de la Montagne, la nature de ses habitants familiarisés depuis longtemps avec la liberté indépendante, sont autant de facteurs qui comportent l'indépendance et la neutralité politique du Liban pour le mettre à l'abri des convoitisés et des agressions;

Attendu qu'il est en outre de son plus grand intérêt, et pour la tranquillité de son peuple, d'être en accord et d'avoir des relations cordiales avec ses voisins, comme cela est prouvé par les consé-quences du désaccord qui ont été le soulèvement des ignorants pour susciter des événements regrettables et troublants qui se sont succédés depuis l'année dernière jusqu'aujourd'hui;

Pour tous ces motifs;

Ledit Conseil a fait tous ses efforts dans le but d'arriver à un accord garantissant les droits des deux pays voisins, le Liban et la Syrie, ainsi que leurs intérêts et la continuité de leurs bons rap-ports dans l'avenir. Apres avoir étudié cette question, le Conseil a trouvé qu'il était possible d'atteindre ce but au moyen des articles suivants:

I. Indépendance complète et absolue du Liban.

II. Sa neutralité politique, en ce sens qu'il ne déclarera pas la guerre, et que la guerre ne lui sera pas déclarée, et qu'il restera à l'écart de tout intervention militaire.

III. La restitution des territoires qui en ont jadis été détachés, et cc en vertu d'un accord à conclure entre lui et le gouvernement syrien.

IV. Les questions économiques seront étudiées et résolues par un comité composé de membres appartenant aux deux parties. Les décisions de ce comité seront exécutoires après l'approbation des deux parlements libanais et syrien.

V. Les deux parties s'entr'aideront dans les démarches à faire auprès des puissances pour que les quatre articles précités soient sanctionnés, et les dispositions qu'ils comportent garanties.

Afin de pouvoir travailler dans ce but en liberté, et en dehors de toute contrainte ou influence étrangère, et pour poursuivre efficacement dans les sphères compétentes l'adoption des dispositions incluses dans les quatre articles sus-mentionnés, qui sont les voeux de la nation libanaise et renferment l'intérêt véritable du Liban en dehors de tous intérêts particuliers, et en raison du mandat conféré légalement par le peuple libanais à ce Conseil et confirmé récemment encore par le suffrage de l'immense majorité du peuple, la majorité des membres du Conseil, signataires de ce mémorandum, ont décidé de se transporter et de partir personnellement afin de poursuivre l'adoption des dispositions incluses dans les articles précités, là ou il faudra et dans les sphères compétentes, et de communiquer cette décision in-extenso aux sphères officielles, et de la proclamer par les moyens possibles à la nation libanaise.

> Signé: Mahmoûd Joumblât
> Soulaïmâne Kan'âne
> Khalîl 'Aql
> Sa'd Allâh Houwaïck
> Mouhammad El Hâj Mouhsine
> Elias Chouaïrî
> Fouâd Abd El Malik

Correspondance d'Orient, 30 October 1920, pp. 260–1.

APPENDIX E MEMORANDUM PRESENTED BY A MUSLIM DELEGATION FROM THE AREAS ANNEXED TO LEBANON, TO HENRY DE JOUVENEL, THE FRENCH HIGH COMMISSIONER, DECEMBER 1925

Memorandum

Présenté au nom de la majorité des habitants des Territoires annexés illégalement au Sandjak autonome du Mont Liban à Monsieur le Haut Commissaire de la République Française en Syrie.

Nous soussignés délégués par des milliers d'habitants, avons l'honneur de présenter à Monsieur le Haut Commissaire de la République Française, les voeux suivants, qui sont incontestablement partagés par la majorité des habitants des villes et contrées-annexées au Sandjak autonome du Mont-Liban.

Ces voeux peuvent se résumer dans la demande de séparation des parties annexées au Sandjak autonome du Mont Liban et leur incorporation dans la Fédération Syrienne.

Notre demande est basée sur les faits et points de droit suivants:

1. L'annexion de la partie restante du vilayet de Beyrouth (le sandjak de Beyrouth et celui de Tripoli sur le littoral) avec les différentes villes de l'intérieur au sandjak autonome du Mont Liban sans le consentement de leurs populations et sans aucun plébiscite, est contraire au principe posé par les Ministres des Affaires Etrangères de France et d'Angleterre, qui, au mois de Novembre 1918, dans un communiqué officiel déclaraient:

DÉCLARATION FAITE CONJOINTEMENT PAR LA FRANCE & LA GRANDE BRETAGNE LE 8 NOVEMBRE 1918 AUX POPULATIONS DE SYRIE ET DE MÉSOPOTAMIE

'Le but de ces deux puissances, en les libérant, est l'établissement de gouvernements nationaux puisant leur autorité dans le libre choix des populations et qui, loin de vouloir leur imposer telles ou telles institutions, ces puissances n'ont d'autres soucis que d'assurer par leur appui, le fonctionnement des gouvernements et administrations qu'elles se seraient librement choisis.'

Malheureusement les habitants des contrées précitées furent complètement privés du droit de libre disposition de leur propre destinée et, bon gré mal gré, se trouvèrent du jour au lendemain annexés au Mont Liban dont l'organisation administrative et les intérêts différaient foncièrement de ceux des parties annexées.

Il est évident que ces différents ne pouvaient pas être éliminés du jour au lendemain par la création d'un état qui, comme son appellation imaginaire, ne pouvait correspondre à aucun besoin ethnique ni même économique.

Car il se trouve que les parties annexées au Mont Liban dans le but de créer l'état appelé 'Grand Liban' ont une importance économique et une fortune plus grandes, un nombre d'habitants supérieur à celui du sandjak autonome du Mont Liban. Jusqu'à la création du Grand Liban, de tout temps, les mêmes lois et règles administratives régissaient le vilayet de Beyrouth avec le reste de la Syrie. Il est vraiment étonnant sinon incompréhensible de voir deux parties homogènes et semblables, séparées et contre le désir de ses habitants, le vilayet de Beyrouth empêché de faire partie de la fédération syrienne, celle-ci présentant des avantages et utilités incontestablement supérieurs à n'importe quel autre système.

Quand le sandjak autonome du Mont Liban refusa de faire partie d'une unité syrienne sous n'importe quelle forme, si bizarre qu'eût été ce refus, il fut et à juste titre, respecté et personne n'eut l'idée de l'y contraindre.

Ne serait-il pas équitable que le même procédé soit appliqué aux habitants du vilayet de Beyrouth et que leurs voeux légitimes soient également respectés?

Nous ne voulons même pas nous arrêter à l'idée que sur la demande des habitants d'une contrée l'annexion d'une autre soit légale si les habitants de celle-ci s'y opposent. Que diraient les habitants du Mont Liban si, sur la demande même unanime de toute la Syrie, on les obligeait à faire partie de l'unité Syrienne?

Alors, pourquoi les habitants du sandjak autonome du Mont Liban veulent-ils nous annexer sur leur propre demande et contre notre volonté?

D'autre part, si nous considérions les revenus de l'état appelé Grand Liban, nous constaterions avec le plus légitime étonnement, qu'à peine les 17% de ces revenus sont payés par le sandjak autonome du Mont Liban tandis que les 83% restants sont perçus dans les parties annexées et que les lourdes charges supportées par les habitants du vilayet servent à entretenir et payer une organisation digne, par le nombre du personnel et l'importance des appointements, d'un grand état comptant plus de 10 millions d'habitants.

Si l'on veut bien constater que la très grande majorité des fonctionnaires du Grand Liban sont des libanais (du sandjak autonome du Mont Liban), on aura peut être une explication sinon légitimant du moins rendant compréhensible l'acharnement que mettent certains libanais à demander et à défendre leur 'Grand Liban'.

2. Si on veut prétendre que le Grand Liban possède les frontières naturelles et géographiques du Mont Liban dont le Gouvernement Impérial Ottoman l'avait injustement privé et que, aujourd'hui le Mont Liban reconquiert de nouveau ses anciennes frontières; un coup d'oeil sur les livres géographiques de tous les temps suffirait à prouver le non fondé de cette allégation. Entre autres, nous pouvons citer les livres des historiens et géographes Aboul Farage, Aboul Kassem Abdallah, auteur du livre (Routes et Pays), Ibni Haoukal, Aboul Fidaa, El Kazwini, El Massoudi, presque tous ayant existé avant la création même de l'Empire Ottoman de 2 à 3 siècles, et parmi les auteurs plus récents Ibni Sabat, l'Emir Haidar Ibni Ahmed Chéhab, etc. et les derniers le célèbre savant Cornelius Van Deck et Georges Zeidan, où tous sont d'accord et unanimes à limiter le Mont Liban: au Nord par le mont Femilmizab, au Sud par la vallée et la rivière de Chkif à l'endroit appelé Djarmak à l'Est, par Mouallaka Zahlé et à l'Ouest, par le fleuve de Beyrouth et Fourn-el-Chebak.

On pourra y constater en plus qu'avant l'occupation ottomane le Mont Liban dans ses limites connues, fut gouverné par les Tennouchites, puis par les Maanites et que quand le Sultan Selim conquit la Syrie, il confia en signe de témoignage de sa satisfaction impériale, à l'Emir du Liban Fakhr El Dine El Maani, le gouvernorat de Saida avec la chaine du Mont Liban. Plus tard, par décret des gouverneurs de Saida et de Saint Jean d'Acre, l'Emir Béchir Chéhab fut désigné comme Emir du Mont Liban, son pouvoir se limitant, comme celui de ses prédécesseurs, au Mont Liban seulement.

Le siège du gouvernement libanais fut transféré par l'Emir

Béchir de Deir El Kamar à Beit El Dine.

Ainsi on voit que jamais un état indépendant n'exista qui put, de loin ou de près, rappeler le Grand Liban ou légitimer sa revendication.

Le Mont Liban et les provinces limitrophes furent toujours sous la dépendance des pachas de Saint Jean d'Acre comme Ahmed Pacha Gezzar, Daher El Omar, Abdullah Pacha, etc., et ce n'est qu'en 1860, après les événements connus et qui amenèrent l'intervention des puissances européennes, que pour la première fois on accorda au Mont Liban une autonomie déterminée avec des prérogatives le différenciant des autres parties de l'Empire Ottoman.

Les limites de ce Sandjak autonome furent fixées par les grandes puissances européennes à la tête desquelles se trouvait la France. Inutile de dire que la Turquie aurait été dans l'impossibilité absolue de s'y opposer si les puissances européennes avaient exigé d'elle la création d'une partie autonome beaucoup plus vaste sous la même appellation ayant pour frontière par exemple: au nord, les monts Taurus, à l'est Moussoul, au sud Gazza ou la presqu'île de Sinai. Ce qui arrêta les grandes puissances aux frontières de 1864 ce n'est certes pas une résistance possible de la part de l'Empire Ottoman mais une considération de droit et d'équité, car un Liban plus grand n'aurait eu ni son explication ni sa raison d'être.

3. *Débouché sur la Mer*. Demander l'annexion du vilayet par force sous prétexte d'avoir un débouché sur la mer quand le Mont Liban a un littoral si long par rapport à sa grandeur et qu'il possède les ports de Chekka, de Batroun, de Djbeil (Biblos) de Djounié, de Nabi Younès, de Damour etc. . .

4. Le nombre des habitants suivant le recensement fait dernièrement est pour le sandjak autonome du Mont Liban de 322608 et pour celui des parties annexées de 388902. Si tel est le nombre des habitants du sandjak autonome du Mont Liban et si ses habitants ne peuvent pas se contenter du long littoral précité, que doivent demander comme débouché, les habitants de la Syrie dont le nombre s'élève à près de 2 millions, surtout si on devrait prendre en considération l'importance agricole et commerciale de leur territoire.

Il saute aux yeux que si le littoral devait être annexé à une partie, c'est bien à l'intérieur auquel il est lié par tant de facteurs d'intérêts vitaux, qu'il devrait l'être et que cela serait sa condamnation à mort que de le laisser sans liens intimes avec la fédération syrienne.

Nous croyons superflu d'insister sur les conséquences nuisibles qu'amena la création du Grand Liban entre autres à Tripoli et à Beyrouth: comment alors admettre qu'une contrée qui de tout temps faisait parti intégrante d'un tout qui s'appelait la Syrie, en soit séparée, et que les habitants appelés Syriens soient obligés par force de se faire appeler des Grands Libanais et ceci sans aucun intérêt pour eux et même à leur grand préjudice.

Nous nous permettons d'insister sur les dépenses énormes par rapport à la richesse du pays et au nombre de ses habitants, que nécessite un état avec ministères, chambre des députés, etc. Avant le Grand Liban, au sandjak autonome du Mont Liban les dépenses totales de l'administration y compris les Travaux Publics ne dépassaient pas 35000 livres turques.

Aujourd'hui cette somme est loin de pouvoir suffire à la plus petite direction de l'état du Grand Liban. Au vilayet, on rencontre la même proportion entre le passé et le présent.

5. Le sandjak autonome du Mont Liban avait des prérogatives accordées par le Gouvernement Ottoman sous la garantie des puissances européennes. Il n'appartiendrait donc pas au Mont Liban ni même à une puissance isolée d'accorder les mêmes prérogatives à une zone, même limitrophe au sandjak du Mont Liban. Les faits nous ont prouvé d'ailleurs que malgré sa création le Grand Liban n'a pas pu unifier ses lois, et tandisqu'au Mont Liban les habitants jouissent toujours de leurs anciennes prérogatives dans le reste de cet état la Régie, la Dette Publique Ottomane, les droits de timbres, etc., continuent comme par le passé à y régner et à peser sur le pauvre contribuable qui, annexé malgré lui, appelé par force Grand Libanais, s'aperçoit qu'il ne fut invité au festin que pour en payer les frais.

En plus, nous pouvons constater qu'en dehors des questions d'ordre international, les simples impôts n'ont pu, jusqu'à maintenant être appliqués au sandjak du Mont Liban malgré leur perception dans les autres parties du nouvel état.

Ainsi on a vu créer sans trop savoir pourquoi, un état de 2 parties où les lois différent, les impôts différent, les habitudes différent et de ces 2 parties hétérogènes que ne lie presqu'aucun intérêt économique, on s'étonne aujourd'hui de ne pas voir se former un état accepté, sinon demandé, par tous ses habitants.

Comment cette acceptation serait-elle possible quand, chiffres en mains, nous pouvons démontrer que dans l'état appelé Grand Liban le sandjak autonome du Mont Liban paie bien moins que les

17% des revenus, tandis que plus de 83% sont perçus dans le reste de cet état et que la majorité des employés et fonctionnaires sont des libanais et qu'en définitive les habitants du vilayet et autres parties annexées se voient obligés de payer des impôts insupportables pour alimenter la caisse d'un état qui a pour but primordial d'assurer l'intérêt du sandjak du Mont Liban et de ses habitants. N'oublions pas d'ailleurs, que l'intérêt commercial du vilayet et de toute la Syrie demanderait impérieusement le rétablissement de l'unité syrienne sous forme d'une fédération pour que, libre, chez soi chaque partie de la fédération puisse traiter en commun toutes les questions d'intérêt général.

6. La majorité écrasante des habitants des parties annexées au Mont Liban, convaincue des sentiments de justice et d'équité des dignes représentants de la République Française en Syrie, n'a pas cessé de demander la réparation d'une erreur commise et le rétablissement de l'unité syrienne.

Nous venons par la présente renouveler notre demande et profitons de l'occasion pour remercier de l'accueil favorable que fit le Haut Commissariat, lors du recensement, à nos justes revendications en rendant facultative l'inscription sur les feuillets de recensement la mention certifiant 'la nationalité de G^d Libanais' à chaque porteur de feuillet.

Confiants en la France, mère patrie de la liberté, en cette France qui toujours fut pour l'opprimé et jamais pour l'oppresseur, qui fit la plus grande des révolutions pour les droits de l'homme et sacrifia un million et demi de ses enfants pour les droits des peuples nous sommes sûrs qu'il ne nous sera jamais refusé le droit de disposer librement de nos propres destinées et que nous ne serons jamais annexés à n'importe quelle partie sans un plébiscite légal comprenant exclusivement les habitants des parties qu'on voudrait annexer.

Veuillez, Monsieur le Haut Commissaire, agréer nos hommages les plus respectueux.

Fonds Henry de Jouvenel

APPENDIX F RESOLUTION PASSED BY THE LEBANESE REPRESENTATIVE COUNCIL, 30 NOVEMBER 1925

CONSIDERANT que les insurgés du Djébel Druze ont envahi la partie Sud-Est du Liban et notamment Hasbaya, Rachaya et la région avoisinante, où les insurgés ont porté leur action en causant des dommages considérables aux biens et aux personnes;

CONSIDERANT qu'aucun motif plausible ne peut être invoqué pour justifier les événements dont nos villes-frontières ont été le théâtre;

CONSIDERANT que le Gouvernement du Grand Liban, qui ne dispose pas d'une armée régulière capable de repousser l'invasion de son territoire, était fermement convaincu que la Puissance Mandataire ne manquerait pas de lui fournir en cas de besoin l'aide nécessaire conformément aux engagements par Elle pris envers la Société des Nations;

CONSIDERANT que la Puissance Mandataire a effectivement tenu ses engagements en défendant, grâce à ses soldats, les frontières du Liban et en prenant toutes les mesures de protection nécessaires;

CONSIDERANT que la gendarmerie libanaise, malgré le petit nombre de ses effectifs, a accompli son devoir au cours des attaques dirigées contre les frontières du Liban;

CONSIDERANT que le Grand Liban qui, politiquement, est indépendant de ses voisins les Etats de Syrie et du Djébel Druze, demeure fermement attaché à son indépendance et à sa neutralité et considère toute violation de son territoire comme une atteinte à son indépendance et un empiètement sur ses droits et sa liberté;

LE CONSEIL REPRESENTATIF DECIDE:

1. de considérer les attaques dirigées par les insurgés contre les localités de Hasbaya, Merjayoun et Rachaya, comme une atteinte à l'indépendance du Grand Liban et à la liberté de ses populations;

2. de remercier au nom du Pays la Noble Puissance Mandataire des sacrifices humains et matériels qu'elle a jusqu'ici consentis pour la défense du territoire libanais, la protection de ses habitants et la

293

sauvegarde de son indépendance;

3. de rendre un juste hommage à la façon dont s'est sacrifiée la gendarmerie libanaise dont la bravoure et la ténacité méritent tout éloge;

4. d'assurer la Puissance Mandataire de l'attachement traditionnel et indéfectible des Libanais à la Noble Nation Française;

5. de prier M. le Gouverneur du Grand Liban de transmettre officiellement cette adresse au Gouvernement de la Puissance Mandataire.

Fonds Henry de Jouvenel, no. 22/CR, Beirut, 1 December 1925, from Mussa Nammur, president of the Lebanese Representative Council, to Cayla, the governor of Lebanon.

APPENDIX G   LETTER FROM THE PATRIARCH HAWAYIK TO BRIAND, THE FRENCH PRIME MINISTER, 15 JULY 1926

A Son Excellence   Neo Kannobin, le 15 Juillet, 1926
Monsieur Briand
Président du Conseil des Ministres
Ministre des Affaires Etrangères
Paris.

Monsieur le Président,

Daignez permettre à un vieil ami de la France de Vous exposer ce qui suit:

Les Libanais entendent, depuis quelques mois, dire que les représentants du Mandat en Syrie et au Liban pensent détacher du Liban la Ville de Tripoli avec les plaines du Akkar e.a.d. de tout le territoire Nord-est libanais, en delà de la ligne du chemin de fer Tripoli-Homs pour le donner à la Syrie, d'aucuns assurent aussi que Baâlbek et son territoire suivront le même sort.

Les derniers événements du Djebel Druze et de la Syrie qui n'ont pas manqué d'avoir leur répercussion dans les régions frontières du Liban et, antérieurement l'union de la Cylicie à la Turquie ont procuré au Liban un excédent de population, que dans ses limites actuelles, il est incapable de faire vivre, comment le deviendra-t-il une fois amputé de la seconde ville commerciale Tripoli et d'une large partie de son territoire le plus fertile?

Une telle amputation ébranlerait très sérieusement la foi de nos populations dans les destinées de la France et surtout dans sa force, quand elles la voient céder devant une froignée d'agitateurs. Le peuple ne connaît pas les influences qui agissent en secret contre la France ici; une telle cession est à ses yeux un triomphe pour la Diplomatie Anglaise dont il voit la main dans tout ce qui se passe actuellement dans ce pays.

C'est avec un amer regret que nous voyons les Chrétiens de la région Sud-Est, Hasbaya-Rachaya-Mardjayoun émigrer en Amérique pendant que leurs assassins, les Druzes, réduits par la force à faire leur soumission, revenir seuls s'installer dans cette région en toute tranquillité.

L'idée primordiale qui a présidé à la formation de l'Etat

Libanais était de constituer un état refuge pour tous les Chrétiens de l'Orient et un foyer de fidélité à toute épreuve à la France, or nous avons la douleur de constater qu'après huit ans d'hésitants essais, on a plutôt perdu que gagné.

Ne serait-il pas opportun de faire ici ce qu'on a fait dans les Balkans et en Sylésie? Quel mal y a-t-il à procéder à un échange de population entre le Djebel Druze et la région Sud-Est Libanaise à une part, pour ce qui concerne les Druzes et entre les Musulmans et les Chrétiens de certaines autres régions d'autre part.

Touts les Hauts Commissaires, qui se sont succédés dans ce pays, ont, chacun à son tour, confirmé au nom de la France, qu'ils ont dûment représentée, la situation actuelle du Liban; le Conseil de la Société des Nations, l'a, à son tour, reconnue; le prestige de la France, en même temps que sa dignité et celle de la Société des Nations, imposent, ce me semble, de s'en tenir à ce qui a été décidé, approuvée et reconnue.

Cette amputation faite contre nos justes réclamations ne résoudrait pas le problème, au contraire, elle encouragerait les exigeances des meneurs Syriens, qui visent au seul but de s'affranchir complètement de la tutelle de la France.

Mon âge et mon expérience des hommes de mon pays, m'obligent à faire ce douloureux aveu.

Quel que soit l'avenir réservé à ce pays, on ne saurait nier que seul le Liban restera à jamais fidèle à la France, le diminuer et l'affaiblir, c'est diminuer d'autant l'influence de la France elle-même.

Il ne serait donc pas prudent de perdre cette occasion pour le maintenir, une fois pour toutes, tel que la France elle-même l'a voulue en 1860 et 1919–1920.

Ceux, qui ont vécu dans nos pays, se rendent bien compte que l'influence de la France est en raison directe de l'importance du patrimoine du Liban.

Avant de terminer, je tiens à attirer l'attention de Votre Excellence sur le tort que ces continuels retours sur ce qui a été solonnellement arrêté et à plusieurs reprises, officiellement confirmé, fait au prestige de la France, chez des populations dont le Gouvernement connaît les intentions malveillantes. Il me semble qu'il faille couper court à toutes les conversations de ce genre, marcher résolument dans la voie qui a été tracée et enlever de l'esprit des ennemis du Mandat de vouloir ainsi diminuer le prestige et l'autorité de la France.

Cette situation incertaine cause un malaise dans le Liban et devant cette incertitude, l'élément sain et fidèle se décide à émigrer.

Telle sont, Monsieur le Président, les observations que dans mon patriotisme et mon dévouement à la France, j'ai eu devoir vous soumettre, dans l'espoir que Vous voudrez bien les prendre en sérieuse considération.

Je prie, Votre Excellence, de vouloir agréer les hommages de mon plus profond respect.

Elias Pierre Hoyek
Patriarche Maronite
d'Antioche et de tout l'Orient

Il y a bientôt six ans que le Général Gouraud alors Haut Commissaire, a proclamé au nom de la France, l'indépendance du Liban dans ses limites actuelles.

En autorisant son Haut Commissaire à faire cette proclamation en son nom, en même temps qu'Elle faisait un acte de justice, la France répondait aux voeux de l'ensemble de la population libanaise que je représentais en 1919 à la Conférence de la Paix, et qui demandait le retour à la Patrie, des provinces qui en avaient été détachées par le gouvernement Turc, et sa reconstitution d'après la charte dressée par l'Etat-Major de l'expédition française de 1860.

Il serait question aujourd'hui d'amputer le Liban Chrétien au profit de la Syrie Musulmane, sous prétexte de vouloir donner à ce pays un débouché à la mer et que le pays qu'on projette de détacher est un pays musulman.

Les Représentants du Sandjak autonome d'Alexandrette viennent en demandant l'annexion de leur pays à la Syrie, de doter ce pays du plus vaste et du plus important des ports syriens.

Sur une population de 85,000 âmes, que comptent Tripoli et le Akkar, il y a environ 40,000 Chrétiens qui vont être noyés dans l'immense majorité musulmane de Syrie.

La ville de Beyrouth, où les intérêts français sont si considérables ne desservant plus que le Liban, ne tardera pas à déchoir et à céder la place à Tripoli.

Toute la banlieue et tout l'arrière plan de Tripoli restent libanais; il y a là une population de 60,000 âmes, exclusivement chrétiennes, qui, tout en restant libanaises, devraient continuer à se ravitailler à Tripoli devenue ville syrienne; autant d'avantages pour la Syrie dont les Finances Libanaises seraient privées.

S'il est permis (ce que nous ne voudrions pas de supposer), que le Mandat prendra un jour fin en Syrie (les événements actuels de Damas nous fixent assez sur les intentions des Syriens), la France, que les voeux des Libanais appellent à toujours rester chez eux, voudrait-elle d'un pays aussi réduit et encerclé au Nord et à l'Est par une Syrie indépendante faisant bloc avec les pays voisins dont on songe à constituer l'immense Empire Arabe sous une égide autre que la Sienne? Au point de vue stratégique, cette amputation n'affaiblirait-elle pas la défense libanaise?

AE, Levant, vol. 263, pp. 114–20.

BIBLIOGRAPHY

I Unpublished primary sources

A. French Archives

1. Archives du Ministère des Affaires Etrangères, Série Levant 1918–29 (Paris).
2. Bibliothèque Nationale, Private Papers of Millerand and Flandin.
3. Centre de Hautes Etudes sur l'Afrique et l'Asie Modernes (Paris).
4. Ministère de la Guerre, Service Historique de l'Armée, Section Outre-Mer (Vincennes).
5. Archives Départementales de la Corrèze, Fonds Henry de Jouvenel (Tulle).

B. British Archives

1 Public Record Office: Foreign Office Papers.

FO 141:	Embassy and Consular correspondence, Egypt.
FO 195:	Consular correspondence, Turkey.
FO 371:	General correspondence, Political, from 1906, Turkey, Syria and Lebanon.
FO 406:	Confidential print, Eastern Affairs.
FO 424:	Confidential print, Turkey.
FO 608:	Paris Peace Conference.
FO 800/221:	Sykes Papers.

2 St. Antony's College, Oxford, Middle East Centre. The Private Papers Collection: Yale Papers, microfilm and photostats of reports from Cairo, Jerusalem, London, etc., 1917–18, and Paris Peace Conference, 1919, and Faisal, miscellaneous documents in Arabic and English.

II Published Primary Sources and Official Publications

Browne, W.L., *The Political History of Lebanon, 1920–1950* (Salisbury, NC, 1976). Collection of documents relating to Lebanon in the State Department, including dispatches from the American consul-general in Beirut.

Butler, R. and Woodward, E.L. (eds.), *Documents on British Foreign Policy, 1919–1939*, First Series, vol. iv (London, 1952).

Great Britain, Admiralty, Naval Intelligence Division, *A Handbook of Syria including Palestine* (London, 1920).

Haut Commissariat de la République Française en Syrie et au Liban, *La Syrie et le Liban en 1922* (Paris, 1922).

Haut-Commissariat de la République Française en Syrie et au Liban, *La Syrie et le Liban sous l'Occupation et Mandat Français 1919–1927* (Paris, 1927).

Maronite Patriarch, *Le Liban et la France: Documents publiés par le Patriarche Maronite* (Bkerki, 23 February 1936).

Turkey, Fourth Army Command (Jamal Pasha) *La Vérité sur la Question Syrienne* (Constantinople, 1916).

United States, Department of State, *Papers related to the Foreign Relations of the United States; Paris Peace Conference, 1919*, vols. iv, v, xii (Washington, 1942–5).

III Books Cited

Abu Rashid, H., *Jabal al Duruze* (Cairo, 1925)

Adib, Auguste Pasha, *Le Liban après la Guerre* (Cairo, 1917).

American University of Beirut, *The Lebanese Constitution* (Beirut, 1960).

Andréa, C.J.E., *La Révolte Druse et l'Insurrection de Damas 1925-1926* (Paris, 1937).

Antonius, G., *The Arab Awakening* (London, 1951).

Atiyah, E., *An Arab Tells His Story* (London, 1946).

Atiyah, N.W., *The Attitude of the Lebanese Sunnites towards the State of Lebanon*, PhD thesis prepared at the University of London (London, 1973).

Barrès, M., *Une Enquête aux Pays du Levant* (Paris, 1923).

Baudicour, L., *La France au Liban* (Paris, 1879).

Bayhum, Muhammad Jamil, *Lubnan baina mushriq wa mughrib, 1920-1969* (Beirut, 1969).

——, *'Urubat Lubnan* (Beirut, 1969).

Bérard, V., *Le Sultan, l'Islam et les Puissances* (Paris, 1907).

Bidwell, R., *Morocco under colonial rule, French administration in tribal areas, 1912-1956* (London, 1973).

Binder, L. (ed.), *Politics in Lebanon* (New York, 1965).

Binion, R., *Defeated Leaders: The political fate of Caillaux, Jouvenel and Tardieu* (New York, 1960).

Bliss, F.J., *The Religions of Modern Syria and Palestine* (New York, 1910).

Bonardi, P., *L'Imbroglio Syrien* (Paris, 1927).

Brémond, E., *Le Hedjaz dans la guerre mondiale* (Paris, 1931).

Bruneau, A., *Traditions et Relations de la France au Levant* (Paris, 1932).

Burckhard, C., *Le Mandat français en Syrie et au Liban* (Nîmes, 1925).

Cambon, P., *Correspondance (1870-1924)* (Paris, 1946).

Carbillet, G., *Au Djebel Druze* (Paris, 1929).

Cassar, G.H., *The French and the Dardanelles* (London, 1971).

Catroux, Général, *Deux missions en Moyen-Orient (1919-1922)* (Paris, 1958).

Chambre de Commerce de Marseilles, *Congrès français de la Syrie: 3, 4 et 5 Janvier 1919, Séances et Travaux* (Marseilles, 1919).

Chevalier, D., *La Société du Mont Liban à l'Époque de la Révolution Industrielle en Europe* (Paris, 1971).

Chiha, M., *Le Liban d'Aujourd'hui* (Beirut, 1942).

——, *Politique Intérieure* (Beirut, 1964).

Cole, S.M., *Italian Policy in the Eastern Mediterranean, 1912-1923*, PhD thesis prepared at Cambridge University (Cambridge, 1975).

Cuinet, V., *Syrie, Liban et Palestine* (Paris, 1896).

Dahir, M., *Ta'rikh Lubnan al-Ijtima'i* (Beirut, 1974).

David, P., *Un gouvernement arabe à Damas* (Paris, 1923).

Desjardins, M., *Le Problème Syrien du point de vue économique* (Lille, 1928).

Djemal (Jamal), Pasha, *Memories of a Turkish Statesman 1913-1919* (New York, 1922).

Entelis, J., *Pluralism and Party Transformation in Lebanon; Al-Kata'ib 1936-1970* (Leiden, 1974).

Fériet, R., *L'Application d'un Mandat* (Beirut, 1926).

Gaulis, B.G., *La Question Arabe* (Paris, 1930).

Gautherot, G., *La France en Syrie et en Cilicie* (Paris, 1920).

——, *Le Général Sarrail Haut-Commissaire en Syrie* (Paris, 1925).

Gontaut-Biron, Comte R. de, *Comment la France s'est installée en Syrie (1918-1919)* (Paris, 1923).

——, *Sur les routes de Syrie après neuf ans du Mandat* (Paris, 1928).

Gordon, H.C., *Syria As It Is* (London, 1939).
Grousset, P., *La Constitution Libanaise du 23 Mai 1926, Révisée le 17 Octobre 1927* (Toulouse, 1928).
Gulick, J., *Tripoli: A Modern Arab City* (Oxford, 1967).
Haddad, R.M., *Syrian Christians in a Muslim Society* (Princeton, 1970).
Haim, S.G., *Arab Nationalism: An Anthology* (London, 1962).
Hakim, Yusuf al-, *Beirut wa Lubnan fi al-'Ahd al-'Uthmani* (Beirut, 1964).
——, *Suriya wal 'Ahd al-Faysali* (Beirut, 1966).
Harik, I.F., *Politics and Change in a Traditional Society, Lebanon 1711–1845* (Princeton, 1968).
Hassan, Hassan al-, *al-Qanun a-dusturi wal-dustur fi Lubnan* (Beirut, 1963).
Himadeh, S.B. (ed.), *Economic Organisation of Syria* (Beirut, 1936).
Hitti, P.K., *Lebanon in History* (London, 1957).
Hobeika, P., *Discours, Allocutions, Articles: Mgr. Michel Feghali* (Junieh, 1938).
Hourani, A.H., *Minorities in the Arab World* (London, 1947).
——, *Syria and Lebanon* (Oxford, 1954).
——, *A Vision of History* (Beirut, 1961).
——, *Arabic Thought in the Liberal Age 1798–1939* (Oxford, 1970).
Howard, H.N., *The King-Crane Commission* (Beirut, 1963).
Hudson, M.C., *The Precarious Republic: Political Modernization in Lebanon* (New York, 1968).
Hurewitz, J.C., *Diplomacy in the Near and the Middle East* (Princeton, 1956).
Husri, Sati al-, *Yawm Maisalun* (Beirut, 1964).
Issawi, C. (ed.), *The Economic History of the Middle East 1800–1919* (Chicago, 1966).
Jalbert, L., *Syrie et Liban — Réussite française?* (Paris, 1934).
Jessup, H., *Fifty-Three Years in Syria* (New York, 1910).
Jouplain, M., *La Question du Liban* (Paris, 1908).
Jung, E., *La Révlote Arabe* (Paris, 1925).
Kautharani, W., *al-Ittijahat al-ijtima'iya-as-Siyasiya fi Jabal Lubnan wal-mashriq al-arabi 1860–1920* (Beirut, 1978).
Kedourie, E., *England and the Middle East* (London, 1956).
——, *In the Anglo-Arab Labyrinth* (London, 1976).
Kerr, D., *The Temporal Authority of the Maronite Patriarchate 1920–1958: A Study in the Relationship of Religious and Secular Power*, PhD thesis prepared at Oxford University (Oxford, 1973).
Kerr, M.H., *Lebanon in the Last Years of Feudalism, 1840–1868: A contemporary Account by Antun Dahir al-Aqiqi and Other Documents* (Beirut, 1959).
Khairallah, K.T., *La Syrie* (Paris, 1912).
Khatib, Anwar al-, *al-'Usul al-barlamaniyah fi Lubnan wa Sa'ir a-duwal al-'arabiyah* (Beirut, 1961).
Khuri, Bishara al-, *Haqa'iq Lubnaniyah* (Beirut, 1960).
Lamy, E., *La France du Levant* (Paris, 1900).
Lewis, B., and Holt, P.N. (eds.), *Historians of the Middle East* (London, 1962).
Lloyd George, D., *The Truth about the Peace Treaties* (London, 1938).
Lohéac, L., *Da'ud 'Ammun et la Création de l'Etat Libanais* (Paris, 1978).
Lyautey, P., *Le Drame Oriental* (Paris, 1923).
——, *Gouraud* (Paris, 1949).
MacCallum, E.P., *The Nationalist Crusade in Syria* (New York, 1928).
Majzoub, M., *Le Liban et l'Orient Arabe, 1943–1956* (Aix-en-Provence, 1956).
Ma'oz, M., *Ottoman Reform in Syria and Palestine 1840–1861* (Oxford, 1968).
——, *Modern Syria* (Tel-Aviv, 1974).
Masson, P., *Elément d'une bibliographie française de la Syrie* (Marseilles, 1919).
Mazière, P., La, *Partant pour la Syrie* (Paris, 1926).
Mélia, J., *Chez les Chrétiens d'Orient* (Paris, 1929).

Monicault, J., *Le Port de Beyrouth et l'Economie des Pays du Levant sous le Mandat Français* (Paris, 1936).

Monroe, E., *The Mediterranean in Politics* (Oxford, 1938).

Mutran, Nadra, *La Syrie de demain* (Paris, 1916).

Muzhir, Yusuf, *Ta'rikh Lubnan al-'Amm* (Beirut, 1957).

Nevakivi, J., *Britain, France and the Arab Middle East, 1914–1920* (London, 1969).

Owen, R. (ed.), *Essays on the Crisis in Lebanon* (London, 1976).

O'Zoux, R., *Les États du Levant sous Mandat français* (Paris, 1931).

Pernot, M., *Rapport sur un voyage d'étude à Constantinople, en Egypte, et en Turquie-d'Asie (Janvier–Août 1912)* (Paris, 1912).

Pichon, J., *Le Partage du Proche-Orient* (Paris, 1938).

Polk, W.R., *The Opening of South Lebanon, 1788–1840* (Harvard University, 1963).

Porter, H., *The History of Beirut* (Beirut, 1912).

Presland, J., *Deedes Bey* (London, 1942).

Qasimiya, Khayriya, *al-Hukuma al-'Arabiya fi Dimashq bayna 1918–1920* (Beirut, 1971).

Rabbath, E., *L'Évolution politique de la Syrie sous mandat* (Paris, 1928).

——, *Unité Syrienne et devenir arabe* (Paris, 1939).

——, *al-Wasit fi al-Qanun al-dustur al-lubnani* (Beirut, 1970).

——, *La Formation Historique du Liban Politique et Constitutionnel* (Beirut, 1973).

Rishayi, Iskandar, *al-Ayyam al-Lubnaniyah* (Beirut, 1957).

Ristelhueber, R., *Les Traditions Françaises au Liban* (Paris, 1925).

Rizk, C., *Le Régime Politique Libanais* (Paris, 1966).

Roberts, S.H., *A History of French Colonial Policy: 1870–1925* (London, 1929).

Rondot, P., *Les Chrétiens d'Orient* (Beirut, 1955).

——, *Les Institutions Politiques du Liban* (Paris, 1947).

Safa, E., *L'Émigration Libanaise* (Beirut, 1960).

Safa, Mahmud Jaber, *Ta'rikh Jabal 'Amil* (Beirut, n.d.).

Sa'id, Amin, *al-Thawra al-'Arabiya al-Kubra* (Cairo, 1933).

Salibi, K.S., *Maronite Historians of Mediaeval Lebanon* (Beirut, 1959).

——, *The Modern History of Lebanon* (London, 1968).

Samné, G., *La Syrie* (Paris, 1920).

Sawda, Yusuf al-, *Fi Sabil al-'Istiqlal* (Beirut, 1967).

Sfer, Abdallah Pasha, *Le Mandat Français et les Traditions Françaises en Syrie et au Liban* (Paris, 1922).

Sorel, J.A., *Le Mandat Français et l'Expansion Economique de la Syrie et du Liban* (Paris, 1929).

Spagnolo, J.P., *France and Ottoman Lebanon 1861–1914* (St Antony's College, Oxford, 1977).

Stein, L., *Syria* (London, 1926).

Tarbin, Ahmad, *Lubnan Mundhu 'Ahd al-Mutassarifiya ila Bidayat al-Intidab* (Damascus, 1968).

Tibawi, A.L., *A Modern History of Syria* (London, 1969).

Toynbee, A.J. (ed.), *Survey of International Affairs, 1925* (London, 1927).

Uwaidat, 'Abdu, *al-Nazum al-dusturiyah fi lubnan wal-bilad al-'arabiyah wal-'alam* (Beirut, 1961).

Véou, P. de, *La Passion de la Cilicie, 1919–1922* (Paris, 1954).

Watson, D.R., *Georges Clemenceau: A Political Biography* (Plymouth, 1974).

Weygand, M., *Mémoires: Mirages et Réalité* (Paris, 1957).

Yamak, L.Z., *The Syrian Social Nationalist Party, An Ideological Analysis* (Harvard, 1966).

Zeine, Z.N., *The Emergence of Arab Nationalism* (Beirut, 1966).

Ziadeh, N., *Syria and Lebanon* (Beirut, 1968).

IV Articles and Pamphlets Cited

Ajay, N.Z., 'Political Intrigue and Suppression in Lebanon during World War I', *International Journal of Middle East Studies*, 5 (1974), pp. 140–60.

'Anniversaire de la Proclamation du Grand-Liban: Discours prononcés le Ier Septembre 1925 par le Gouverneur de l'Etat et par le Président du Conseil Représentatif' (Beirut, 1925).

Anon., 'Les Chiites du Liban Sud', CHEAM (n.d.).

——, 'Une Opinion chrétienne libanaise sur le rôle du Liban auprès des pays arabes', CHEAM (n.d.).

——, 'L'Oeuvre de la France en Syrie', *Revue des Deux Mondes* (Paris, 15 February 1921), pp. 801–40.

——, 'L'Organisation de la Syrie sous le Mandat français', *Revue des Deux Mondes* (Paris, 1 December 1921), pp. 633–63.

Arslan, Shekib, 'La mort du Patriarche maronite', *Nation Arabe* (Geneva, November–December 1931), pp. 50–7.

Association 'Le Jeune Liban', 'Mémoire sur la Question libanaise' (Cairo, April, 1922).

Burke, E., 'A Comparative View of French Native Policy in Morocco and Syria, 1912–1925', *Middle Eastern Studies* (May 1973), pp. 175–86.

Chambre de Commerce de Marseille, *Bulletin de la Chambre de Commerce de Marseille: Correspondance et Documents* (Marseilles, October 1919).

Comité Central Syrien, 'La Question syrienne exposée par les Syriens' (Paris, 1919).

Cressaty, Count, 'Les intérêts de la France en Syrie, Conférence prononcée par le Comte Cressaty sous la Présidence de M. Paul Doumer et sous les auspices de l'Alliance française' (Paris, 21 May 1913).

Dahdah, Salim al-, 'Lubnan al-Kabir wa Suriya', *al-Mashriq* (1923), pp. 454–62.

Dawn, C.E., 'The Question of Nationalism in Syria and Lebanon', *Tensions in the Middle East* (Washington, 1956) Middle East Institute, pp. 11–17.

Deebs, J., 'Les Maronites du Liban, Appel aux Catholiques' (Paris, April, 1875).

Epstein, E., 'The Lebanon: Demographic and Political Survey' (Jerusalem, 1943) in CHEAM.

Giscard, R.V., 'La Syrie et le Liban sous le Mandat Français, mai 1923 — novembre 1924', *Revue des Deux Mondes* (15 April 1924), pp. 838–65.

Gouraud, Général, 'La France en Syrie', *Revue de la France* (1 April 1922).

Hess, C.G., and Bodman, H.L., 'Confessionalism and Feudality in Lebanese Politics', *Middle East Journal* (1954), pp. 10–26.

Hourani, A.H., 'Lebanon from Feudalism to Modern State', *Middle Eastern Studies* (April 1966), pp. 256–63.

Huvelin, P., 'Que veut la Syrie?' Supplement to *L'Asie Française*, December 1921.

Johnson, M., 'Factional Politics in Lebanon: The case of the "Islamic Society of Benevolent Intention" (Al-Maqasid) in Beirut', *Middle Eastern Studies* (January 1978), pp. 56–75.

Kedourie, E., 'Lebanon: The Perils of Independence', *The Washington Review of Strategic and International Studies*, vol. I, no. 3, July 1978, pp. 84–9.

Khalaf, S., 'Primordial Ties and Politics in Lebanon', *Middle Eastern Studies* (April 1968), pp. 243–69.

Landau, J.M., 'Elections in Lebanon', *The Western Political Quarterly* (University of Utah, March, 1961), pp. 121–47.

Al-mu'atamar al-suri al-falastini, 'Nida ila al-mujtama' al-'amm li-usmat al-'umam' (Cairo, February 1922).

——, 'Mudakirat a'mal al-wafd al-suri al-falastini' (Cairo, January 1923).

Porat, Y., 'The Peasant Revolt of 1858–1861 in Kisrawan', *Hamizrah Hehadash*, vol. XV, no. 4 (1965), pp. 379–400; vol. XVI, no. 1 (1966), pp. 31–57.

Rondot, P., 'L'Expérience du Mandat français en Syrie et au Liban', *Revue Générale de Droit International Public* (Paris, 1948), pp. 387–409.
——, 'Les structures socio-politiques de la nation libanaise', *Revue française du Science Politique* (Paris, 1953), pp. 80–104.
Salibi, K.S., 'Beirut under the Young Turks as Depicted in the Political Memoirs of Salim Ali Salam' (Beirut, 1974).
——, 'The Lebanese Identity', *The Journal of Contemporary History*, vol. 6, no. 1 (1971), pp. 76–88.
Salmon, E., 'La communauté musulmane au Liban', CHEAM, Doc. no. 291, n.d.
Samné, G., 'Comité de l'Orient: La question syrienne, exposé — solution, statut politique' (Paris, August 1918).
——, 'Le Liban Autonome de 1861 à Nos Jours' (Paris, 1919).
Spagnolo, J.P., 'Constitutional Change in Mount Lebanon: 1861–1864', *Middle Eastern Studies* (January 1971), pp. 25–48.
Sulh, Khatem al-, 'Mushkilat al Ittisal wal-Infissal fi Lubnan' (Beirut, 1937).
Taillandier, S.R., 'La France et la Syrie — Notre oeuvre dans le Levant et son avenir', *Revue des Deux Mondes* (Paris, 15 February 1919), pp. 771–804.
Tannous, A.I., 'The Village in the National Life of Lebanon', *Middle East Journal* (January 1949), pp. 151–63.
Weygand, M., 'L'Avenir de la Syrie', *Marche de France* (September 1924).
Zamir, M., 'Emile Eddé and the Territorial Integrity of Lebanon', *Middle Eastern Studies* (May, 1978), pp. 232–5.
——, 'Smaller and Greater Lebanon — The Squaring of a Circle?', *The Jerusalem Quarterly*, no. 23 (Spring 1982), pp. 34–53.
——, 'Faisal and the Lebanese Question, 1918–1920' (to be published in *Middle Eastern Studies*).
Ziadeh, N. 'The Lebanese Elections, 1960' *Middle East Journal* (1960), p. 367–81.

V Periodicals

L'Asie arabe, Paris.
L'Asie Française, Paris.
Bairut al-Massa, Beirut.
Bulletin Officiel du Comité 'France-Orient', Paris.
Correspondance d'Orient, Paris.
Revue des Deux Mondes, Paris.
The Near East, London.

INDEX

Adib Pasha, Auguste 50, 157, 181, 204, 215, 264n104, 265n108
'Adra, Khair a-Din 167, 187, 211
'Ain Ibel 2, 85
'Akkar 13, 14, 73, 92, 94, 99, 101, 181, 194, 196, 219
'Alawites 57, 82, 92, 106, 108, 198
Allenby, General Edmund 53, 56, 57, 63, 74
Alliance Française 38-9
Alliance Libanaise 18, 23, 49, 50, 54, 228n60
'Ammun, Da'ud 53-4, 89, 141, 234n42, 252n97
'Ammun, Iskandar 32, 49, 50, 65
Arab Congress in Paris 1913 32-3
Arab League 222
Arab nationalism 2-4, 28, 34, 59, 77, 80-1, 108, 129, 180
Armenians 27, 40, 59, 80, 86, 98, 99, 100-1, 120, 165, 173, 198, 243n3, 259n57
Arslan, 'Adel 174, 181, 239n117, 240n124
Arslan, Amin 89, 135, 175, 183, 240n124, 259n60
Arslan, Fu'ad 174, 175, 203, 207, 265n108, 266n117
Arslan, Shekib 27, 70, 182, 198, 229n67
Arslan, Tawfik 68, 174, 239n110
Arwad 40, 51, 230n91
As'ad, Kamal al- 57, 68, 85, 86, 135, 136, 251n84
As'ad, Khurshid 131, 132
Atrash, Salim al- 168
Atrash, Sultan al- 169, 170, 174, 181
Atrash, Zayd al- 171-2, 173, 175, 181, 260n66
autonomous Sanjak of Mount Lebanon 98, 99, 101, 220
  Administrative Council 11, 18-22, 36, 52-3, 63, 66, 70, 88-91, 228n55
  and France 16-17, 20-1
  borders 12-15
  civil war 1860 7-8

  during First World War 34-7, 230n89
  Règlement Organique 9-10
  see also Mount Lebanon
Ayubi, Shukri al- 51
'Azmah, Yusuf al- 85

Ba'albek 51, 73, 100, 116, 136, 151, 190, 194-5, 196
Barakat, Subhi 180, 246n32, 255n13
Barrès, Maurice 43
Barthou, Louis 45
Bashir II 5, 8
Bayhum, 'Abdullah 211
Bayhum, Ahmad Mukhtar 33, 127, 130, 229n84
Bayhum, Jamil 211
Bayhum, 'Umar 167, 211, 212
Beirut 13, 14-15, 26, 50-1, 67, 77, 87, 92-3, 94, 97, 100, 101, 111, 118, 122, 123, 127, 128, 136, 151-2, 172, 173, 199, 210, 211, 229n65, 229n70, 243n3
  vilayet of 24, 30-1, 227n36
Beirut Reform Society 30, 31, 32, 33
Bejani, 'Abbas 50
Beqa'a Valley 13, 14, 41, 42, 51, 59, 73, 74, 78, 81, 92, 93, 101, 116, 135-6, 169, 173, 175, 176, 179, 180, 181, 183, 190, 194, 198, 219, 228n62
Bérard, Victor 43, 45, 75, 231n15, 240n10
Berthelot, Philippe 45, 73, 167
Boncour, Joseph Paul- 203, 205-6, 261n79
Briand, Aristide 45, 104, 105-6, 109, 115-16, 119, 142, 184-5, 191, 198, 202, 205, 213, 267n127
Britain 3, 27, 29, 31-2, 40, 41, 52-3, 56, 58, 60, 63, 72, 80, 86, 93, 108, 220-1
Brunet, Auguste 202, 203

Cachin, Marcel 231n12
Caix, Robert de 45, 46, 65, 74, 147, 223
  and Faisal 60, 61, 64, 75, 85, 238n101